Florida Probate Rules
2014

Florida Probate Code
2014

ALSO AVAILABLE FROM
SUAVE FISH PUBLISHING, LEGAL DIVISION

Florida Rules of Civil Procedure and Florida Evidence Code

Florida Rules of Criminal Procedure and Florida Evidence Code

Florida Standard Jury Instructions in Criminal Cases

Other States

Illinois Code of Civil Procedure and Illinois Rules of Evidence

Illinois Code of Criminal Procedure and Illinois Rules of Evidence

Michigan Rules of Civil Procedure and Michigan Rules of Evidence

Michigan Rules of Criminal Procedure and Michigan Rules of Evidence

Michigan Rules of Probate Court and Michigan Rules of Evidence

Texas Rules of Civil Procedure and Texas Rules of Evidence

TABLE OF CONTENTS

FLORIDA PROBATE RULES

TABLE OF CONTENTS

FLORIDA PROBATE CODE

TITLE XLII
ESTATES AND TRUSTS

CHAPTER 731
PROBATE CODE: GENERAL
PROVISIONS

PART I
SHORT TITLE; CONSTRUCTION

PART II

DEFINITIONS

PART III
NOTICE AND REPRESENTATION

CHAPTER 732
PROBATE CODE: INTESTATE SUCCESSION AND WILLS

PART I
INTESTATE SUCCESSION

PART II
ELECTIVE SHARE OF SURVIVING SPOUSE; RIGHTS IN COMMUNITY PROPERTY

PART VI
RULES OF CONSTRUCTION

PART VII
CONTRACTUAL ARRANGEMENTS RELATING TO DEATH

PART VIII
GENERAL PROVISIONS

PART IX
PRODUCTION OF WILLS

CHAPTER 733
PROBATE CODE: ADMINISTRATION
OF ESTATES

PART I
GENERAL PROVISIONS

PART II
COMMENCING ADMINISTRATION

PART III
PREFERENCE IN APPOINTMENT
AND QUALIFICATIONS OF
PERSONAL REPRESENTATIVE

PART VII
CREDITORS' CLAIMS

CHAPTER 734
PROBATE CODE: FOREIGN PERSONAL REPRESENTATIVES; ANCILLARY ADMINISTRATION

PART I
GENERAL PROVISIONS

PART II
JURISDICTION OVER FOREIGN PERSONAL REPRESENTATIVES

CHAPTER 735
PROBATE CODE: SMALL ESTATES

PART I
SUMMARY ADMINISTRATION

Florida Probate Rules

NOTE TO USERS: Rules in this pamphlet are current through 38 FLW S868. Subsequent amendments, if any, can be found at www.floridasupremecourt.org/decisions/rules.shtml. The Florida Bar also updates the rules on its website at www.FloridaBar.org (on the homepage click "Rules Updates").

Florida Probate Rules

PART I — GENERAL

RULE 5.010.   SCOPE

These rules govern the procedure in all probate and guardianship proceedings and shall be known as the Florida Probate Rules and may be cited as Fla. Prob. R. Part I applies to all proceedings. Part II applies to probate alone, Part III applies to guardianship alone, and Part IV applies to expedited judicial intervention concerning medical treatment procedures. The Florida Rules of Civil Procedure apply only as provided herein.

Committee Notes

Rule History

1975 Revision: These rules shall govern the procedures to be followed in all matters pending on or commenced after January 1, 1976, including procedures for the enforcement of substantive rights that have vested before that date. See section 731.011, Florida Statutes.

1977 Revision: The changes in these rules shall take effect on July 1, 1977.

1988 Revision: In the opinion reported at 460 So. 2d 906, the Florida Supreme Court directed the Probate and Guardianship Rules Committee to study the statutes and attempt to identify those portions of the Florida Probate Code, the Florida Guardianship Law, and other statutes that contained procedural provisions. When those procedural provisions were identified, the committee was charged to promulgate rules incorporating those procedures.

The committee has reviewed the statutes and has found a substantial measure of procedure that was contained only in the statutes for which there were no corresponding rules. The committee also determined that much of the procedure in the statutes already had a rule counterpart.

New rules added, or prior rules amended, in 1988 to add procedural matters previously found only in the statutes are rules 5.050, 5.122, 5.171, 5.180, 5.201, 5.235, 5.270, 5.275, 5.355, 5.360, 5.385, 5.386, 5.400, 5.440, 5.475, 5.490, and 5.510. With only one exception (see rule 5.050), the only portion of the statutes that has been reviewed in detail, and for which rules have been created, is the Florida Probate Code. Other portions of the statutes mentioned in the opinion cited above remain for the next cycle of this committee to review.

As the committee wrote rules to transfer the statutory procedure into these rules, an attempt was made to write the rule without changing the meaning of the statute. It was not possible or advisable to use the exact wording of the statute in some instances, and in those instances the committee rewrote the statutory language in the format used in the rules generally. Even under those circumstances, the committee attempted to transfer the entire procedural portion of the statute without changing its meaning. Where it was specifically intended in a few instances to add to existing statutory procedure, that fact is noted in the relevant committee note. The committee felt strongly that it would be detrimental to the orderly process of estate probate and related procedures if a rule specified a different procedure than was specified in the related statute, even though the statute must, under the Florida Constitution, yield to the rule when there is a conflict.

The committee, through the proper channels in The Florida Bar (initially, the Probate Law Committee of the Real Property, Probate and Trust Law Section), intends to ask the legislature to repeal those portions of the statutes that are procedural when there are similar rules already in place, or when similar new rules are added by this opinion. It is the opinion of the committee that continuing to maintain procedure in the statutes when there is a rule specifying that procedure is detrimental to the orderly process of the court and the public that it serves, especially when, over time, the statute and the rule may diverge.

Although the supreme court has adopted these recommended rules, it has not specifically determined that all of the provisions of the statutes that were procedural have now been adopted as a rule. This is a continuing project for the committee and although these new rules and changes represent a substantial transition of procedure into the rules, the committee does not suggest that the transition is complete. The court is not precluded from examining any particular statute or rule in the context of a particular actual dispute.

1991 Revision: Rule revised to reflect addition of new Part IV dealing with expedited judicial intervention concerning medical treatment procedures.

1992 Revision: In 1989, the Florida Legislature enacted a comprehensive revision to Florida's guardianship law. In response, the Florida Supreme Court appointed an ad hoc committee to recommend temporary rules of procedure for the new law. In an opinion at 551 So. 2d 452 (Fla. 1989), the court adopted the temporary rules recommended by the ad hoc committee, to replace Part III of the then-existing Florida Probate Rules, effective October 1, 1989. In its opinion, the court also directed the Florida Probate Rules Committee to review the new laws and, on a priority basis, to recommend permanent rules of procedure.

The committee reviewed the Florida Guardianship Law enacted in 1989, as well as revisions to the law enacted in 1990, and presented its rule recommendations to the court in 1991. The court, in an opinion at 584 So. 2d 964, adopted the recommendations with minor exceptions, to be effective October 1, 1991.

In 1990, the court also rendered its opinion in In re Guardianship of Browning, 568 So. 2d 4 (Fla. 1990), regarding a person's right to refuse life-prolonging medical procedures. In that decision, the court directed the committee to recommend a rule to provide for expedited judicial intervention. In response, the committee created a new Part IV of these rules and recommended rule 5.900, which was adopted by the court, with minor changes, in its opinion at 584 So. 2d 964, effective October 1, 1991.

The committee continued its efforts to review the Florida Probate Code and to promulgate or amend rules regarding any procedural portions of those statutes. As a result of those efforts, as well as the efforts described above, the committee recommended amendments to rules 5.010, 5.025, 5.040, 5.050, 5.200, 5.240, 5.310, 5.346, 5.400, 5.470, 5.550, 5.560, 5.590, 5.600, 5.610, 5.620, 5.630, 5.640, 5.650, 5.660, 5.670, 5.680, 5.695, 5.700, 5.710, and 5.800; creation of new rules 5.496, 5.540, 5.541, 5.555, 5.635, 5.636, 5.690, 5.696, 5.697, 5.705, and 5.900; and deletion of rule 5.495. In addition, the committee recommended editorial changes in virtually all the rules so that they would conform stylistically to one another and to all other rules promulgated by the supreme court.

2003 Revision: The committee has promulgated numerous changes in the rules and in the committee notes to many of the rules, in response to legislative amendments that deleted procedural aspects of a number of statutes in the Florida Probate Code, including deletion and re-titling of some statutes. See Ch. 2001-226, Laws of Fla.

Rule References

Fla. Prob. R. 5.025 Adversary proceedings.
Fla. Prob. R. 5.040(a)(3)(B) Notice.
Fla. Prob. R. 5.050 Transfer of proceedings.
Fla. Prob. R. 5.080 Discovery and subpoena.
Fla. Prob. R. 5.230(e) Commission to prove will.
Fla. R. App. P. 9.800 Uniform citation system.

RULE 5.015. GENERAL DEFINITIONS

(a) **General.** The definitions and rules of construction stated or referred to in sections 1.01 and 393.12, Florida Statutes, and chapters 731, 732, 733, 734, 735, 736, 738, 739, and 744, Florida Statutes, as amended from time to time, shall apply to these rules, unless otherwise defined in these rules.

(b) **Specific Definitions.** When used in these rules

(1) "certified copy" means a copy of a document signed and verified as a true copy by the officer to whose custody the original is entrusted;

(2) "formal notice" means notice under rule 5.040(a);

(3) "informal notice" means notice under rule 5.040(b);

(4) "judge" means a judge of the circuit court, including any judge elected, appointed, substituted, or assigned to serve as judge of the court;

(5) "guardian advocate" means a person appointed for a person with a developmental disability pursuant to section 393.12, Florida Statutes;

(6) "guardian" means a person appointed pursuant to chapter 744, Florida Statutes, or a guardian advocate unless a rule indicates otherwise;

(7) "ward" means an individual for whom a guardian is appointed.

Committee Notes

Rule History

1977 Revision: No change in rule. Correction of typographical error in committee note.

This is intended to simplify drafting of these rules and should be liberally construed. See Fla. Prob. R. 5.190 and 5.540 and also §§ 731.201 and 744.102, Fla. Stat.

1988 Revision: Rule was expanded due to deletion of rule 5.190. Committee notes expanded. Citation form changes in rule and committee notes.

1992 Revision: Citation form changes in rule and committee notes.

2000 Revision: Subdivision (b)(2) amended to delete outdated reference to rule 5.550(c).

2007 Revision: Subdivision (a) amended to add reference to chapter 736, Florida Statutes, which was added to the statutes effective July 1, 2007 and which replaces deleted chapter 737, and to add reference to chapter 739, Florida Statutes, which was added effective July 1, 2005. Committee notes revised.

2008 Revision: Subdivision (a) amended to add reference to section 393.12, Florida Statutes, which governs guardian advocates for persons with developmental disabilities. As provided by section 744.102(11), the term "guardian advocate" as used in the Florida Guardianship Law and these rules does not include a guardian advocate appointed for a person determined to lack capacity to consent to treatment under section 394.4598, Florida Statutes. Subdivisions (b)(5) through (b)(7) added to reflect 2008 amendments to section 393.12, Florida Statutes. Committee notes revised.

Statutory References

§ 1.01, Fla. Stat. Definitions.
§ 393.063, Fla. Stat. Definitions.
§ 393.12, Fla. Stat. Capacity; appointment of guardian advocate.
§ 731.201, Fla. Stat. General definitions.
§ 736.0103, Fla. Stat. Definitions.
§ 738.102, Fla. Stat. Definitions.
§ 739.102, Fla. Stat. Definitions.
§ 744.102, Fla. Stat. Definitions.

RULE 5.020. PLEADINGS; VERIFICATION; MOTIONS

(a) Forms of Pleading. Pleadings shall be signed by the attorney of record, and by the pleader when required by these rules. All technical forms of pleadings are abolished. No defect of form impairs substantial rights, and no defect in the statement of jurisdictional facts actually existing renders any proceeding void.

(b) Petition. A petition shall contain a short and plain statement of the relief sought, the grounds therefor, and the jurisdiction of the court where the jurisdiction has not already been shown.

(c) Motions. Any other application to the court for an order shall be by written motion, unless made orally during a hearing or trial. The motion shall state with particularity the grounds therefor and shall set forth the relief or order sought.

(d) Rehearing. A motion for rehearing of any order or judgment shall be served not later than 10 days after the date of filing the order or judgment with the clerk as shown on the face of the order or judgment.

(e) Verification. When verification of a document is required, the document filed shall include an oath, affirmation, or the following statement:

"Under penalties of perjury, I declare that I have read the foregoing, and the facts alleged are true, to the best of my knowledge and belief."

Committee Notes

The time for determining when a motion for rehearing must be served has been clarified in view of *Casto v. Casto*, 404 So. 2d 1046 (Fla. 1981).

Rule History

1977 Revision: Editorial change (rule) and expansion of committee note. Subdivisions (a), (b), and (d) substantially the same as subdivisions (a), (b), and (f) of prior rule 5.030. Subdivision (c) taken from section 731.104, Florida Statutes. For adversary proceedings see new rule 5.025. Notice of administration is not a pleading within the meaning of this rule.

1980 Revision: Subdivisions (c) and (d) have been redesignated as (e) and (f). New subdivisions (c) and (d) are added to provide for the use of motions in probate proceedings other than adversary proceedings and to specifically authorize a procedure for rehearing.

1984 Revision: Minor editorial changes. Subdivision (f) of prior rule has been deleted as it is now covered under the adversary rules.

1988 Revision: Editorial change in caption of (a). Committee notes revised. Citation form change in committee notes.

1992 Revision: Editorial changes. Committee notes revised. Citation form changes in rule and committee notes.

2003 Revision: Committee notes revised.

2008 Revision: Committee notes revised.

2010 Revision: Committee notes revised.

Statutory References

§ 393.12, Fla. Stat. Capacity; appointment of guardian advocate.
§ 731.104, Fla. Stat. Verification of documents.
§ 731.201, Fla. Stat. General definitions.
§ 733.202, Fla. Stat. Petition.
§ 733.604(1), Fla. Stat. Inventories and accountings; public records exemptions.
§ 733.901, Fla. Stat. Final discharge.
§ 735.203, Fla. Stat. Petition for summary administration.
§ 744.104, Fla. Stat. Verification of documents.
§ 744.3085, Fla. Stat. Guardian advocates.
§ 744.3201, Fla. Stat. Petition to determine incapacity.
§ 744.331, Fla. Stat. Procedures to determine incapacity.
§ 744.334, Fla. Stat. Petition for appointment of guardian or professional guardian; contents.

Rule References

Fla. Prob. R. 5.025 Adversary proceedings.
Fla. Prob. R. 5.200 Petition for administration.
Fla. Prob. R. 5.205(b) Filing evidence of death.
Fla. Prob. R. 5.320 Oath of personal representative.
Fla. Prob. R. 5.330 Execution by personal representative.
Fla. Prob. R. 5.350 Continuance of unincorporated business or venture.
Fla. Prob. R. 5.370(a) Sales of real property where no power conferred.
Fla. Prob. R. 5.405(b) Proceedings to determine homestead real property.
Fla. Prob. R. 5.530 Summary administration.
Fla. Prob. R. 5.550 Petition to determine incapacity.
Fla. Prob. R. 5.560 Petition for appointment of guardian of an incapacitated person.
Fla. Prob. R. 5.600 Oath.
Fla. Prob. R. 5.649 Guardian advocate.

RULE 5.025. ADVERSARY PROCEEDINGS

(a) **Specific Adversary Proceedings.** The following are adversary proceedings unless otherwise ordered by the court: proceedings to remove a personal representative, surcharge a personal representative, remove a guardian, surcharge a guardian, probate a lost or destroyed will or later-discovered will, determine beneficiaries, construe a will, reform a will, modify a will, cancel a devise, partition property for the purposes of distribution, determine pretermitted status, determine pretermitted share, determine amount of elective share and contribution, and for revocation of probate of a will.

(b) **Declared Adversary Proceedings.** Other proceedings may be declared adversary by service on interested persons of a separate declaration that the proceeding is adversary.

(1) If served by the petitioner, the declaration must be served with the petition to which it relates.

(2) If served by the respondent, the declaration and a written response to the petition must be served at the earlier of:

(A) within 20 days after service of the petition, or

(B) prior to the hearing date on the petition.

(3) When the declaration is served by a respondent, the petitioner must promptly serve formal notice on all other interested persons.

(c) **Adversary Status by Order.** The court may determine any proceeding to be an adversary proceeding at any time.

(d) **Notice and Procedure in Adversary Proceedings.**

(1) Petitioner must serve formal notice.

(2) After service of formal notice, the proceedings, as nearly as practicable, must be conducted similar to suits of a civil nature, including entry of defaults.

The Florida Rules of Civil Procedure govern, except for rule 1.525.

(3)   The court on its motion or on motion of any interested person may enter orders to avoid undue delay in the main administration.

(4)   If a proceeding is already commenced when an order is entered determining the proceeding to be adversary, it must thereafter be conducted as an adversary proceeding. The order must require interested persons to serve written defenses, if any, within 20 days from the date of the order. It is not necessary to re- serve the petition except as ordered by the court.

(5)   When the proceedings are adversary, the caption of subsequent pleadings, as an extension of the probate caption, must include the name of the first petitioner and the name of the first respondent.

Committee Notes

The court on its initiative or on motion of any party may order any proceeding to be adversary or nonadversary or enter any order that will avoid undue delay. The personal representative would be an interested person in all adversary proceedings. A prescribed form for the caption is provided that will facilitate the clerk's and the court's ability to segregate such adversary proceeding from other adversary proceedings and from the main probate file:

		Court Case #
In Re Estate of John B. Jones	)	
	)	
Julia Jones,	)	
	)	
Petitioner,	)	
	)	
v.	)	
	)	
Harold Jones, as Personal	)	
Representative, et al.,	)	
	)	
Respondents.	)	

Rule History

1975 Revision: New rule. 324 So. 2d 38.

1977 Revision: Editorial changes to (a)(1).

1984 Revision: Extensive changes, committee notes revised and expanded.

1988 Revision: Changes in (a) add proceedings to remove a guardian and to surcharge a guardian to the list of specific adversary proceedings and delete proceedings to determine and award the elective share from the list. Change in (b)(4) clarifies on whom the petitioner must serve formal notice. Editorial change in (d)(2) and (d)(5). Committee notes revised. Citation form changes in committee notes.

1992 Revision: Deletion of (b)(3) as unnecessary. Former (b)(4) renumbered as new (b)(3). Committee notes revised. Citation form changes in committee notes.

2001 Revision: Change in (a) to add determination of amount of elective share and contribution as specific adversary proceedings. Committee notes revised.

2003 Revision: Committee notes revised.

2008 Revision: Committee notes revised.

2011 Revision: Subdivision (a) revised to add "reform a will, modify a will" and "determine pretermitted status." Subdivision (d)(2) modified to insure that an award of attorneys' fees in a probate or guardianship proceeding follows the law and procedures established for such proceedings, rather than the law and procedures for civil proceedings. See Amendments to the Florida Family Law Rules of Procedure (Rule 12.525), 897 So. 2d 467 (Fla. 2005). Editorial changes to conform to the court's guidelines for rules submissions as set forth in Administrative Order AOSC06-14. Committee Notes revised.

Statutory References

§ 393.12, Fla. Stat. Capacity; appointment of guardian advocate.
§§ 732.201–732.2155, Fla. Stat. Elective share of surviving spouse.
§ 732.301, Fla. Stat. Pretermitted spouse.
§ 732.302, Fla. Stat. Pretermitted children.
§ 732.507, Fla. Stat. Effect of subsequent marriage, birth, adoption, or dissolution of marriage.
§§ 732.6005–732.611, Fla. Stat. Rules of construction.
§ 732.615, Fla. Stat. Reformation to correct mistakes.
§ 732.616, Fla. Stat. Modification to achieve testator's tax objectives.
§ 733.105, Fla. Stat. Determination of beneficiaries.
§ 733.107, Fla. Stat. Burden of proof in contests; presumption of undue influence.
§ 733.109, Fla. Stat. Revocation of probate.
§ 733.207, Fla. Stat. Establishment and probate of lost or destroyed will.
§ 733.208, Fla. Stat. Discovery of later will.
§ 733.504, Fla. Stat. Removal of personal representative; causes for removal.
§ 733.505, Fla. Stat. Jurisdiction in removal proceedings.
§ 733.506, Fla. Stat. Proceedings for removal.
§ 733.5061, Fla. Stat. Appointment of successor upon removal.
§ 733.603, Fla. Stat. Personal representative to proceed without court order.
§ 733.609, Fla. Stat. Improper exercise of power; breach of fiduciary duty.
§ 733.619(2), (4), Fla. Stat. Individual liability of personal representative.
§ 733.814, Fla. Stat. Partition for purpose of distribution.
§ 744.3085, Fla. Stat. Guardian advocates.
§ 744.474, Fla. Stat. Reasons for removal of guardian.
§ 744.477, Fla. Stat. Proceedings for removal of a guardian.

Rule References

Fla. Prob. R. 5.040 Notice.

Fla. Prob. R. 5.270 Revocation of probate.
Fla. Prob. R. 5.360 Elective share.
Fla. Prob. R. 5.365 Petition for dower.
Fla. Prob. R. 5.440 Proceedings for removal.
Fla. Prob. R. 5.649 Guardian advocate.
Fla. Prob. R. 5.660 Proceedings for removal of guardian.
Fla. Prob. R. 5.681 Restoration of rights of person with developmental disability.
Fla. R. Civ. P. 1.140 Defenses.
Fla. R. Civ. P. 1.160 Motions.
Fla. R. Civ. P. 1.200 Pretrial procedure.
Fla. R. Civ. P. 1.280 General provisions governing discovery.
Fla. R. Civ. P. 1.290 Depositions before action or pending appeal.
Fla. R. Civ. P. 1.310 Depositions upon oral examination.
Fla. R. Civ. P. 1.340 Interrogatories to parties.
Fla. R. Civ. P. 1.380 Failure to make discovery; sanctions.

RULE 5.030.   ATTORNEYS

(a)   **Required; Exception.** Every guardian and every personal representative, unless the personal representative remains the sole interested person, shall be represented by an attorney admitted to practice in Florida. A guardian or personal representative who is an attorney admitted to practice in Florida may represent himself or herself as guardian or personal representative. A guardian advocate is not required to be represented by an attorney unless otherwise required by law or the court.

(b)   **Limited Appearance without Court Order.** An attorney of record for an interested person in a proceeding governed by these rules shall be the attorney of record in all other proceedings in the administration of the same estate or guardianship, except service of process in an independent action on a claim, unless at the time of appearance the attorney files a notice specifically limiting the attorney's appearance only to the particular proceeding or matter in which the attorney appears. At the conclusion of that proceeding or matter, the attorneys role terminates upon the attorney filing notice of completion of limited appearance and serving a copy on the client and other interested persons.

(c)   **Withdrawal or Limited Appearance with Court Order.** An attorney of record may withdraw or limit the attorney's appearance with approval of the court, after filing a motion setting forth the reasons and serving a copy on the client and other interested persons.

Committee Notes

The appearance of an attorney in an estate is a general appearance unless (i) specifically limited at the time of such appearance or (ii) the court orders otherwise. This rule does not affect the right of a party to employ additional attorneys who, if members of The Florida Bar, may appear at any time.

Rule History

1975 Revision: Subdivision (a) is same as prior rule 5.040 with added provision for withdrawal of attorney similar to Florida Rule of Appellate Procedure 2.3(d)(2). Subdivision (b) reflects ruling in case of State ex rel.
Falkner v. Blanton, 297 So. 2d 825 (Fla. 1974).

1977 Revision: Editorial change requiring filing of petition for withdrawal and service of copy upon interested persons. Editorial change in citation forms in rule and committee note.

1984 Revision: Minor editorial changes and addition of subdivision (c). Committee notes expanded.

1988 Revision: Editorial changes and order of subdivisions rearranged. Committee notes expanded. Citation form changes in committee notes.

1992 Revision: Editorial changes. Committee notes revised. Citation form changes in committee notes.

2003 Revision: Committee notes revised.

2005 Revision: Committee notes revised.

2006 Revision: Committee notes revised.

2008 Revision: Subdivision (a) amended to reflect that a guardian advocate may not be required to be represented by an attorney in some instances. Committee notes revised.

2010 Revision: Subdivision (b) and (c) amended to clarify the procedure for termination of an attorney's representation of an interested person either with or without court order.

2012 Revision: Committee notes revised.

Statutory References

§ 393.12, Fla. Stat. Capacity; appointment of guardian advocate.
§ 731.301, Fla. Stat. Notice.
§ 733.106, Fla. Stat. Costs and attorney's fees.
§ 733.212, Fla. Stat. Notice of administration; filing of objections.
§ 733.6175, Fla. Stat. Proceedings for review of employment of agents and compensation of personal representatives and employees of estate.
§ 744.108, Fla. Stat. Guardian's and attorney's fees and expenses.
§ 744.3085, Fla. Stat. Guardian advocates.

Rule References

Fla. Prob. R. 5.041(b) Service of pleadings and papers.
Fla. Prob. R. 5.110(b), (c) Resident agent.
Fla. R. Jud. Admin. 2.505 Attorneys.
Fla. R. Jud. Admin. 2.516 Service of pleadings and documents.
Fla. R. App. P. 9.440 Attorneys.

RULE 5.040.   NOTICE

(a)   Formal Notice.

(1)   When formal notice is given, a copy of the pleading or motion shall be served on interested persons, together with a notice requiring the person served to serve written defenses on the person giving notice within 20 days after service of the notice, exclusive of the day of service, and to file the original of the written defenses with the clerk of the court either before service or immediately thereafter, and notifying the person served that failure to serve written defenses as required may result in a judgment or order for the relief demanded in the pleading or motion, without further notice.

(2)   After service of formal notice, informal notice of any hearing on the pleading or motion shall be served on interested persons, provided that if no written defense is served within 20 days after service of formal notice on an interested person, the pleading or motion may be considered ex parte as to that person, unless the court orders otherwise.

(3)   Formal notice shall be served:

(A)   by sending a copy by any commercial delivery service requiring a signed receipt or by any form of mail requiring a signed receipt as follows:

(i)   to the attorney representing an interested person; or

(ii)   to an interested person who has filed a request for notice at the address given in the request for notice; or

(iii)   to an incapacitated person or a person with a developmental disability to the person's usual place of abode and to the person's legal guardian, if any, at the guardian's usual place of abode or regular place of business; or, if there is no legal guardian, to the incapacitated person or person with a developmental disability at the person's usual place of abode and on the person, if any, having care or custody of the incapacitated person or person with a developmental disability at the usual place of abode or regular place of business of such custodian; or

(iv)   to a minor whose disabilities of nonage are not removed, by serving the persons designated to accept service of process on a minor under chapter 48, Florida Statutes; or

(v)   on any other individual to the individual's usual place of abode or to the place where the individual regularly conducts business; or

(vi)   on a corporation or other business entity to its registered office in Florida or its principal business office in Florida or, if neither is known after reasonable inquiry, to its last known address; or

(B)   as provided in the Florida Rules of Civil Procedure for service of process; or

(C)   as otherwise provided by Florida law for service of process.

11

(4)   Service of formal notice pursuant to subdivision (3)(A) shall be complete on receipt of the notice. Proof of service shall be by verified statement of the person giving the notice; and there shall be attached to the verified statement the signed receipt or other evidence satisfactory to the court that delivery was made to the addressee or the addressee's agent.

(5)   If service of process is made pursuant to Florida law, proof of service shall be made as provided therein.

(b)   Informal Notice. When informal notice of a petition or other proceeding is required or permitted, it shall be served as provided in rule 5.041.

(c)   "Notice" Defined. In these rules, the Florida Probate Code, and the Florida Guardianship Law "notice" shall mean informal notice unless formal notice is specified.

(d)   Formal Notice Optional. Formal notice may be given in lieu of informal notice at the option of the person giving notice unless the court orders otherwise. When formal notice is given in lieu of informal notice, formal notice shall be given to all interested persons entitled to notice. When formal notice is given in lieu of informal notice, that notice does not modify any time period otherwise specified by statute or these rules.

Committee Notes

Formal notice is the method of service used in probate proceedings and the method of service of process for obtaining jurisdiction over the person receiving the notice. "The manner provided for service of formal notice" is as provided in rule 5.040(a)(3).

Informal notice is the method of service of notice given to interested persons entitled to notice when formal notice is not given or required.

Reference in this rule to the terms "mail" or "mailing" refers to use of the United States Postal Service.

Rule History

1975 Revision: Implements section 731.301, Florida Statutes.

1977 Revision: Reference to elisor.

1980 Revision: Editorial changes. Clarification of time for filing defenses after formal notice. Authorizes court to give relief to delinquent respondent from ex parte status; relief from service on numerous persons; allows optional use of formal notice.

1984 Revision: Editorial changes. Eliminates deadline for filing as opposed to serving defenses after formal notice; defines procedure subsequent to service of defenses after formal notice; new requirements for service of formal notice on incompetents and corporations; defines when service of formal notice is deemed complete; provisions relating to method of service of informal notice transferred to new rules 5.041 and 5.042; eliminates waiver of notice by will.

1988 Revision: Editorial changes. Committee notes revised. Citation form changes in committee notes.

1991 Revision: Subdivision (b) amended to define informal notice more clearly.

1992 Revision: Editorial changes. Committee notes revised. Citation form changes in committee notes.

1996 Revision: Subdivision (a) amended to permit service of formal notice by commercial delivery service to conform to 1993 amendment to section 731.301(1), Florida Statutes. Editorial changes.

2001 Revision: Editorial changes in subdivision (a)(3)(A) to clarify requirements for service of formal notice.

2003 Revision: Committee notes revised.

2005 Revision: Subdivision (a)(3)(A) amended to delete requirement of court approval of commercial delivery service.

2006 Revision: Committee notes revised.

2007 Revision: Committee notes revised.

2007 Revision: New subdivision (a)(3)(A)(iv) inserted in response to Cason ex rel. Saferight v. Hammock, 908 So.2d 512 (Fla. 5th DCA 2005), and subsequent subdivisions renumbered accordingly. Committee notes revised.

2008 Revision: Subdivision (a)(3)(A)(iii) revised to include "person with a developmental disability." Committee notes revised.

2010 Revision: Subdivision (d) amended to clarify that the optional use of formal notice when only informal notice is required does not modify any time period otherwise specified by statutes or rule. Committee notes revised.

2012 Revision: Subdivision (b) revised to reflect amendment to rule 5.041.

Statutory References

§ 1.01(3), Fla. Stat. Definitions.
ch. 48, Fla. Stat. Process and service of process.
ch. 49, Fla. Stat. Constructive service of process.
§ 393.12, Fla. Stat. Capacity; appointment of guardian advocate.
§ 731.105, Fla. Stat. In rem proceeding.
§ 731.201(18), (22), Fla. Stat. General definitions.
§ 731.301, Fla. Stat. Notice.
§ 731.302, Fla. Stat. Waiver and consent by interested person.
§ 733.212, Fla. Stat. Notice of administration; filing of objections.
§ 733.2123, Fla. Stat. Adjudication before issuance of letters.
§ 733.502, Fla. Stat. Resignation of personal representative.
§ 733.613, Fla. Stat. Personal representative's right to sell real property.
§ 733.6175, Fla. Stat. Proceedings for review of employment of agents and compensation of personal representatives and employees of estate.

§ 733.901, Fla. Stat. Final discharge.

ch. 743, Fla. Stat. Disability of nonage of minors removed.

§ 744.106, Fla. Stat. Notice.

§ 744.301, Fla. Stat. Natural guardians.

§ 744.3085, Fla. Stat. Guardian advocates.

§ 744.3201, Fla. Stat. Petition to determine incapacity.

§ 744.331, Fla. Stat. Procedures to determine incapacity.

§ 744.3371, Fla. Stat. Notice of petition for appointment of guardian and hearing.

§ 744.441, Fla. Stat. Powers of guardian upon court approval.

§ 744.447, Fla. Stat. Petition for authorization to act.

§ 744.477, Fla. Stat. Proceedings for removal of a guardian.

Rule References

Fla. Prob. R. 5.025 Adversary proceedings.

Fla. Prob. R. 5.030 Attorneys.

Fla. Prob. R. 5.041 Service of pleadings and documents.

Fla. Prob. R. 5.042 Time.

Fla. Prob. R. 5.060 Request for notices and copies of pleadings.

Fla. Prob. R. 5.180 Waiver and consent.

Fla. Prob. R. 5.560 Petition for appointment of guardian of an incapacitated person.

Fla. Prob. R. 5.649 Guardian advocate.

Fla. Prob. R. 5.681 Restoration of rights of person with developmental disability.

Fla. R. Jud. Admin. 2.505 Attorneys.

Fla. R. Jud. Admin. 2.516 Service of pleadings and documents.

Fla. R. Civ. P. 1.070 Process.

Fla. R. Civ. P. Form 1.902 Summons.

RULE 5.041.   SERVICE OF PLEADINGS AND DOCUMENTS

Unless the court orders otherwise, every petition or motion for an order determining rights of an interested person, and every other pleading or document filed in the particular proceeding which is the subject matter of such petition or motion, except applications for witness subpoenas, shall be served on interested persons as set forth in Florida Rule of Judicial Administration 2.516 unless these rules, the Florida Probate Code, or the Florida Guardianship Law provides otherwise. No service need be made on interested persons against whom a default has been entered, or against whom the matter may otherwise proceed ex parte, unless a new or additional right or demand is asserted. For purposes of this rule an interested person shall be deemed a party under rule 2.516.

If the interested person is a minor whose disabilities of nonage are not removed, and who is not represented by an attorney, then service shall be on the persons designated to accept service of process on a minor under chapter 48, Florida Statutes.

Committee Notes

Derived from Florida Rule of Civil Procedure 1.080. Regulates the service of pleadings and papers in proceedings on petitions or motions for determination of rights. It is not applicable to every pleading and paper served or filed in the administration of a guardianship or decedent's estate.

Rule History

1984 Revision: New rule. Subdivision (c) is same as former rule 5.040(d).

1988 Revision: Committee notes revised. Citation form changes in committee notes.

1992 Revision: Editorial changes. Committee notes revised. Citation form changes in committee notes.

1996 Revision: Subdivision (b) amended to allow service to be made by facsimile. Committee notes revised.

2000 Revision: Subdivision (b) amended to clarify requirements for service of pleadings and papers. Subdivision (e) amended to clarify date of filing. Editorial changes in subdivision (f).

2003 Revision: Committee notes revised.

2005 Revision: Changes in subdivisions (b) and (f) to clarify service requirements, and editorial changes in (e).

2006 Revision: Committee notes revised.

2007 Revision: Provisions regarding service on a minor added in subdivision (b) in response to *Cason ex rel. Saferight v. Hammock*, 908 So.2d 512 (Fla. 5th DCA 2005). Committee notes revised.

2008 Revision: Committee notes revised. 2010 Revision: Committee notes revised.

2012 Revision: Portions of subdivision (b) and all of subdivisions (d), (e), (f), and (g) deleted in response to creation of Rule 2.516 of the Rules of Judicial Administration. Committee notes revised.

Statutory References

ch. 39, Fla. Stat. Proceedings relating to children.
ch. 48, Fla. Stat. Process and service of process.
ch. 61, Fla. Stat. Dissolution of marriage; support; time-sharing.
ch. 63, Fla. Stat. Adoption.
§ 393.12, Fla. Stat. Capacity; appointment of guardian advocate.
§ 731.201, Fla. Stat. General definitions.
§ 731.301, Fla. Stat. Notice.
§ 733.212, Fla. Stat. Notice of administration; filing of objections.
§ 733.2123, Fla. Stat. Adjudication before issuance of letters.
§ 733.705(2), (4), Fla. Stat. Payment of and objection to claims.
ch. 743, Fla. Stat. Disability of nonage of minors removed.
§ 744.3085, Fla. Stat. Guardian advocates.
§ 744.3201, Fla. Stat. Petition to determine incapacity.
§ 744.331, Fla. Stat. Procedures to determine incapacity.
§ 744.3371, Fla. Stat. Notice of petition for appointment of guardian and hearing.
§ 744.447, Fla. Stat. Petition for authorization to act.

Florida Probate Rules

ch. 751, Fla. Stat. Temporary custody of minor children by extended family.

Rule References

Fla. Prob. R. 5.020 Pleadings; verification; motions.
Fla. Prob. R. 5.025 Adversary proceedings.
Fla. Prob. R. 5.030 Attorneys. Fla. Prob. R. 5.040 Notice.
Fla. Prob. R. 5.042 Time.
Fla. Prob. R. 5.150(c) Order requiring accounting.
Fla. Prob. R. 5.180 Waiver and consent.
Fla. Prob. R. 5.240(a) Notice of administration.
Fla. Prob. R. 5.340(d) Inventory.
Fla. Prob. R. 5.550 Petition to determine incapacity.
Fla. Prob. R. 5.560 Petition for appointment of guardian of an incapacitated person.
Fla. Prob. R. 5.649 Guardian advocate.
Fla. Prob. R. 5.681 Restoration of rights of person with developmental disability.
Fla. R. Civ. P. 1.080 Service of pleadings and papers.
Fla. R. Jud. Admin. 2.505 Attorneys.
Fla. R. Jud. Admin. 2.516 Service of pleadings and documents.

RULE 5.042.   TIME

(a)   Computation. Computation of time shall be governed by Florida Rule of Judicial Administration 2.514.

(b)   Enlargement. When an act is required or allowed to be done at or within a specified time by these rules, by order of court, or by notice given thereunder, for cause shown the court at any time in its discretion

(1)   with or without notice may order the period enlarged if request therefor is made before the expiration of the period originally prescribed or as extended by a previous order, or

(2)   on motion made and notice after the expiration of the specified period may permit the act to be done when failure to act was the result of excusable neglect. The court under this rule may not extend the time for serving a motion for rehearing or to enlarge any period of time governed by the Florida Rules of Appellate Procedure.

(c)   Service for Hearings. A copy of any written petition or motion which may not be heard ex parte and a copy of the notice of the hearing thereon shall be served a reasonable time before the time specified for the hearing.

(d)   Additional Time After Service by Mail Or E-mail. Except when serving formal notice, or when serving a motion, pleading, or other document in the manner provided for service of formal notice, Florida Rule of Judicial Administration 2.514 shall apply to the computation of time following service.

Committee Notes

This rule is derived from Florida Rule of Civil Procedure 1.090.

Rule History

1984 Revision: New rule.

1988 Revision: Editorial changes in (a) and (b). Subdivision (a) enlarged to include closing of the clerk's office as a legal holiday. In *Clara P. Diamond, Inc. v. Tam-Bay Realty, Inc.*, 462 So. 2d 1168 (Fla. 2d DCA 1984), the Second District Court of Appeal suggested that Florida Rule of Civil Procedure 1.090(b) be clarified to leave no question that the court may not extend the time for rehearing, appeal, or petition for certiorari regardless of whether a request to enlarge the time therefor was made before the expiration of the time allowed. Because the format of rule 5.042(b) was substantially the same as the format of rule 1.090(b), subdivision (b) is amended to conform for the sake of clarity. Committee notes revised.

1992 Revision: Editorial changes. Committee notes revised. Citation form changes in committee notes. 2003 Revision: Committee notes revised.

2005 Revision: Subdivision (d) amended to clarify exception to mailing rule for service of formal notice and service in the manner provided for service of formal notice. Committee notes revised.

2008 Revision: Committee notes revised.

2012 Revision: Subdivision (a) revised to refer to Rule 2.514 and delete duplicative provisions. Subdivision (d) revised to incorporate service by e-mail and the filing and service of documents, rather than papers. Committee notes revised.

Statutory References

§ 393.12, Fla. Stat. Capacity; appointment of guardian advocate.
§ 683.01, Fla. Stat. Legal holidays.
§ 731.301, Fla. Stat. Notice.
§ 732.107, Fla. Stat. Escheat.
§ 732.2135, Fla. Stat. Time of election; extensions; withdrawal.
§ 732.402, Fla. Stat. Exempt property.
§ 732.901, Fla. Stat. Production of wills.
§ 733.104, Fla. Stat. Suspension of statutes of limitation in favor of the personal representative.
§ 733.212, Fla. Stat. Notice of administration; filing of objections.
§ 733.2121, Fla. Stat. Notice to creditors; filing of claims.
§ 733.701, Fla. Stat. Notifying creditors.
§ 733.702, Fla. Stat. Limitations on presentation of claims.
§ 733.705, Fla. Stat. Payment of and objection to claims.
§ 733.710, Fla. Stat. Limitations on claims against estates.
§ 733.816, Fla. Stat. Disposition of unclaimed property held by personal representatives.
§ 744.3085, Fla. Stat. Guardian advocates.

Rule References

Fla. Prob. R. 5.040(a)(1) Notice.
Fla. Prob. R. 5.150 Order requiring accounting.

Fla. Prob. R. 5.240 Notice of administration.
Fla. Prob. R. 5.241 Notice to creditors.
Fla. Prob. R. 5.340(a)–(b) Inventory.
Fla. Prob. R. 5.345 Accountings other than personal representatives' final accountings.
Fla. Prob. R. 5.395 Notice of federal estate tax return.
Fla. Prob. R. 5.400 Distribution and discharge.
Fla. Prob. R. 5.649 Guardian advocate.
Fla. Prob. R. 5.681 Restoration of rights of person with developmental disability.
Fla. Prob. R. 5.700 Objection to guardianship reports.
Fla. R. Civ. P. 1.090 Time.
Fla. R. Jud. Admin. 2.514 Computing and extending time.

RULE 5.043. DEPOSIT OF WILLS AND CODICILS

Text of rule as amended by Florida Supreme Court Opinion SC11-399.

Notwithstanding any rule to the contrary, and unless the court orders otherwise, any original executed will or codicil deposited with the court must be retained by the clerk in its original form and must not be destroyed or disposed of by the clerk for 20 years after submission regardless of whether the will or codicil has been permanently recorded as defined by Florida Rule of Judicial Administration 2.430.

Committee Notes

2012 Adoption. Florida Rule of Judicial Administration 2.525 requires that all documents be filed with the court electronically. Although the Florida Statutes direct deposit of a will, rather than the filing of the will, the committee believes that original wills and codicils should be retained in their original form longer than other documents filed with the court due to the unique evidentiary aspects of the actual document. These unique aspects could be lost forever if the original document were converted to electronic form and the original destroyed.

Rule History

2012 Revision: New Rule.

Statutory References

§ 731.201(16), Fla. Stat. General definitions.
§ 732.901, Fla. Stat. Production of wills.

Rule References

Fla. R. Jud. Admin. 2.430 Retention of court records.
Fla. R. Jud. Admin. 2.525 Electronic filing.

Editor's Note

On October 18, 2012, the Supreme Court of Florida issued a revised opinion in case number SC11-399, which was originally issued on June 21, 2012. See *In re Amendments to the Florida Rules of Judicial Administration*, 102 So. 3d 451 (Fla. 2012).

Florida Probate Rules

The opinion provides in relevant part:

"First, the new electronic filing requirements the Courts adopts will become effective in the civil, probate, small claims, and family law divisions of the trial courts, as well as for appeals to the circuit courts in these categories of cases, on April 1, 2013, at 12:01 a.m., except as may be otherwise provided by administrative order. Electronic filing will be mandatory in these divisions pursuant to rule 2.525 on that date. However, until the new rules take effect in these divisions, any clerk who is already accepting documents filed by electronic transmission under the current rules should continue to do so; attorneys in these counties are encouraged to file documents electronically under the current rules.

"Next, the new electronic filing requirements the Court adopts will become effective in the criminal, traffic, and juvenile divisions of the trial courts, as well as for appeals to the circuit court in these categories of cases, on October 1, 2013, at 12:01 a.m., except as may be otherwise provided by administrative order. Electronic filing will be mandatory in these divisions under rule 2.525 on that date. The new e-filing requirements, as they apply in proceedings brought pursuant to the Florida Mental Health Act (Baker Act), Chapter 394, Part I, Florida Statutes, and the Involuntary Commitment of Sexually Violent Predators Act (Jimmy Ryce), Chapter 394, Part V, Florida Statutes, will also not be mandatory in these cases until October 1, 2013. As stated above, until the new rules take effect in these divisions and proceedings, any clerk who is already accepting electronically filed documents under the current rules should continue to do so; attorneys are again encouraged to utilize existing electronic filing procedures under the current rules.

"However, until the new rules and procedures take effect in the district courts, any clerk who is already accepting documents filed by electronic transmission may continue to do so; attorneys in these districts are encouraged to file documents electronically. Clerks will not be required to electronically transmit the record on appeal until July 1, 2013, at 12:01 a.m. Until July 1, we encourage clerks, whenever possible, to electronically transmit the record under the new rules and requirements.

"(W)e note that, in all types of cases, pursuant to amended rule 2.525(d) self-represented parties and self- represented nonparties, including nonparty governmental or public agencies, and attorneys excused from e-mail service under Florida Rule of Judicial Administration 2.516 will be permitted, but nor required, to file documents electronically.

By order of November 28, 2012, in case number SC11-399, the Court released a revised implementation schedule, which provides, in pertinent part: "The e-filing rules adopted in the October 2012 opinion will be mandatory in this (Supreme) Court on February 27, 2013, at 12:01 a.m.; and effective earlier on a voluntary basis as will be indicated by further administrative order of the chief justice.

"Thereafter, the e-filing rules will be mandatory in the Second District Court of Appeal on July 22, 2013, at 12:01 a.m.; in the Third District Court of Appeal on September 27, 2013, at 12:01 a.m.; in the Fourth District Court of Appeal on October 31, 2013, at 12:01 a.m.; in the Fifth District Court of Appeal on November 27, 2013 at 12:01 a.m.; and in the First District Court of Appeal on December 27, 2013, at 12:01 a.m., unless made mandatory earlier by the chief judge of the applicable district court of appeal. The e-filing rules will be effective earlier on a voluntary trial basis in the district courts of appeal as will be indicated by further administrative order by the chief judge of the applicable district court."

RULE 5.050.   **TRANSFER OF PROCEEDINGS**

(a)   **Incorrect Venue.** When any proceeding is filed laying venue in the wrong county, the court may transfer the proceeding in the same manner as provided in the Florida Rules of Civil Procedure. Any action taken by the court or the parties before the transfer is not affected because of the improper venue.

(b)   **Change of Residence of Ward.** When the residence of a ward is changed to another county, the guardian of the person or the guardian advocate shall have the venue of the guardianship changed to the county of the acquired residence.

Committee Notes

Subdivision (b) of this rule represents a rule implementation of the procedure found in section 744.202(3), Florida Statutes.

Rule History

1975 Revision: Same as section 733.101(3), Florida Statutes.

1977 Revision: Title changed to indicate that the rule is one dealing with transfer.

1988 Revision: Prior rule renumbered as (a). New (b) is rule implementation of procedure in section 744.202(2), Florida Statutes. Editorial changes. Committee notes expanded. Citation form changes in rule and committee notes.

1991 Revision: Editorial changes.

1992 Revision: Committee notes revised. Citation form changes in committee notes.

2003 Revision: Committee notes revised.

2008 Revision: Change in (b) to add reference to guardian advocate. Committee notes revised.

Statutory References

ch. 47, Fla. Stat. Venue.
§ 393.12, Fla. Stat. Capacity; appointment of guardian advocate.
§ 733.101, Fla. Stat. Venue of probate proceedings.
§ 744.106, Fla. Stat. Notice.
§ 744.201, Fla. Stat. Domicile of ward.
§ 744.202, Fla. Stat. Venue.
§ 744.2025, Fla. Stat. Change of ward's residence.
§ 744.306, Fla. Stat. Foreign guardians.
§ 744.3085, Fla. Stat. Guardian advocates.
§ 744.3201, Fla. Stat. Petition to determine incapacity.

Rule References

Fla. Prob. R. 5.200(d) Petition for administration.

Fla. Prob. R. 5.240(b)(3), (d) Notice of administration.
Fla. Prob. R. 5.649 Guardian advocate.
Fla. R. Civ. P. 1.060 Transfers of actions.

RULE 5.060.   **REQUEST FOR NOTICES AND COPIES OF PLEADINGS**

     (a)   **Request.** Any interested person who desires notice of proceedings in the estate of a decedent or ward may file a separate written request for notice of further proceedings, designating therein such person's residence and post office address. When such person's residence or post office address changes, a new designation of such change shall be filed in the proceedings. A person filing such request, or address change, shall also deliver a copy thereof to the clerk, who shall forthwith mail it to the attorney for the personal representative or guardian, noting on the original the fact of mailing.

     (b)   **Notice and Copies.** A party filing a request shall be served thereafter by the moving party with notice of further proceedings and with copies of subsequent pleadings and papers as long as the party is an interested person.

Committee Notes

Rule History

     1975 Revision: This rule substantially incorporates the provisions of prior rule 5.060 except that now a copy of the request shall be mailed by the clerk only to the attorney for the personal representative or guardian. Even though a request under this rule has not been made, informal notice as provided in rule 5.040(b)(3) may still be required.

     1977 Revision: Editorial and citation form change in committee note.

     1980 Revision: Caveat, the personal representative may want to give notice to parties even though not required, for example, where an independent action has been filed on an objected claim.

     1988 Revision: Captions added to subdivisions. Committee notes expanded. Citation form changes in committee notes.

     1992 Revision: Editorial changes. Committee notes revised. Citation form changes in committee notes.

     2003 Revision: Committee notes revised.

     2010 Revision: Committee notes revised.

     2012 Revision: Committee notes revised.

Statutory References

§ 731.201, Fla. Stat. General definitions.
§ 733.604, Fla. Stat. Inventories and accountings; public records exemptions.

Rule References

Fla. Prob. R. 5.040 Notice.
Fla. Prob. R. 5.041 Service of pleadings and documents.
Fla. Prob. R. 5.340 Inventory.
Fla. Prob. R. 5.341 Estate information.
Fla. R. Jud. Admin. 2.516 Service of pleadings and documents.

RULE 5.065. NOTICE OF CIVIL ACTION OR ANCILLARY ADMINISTRATION

(a) Civil Action. A personal representative and a guardian shall file a notice when a civil action has been instituted by or against the personal representative or the guardian. The notice shall contain:

> (1) the names of the parties;

> (2) the style of the court and the case number;

> (3) the county and state where the proceeding is pending;

> (4) the date of commencement of the proceeding; and

> (5) a brief statement of the nature of the proceeding.

(b) Ancillary Administration. The domiciliary personal representative shall file a notice when an ancillary administration has commenced, which notice shall contain:

> (1) the name and residence address of the ancillary personal representative; and

> (2) the information required in subdivisions (a)(2), (3), and (4) above

(c) Copies Exhibited. A copy of the initial pleading may be attached to the notice. To the extent an attached initial pleading states the required information, the notice need not restate it.

Committee Notes

This rule reflects a procedural requirement not founded on a statute or rule.

Rule History

1984 Revision: New rule.
1988 Revision: Committee notes expanded.
1992 Revision: Editorial change. Citation form changes in committee notes.
2000 Revision: Subdivision (b) amended to eliminate requirement to set forth nature and value of ancillary assets.

Statutory References

§ 733.612(20), Fla. Stat. Transactions authorized for the personal representative; exceptions.

§ 744.441(11), Fla. Stat. Powers of guardian upon court approval.

RULE 5.080.   DISCOVERY AND SUBPOENA

(a)   Adoption of Civil Rules. The following Florida Rules of Civil Procedure shall apply in all probate and guardianship proceedings:

(1)   Rule 1.280, general provisions governing discovery.

(2)   Rule 1.290, depositions before action or pending appeal.

(3)   Rule 1.300, persons before whom depositions may be taken.

(4)   Rule 1.310, depositions upon oral examination.

(5)   Rule 1.320, depositions upon written questions.

(6)   Rule 1.330, use of depositions in court proceedings.

(7)   Rule 1.340, interrogatories to parties.

(8)   Rule 1.350, production of documents and things and entry upon land for inspection and other purposes.

(9)   Rule 1.351, production of documents and things without deposition.

(11)   Rule 1.370, requests for admission.

(12)   Rule 1.380, failure to make discovery; sanctions.

(13)   Rule 1.390, depositions of expert witnesses.

(14)   Rule 1.410, subpoena.

(b)   Limitations and Costs. In order to conserve the assets of the estate, the court has broad discretion to limit the scope and the place and manner of the discovery and to assess the costs, including attorneys' fees, of the discovery against the party making it or against 1 or more of the beneficiaries of the estate or against the ward in such proportions as the court determines, considering, among other factors, the benefit derived therefrom.

(c)   Application. It is not necessary to have an adversary proceeding under rule 5.025 to utilize the rules adopted in subdivision (a) above. Any interested person may utilize the rules adopted in subdivision (a).

Committee Notes

Subdivision (b) is not intended to result in the assessment of costs, including attorney's fees, in every instance in which discovery is sought. Subdivision (c) is not intended to overrule the holdings in *In re Estate of Shaw*, 340 So. 2d 491 (Fla. 3d DCA 1976), and *In re Estate of Posner*, 492 So. 2d 1093 (Fla. 3d DCA 1986).

Rule History

1975 Revision: This rule is the same as prior rule 5.080, broadened to include guardianships and intended to clearly permit the use of discovery practices in nonadversary probate and guardianship matters.

1977 Revision: Editorial change in citation form in committee note.

1984 Revision: Florida Rules of Civil Procedure 1.290, 1.300, 1.351, and 1.410 have been added.

1988 Revision: Subdivision (a)(15) deleted as duplicative of rule 5.070 Subpoena. Editorial change in (b). Citation form change in committee notes.

1992 Revision: Editorial changes. Committee notes revised. Citation form changes in committee notes.

1996 Revision: Reference to rule 1.400 eliminated because of deletion of that rule from the Florida Rules of Civil Procedure. Editorial change.

2002 Revision: Reference to rule 1.410 transferred to subdivision (a) from former rule 5.070. Subdivision (b) amended to give court discretion to assess attorneys' fees. Subdivision (c) added. Committee notes revised.

2006 Revision: Committee notes revised.

2007 Revision: Committee notes revised.

Statutory References

§ 731.201(23), Fla. Stat. General definitions.
§ 733.106, Fla. Stat. Costs and attorney's fees.
§ 744.105, Fla. Stat. Costs.
§ 744.108, Fla. Stat. Guardian's and attorney's fees and expenses.

Rule References

Fla. Prob. R. 5.025 Adversary proceedings.
Fla. R. Jud. Admin. 2.535 Court reporting.

RULE 5.095.   GENERAL AND SPECIAL MAGISTRATES

(a)   **General Magistrates.** The court may appoint general magistrates as the court finds necessary. General magistrates shall be members of The Florida Bar and shall continue in office until removed by the court. The order making an appointment shall be recorded. Each general magistrate shall take the oath required of officers by the Florida Constitution. The oath shall be recorded before the magistrate begins to act.

(b) **Special Magistrates.** The court may appoint members of The Florida Bar as special magistrates for any particular service required by the court. Special magistrates shall be governed by all laws and rules relating to general magistrates, except special magistrates shall not be required to make oath unless specifically required by the court. For good cause shown, the court may appoint a person other than a member of The Florida Bar as a special magistrate.

(c) **Reference.** No referral shall be made to a magistrate without the consent of the parties. When a referral is made to a magistrate, either party may set the action for hearing before the magistrate.

(d) **General Powers and Duties.** Every magistrate shall act under the direction of the court. Process issued by a magistrate shall be directed as provided by law. All grounds for disqualification of a judge shall apply to magistrates.

(e) **Bond.** When not otherwise provided by law, the court may require magistrates who are appointed to dispose of real or personal property to give bond and surety conditioned for the proper payment of all money that may come into their hands and for the due performance of their duties. The bond shall be made payable to the State of Florida and shall be for the benefit of all persons aggrieved by any act of the magistrate.

(f) **Hearings.** Hearings before any magistrate may be held in the county where the action is pending or at any other place by order of the court for the convenience of the witnesses or the parties. The magistrate shall assign a time and place for proceedings as soon as reasonably possible after a referral is made and give notice to all parties. If any party fails to appear, the magistrate may proceed ex parte or may continue the hearing to a future day, with notice to the absent party. The magistrate shall proceed with reasonable diligence and the least practicable delay. Any party may apply to the court for an order directing the magistrate to accelerate the proceedings and to make a report promptly. Evidence shall be taken in writing or by electronic recording by the magistrate or by some other person under the magistrate's authority in the magistrate's presence and shall be filed with the magistrate's report. The magistrate may examine and take testimony from the parties and their witnesses under oath on all matters contained in the referral and may require production of all books, papers, writings, vouchers, and other documents applicable to those matters. The magistrate shall admit only evidence that would be admissible in court. The magistrate may take all actions concerning evidence that may be taken by the court. All parties accounting before a magistrate shall bring in their accounts in the form of accounts payable and receivable, and any other parties who are not satisfied with the account may examine the accounting party orally or by interrogatories or deposition as the magistrate directs. All depositions and documents that have been taken or used previously in the action may be used before the magistrate.

(g) **Magistrate's Report.** The magistrate's report shall contain a description of the matters considered and the magistrate's conclusion and any recommendations. No part of any statement of facts, account, charge, deposition, examination, or answer used before the magistrate shall be recited.

(h) **Filing Report; Notice; Exceptions.** The magistrate shall file the report and serve copies on the parties. The parties may serve exceptions to the report within 10 days from the time it is served on them. If no exceptions are filed within that period, the court shall take appropriate action on the report. All timely filed exceptions shall be heard on reasonable notice by either party.

(i) **Application of Rule.** This rule shall not apply to the appointment of magistrates for the specific purpose of reviewing guardianship inventories, accountings, and plans as otherwise governed by law and these rules.

Committee Notes

Rule History

2007 Revision: This rule, patterned after Florida Rule of Civil Procedure 1.490, is created to implement the use of magistrates in probate and guardianship proceedings other than those specifically addressed in rule 5.697.

Rule References

Fla. Prob. R. 5.697 Magistrates' review of guardianship inventories, accountings, and plans.
Fla. R. Civ. P. 1.490 Magistrates.

RULE 5.100.   RIGHT OF APPEAL

Appeal of final orders and discretionary appellate review of non-final orders are governed by the Florida Rules of Appellate Procedure.

Committee Notes

For purposes of appellate review, the service of a motion for rehearing postpones rendition of final orders only. A motion for rehearing of a non-final order does not toll the running of the time to seek review of that order.

Rule History

1975 Revision: Same as prior rule 5.100 with editorial changes.

1977 Revision: Citation form change in committee note.

1988 Revision: Committee notes expanded. Citation form changes in rule and committee notes.

1992 Revision: Editorial changes. Citation form changes in committee notes.

1996 Revision: Superseded by Florida Rule of Appellate Procedure 9.110(a)(2).

2000 Revision: Rewritten because former rule was superseded. Revisions to committee notes to amend text and to include cross-references to other rules.

2003 Revision: Committee notes revised.

Rule References

Fla. Prob. R. 5.020(d) Pleadings; verifications; motions.
Fla. R. App. P. 9.020(h) Definitions.

Fla. R. App. P. 9.110(a)(2), (b) Appeal proceedings to review final orders of lower tribunals and orders granting new trial in jury and non-jury cases.

Fla. R. App. P. 9.130(b) Proceedings to review non-final orders and specified final orders.

RULE 5.110. **ADDRESS DESIGNATION FOR PERSONAL REPRESENTATIVE OR GUARDIAN; DESIGNATION OF RESIDENT AGENT AND ACCEPTANCE**

(a) **Address Designation of Personal Representative or Guardian.** Before letters are issued, the personal representative or guardian shall file a designation of its residence street address and mailing address. The personal representative or guardian shall notify the court of any change in its residence street address or mailing address within 20 days of the change.

(b) **Designation of Resident Agent.** Before letters are issued, a personal representative or guardian shall file a designation of resident agent for service of process or notice, and the acceptance by the resident agent. A designation of resident agent is not required if a personal representative or guardian is (1) a corporate fiduciary having an office in Florida, or (2) a Florida Bar member who is a resident of and has an office in Florida. The designation shall contain the name, residence street address, and mailing address of the resident agent. A Florida office street address and mailing address for the attorney as resident agent may be designated in lieu of a residence address.

(c) **Residency Requirement.** A resident agent, other than a member of The Florida Bar who is a resident of Florida, must be a resident of the county where the proceedings are pending.

(d) **Acceptance by Resident Agent.** The resident agent shall sign a written acceptance of its designation.

(e) **Incorporation in Other Pleadings.** The designation of the address of the personal representative or guardian, the designation of resident agent, or acceptance may be incorporated in the petition for administration, the petition for appointment of guardian, or the personal representative's or guardian's oath.

(f) **Effect of Designation and Acceptance.** The designation of and acceptance by the resident agent shall constitute consent to service of process or notice on the agent and shall be sufficient to bind the personal representative or guardian:

(1) in its representative capacity in any action; and

(2) in its personal capacity only in those actions in which the personal representative or guardian is sued personally for claims arising from the administration of the estate or guardianship.

(g) **Successor Agent.** If the resident agent dies, resigns, or is unable to act for any other reason, the personal representative or guardian shall appoint a successor agent within 10 days after receiving notice that such event has occurred.

Florida Probate Rules

Rule History

1977 Revision: Change in committee note to conform to statutory renumbering. Substantially the same as prior rule 5.210, except that under prior rule, designation was required to be filed within 10 days after letters issued.

1984 Revision: Captions added to subdivisions. New subdivision (b) added. Requires filing acceptance at the same time as filing designation. Committee notes revised.

1988 Revision: Change in (c) to clarify that the personal representative, if a member of The Florida Bar, may not also serve as resident agent for service of process or notice. Citation form change in committee notes.

1992 Revision: Editorial changes. Committee notes revised. Citation form changes in committee notes.

2000 Revision: Extensive editorial changes to rule. Rule reformatted for clarity and revised to permit an attorney serving as resident agent to designate a business address in lieu of a residence address.

2003 Revision: Committee notes revised.

2008 Revision: Committee notes revised.

2010 Revision: Subdivision (a) amended to require the personal representative or guardian to notify the court of any change of address to facilitate timely communication with the personal representative or guardian.

Rule References

Fla. Prob. R. 5.200 Petition for administration.
Fla. Prob. R. 5.320 Oath of personal representative.
Fla. Prob. R. 5.560 Petition for appointment of guardian of an incapacitated person.
Fla. Prob. R. 5.649 Guardian advocate.

RULE 5.120.   ADMINISTRATOR AD LITEM AND GUARDIAN AD LITEM

(a)   **Appointment.** When it is necessary that the estate of a decedent or a ward be represented in any probate or guardianship proceeding and there is no personal representative of the estate or guardian of the ward, or the personal representative or guardian is or may be interested adversely to the estate or ward, or is enforcing the personal representative's or guardian's own debt or claim against the estate or ward, or the necessity arises otherwise, the court may appoint an administrator ad litem or a guardian ad litem, as the case may be, without bond or notice for that particular proceeding. At any point in a proceeding, a court may appoint a guardian ad litem to represent the interests of an incapacitated person, an unborn or unascertained person, a minor or any other person otherwise under a legal disability, a person with a developmental disability, or a person whose identity or address is unknown, if the court determines that representation of the interest otherwise would be inadequate. If not precluded by conflict of interest, a guardian ad litem may be appointed to represent several persons or interests. The administrator ad litem or guardian ad litem shall file an oath to discharge all duties faithfully and upon the filing shall be qualified to act. No process need be served upon the administrator ad litem or guardian ad litem, but such person shall appear and defend as directed by the court.

(b) **Petition.** The petition for appointment of a guardian ad litem shall state to the best of petitioner's information and belief:

(1) the name and residence address of each minor, person with a developmental disability, or incapacitated person and birth date of each minor who has an interest in the proceedings;

(2) the name and address of any guardian appointed for each minor, person with a developmental disability, or incapacitated person;

(3) the name and residence address of any living natural guardians or living natural guardian having legal custody of each minor, person with a developmental disability, or incapacitated person;

(4) a description of the interest in the proceedings of each minor, person with a developmental disability, or incapacitated person; and

(5) the facts showing the necessity for the appointment of a guardian ad litem.

(c) **Notice.** Within 10 days after appointment, the petitioner shall serve conformed copies of the petition for appointment of a guardian ad litem and order to any guardian, or if there is no guardian, to the living natural guardians or the living natural guardian having legal custody of the minor, person with a developmental disability, or incapacitated person.

(d) **Report.** The guardian ad litem shall serve conformed copies of any written report or finding of the guardian ad litem's investigation and answer filed in the proceedings, petition for compensation and discharge, and the notice of hearing on the petition to any guardian, or in the event that there is no guardian, to the living natural guardians or the living natural guardian having legal custody of the minor, person with a developmental disability, or incapacitated person.

(e) **Service of Petition and Order.** Within 10 days after appointment, the petitioner for an administrator ad litem shall serve conformed copies of the petition for appointment and order to the attorney of record of each beneficiary and to each known beneficiary not represented by an attorney of record.

(f) **Enforcement of Judgments.** When an administrator ad litem or guardian ad litem recovers any judgment or other relief, it shall be enforced as other judgments. Execution shall issue in favor of the administrator ad litem or guardian ad litem for the use of the estate or ward and the money collected shall be paid to the personal representative or guardian, or as otherwise ordered by the court.

(g) **Claim of Personal Representative.** The fact that the personal representative is seeking reimbursement for claims against the decedent paid by the personal representative does not require appointment of an administrator ad litem.

Committee Notes

Rule History

1977 Revision: Editorial change in (a) limiting application of rule to probate and guardianship proceedings. In (b) the petition for appointment of a guardian need not be verified. Deletion of (g) as being substantive rather than procedural and changing former (h) to new (g). Change in committee note to conform to statutory renumbering.

This rule implements sections 731.303(5), 733.308, and 744.391, Florida Statutes, and includes some of the provisions of prior rule 5.230.

1988 Revision: Editorial changes; captions added to paragraphs. Citation form changes in committee notes.

1992 Revision: Addition of phrase in subdivision (a) to conform to 1992 amendment to section 731.303(5), Florida Statutes. Editorial changes. Committee notes revised. Citation form changes in committee notes.

2003 Revision: Committee notes revised. 2006 Revision: Committee notes revised.

2008 Revision: Subdivisions (a), (b), (c), and (d) amended to include persons with a developmental disability. Committee notes revised.

2012 Revision: The phrase "deliver or mail" in subdivisions (c), (d), and (e) has been replaced with the word "serve" to comply with other rules relating to service of pleadings and documents. Committee notes revised.

Statutory References

§ 393.12, Fla. Stat. Capacity; appointment of guardian advocate.
§ 731.303, Fla. Stat. Representation.
§ 733.308, Fla. Stat. Administrator ad litem.
§ 733.708, Fla. Stat. Compromise.
§ 744.3025, Fla. Stat. Claims of minors.
§ 744.3085, Fla. Stat. Guardian advocates.
§ 744.387, Fla. Stat. Settlement of claims.
§ 744.391, Fla. Stat. Actions by and against guardian or ward.
§ 744.446, Fla. Stat. Conflicts of interest; prohibited activities; court approval; breach of fiduciary duty.

Rule References

Fla. Prob. R. 5.041 Service of pleadings and documents.
Fla. R. Jud. Admin. 2.516 Service of pleadings and documents.

RULE 5.122.   CURATORS

(a)   Petition for Appointment. The petition for appointment of a curator shall be verified and shall contain:

        (1)   the petitioner's name, address, and interest, if any, in the estate;

        (2)   the decedent's name, address, date and place of death, and state and county of domicile;

        (3)   the names and addresses of the persons apparently entitled to letters of administration and any known beneficiaries;

        (4)   the nature and approximate value of the assets;

        (5)   a statement showing venue;

        (6)   a statement as to why a curator should be appointed; and

        (7)   the name and address of any proposed curator. The court may appoint a curator sua sponte.

(b) **Appointment.** Before letters of curatorship are issued, the curator shall file a designation of resident agent and acceptance, and an oath, as is required for personal representatives under these rules. The court shall issue letters of curatorship that shall entitle the curator to possess or control the decedent's property, which the court may enforce through contempt proceedings.

(c) **Notice.** Formal notice shall be given to the person apparently entitled to letters, if any. If it is likely that the decedent's property will be wasted, destroyed, or removed beyond the jurisdiction of the court and if the appointment of a curator would be delayed by giving notice, the court may appoint a curator without notice.

(d) **Powers.** By order, the court may authorize the curator to perform any duty or function of a personal representative, including publication and service of notice to creditors, or if a will has been admitted, service of notice of administration.

(e) **Inventory and Accounting.** The curator shall file an inventory within 30 days after issuance of letters of curatorship. When the personal representative is appointed, the curator shall account for and deliver all estate assets in the curator's possession to the personal representative within 30 days after issuance of letters of administration.

(f) **Petition to Reconsider.** If a curator has been appointed without notice, any interested party who did not receive notice may, at any time, petition to reconsider the appointment.

(g) **Subject to Other Provisions.** Curators shall be subject to the provisions of these rules and other applicable law concerning personal representatives.

Committee Notes

This rule implements of the procedure found in section 733.501, Florida Statutes, as amended in 1997 and 2001. The rule has been modified, in part, to reflect the addition of new rule 5.241 regarding notice to creditors. Because the fundamental concern of curatorship is protection of estate property, the procedure facilitates speed and flexibility while recognizing due process concerns. It is not intended that this rule change the effect of the statute from which it has been derived, but the rule has been reformatted to conform to the structure of these rules. Furthermore, the Committee does not intend to create a new procedure, except that subdivision (d) specifies certain acts that the court may authorize the curator to perform. This specificity of example, while not included in the statute, is not intended to limit the authorized acts to those specified in the rule. The appointment of a curator without notice is tantamount to a temporary injunction. Thus, due process considerations suggest an expedited hearing to reconsider the appointment of a curator by any interested party who did not receive notice.

Rule History

1988 Revision: New rule.

1992 Revision: Editorial changes. Citation form changes in committee notes.

2003 Revision: Extensive changes to rule to clarify procedure for appointment of curator. Committee notes revised.

Statutory References

§ 733.402, Fla. Stat. Bond of fiduciary; when required; form.
§ 733.501, Fla. Stat. Curators.

Rule Reference

Fla. Prob. R. 5.020 Pleadings; verification; motions.

RULE 5.150.   ORDER REQUIRING ACCOUNTING

(a)   **Accountings Required by Statute.** When any personal representative or guardian fails to file an accounting or return required by statute or rule, the court on its own motion or on the petition of an interested person shall order the personal representative or guardian to file the accounting or return within 15 days from the service on the personal representative or guardian of the order, or show cause why he or she should not be compelled to do so.

(b)   **Accountings Not Required by Statute.** On the petition of an interested person, or on its own motion, the court may require the personal representative or guardian to file an accounting or return not otherwise required by statute or rule. The order requiring an accounting or return shall order the personal representative or guardian to file the accounting or return within a specified time from service on the personal representative or guardian of the order, or show cause why he or she should not be compelled to do so.

(c)   **Service.** A copy of the order shall be served on the personal representative or guardian and the personal representative's or guardian's attorney.

Committee Notes

The court on its motion or on petition of an interested person may require a personal representative or guardian to file an accounting or return not otherwise required by statute.

Rule History

1977 Revision: Change in committee notes.

1984 Revision: Extensive editorial changes. Committee notes revised and expanded.

1992 Revision: Editorial changes. Committee notes revised. Citation form changes in committee notes.

2003 Revision: Committee notes revised.

2008 Revision: Committee notes revised.

Statutory References

§ 38.22, Fla. Stat. Power to punish contempts.
§ 38.23, Fla. Stat. Contempts defined.
§ 393.12(2)(h), Fla. Stat. Capacity; appointment of guardian advocate.
§ 733.5036, Fla. Stat. Accounting and discharge following resignation.
§ 733.508, Fla. Stat. Accounting and discharge of removed personal representatives upon removal.
§ 733.901, Fla. Stat. Final discharge.
ch. 738, Fla. Stat. Principal and income.
§ 744.3085, Fla. Stat. Guardian advocates.
§ 744.367, Fla. Stat. Duty to file annual guardianship report.
§ 744.3678, Fla. Stat. Annual accounting.
§ 744.3685, Fla. Stat. Order requiring guardianship report; contempt.
§ 744.369, Fla. Stat. Judicial review of guardianship reports.
§ 744.467, Fla. Stat. Resignation of guardian.
§ 744.511, Fla. Stat. Accounting upon removal.
§ 744.517, Fla. Stat. Proceedings for contempt.
§ 744.521, Fla. Stat. Termination of guardianship.
§ 744.524, Fla. Stat. Termination of guardianship on change of domicile of resident ward.
§ 744.527, Fla. Stat. Final reports and applications for discharge; hearing.

Rule References

Fla. Prob. R. 5.649 Guardian advocate.
Fla. Prob. R. 5.650 Resignation or disqualification of guardian; appointment of successor. Fla. Prob. R. 5.660 Proceedings for removal of guardian.
Fla. Prob. R. 5.670 Termination of guardianship on change of domicile of resident ward.
Fla. Prob. R. 5.680 Termination of guardianship.
Fla. Prob. R. 5.681 Restoration of rights of person with developmental disability.
Fla. Prob. R. 5.695 Annual guardianship report.
Fla. Prob. R. 5.696 Annual accounting.
Fla. Prob. R. 5.697 Magistrates' review of guardianship accountings and plans.

RULE 5.160.   **PRODUCTION OF ASSETS**

On the petition of an interested person, or on its own motion, the court may require any personal representative or guardian to produce satisfactory evidence that the assets of the estate are in the possession or under the control of the personal representative or guardian and may order production of the assets in the manner and for the purposes directed by the court.

Committee Notes

Rule History

1977 Revision: Change in committee notes.

1984 Revision: Minor editorial changes. Committee notes revised.

1988 Revision: Editorial changes.

1992 Revision: Editorial changes. Committee notes revised.

Statutory Reference

§ 744.373, Fla. Stat. Production of property.

RULE 5.170.   **EVIDENCE**

In proceedings under the Florida Probate Code and the Florida Guardianship Law the rules of evidence in civil actions are applicable unless specifically changed by the Florida Probate Code, the Florida Guardianship Law, or these rules.

Committee Notes

Rule History

1977 Revision: New rule.

1984 Revision: To further clarify the intent of the rule to incorporate the provisions of the Florida Evidence Code (chapter 90, Florida Statutes) when not in conflict with the Florida Probate Code or Florida Guardianship Law, or rules applicable to these particular proceedings.

1992 Revision: Citation form changes in committee notes.

2003 Revision: Committee notes revised.

Statutory References

ch. 90, Fla. Stat. Florida Evidence Code.
§ 733.107, Fla. Stat. Burden of proof in contests; presumption of undue influence.

RULE 5.171.   EVIDENCE OF DEATH

In a proceeding under these rules, the following shall apply:

(a)   Death Certificate. An authenticated copy of a death certificate issued by an official or agency of the place where the death purportedly occurred or by an official or agency of the United States is prima facie proof of the fact, place, date, and time of death and the identity of the decedent.

(b)   Other Records. A copy of any record or report of a governmental agency, domestic or foreign, that a person is dead, alive, missing, detained, or, from the facts related, presumed dead is prima facie evidence of the status, dates, circumstances, and places disclosed by the record or report.

(c)   Extended Absence. A person who is absent from the place of that person's last known domicile for a continuous period of 5 years and whose absence is not satisfactorily explained after diligent search and inquiry is presumed dead. The person's death is presumed to have occurred at the end of the period unless there is evidence establishing that death occurred earlier.

Committee Notes

This rule represents a rule implementation of the procedure found in section 731.103, Florida Statutes. It is not intended to change the effect of the statute from which it was derived but has been reformatted to conform with the structure of these rules. It is not intended to create a new procedure or modify an existing procedure, except that additional language has been added which was not in the statute, to permit issuance of a death certificate by an official or agency of the United States. An example would be such a certificate issued by the Department of State or the Department of Defense.

Rule History

1988 Revision: New rule.

1992 Revision: Editorial changes. Committee notes revised. Citation form changes in committee notes.

Statutory References

§ 731.103, Fla. Stat. Evidence as to death or status.
§ 744.521, Fla. Stat. Termination of guardianship.

Rule References

Fla. Prob. R. 5.205 Filing evidence of death.
Fla. Prob. R. 5.680 Termination of guardianship.

RULE 5.180.   WAIVER AND CONSENT

(a)   Manner of Execution. A waiver or consent as authorized by law shall be in writing and signed by the person executing the waiver or consent.

(b)   **Contents.** The waiver or consent shall state:

    (1)   the person's interest in the subject of the waiver or consent;

    (2)   if the person is signing in a fiduciary or representative capacity, the nature of the capacity;

    (3)   expressly what is being waived or consented to; and

    (4)   if the waiver pertains to compensation, language declaring that the waiving party has actual knowledge of the amount and manner of determining the compensation and, in addition, either:

    (A)   that the party has agreed to the amount and manner of determining that compensation and waives any objection to payment; or

    (B)   that the party has the right to petition the court to determine the compensation and waives that right.

(c)   **Filing.** The waiver or consent shall be filed.

Committee Notes

One person who serves in two fiduciary capacities may not waive or consent to the person's acts without the approval of those whom the person represents. This rule represents a rule implementation of the procedure found in section 731.302, Florida Statutes.

Rule History

1977 Revision: Extends right of waiver to natural guardian; clarifies right to waive service of notice of administration.

1984 Revision: Extends waiver to disclosure of compensation and distribution of assets. Committee notes revised.

1988 Revision: Procedure from section 731.302, Florida Statutes, inserted as new (1)(f), and a new requirement that the waiver be in writing has been added. Editorial changes. Committee notes expanded. Citation form changes in committee notes.

1992 Revision: Editorial changes. Committee notes revised. Citation form changes in committee notes.

1996 Revision: Addition of specific fee waiver disclosure requirements found in § 733.6171(9), Florida Statutes, and expanded to cover all fees. Committee notes revised.

2003 Revision: Committee notes revised.

2006 Revision: Rule extensively amended to remove references to interested persons' right to waive or consent, which is governed by section 731.302, Florida Statutes, and to address manner of execution and contents of waiver. Committee notes revised.

Statutory References

§ 731.302, Fla. Stat. Waiver and consent by interested person.
§ 731.303, Fla. Stat. Representation.
§ 733.6171, Fla. Stat. Compensation of attorney for the personal representative.

PART II — PROBATE

RULE 5.200.   PETITION FOR ADMINISTRATION

The petition for administration shall be verified by the petitioner and shall contain:

(a)   a statement of the interest of the petitioner, the petitioner's name and address, and the name and office address of the petitioner's attorney;

(b)   the name and last known address of the decedent, last 4 digits of the decedent's social security number, date and place of death of the decedent, and state and county of the decedent's domicile;

(c)   so far as is known, the names and addresses of the surviving spouse, if any, and the beneficiaries and their relationship to the decedent and the date of birth of any who are minors;

(d)   a statement showing venue;

(e)   the priority, under the Florida Probate Code, of the person whose appointment as the personal representative is sought and a statement that the person is qualified to serve under the laws of Florida;

(f)   a statement whether domiciliary or principal proceedings are pending in another state or country, if known, and the name and address of the foreign personal representative and the court issuing letters;

(g)   a statement of the approximate value and nature of the assets;

(h)   in an intestate estate, a statement that after the exercise of reasonable diligence the petitioner is unaware of any unrevoked wills or codicils, or if the petitioner is aware of any unrevoked wills or codicils, a statement why the wills or codicils are not being probated;

(i)   in a testate estate, a statement identifying all unrevoked wills and codicils being presented for probate, and a statement that the petitioner is unaware of any other unrevoked wills or codicils or, if the petitioner is aware of any other unrevoked wills or codicils, a statement why the other wills or codicils are not being probated; and

(j)   in a testate estate, a statement that the original of the decedent's last will is in the possession of the court or accompanies the petition, or that an authenticated copy of a will deposited with or probated in another jurisdiction or that an authenticated copy of a notarial will, the original of which is in the possession of a foreign notary, accompanies the petition.

Florida Probate Rules

Rule History

1977 Revision: Addition to (b)(5) to require an affirmative statement that the person sought to be appointed   as personal representative is qualified to serve. Committee note expanded to include additional statutory references.

Substantially the same as section 733.202, Florida Statutes, and implementing sections 733.301 through   733.305, Florida Statutes.

1988 Revision: Editorial changes. Committee notes revised.

1992 Revision: Addition of phrase in subdivision (b) to conform to 1992 amendment to section   733.202(2)(b), Florida Statutes. Reference to clerk ascertaining the amount of the filing fee deleted in subdivision (g) because of repeal of sliding scale of filing fees. The remaining language was deemed unnecessary. Editorial   changes. Committee notes revised. Citation form changes in committee notes.

2002 Revision: Addition of phrases in subdivision (j) to add references to wills probated in Florida where   the original is in the possession of a foreign official. Editorial changes. Committee notes revised.

2003 Revision: Committee notes revised.

2007 Revision: Committee notes revised.

2007 Revision: Editorial changes in (h) and (i).

2010 Revision: Editorial change in (e) to clarify reference to Florida Probate Code.

2011 Revision: Subdivision (b) amended to limit listing of decedent's social security number to last four digits.

2012 Revision: Committee notes revised.

Statutory References

§ 731.201(23), Fla. Stat. General definitions.
§ 731.301, Fla. Stat. Notice.
§ 733.202, Fla. Stat. Petition.
§ 733.301, Fla. Stat. Preference in appointment of personal representative.
§ 733.302, Fla. Stat. Who may be appointed personal representative.
§ 733.303, Fla. Stat. Persons not qualified.
§ 733.304, Fla. Stat. Nonresidents.
§ 733.305, Fla. Stat. Trust companies and other corporations and associations.

Rule References

Fla. Prob. R. 5.020 Pleadings; verification; motions.
Fla. Prob. R. 5.040 Notice.
Fla. Prob. R. 5.041 Service of pleadings and documents.

Fla. Prob. R. 5.180 Waiver and consent.
Fla. Prob. R. 5.201 Notice of petition for administration.
Fla. R. Jud. Admin. 2.516 Service of pleadings and documents.

RULE 5.201.   NOTICE OF PETITION FOR ADMINISTRATION

(a)   Petitioner Entitled to Preference of Appointment. Except as may otherwise be required by these rules or the Florida Probate Code, no notice need be given of the petition for administration or the issuance of letters when it appears that the petitioner is entitled to a reference of appointment as personal representative.

(b)   Petitioner Not Entitled to Preference. Before letters shall be issued to any person who is not entitled to preference, formal notice must be served on all known persons qualified to act as personal representative and entitled to preference equal to or greater than the applicant, unless those entitled to preference waive it in writing.

(c)   Service of Petition by Formal Notice. If the petitioner elects or is required to serve formal notice of the petition for administration prior to the issuance of letters, a copy of the will offered for probate must be attached to the notice.

Committee Notes

This rule represents a rule implementation of the procedure formerly found in section 733.203(2), Florida Statutes, which was repealed as procedural in 2001.

Rule History

1988 Revision: New rule.

1992 Revision: Committee notes revised. Citation form changes in committee notes.

2003 Revision: Committee notes revised.

2010 Revision: Subdivision (c) added to require service of a copy of the will offered for probate. This requirement was included in section 733.2123, Florida Statutes, but was removed in 2010 because it was deemed to be a procedural requirement. Committee notes revised. Editorial changes.

Statutory References

§ 731.301, Fla. Stat. Notice.
§ 733.212, Fla. Stat. Notice of administration; filing of objections.
§ 733.2123 Fla. Stat. Adjudication before issuance of letters.

Rule References

Fla. Prob. R. 5.040 Notice.
Fla. Prob. R. 5.060 Request for notices and copies of pleadings.
Fla. Prob. R. 5.200 Petition for administration.

RULE 5.205.   **FILING EVIDENCE OF DEATH**

   (a)   **Requirements for Filing.** A copy of an official record of the death of a decedent shall be filed by the personal representative, if any, or the petitioner in each of the following proceedings and at the times specified:

   (1)   Administration of decedent's estate: not later than 3 months following the date of the first publication of the notice to creditors.

   (2)   Ancillary proceedings: not later than 3 months following the date of first publication of notice to creditors.

   (3)   Summary administration: at any time prior to entry of the order of summary administration.

   (4)   Disposition without administration: at the time of filing the application for disposition without administration.

   (5)   Determination of beneficiaries: at any time prior to entry of the final judgment determining beneficiaries.

   (6)   Determination of protected homestead: at any time prior to entry of the final judgment determining protected homestead status of real property.

   (7)   Probate of will without administration: at any time prior to entry of the order admitting will to probate.

   (b)   **Waiver.** On verified petition by the personal representative, if any, or the petitioner the court may enter an order dispensing with this rule, without notice or hearing.

   (c)   **Authority to Require Filing.** The court may, without notice or hearing, enter an order requiring the personal representative, if any, or the petitioner to file a copy of an official record of death at any time during the proceedings.

Committee Notes

   A short form certificate of death, which does not disclose the cause of death, should be filed.

Rule History

   1980 Revision: This rule is intended to provide a uniform procedure for filing an official record of death in any judicial or statutory proceeding upon the death of a decedent. The court may, upon ex parte application, waive compliance with this rule or require filing at any stage in the proceedings.

   1984 Revision: Captions and minor editorial changes. Committee notes revised.

   1988 Revision: Editorial and substantive changes. Adds (a)(8) to require filing when will is admitted to probate without administration of the estate or an order disposing of property. Committee notes revised.

1992 Revision: Editorial changes. Committee notes revised. Citation form changes in committee notes.

2002 Revision: Replaces "homestead" with "protected homestead" in (a)(7) to conform to addition of term in section 731.201(29), Florida Statutes. Committee notes revised.

2003 Revision: Revises subdivision (a)(1) to change notice of administration to notice to creditors. Deletes subdivision (a)(3) referring to family administration, and renumbers subsequent subdivisions. Committee notes revised.

2010 Revision: Committee notes revised.

Statutory References

§ 28.222(3)(g), Fla. Stat. Clerk to be county recorder.
§ 382.008(6), Fla. Stat. Death and fetal death registration.
§ 731.103, Fla. Stat. Evidence as to death or status.
§ 733.2121, Fla. Stat. Notice to creditors; filing of claims.

Rule References

Fla. Prob. R. 5.042(a) Time.
Fla. Prob. R. 5.171 Evidence of death.
Fla. Prob. R. 5.241 Notice to creditors.

RULE 5.210.   PROBATE OF WILLS WITHOUT ADMINISTRATION

(a)   **Petition and Contents.** A petition to admit a decedent's will to probate without administration shall be verified by the petitioner and shall contain:

(1)   a statement of the interest of the petitioner, the petitioner's name and address, and the name and office address of the petitioner's attorney;

(2)   the name and last known address of the decedent, last 4 digits of the decedent's social security number, date and place of death of the decedent, and state and county of the decedent's domicile;

(3)   so far as is known, the names and addresses of the surviving spouse, if any, and the beneficiaries and their relationships to the decedent, and the date of birth of any who are minors;

(4)   a statement showing venue;

(5)   a statement whether domiciliary or principal proceedings are pending in another state or country, if known, and the name and address of the foreign personal representative and the court issuing letters;

(6)   a statement that there are no assets subject to administration in Florida;

41

(7)   a statement identifying all unrevoked wills and codicils being presented for probate and a statement that the petitioner is unaware of any other unrevoked wills or codicils or, if the petitioner is aware of any other unrevoked wills or codicils, a statement why the other wills or codicils are not being probated; and

(8)   a statement that the original of the decedent's last will is in the possession of the court or accompanies the petition, or that an authenticated copy of a will deposited with or probated in another jurisdiction or that an authenticated copy of a notarial will, the original of which is in the possession of a foreign notary, accompanies the petition.

(b)   Service. The petitioner shall serve a copy of the petition on those persons who would be entitled to service under rule 5.240.

(c)   Objections. Objections to the validity of the will shall follow the form and procedure set forth in these rules pertaining to revocation of probate. Objections to the venue or jurisdiction of the court shall follow the form and procedure set forth in the Florida Rules of Civil Procedure.

(d)   Order. An order admitting the will to probate shall include a finding that the will has been executed as required by law.

Committee Notes

Examples illustrating when a will might be admitted to probate are when an instrument (such as a will or trust agreement) gives the decedent a power exercisable by will, such as the power to appoint a successor trustee or a testamentary power of appointment. In each instance, the will of the person holding the power has no legal significance until admitted to probate. There may be no assets, creditors' issues, or other need for a probate beyond admitting the will to establish the exercise or non-exercise of such powers.

Rule History

1975 Revision: Proof of will may be taken by any Florida circuit judge or clerk without issuance of commission.

1984 Revision: This rule has been completely revised to set forth the procedure for proving all wills except lost or destroyed wills and the title changed. The rule requires an oath attesting to the statutory requirements for execution of wills and the will must be proved before an order can be entered admitting it to probate. Former rules 5.280, 5.290, and 5.500 are included in this rule. Committee notes revised.

1988 Revision: Editorial and substantive changes. Change in (a)(3) to clarify which law determines validity of a notarial will; change in (a)(4) to clarify requirement that will of a Florida resident must comply with Florida law; adds new subdivision (b) to set forth required contents of petition for probate of will; moves former (b) to (c). Committee notes expanded; citation form change in committee notes.

1992 Revision: Editorial changes. Committee notes revised. Citation form changes in committee notes.

1996 Revision: Subdivision (a)(4) changed to allow authenticated copies of wills to be admitted to probate if the original is filed or deposited in another jurisdiction.

2002 Revision: Substantial revision to the rule setting forth the requirements of a petition to admit a will to probate when administration is not required. Self proof of wills is governed by the Florida Statutes. Former subdivision (a)(4) amended and transferred to new rule 5.215. Former subdivision (a)(5) amended and transferred to new rule 5.216.

2003 Revision: Committee notes revised.

2007 Revision: Existing text redesignated as subdivision (a) and editorial change made in (a)(7). New subdivisions (b) and (c) added to provide for service of the petition and the procedure for objections consistent with the procedures for probate of a will with administration. Committee notes revised.

2010 Revision: Subdivision (b) amended to reflect that service of the petition to admit a decedent's will to probate without administration shall be served on the persons who would be entitled to service of the notice of administration in a formal administration as set forth in rule 5.240. New subdivision (d) added to provide that any order admitting the decedent's will to probate without administration contain a finding that the will was executed as required by law. Committee notes revised.

2011 Revision: Subdivision (a)(2) amended to limit listing of decedent's social security number to last four digits.

Statutory References

§ 731.201, Fla. Stat. General definitions.
§ 731.301, Fla. Stat. Notice.
§ 732.502, Fla. Stat. Execution of wills.
§ 732.503, Fla. Stat. Self-proof of will.
§ 733.103, Fla. Stat. Effect of probate.
§ 733.201, Fla. Stat. Proof of wills.
§ 733.202, Fla. Stat. Petition.
§ 733.204, Fla. Stat. Probate of a will written in a foreign language.
§ 733.205, Fla. Stat. Probate of notarial will.
§ 733.206, Fla. Stat. Probate of will of resident after foreign probate.
§ 733.207, Fla. Stat. Establishment and probate of lost or destroyed will.
§ 734.104, Fla. Stat. Foreign wills; admission to record; effect on title.

Rule References

Fla. Prob. R. 5.015 General definitions.
Fla. Prob. R. 5.020 Pleadings, verification; motions.
Fla. Prob. R. 5.205(a)(7) Filing evidence of death.
Fla. Prob. R. 5.215 Authenticated copy of will.
Fla. Prob. R. 5.216 Will written in foreign language.
Fla. Prob. R. 5.230 Commission to prove will.
Fla. Prob. R. 5.240 Notice of administration.
Fla. Prob. R. 5.270 Revocation of probate.

RULE 5.215.   AUTHENTICATED COPY OF WILL

An authenticated copy of a will may be admitted to probate if the original could be admitted to probate in Florida.

Committee Notes

Rule History

2002 Revision: New rule, derived from former rule 5.210(a)(4).

2003 Revision: Committee notes revised.

Statutory References

§ 733.205, Fla. Stat. Probate of notarial will.
§ 733.206, Fla. Stat. Probate of will of resident after foreign probate.
§ 734.102, Fla. Stat. Ancillary administration.
§ 734.1025, Fla. Stat. Nonresident decedent's testate estate with property not exceeding $50,000 in this state; determination of claims.
§ 734.104, Fla. Stat. Foreign wills; admission to record; effect on title.

Rule References

Fla. Prob. R. 5.200 Petition for administration.
Fla. Prob. R. 5.210 Probate of wills without administration.
Fla. Prob. R. 5.470 Ancillary administration.
Fla. Prob. R. 5.475 Ancillary administration, short form.

RULE 5.216.   WILL WRITTEN IN FOREIGN LANGUAGE

A will written in a foreign language being offered for probate shall be accompanied by a true and complete English translation. In the order admitting the foreign language will to probate, the court shall establish the correct English translation. At any time during administration, any interested person may have the correctness of the translation redetermined after formal notice to all other interested persons.

Committee Notes

Rule History

2002 Revision: New rule, derived from former rule 5.210(a)(5) and section 733.204(2), Florida Statutes.

Statutory Reference

§ 733.204, Fla. Stat. Probate of a will written in a foreign language.

RULE 5.230.   COMMISSION TO PROVE WILL

(a)   Petition. On petition the court may appoint a commissioner to take the oath of any person qualified to prove the will under Florida law. The petition shall set forth the date of the will and the place where it was executed, if known; the names of the witnesses and address of the witness whose oath is to be taken; and the name, title, and address of the proposed commissioner.

(b) **Commission.** The commission shall be directed to any person who is authorized to administer an oath by the laws of Florida, the United States of America, or the state or country where the witness may be found, and it shall empower the commissioner to take the oath of the witness to prove the will and shall direct the commissioner to certify the oath and file the executed commission, copy of the will, oath of the witness, and certificate of commissioner. An oath of the commissioner is not required.

(c) **Mailing or Delivery.** The petitioner or the petitioner's attorney shall cause the commission, together with a copy of the will, the oath, and the certificate of commissioner, to be mailed or delivered to the commissioner.

(d) **Filing.** The executed commission, copy of the will, oath of the witness, and certificate of commissioner shall be filed.

(e) **Objections.** Objections to the validity of the will shall follow the form and procedure set forth in these rules pertaining to revocation of probate. Objections to the qualifications of the personal representative shall follow the form and procedure set forth in these rules pertaining to removal of personal representatives. Objections to the venue or jurisdiction of the court shall follow the form and procedure set forth in the Florida Rules of Civil Procedure.

Committee Notes

Rule History

1975 Revision: Substantially the same as prior rule 5.130(a) and (b) and carries forward prior procedures as to a matter upon which Florida Probate Code is silent.

1984 Revision: This rule has been completely changed to set forth the procedure for the issuance and return of a commission. The rule has been broadened to allow anyone authorized by Florida Statutes or by the U.S. Code to be a commissioner as well as those authorized by the state or country where the witness resides.

The rule now provides that the petitioner or his attorney shall forward the commission to the commissioner. The rule also contemplates that a Florida notary may be appointed as commissioner to take the proof of a witness outside the State of Florida. Committee notes revised and expanded.

1988 Revision: Editorial and substantive changes. Change in (a) to provide that the commissioner may take the oath of not only the attesting witness to the will but also the oath of any other person qualified to prove the will; change in (c) to permit copies other than photographic copies to be furnished to the commissioner, and to permit delivery of documents in a manner other than by mailing; change in (d) to require the filing of documents with the court. Committee notes revised. Citation form changes in rule and committee notes.

1992 Revision: Editorial change. Committee notes revised. Citation form changes in committee notes.

2003 Revision: Committee notes revised.

Statutory References

§ 92.50, Fla. Stat. Oaths, affidavits, and acknowledgments; who may take or administer; requirements.
§ 733.101, Fla. Stat. Venue of probate proceedings.
§ 733.109, Fla. Stat. Revocation of probate.
§ 733.201, Fla. Stat. Proof of wills.
§ 733.504, Fla. Stat. Removal of personal representative; causes for removal.
§ 733.506, Fla. Stat. Proceedings for removal.
22 U.S.C. § 4215 Notarial acts, oaths, affirmations, affidavits, and depositions; fees.

Rule References

Fla. Prob. R. 5.050 Transfer of proceedings.
Fla. Prob. R. 5.270 Revocation of probate.
Fla. Prob. R. 5.440 Proceedings for removal.
Fla. R. Civ. P. 1.060 Transfers of actions.

RULE 5.235.   ISSUANCE OF LETTERS, BOND

(a)   Appointment of Personal Representative. After the petition for administration is filed and the will, if any, is admitted to probate:

(1)   the court shall appoint the person entitled and qualified to be personal representative;

(2)   the court shall determine the amount of any bond required. The clerk may approve the bond in the amount determined by the court; and

(3)   any required oath or designation of, and acceptance by, a resident agent shall be filed.

(b)   Issuance of Letters. Upon compliance with all of the foregoing, letters shall be issued to the personal representative.

(c)   Bond. On petition by any interested person or on the court's own motion, the court may waive the requirement of filing a bond, require a personal representative or curator to give bond, increase or decrease the bond, or require additional surety.

Committee Notes

This rule represents a rule implementation of the procedure formerly found in sections 733.401 and 733.403(2), Florida Statutes, both of which were repealed in 2001. It is not intended to change the effect of the   statutes from which it was derived but has been reformatted to conform with the structure of these rules. It is not intended to create a new procedure or modify an existing procedure.

Rule History

1988 Revision: New rule.

1992 Revision: Editorial changes. Committee notes revised. Citation form changes in committee notes.

1996 Revision: Mandate in subdivision (a)(2) prohibiting charge of service fee by clerk deleted. Statutory references added.

2003 Revision: Committee notes revised.

2010 Revision: Committee notes revised.

Statutory References

§ 28.24(19), Fla. Stat. Service charges by clerk of the circuit court.
§ 28.2401, Fla. Stat. Service charges in probate matters.
§ 733.402, Fla. Stat. Bond of fiduciary; when required; form.
§ 733.403, Fla. Stat. Amount of bond.
§ 733.405, Fla. Stat. Release of surety.
§ 733.501, Fla. Stat. Curators.

Rule References

Fla. Prob. R. 5.110 Address designation for personal representative or guardian; designation of resident agent and acceptance.
Fla. Prob. R. 5.122 Curators.
Fla. Prob. R. 5.320 Oath of personal representative.

RULE 5.240.   NOTICE OF ADMINISTRATION

(a)   **Service.** The personal representative shall promptly serve a copy of the notice of administration on the following persons who are known to the personal representative and who were not previously served under section 733.2123, Florida Statutes:

(1)   the decedent's surviving spouse;

(2)   all beneficiaries;

(3)   a trustee of any trust described in section 733.707(3), Florida Statutes and each qualified beneficiary of the trust as defined in section 736.0103(16), if each trustee is also a personal representative of the estate; and

(4)   persons who may be entitled to exempt property

in the manner provided for service of formal notice. The personal representative may similarly serve a copy of the notice on any devisee under another will or heirs or others who claim or may claim an interest in the estate.

(b)   **Contents.** The notice shall state:

(1)   the name of the decedent, the file number of the estate, the designation and address of the court in which the proceedings are pending, whether the estate is testate or intestate, and, if testate, the date of the will and any codicils;

(2)   the name and address of the personal representative and of the personal representative's attorney, and that the fiduciary lawyer-client privilege in section 90.5021, Florida Statutes, applies with respect to the personal representative and any attorney employed by the personal representative;

(3)   that any interested person on whom the notice is served who challenges the validity of the will, the qualifications of the personal representative, venue, or jurisdiction of the court must file any objections with the court in the manner provided in the Florida Probate Rules within the time required by law or those objections are forever barred;

(4)   that any person entitled to exempt property must file a petition for determination of exempt property within the time provided by law or the right to exempt property is deemed waived; and

(5)   that an election to take an elective share must be filed within the time provided by law.

(c)   Copy of Will. Unless the court directs otherwise, the personal representative of a testate estate must, upon written request, furnish a copy of the will and all codicils admitted to probate to any person on whom the notice of administration was served.

(d)   Objections. Objections to the validity of the will shall follow the form and procedure set forth in these rules pertaining to revocation of probate. Objections to the qualifications of the personal representative shall follow the form and procedure set forth in these rules pertaining to removal of a personal representative. Objections to the venue or jurisdiction of the court shall follow the form and procedure set forth in the Florida Rules of Civil Procedure.

(e)   Waiver of Service. For the purpose of determining deadlines established by reference to the date of service of a copy of the notice of administration in cases in which service has been waived, service on a person who has waived notice is deemed to occur on the date the waiver is filed.

Committee Notes

Rule History

1977 Revision: Former subdivision (c) is deleted as being substantive rather than procedural.

1984 Revision: Editorial changes; new requirement to file proof of publication; new requirements as to form of objections to will and qualifications of personal representative. Committee notes revised.

1988 Revision: The obligation to mail notice of administration to all known or reasonably ascertainable creditors has been added to comply with the dictates of *Tulsa Professional Collection Services, Inc. v. Pope*, 485 U.S. 478, 108 S. Ct. 1340, 99 L. Ed. 2d 565 (1988).

This rule does not require sending notice of administration to creditors in estates where the time for filing claims has expired before the effective date of this rule. However, no opinion is offered whether such claims are barred by the provisions of section 733.702, Florida Statutes.

Committee notes revised. Citation form changes in committee notes.

1991 Revision: Subdivision (a) modified to make it consistent with recent changes to sections 733.212 and 733.702, Florida Statutes. Those statutes were amended to comply with the dictates of Tulsa Professional Collection Services, Inc. v. Pope, 485 U.S. 478, 108 S. Ct. 1340, 99 L. Ed. 2d 565 (1988). For the same reason, subdivision (e) was eliminated.

1992 Revision: Former subdivision (e) revised and reinstated to emphasize need for personal representative to determine all known or reasonably ascertainable creditors. Editorial changes; committee notes revised; citation form changes in committee notes.

1996 Revision: Subdivision (a) amended to require service of notice of administration on trustees of certain revocable trusts as defined by Florida statute. Editorial changes.

2002 Revision: Procedures for notifying creditors are now governed by new rule 5.241. Committee notes revised.

2003 Revision: Change in title of (a) to reflect elimination of publication of notice. Committee notes revised.

2005 Revision: Subdivision (a)(3) amended to make it consistent with 2003 change to section 733.212(1)(c), Florida Statutes, regarding when service on trust beneficiaries is required, and clarifying editorial change made in (a). New subdivision (b)(5) added regarding notice to file election to take elective share. Committee notes revised.

2007 Revision: Subdivision (a)(3) amended to replace reference to "beneficiary" with "qualified beneficiary" and to change reference from former section 737.303(4)(b) to new section 736.0103(14), which defines that term. Subdivision (b)(5) amended to delete the reference to the surviving spouse filing the election as another person can file the election on behalf of the surviving spouse. New subdivision (e) added to provide a deadline for objection by a person who waives service. Committee notes revised.

2011 Revision: Subdivision (b)(2) amended to conform to amendment to section 732.212, Florida Statutes, relating to attorney-client privilege for fiduciaries and their attorneys. Editorial changes to conform to the court's guidelines for rules submissions as set forth in Administrative Order AOSC06-14. Statutory references to section 732.402, Florida Statutes, added. Committee Notes revised.

2013 Revision: Updated statutory reference in subdivision (a)(3). Committee notes revised.

Statutory References

§ 731.201(23), Fla. Stat. General definitions.
§ 731.301, Fla. Stat. Notice.

§ 731.302, Fla. Stat. Waiver and consent by interested person.
§ 732.2135, Fla. Stat. Time of election; extensions; withdrawal.
§ 732.402, Fla. Stat. Exempt property.
§ 732.5165, Fla. Stat. Effect of fraud, duress, mistake, and undue influence.
§ 733.101, Fla. Stat. Venue of probate proceedings.
§ 733.109, Fla. Stat. Revocation of probate.
§ 733.212, Fla. Stat. Notice of administration; filing of objections.
§ 733.2123, Fla. Stat. Adjudication before issuance of letters.
§ 733.302, Fla. Stat. Who may be appointed personal representative.
§ 733.303, Fla. Stat. Persons not qualified.
§ 733.305, Fla. Stat. Trust companies and other corporations and associations.
§ 733.504, Fla. Stat. Removal of personal representative; causes for removal.
§ 733.506, Fla. Stat. Proceedings for removal.

Rule References

Fla. Prob. R. 5.025 Adversary proceedings.
Fla. Prob. R. 5.040 Notice.
Fla. Prob. R. 5.050 Transfer of proceedings.
Fla. Prob. R. 5.180 Waiver and consent.
Fla. Prob. R. 5.270 Revocation of probate.
Fla. Prob. R. 5.440 Proceedings for removal.
Fla. R. Civ. P. 1.060 Transfers of actions.

RULE 5.241.   NOTICE TO CREDITORS

(a)   **Publication and Service.** Unless creditors' claims are otherwise barred by law, the personal representative shall promptly publish a notice to creditors and serve a copy of the notice on all creditors of the decedent who are reasonably ascertainable and, if required by law, on the Agency for Health Care Administration. Service of the notice shall be either by informal notice, or in the manner provided for service of formal notice at the option of the personal representative. Service on one creditor by a chosen method shall not preclude service on another creditor by another method.

(b)   **Contents.** The notice to creditors shall contain the name of the decedent, the file number of the estate, the designation and address of the court, the name and address of the personal representative and of the personal representative's attorney, and the date of first publication of the notice to creditors. The notice shall require all creditors to file all claims against the estate with the court, within the time provided by law.

(c)   **Method of Publication and Proof.** Publication shall be made as required by law. The personal representative shall file proof of publication with the court within 45 days after the date of first publication of the notice to creditors.

(d)   **Statement Regarding Creditors.** Within 4 months after the date of the first publication of notice to creditors, the personal representative shall file a verified statement that diligent search has been made to ascertain the name and address of each person having a claim against the estate. The statement shall indicate the name and address of each person at that time known to the personal representative who has or may have a claim against the estate and whether such person was served with the notice to creditors or otherwise received actual notice of the information contained in the notice to creditors; provided that the statement need not include persons who have filed a timely claim or who were included in the personal representative's proof of claim.

(e) **Service of Death Certificate.** If service of the notice on the Agency for Health Care Administration is required, it shall be accompanied by a death certificate.

Committee Notes

It is the committee's opinion that the failure to timely file the proof of publication of the notice to creditors shall not affect time limitations for filing claims or objections.

On April 19, 1988, the United States Supreme Court decided *Tulsa Professional Collection Services, Inc. v. Pope*, 485 U.S. 478, 108 S. Ct. 1340, 99 L. Ed. 2d 565. This case substantially impacted the method for handling (and barring) creditors' claims. This case stands for the proposition that a creditor may not be barred by the usual publication if that creditor was actually known to or reasonably ascertainable by the personal representative, and the personal representative failed to give notice to the creditor by mail or other means as certain to ensure actual notice. Less than actual notice in these circumstances would deprive the creditor of due process rights under the 14th Amendment to the U.S. Constitution. Probably actual notice of the death (as in the case of a hospital where the decedent died as a patient) without notice of the institution of probate proceedings is not sufficient.

An elementary and fundamental requirement of due process in any proceeding which is to be accorded finality is notice reasonably calculated, under all the circumstances, to apprise interested persons of the pendency of the proceeding and afford them an opportunity to present their claims.

The steps to be taken by a personal representative in conducting a diligent search for creditors depends, in large measure, on how familiar the personal representative is with the decedent's affairs. Therefore, the committee believes it is inappropriate to list particular steps to be taken in each estate, since the circumstances will vary from case to case.

The statement required by this rule is not intended to be jurisdictional but rather to provide evidence of satisfaction (or lack thereof) of the due process requirements.

Rule History

2002 Revision: New rule to implement procedures consistent with new section 733.2121, Florida Statutes.

2003 Revision: Committee notes revised.

2005 Revision: Subdivision (a) amended to clarify approved methods of service on creditors. Committee notes revised.

2007 Revision: New subdivision (e) added to require service of a copy of the decedent's death certificate on the Agency for Health Care Administration, as is now required by section 733.2121(3)(d), Florida Statutes.

2007 Revision: Editorial change in (a).

Florida Probate Rules

Statutory References

ch. 50, Fla. Stat. Legal and official advertisements.
§ 731.301, Fla. Stat. Notice.
§ 733.2121, Fla. Stat. Notice to creditors; filing of claims.
§ 733.702, Fla. Stat. Limitations on presentation of claims.
§ 733.703, Fla. Stat. Form and manner of presenting claim.
§ 733.704, Fla. Stat. Amendment of claims.
§ 733.705, Fla. Stat. Payment of and objection to claims.
§ 733.708, Fla. Stat. Compromise.

Rule Reference

Fla. Prob. R. 5.490 Form and manner of presenting claim.

RULE 5.260.   CAVEAT; PROCEEDINGS

(a)   Filing. Any creditor or interested person other than a creditor may file a caveat with the court. The caveat of an interested person, other than a creditor, may be filed before or after the death of the person for whom the estate will be, or is being, administered. The caveat of a creditor may be filed only after the person's death.

(b)   Contents. The caveat shall contain the name of the person for whom the estate will be, or is being, administered, the last 4 digits of the person's social security number or year of birth, if known, a statement of the interest of the caveator in the estate, and the name and specific mailing address of the caveator.

(c)   Resident Agent of Caveator; Service. If the caveator is not a resident of Florida, the caveator must file a designation of the name and specific mailing address and residence address of a resident in the county where the caveat is filed as the caveator's agent for service of notice. The written acceptance by the person appointed as resident agent must be filed with the designation or included in the caveat. The designation and acceptance shall constitute the consent of the caveator that service of notice upon the designated resident agent shall bind the caveator. If the caveator is represented by an attorney admitted to practice in Florida who signs the caveat, it shall not be necessary to designate a resident agent under this rule.

(d)   Filing After Commencement. If at the time of the filing of any caveat the decedent's will has been admitted to probate or letters of administration have been issued, the clerk must promptly notify the caveator in writing of the date of issuance of letters and the names and addresses of the personal representative and the personal representative's attorney.

(e)   Creditor. When letters of administration issue after the filing of a caveat by a creditor, the clerk must promptly notify the caveator, in writing, advising the caveator of the date of issuance of letters and the names and addresses of the personal representative and the personal representative's attorney, unless notice has previously been served on the caveator. A copy of any notice given by the clerk, together with a certificate of the mailing of the original notice, must be filed in the estate proceedings.

(f)   Other Interested Persons; Before Commencement. After the filing of a caveat by an interested person other than a creditor, the court must not admit a will of the decedent to probate or appoint a personal representative without service of formal notice on the caveator or the caveator's designated agent. A caveator is not required to be served with formal notice of its own petition for administration.

Committee Notes

Caveat proceedings permit a decedent's creditor or other interested person to be notified when letters of administration are issued. Thereafter, the caveator must take appropriate action to protect the caveator's interests.

This rule treats the creditor caveator differently from other caveators.

An attorney admitted to practice in Florida who represents the caveator may sign the caveat on behalf of the client.

Rule History

1977 Revision: Carried forward prior rule 5.150.

1984 Revision: Changes in (a), (b), and (d) are editorial. Change in (c) eliminates resident agent requirement for Florida residents and for nonresidents represented by a Florida attorney. Service on the attorney binds caveator. Former (e) is now subdivisions (e) and (f) and treats creditor caveator differently from other interested persons. Change in (f) requires formal notice. Committee notes revised.

1988 Revision: Committee notes revised. Citation form changes in committee notes.

1992 Revision: Addition of language in subdivision (b) to implement 1992 amendment to section 731.110(2), Florida Statutes. Editorial changes. Citation form changes in committee notes.

2003 Revision: Committee notes revised.

2010 Cycle Report Revision: Subdivision (c) amended to clarify that a state agency filing a caveat need not designate an agent for service of process, and to provide that a caveator who is not a resident of the county where the caveat is filed must designate either a resident of that county or an attorney licensed and residing in Florida as the caveator's agent. Editorial changes in (d) and (e). Committee notes revised.

2010 Out-of-Cycle Report Revision: Subdivisions (a) and (b) amended to conform with statutory changes. Subdivision (c) amended to read as it existed prior to SC10-171 (35 FLW S482) due to a subsequent legislative amendment (Chapter 2010-132, § 3, Laws of Fla.). Editorial changes in (d), (e), and (f). Committee notes revised.

2011 Revision: Subdivision (b) amended to replace language removed in 2010 out-of-cycle revision, to replace term "decedent" with "person for whom the estate will be, or is being, administered," and to limit listing of a social security number to the last four digits and a date of birth to the year of birth.

2013 Revision: Subdivision (f) is updated to provide that a caveator is not required to be served with formal notice of its own petition for administration. Committee notes revised.

Statutory Reference

§ 731.110, Fla. Stat. Caveat; proceedings.

Rule Reference

Fla. Prob. R. 5.040(a) Notice.

RULE 5.270.   **REVOCATION OF PROBATE**

(a)   **Petition and Contents.** A petition for revocation of probate shall state the interest of the petitioner in the estate and the facts constituting the grounds on which revocation is demanded.

(b)   **Continued Administration.** Pending the determination of any issue for revocation of probate, the personal representative shall proceed with the administration of the estate as if no revocation proceeding had been commenced, except that no distribution may be made to beneficiaries in contravention of the rights of those who, but for the will, would be entitled to the property disposed of.

Committee Notes

This rule represents a rule implementation of the procedure found in section 733.109(2), Florida Statutes. It is not intended to change the effect of the statute from which it was derived but has been reformatted to conform with the structure of these rules. It is not intended to create a new procedure or modify an existing procedure. The committee believes that subsections (1) and (3) of the statute are substantive, and have therefore not been included. Further, this rule revises subdivision (b) of the prior similar rule to track the language in the statute from which it was derived.

Rule History

1984 Revision: Extensive changes. Committee notes revised.

1988 Revision: Language of subdivision (b) of the rule rewritten to track the statute more closely. Committee notes expanded. Citation form change in committee notes.

1992 Revision: Committee notes revised. Citation form changes in committee notes.

2003 Revision: Committee notes revised.

2005 Revision: "Beneficiaries" substituted for "devisees" in subdivision (b) to conform language to section 733.109(2), Florida Statutes.

2007 Revision: Committee notes revised.

Statutory References

§ 731.201(23), Fla. Stat. General definitions.

§ 732.5165, Fla. Stat. Effect of fraud, duress, mistake, and undue influence.
§ 733.109, Fla. Stat. Revocation of probate.
§ 733.212, Fla. Stat. Notice of administration; filing of objections.
§ 733.2123, Fla. Stat. Adjudication before issuance of letters.

Rule References

Fla. Prob. R. 5.025 Adversary proceedings.
Fla. Prob. R. 5.040 Notice.
Fla. Prob. R. 5.240 Notice of administration.

RULE 5.275.   BURDEN OF PROOF IN WILL CONTESTS

In all proceedings contesting the validity of a will, the burden shall be upon the proponent of the will to establish prima facie its formal execution and attestation. Thereafter, the contestant shall have the burden of establishing the grounds on which the probate of the will is opposed or revocation sought.

Committee Notes

This rule represents a rule implementation of the procedure found in section 733.107, Florida Statutes. The presumption of undue influence implements public policy against abuse of fiduciary or confidential relationships and is therefore a presumption shifting the burden of proof under sections 90.301–90.304, Florida Statutes.

Rule History

1988 Revision: New rule.

1992 Revision: Citation form changes in committee notes.

2003 Revision: Committee notes revised.

Statutory References

§ 90.301, Fla. Stat. Presumption defined; inferences.
§ 90.302, Fla. Stat. Classification of rebuttable presumptions.
§ 90.303, Fla. Stat. Presumption affecting the burden of producing evidence
defined.
§ 90.304, Fla. Stat. Presumption affecting the burden of proof defined.
§ 733.107, Fla. Stat. Burden of proof in contests; presumption of undue influence.

RULE 5.310.   DISQUALIFICATION OF PERSONAL
REPRESENTATIVE; NOTIFICATION

Any personal representative who was not qualified to act at the time of appointment or who would not be qualified for appointment if application for appointment were then made shall immediately file and serve on all interested persons a notice describing:

(a)   the reason the personal representative was not qualified at the time of appointment; or

(b)   the reason the personal representative would not be qualified for appointment if application for appointment were then made and the date on which the disqualifying event occurred.

The personal representative's notice shall state that any interested person may petition to remove the personal representative.

Committee Notes

Notification under this rule or section 733.3101, Florida Statutes, does not automatically affect the authority of the personal representative to act. The personal representative may resign or interested persons or the court must act to remove the personal representative.

Rule History

1975 Revision: This is same as old rule 5.220 and old section 732.47(3), Florida Statutes. The rule sets forth the imperative need for timely action and the inherent responsibility of a fiduciary to effect orderly succession. It further implies the inherent jurisdiction of the court to control by judicial overview the succession.

1977 Revision: Citation form change in committee note.

1988 Revision: Committee notes revised. Citation form changes in committee notes.

1992 Revision: Editorial changes to clarify rule. Committee notes revised. Citation form changes in committee notes.

2002 Revision: Rule amended to implement procedures found in section 733.3101, Florida Statutes. Committee notes revised.

Statutory References

§ 731.301, Fla. Stat. Notice.
§ 733.302, Fla. Stat. Who may be appointed personal representative.
§ 733.303, Fla. Stat. Persons not qualified.
§ 733.3101, Fla. Stat. Personal representative not qualified.
§ 733.502, Fla. Stat. Resignation of personal representative.
§ 733.504, Fla. Stat. Removal of personal representative; causes for removal.
§ 733.505, Fla. Stat. Jurisdiction in removal proceedings.
§ 733.506, Fla. Stat. Proceedings for removal.

Rule References

Fla. Prob. R. 5.040 Notice.
Fla. Prob. R. 5.430 Resignation of personal representative.
Fla. Prob. R. 5.440 Proceedings for removal.

RULE 5.320.   OATH OF PERSONAL REPRESENTATIVE

Before the granting of letters of administration, the personal representative shall file an oath to faithfully administer the estate of the decedent. If the petition is verified by the prospective personal representative individually, the oath may be incorporated in the petition or in the designation of resident agent.

Committee Notes

It is contemplated the oath may be signed concurrently with the petition for administration and will be valid even if it predates the order appointing the personal representative.

Rule History

1977 Revision: No change in rule. Change in committee note to conform to statutory renumbering.

This rule establishes the uniform requirement for an oath of faithful performance of fiduciary duties within the permissiveness of section 733.401(1)(d), Florida Statutes. Should be taken together with new rule 5.110, Resident Agent.

1988 Revision: Committee notes expanded. Citation form changes in committee notes.

1992 Revision: Editorial change. Committee notes revised. Citation form changes in committee notes.

2003 Revision: Committee notes revised.

Rule References

Fla. Prob. R. 5.110 Address designation for personal representative or guardian; designation of resident agent and acceptance.

Fla. Prob. R. 5.235 Issuance of letters, bond.

RULE 5.330.   EXECUTION BY PERSONAL REPRESENTATIVE

Notwithstanding any other provisions of these rules, the personal representative shall sign the:

(a)   inventory;

(b)   accountings;

(c)   petition for sale or confirmation of sale or encumbrance of real or personal property;

(d)   petition to continue business of decedent;

(e)   petition to compromise or settle claim;

(f)　　　　petition to purchase on credit;

(g)　　　　petition for distribution and discharge; and

(h)　　　　resignation of personal representative.

Committee Notes

Rule History

1975 Revision: Where the jurisdiction of the court is invoked voluntarily pursuant to section 733.603, Florida Statutes, or otherwise, the rule requires that the personal representative have actual knowledge of the more important steps and acts of administration.

1977 Revision: Citation form change in committee note.

1988 Revision: Editorial changes. Citation form changes in committee notes.

1992 Revision: Editorial changes. Committee notes revised. Citation form changes in committee notes.

2003 Revision: Committee notes revised.

2010 revision: Committee notes revised.

Statutory References

§ 733.502, Fla. Stat. Resignation of personal representative.
§ 733.604, Fla. Stat. Inventories and accountings; public records exemptions.
§ 733.612(5), (22), (24), Fla. Stat. Transactions authorized for the personal representative; exceptions.
§ 733.613, Fla. Stat. Personal representative's right to sell real property.
§ 733.708, Fla. Stat. Compromise.
§ 733.901, Fla. Stat. Final discharge.

Rule References

Fla. Prob. R. 5.340 Inventory.
Fla. Prob. R. 5.345 Accountings other than personal representatives' final accountings.
Fla. Prob. R. 5.346 Fiduciary accounting.
Fla. Prob. R. 5.350 Continuance of unincorporated business or venture.
Fla. Prob. R. 5.370 Sales of real property where no power conferred.
Fla. Prob. R. 5.400 Distribution and discharge.
Fla. Prob. R. 5.430 Resignation of personal representative.

RULE 5.340.　　　INVENTORY

(a)　　Contents and Filing. Unless an inventory has been previously filed, the personal representative shall file an inventory of the estate within 60 days after issuance of letters. The inventory shall contain notice of the beneficiaries' rights under subdivision (e), list the estate with reasonable detail, and include for each listed item (excluding real property appearing to be protected homestead property) its estimated fair market value at the date of the decedent's death. Real property appearing to be protected homestead property shall be listed and so designated.

(b) **Extension.** On petition the time for filing the inventory may be extended by the court for cause shown without notice, except that the personal representative shall serve copies of the petition and order on the persons described in subdivision (d).

(c) **Amendments.** A supplementary or amended inventory containing the information required by subdivision (a) as to each affected item shall be filed and served by the personal representative if:

(1) the personal representative learns of property not included in the original inventory; or

(2) the personal representative learns that the estimated value or description indicated in the original inventory for any item is erroneous or misleading; or

(3) the personal representative determines the estimated fair market value of an item whose value was described as unknown in the original inventory.

(d) **Service.** The personal representative shall serve a copy of the inventory and all supplemental and amended inventories on the surviving spouse, each heir at law in an intestate estate, each residuary beneficiary in a testate estate, and any other interested person who may request it in writing

(e) **Information.** On request in writing, the personal representative shall provide the following:

(1) To the requesting residuary beneficiary or heir in an intestate estate, a written explanation of how the inventory value for an asset was determined or, if an appraisal was obtained, a copy of the appraisal.

(2) To any other requesting beneficiary, a written explanation of how the inventory value for each asset distributed or proposed to be distributed to that beneficiary was determined or, if an appraisal of that asset was obtained, a copy of the appraisal.

(f) **Notice to Nonresiduary Beneficiaries.** The personal representative shall provide to each nonresiduary beneficiary written notice of that beneficiary's right to receive a written explanation of how the inventory value for each asset distributed or proposed to be distributed to that beneficiary was determined or a copy of an appraisal, if any, of the asset.

(g) **Elective Share Proceedings.** Upon entry of an order determining the surviving spouse's entitlement to the elective share, the personal representative shall file an inventory of the property entering into the elective estate which shall identify the direct recipient, if any, of that property. The personal representative shall serve the inventory of the elective estate as provided in rule 5.360. On request in writing, the personal representative shall provide an interested person with a written explanation of how the inventory value for an asset was determined and shall permit an interested person to examine appraisals on which the inventory values are based.

(h)   **Verification.** All inventories shall be verified by the personal representative.

Committee Notes

Inventories of the elective estate under subdivision (f) shall be afforded the same confidentiality as probate inventories. § 733.604(1) and (2), Fla. Stat.

Inventories are still required to be filed. Once filed, however, they are subject to the confidentiality provisions found in sections 733.604(1) and (2), Florida Statutes.

Constitutional protected homestead real property is not necessarily a probatable asset. Disclosure on the inventory of real property appearing to be constitutional protected homestead property informs interested persons of the homestead issue.

Interested persons are entitled to reasonable information about estate proceedings on proper request, including a copy of the inventory, an opportunity to examine appraisals, and other information pertinent to their interests in the estate. The rights of beneficiaries to information contained in estate inventories is limited by section 733.604(3), Florida Statutes. Inventories of the elective estate under subdivision (f) affects a broader class of interested persons who may obtain information regarding the assets disclosed therein subject to control by the court and the confidentiality afforded such inventories under section 733.604(1) and (2).

Rule History

1980 Revision: Eliminated the time limit in requesting a copy of the inventory by an interested person or in furnishing it by the personal representative.

1984 (First) Revision: Extensive changes. Committee notes revised.

1984 (Second) Revision: Subdivision (a) modified to clarify or re-insert continued filing requirement for inventory.

1988 Revision: Editorial changes in (b) and (d). Committee notes revised. Citation form changes in committee notes.

1992 Revision: Editorial changes. Committee notes revised. Citation form changes in committee notes.

2001 Revision: Subdivision (a) amended to conform to statutory changes. Subdivision (d) amended to add requirement of filing of proof of service. Subdivision (e) amended to clarify personal representative's duty to furnish explanation of how inventory values were determined. Subdivision (f) added to require personal representative to file inventory of property entering into elective share. Subdivision (g) added to require verification of inventories. Committee notes revised.

2002 Revision: Subdivision (e) amended to conform to section 733.604(3), Florida

Statutes. Subdivision (f) amended to establish procedures for interested persons to obtain information about assets and values listed in the inventory of the elective estate. Committee notes revised.

2003 Revision: Committee notes revised.

2010 Revision: Subdivisions (d) and (g) (former (f)) amended to delete the requirement to serve a copy of the inventory on the Department of Revenue. Subdivision (e) amended, and new (f) created, to limit the kind of information available to nonresiduary beneficiaries, and subsequent subdivisions relettered. Editorial changes in (a), (e), and (g). Committee notes revised.

2012 Revision: The last sentence of subdivision (d) is deleted to remove duplicative requirement of filing a proof of service for a document which includes a certificate of service as provided in Fla. R. Jud. Admin. 2.516. If service of the inventory is by service in the manner provided for service of formal notice, then proof of service should be filed as provided in rule 5.040(a)(5). Committee notes revised.

Constitutional Reference

Art. X, § 4, Fla. Const.

Statutory References

§ 732.401, Fla. Stat. Descent of homestead.
§ 732.4015, Fla. Stat. Devise of homestead.
§ 733.604, Fla. Stat. Inventories and accounting; public records exemptions.

Rule References

Fla. Prob. R. 5.041 Service of pleadings and documents.
Fla. Prob. R. 5.060 Request for notices and copies of pleadings.
Fla. Prob. R. 5.330 Execution by personal representative.
Fla. Prob. R. 5.360 Elective share.
Fla. Prob. R. 5.405 Proceedings to determine homestead real property.
Fla. R. Jud. Admin. 2.516 Service of pleadings and documents.

RULE 5.341.   ESTATE INFORMATION

On reasonable request in writing, the personal representative shall provide an interested person with information about the estate and its administration.

Committee Notes

This rule is not intended to overrule the holdings in *In re Estate of Shaw*, 340 So. 2d 491 (Fla. 3d DCA 1976), and *In re Estate of Posner*, 492 So. 2d 1093 (Fla. 3d DCA 1986).

Rule History

2002 Revision: New rule.

RULE 5.342.   INVENTORY OF SAFE-DEPOSIT BOX

(a)   Filing. The personal representative shall file an inventory of the contents of the decedent's safe-deposit box within 10 days of the initial opening of the box by the personal representative or the personal representative's attorney of record. The inventory shall include a copy of the financial institution's entry record for the box from a date that is six months prior to the decedent's date of death to the date of the initial opening by the personal representative or the personal representative's attorney of record.

(b)   Verification. Each person who was present at the initial opening must verify the contents of the box by signing a copy of the inventory under penalties of perjury.

(c)   Service. The personal representative shall serve a copy of the inventory on the surviving spouse, each heir at law in an intestate estate, each residuary beneficiary in a testate estate, and any other interested person who may request it in writing.

Committee Notes

Inventories and entry records, once filed, shall be afforded the same confidentiality as probate inventories.

If a safe-deposit box is opened pursuant to section 655.935 of the Florida Statutes, no written inventory of the box need be prepared or filed.

Rule History

2003 Revision: New rule.

2012 Revision: The last sentence of subdivision (c) is deleted to remove duplicative requirement of filing a proof of service for a document which includes a certificate of service as provided in Fla. R. Jud. Admin. 2.516. In service of the inventory is by service in the manner provided for service of formal notice, then proof of service should be filed as provided in rule 5.040(a)(5). Committee notes revised.

Statutory References

§ 655.935, Fla. Stat. Search procedure on death of lessee.
§ 655.936, Fla. Stat. Delivery of safe-deposit box contents or property held in safekeeping to personal representative.
§ 733.6065, Fla. Stat. Opening safe-deposit box.

Rule References

Fla. Prob. R. 5.041 Service of pleadings and documents.
Fla. Prob. R. 5.340 Inventory.
Fla. R. Jud. Admin. 2.516 Service of pleadings and documents.

RULE 5.3425.   SEARCH OF SAFE DEPOSIT BOX

(a)   Petition for Order Authorizing Search. The petition for an order authorizing the search of a safe deposit box leased or co-leased by a decedent must be verified and must contain:

        (1)   The petitioner's name, address, and interest, if any, in the estate;

        (2)   The decedent's name, address, date and place of death, and state and county of domicile;

        (3)   A description of the safe deposit box leased by the decedent and, if known, the name of any co-lessee;

        (4)   The name and address of the institution where the safe deposit box is located; and

        (5)   A statement that the petitioner believes that the decedent may have left in the safe deposit box one or more of the following:

        (A)   A will or codicil of the decedent, or a writing described in section 732.515 of the Code;

        (B)   A deed to a burial plot;

        (C)   A writing giving burial instructions; or

        (D)   Insurance policies on the life of the decedent.

    (b)   **Order.** If the Court determines that the petitioner is entitled to an order authorizing a search of the decedent's safe deposit box, it must enter an order

        (1)   authorizing the petitioner to open the safe deposit box in the presence of an officer of the lessor and, if requested by the petitioner, to remove and deliver

        (A)   to the court having probate jurisdiction in the county where the lessor is located any writing purporting to be a will or codicil of the decedent and any writing purporting to identify devises of tangible property;

        (B)   to the petitioner, any writing purporting to be a deed to a burial plot to give burial instructions; and

        (C)   to the beneficiary named therein, any document purporting to be an insurance policy on the life of the decedent.

        (2)   directing the officer of the lessor to make a complete copy of any document removed and delivered pursuant to the court order, together with a memorandum of delivery identifying the name of the officer, the person to whom the document was delivered, and the date of delivery, to be placed in the safe deposit box leased or co-leased by the decedent.

Committee Notes

    The search of the safe deposit box is not considered an initial opening and is not subject to the inventory requirements of rule 5.342.

Rule History

2010 Revision: New rule.

Statutory References

§ 655.935, Fla. Stat. Search procedure on death of lessee.

RULE 5.345. ACCOUNTINGS OTHER THAN PERSONAL REPRESENTATIVES' FINAL ACCOUNTINGS

(a) **Applicability and Accounting Periods.** This rule applies to the interim accounting of any fiduciary of a probate estate, the accounting of a personal representative who has resigned or been removed, and the accounting of a curator upon the appointment of a successor fiduciary. The fiduciary may elect to file an interim accounting at any time, or the court may require an interim or supplemental accounting. The ending date of the accounting period for any accounting to which this rule applies shall be as follows:

(1) For an interim accounting, any date selected by the fiduciary, including a fiscal or calendar year, or as may be determined by the court.

(2) For the accounting of a personal representative who has resigned or has been removed, the date the personal representative's letters are revoked.

(3) For a curator who has been replaced by a successor fiduciary, the date of appointment of the successor fiduciary.

(b) **Notice of Filing.** Notice of filing and a copy of any accounting to which this rule applies shall be served on all interested persons. The notice shall state that objections to the accounting must be filed within 30 days from the date of service of notice.

(c) **Objection.** Any interested person may file an objection to any accounting to which this rule applies within 30 days from the date of service of notice on that person. Any objection not filed within 30 days from the date of service shall be deemed abandoned. An objection shall be in writing and shall state with particularity the item or items to which the objection is directed and the grounds upon which the objection is based.

(d) **Service of Objections.** The objecting party shall serve a copy of the objection on the fiduciary filing the accounting and other interested persons.

(e) **Disposition of Objections and Approval of Accountings.** The court shall sustain or overrule any objection filed as provided in this rule. If no objection is filed, any accounting to which this rule applies shall be deemed approved 30 days from the date of service of the accounting on interested persons.

(f) **Substantiating Papers.** On reasonable written request, the fiduciary shall permit an interested person to examine papers substantiating items in any accounting to which this rule applies.

(g) **Supplemental Accountings.** The court, on its own motion or on that of any interested person, may require a fiduciary who has been replaced by a successor fiduciary to file a supplemental accounting, the beginning date of which shall be the ending date of the accounting as specified in subdivision (a) of this rule and the ending date of which is the date of delivery of all of the estate's property to the successor fiduciary, or such other date as the court may order.

(h) **Verification.** All accountings shall be verified by the fiduciary filing the accounting.

Committee Notes

The personal representative is required to file a final accounting when administration is complete, unless filing is waived by interested persons. Additionally, a fiduciary of a probate estate may elect, but is not required, to file interim accountings at any time. An accounting is required for resigning or removed fiduciaries. The filing, notice, objection, and approval procedure is similar to that for final accounts.

Rule History

1977 Revision: Change in (a) to authorize selection of fiscal year.

1980 Revision: Change in (d) of prior rule to require the notice to state that the basis for an objection is necessary. Change in (e) of prior rule to require any person filing an objection to set forth the basis of such objection.

1984 Revision: Extensive changes. Committee notes revised. 1988 Revision: Citation form change in committee notes.

1992 Revision: Editorial change. Committee notes revised. Citation form changes in committee notes.

2002 Revision: Implements procedures for interim accountings and accountings by resigning or removed fiduciaries. Committee notes revised.

2003 Revision: Committee notes revised.

2005 Revision: Verification requirement added as new (h). Committee notes revised.

Statutory References

§ 733.3101, Fla. Stat. Personal representative not qualified.
§ 733.501, Fla. Stat. Curators.
§ 733.5035, Fla. Stat. Surrender of assets after resignation.
§ 733.5036, Fla. Stat. Accounting and discharge following resignation.
§ 733.508, Fla. Stat. Accounting and discharge of removed personal representatives upon removal.
§ 733.509, Fla. Stat. Surrender of assets upon removal.
ch. 738, Fla. Stat. Principal and income.

Rule References

Fla. Prob. R. 5.020 Pleadings; verification; motions.
Fla. Prob. R. 5.122 Curators.

Fla. Prob. R. 5.150 Order requiring accounting.
Fla. Prob. R. 5.330 Execution by personal representative.
Fla. Prob. R. 5.346 Fiduciary accounting.
Fla. Prob. R. 5.430 Resignation of personal representative.
Fla. Prob. R. 5.440 Proceedings for removal.

RULE 5.346.   **FIDUCIARY ACCOUNTING**

     (a)   **Contents.** A fiduciary accounting shall include:

     (1)   all cash and property transactions since the date of the last accounting or, if none, from the commencement of administration, and

     (2)   a schedule of assets at the end of the accounting period.

     (b)   **Accounting Standards.** The following standards are required for the accounting of all transactions occurring on or after January 1, 1994:

     (1)   Accountings shall be stated in a manner that is understandable to persons who are not familiar with practices and terminology peculiar to the administration of estates and trusts.

     (2)   The accounting shall begin with a concise summary of its purpose and content.

     (3)   The accounting shall contain sufficient information to put interested persons on notice as to all significant transactions affecting administration during the accounting period.

     (4)   The accounting shall contain 2 values in the schedule of assets at the end of the accounting period, the asset acquisition value or carrying value, and estimated current value.

     (5)   Gains and losses incurred during the accounting period shall be shown separately in the same schedule.

     (6)   The accounting shall show significant transactions that do not affect the amount for which the fiduciary is accountable.

     (c)   **Accounting Format.** A model format for an accounting is attached to this rule as Appendix A.

     (d)   **Verification.** All accountings shall be verified by the fiduciary filing the accounting.

Committee Notes

This rule substantially adopts the Uniform Fiduciary Accounting Principles and Model Formats adopted by the Committee on National Fiduciary Accounting Standards of the American Bar Association: Section of Real Property, Probate and Trust Law, the American College of Probate Counsel, the American Bankers Association: Trust Division, and other organizations.

Accountings shall also comply with the Florida principal and income law, chapter 738, Florida Statutes.

Attached as Appendix B to this rule are an explanation and commentary for each of the foregoing standards, which shall be considered as a Committee Note to this rule.

Accountings that substantially conform to the model formats are acceptable. The model accounting format included in Appendix A is only a suggested form.

Rule History

1988 Revision: New rule.

1992 Revision: Editorial changes throughout. Rule changed to require compliance with the Uniform Fiduciary Accounting Principles and Model Formats for accounting of all transactions occurring on or after January 1, 1994. Committee notes revised. Citation form changes in committee notes.

1996 Revision: Committee notes revised.

1999 Revision: Committee notes revised to correct rule reference and to reflect formatting changes in accounting formats.

2002 Revision: Subdivisions (a) and (b) amended to clarify contents of accounting. Committee notes revised.

2003 Revision: Committee notes revised.

2005 Revision: Verification requirement added as new (d). Committee notes revised.

2007 Revision: Committee notes revised.

2010 Revision: Committee notes revised.

Statutory References

§ 733.501, Fla. Stat. Curators.
§ 733.5036, Fla. Stat. Accounting and discharge following resignation.
§ 733.508, Fla. Stat. Accounting and discharge of removed personal representatives upon removal.
§ 733.602(1), Fla. Stat. General duties.
§ 733.612(18), Fla. Stat. Transactions authorized for the personal representative; exceptions.
ch. 738, Fla. Stat. Principal and income.

Rule References

Fla. Prob. R. 5.020 Pleadings; verification; motions.
Fla. Prob. R. 5.040 Notice.
Fla. Prob. R. 5.122 Curators.

Fla. Prob. R. 5.180 Waiver and consent.
Fla. Prob. R. 5.330 Execution by personal representative.
Fla. Prob. R. 5.345 Accountings other than personal representatives' final accountings.
Fla. Prob. R. 5.400 Distribution and discharge.
Fla. Prob. R. 5.430 Resignation of personal representative.
Fla. Prob. R. 5.440 Proceedings for removal.

APPENDIX A

IN THE CIRCUIT COURT FOR_____COUNTY, FLORIDA

IN RE: ESTATE OF

PROBATE DIVISION

File Number _____

Deceased.

Division _____

_____ ACCOUNTING OF PERSONAL REPRESENTATIVE(S)

From: _____, _____, Through:_____, _____

  The purpose of this accounting is to acquaint all interested persons with the transactions that have occurred during the period covered by the accounting and the assets that remain on hand. It consists of a SUMMARY sheet and Schedule A showing all Receipts, Schedule B showing all Disbursements, Schedule C showing all Distributions, Schedule D showing all Capital Transactions and Adjustments (the effect of which are also reflected in other schedules, if appropriate), and Schedule E showing assets on hand at the end of the accounting period.

  It is important that this accounting be carefully examined. Requests for additional information and any questions should be addressed to the personal representative(s) or the attorneys for the personal representative(s), the names and addresses of whom are set forth below.

  Under penalties of perjury, the undersigned personal representative(s) declare(s) that I (we) have read and examined this accounting and that the facts and figures set forth in the Summary and the attached Schedules are true, to the best of my (our) knowledge and belief, and that it is a complete report of all cash and property transactions and of all receipts and disbursements by me (us) as personal representative(s) of the estate of_____ _____ deceased, from, _____, _____ through _____, _____.

Signed on _____, _____.

Florida Probate Rules

Attorney for Personal Representative: Personal Representative:

_____
Attorney

                     _____
                     Name

Florida Bar No. _____

_____
(address)
Telephone:_____

                     _____

                     _____
                     (address)
                     [Print or Type Names Under All Signature Lines]

IN THE CIRCUIT COURT FOR_____COUNTY, FLORIDA

IN RE: ESTATE OF

                     PROBATE DIVISION

                     File Number _____

      Deceased.

                     Division _____

_____ ACCOUNTING OF PERSONAL REPRESENTATIVE(S)

From: _____, _____, Through: _____. _____

===

SUMMARY

		Income	Principal	Totals
I.	Starting Balance Assets per Inventory or on Hand at Close of Last Accounting Period	_____	_____	_____
II.	Receipts Schedule A:	_____	_____	_____
III.	Disbursements Schedule B:	_____	_____	_____
IV.	Distributions Schedule C:	_____	_____	_____
V.	Capital Transactions and Adjustments			

	Schedule D: Net Gain or (Loss)	$_____ _____	
VI.	Assets on Hand at Close of Accounting Period Schedule E: Cash and Other Assets	_____ _____ _____	

NOTE: Refer to Fla. Prob. R. 5.330(b), 5.345, 5.346, and 5.400.

Also see Accountings, Chapter 12 of Practice Under Florida Probate Code (Fla. Bar CLE).

Entries on Summary are to be taken from totals on Schedules A, B, C, D and E.

The Summary and Schedules A, B, C, D and E are to constitute the full accounting. Every transaction occurring during the accounting period should be reflected on the Schedules.

All purchases and sales, all adjustments to the inventory or carrying value of any asset, and any other changes in the assets (such as stock splits) should be described on Schedule D.

The amount in the "Total" column for Item VI must agree with the total inventory or adjusted carrying value of all assets on hand at the close of the accounting period on Schedule E.

_____ ACCOUNTING OF PERSONAL REPRESENTATIVE,

ESTATE OF_____

From: _____, _____, Through: _____, _____

SCHEDULE A   Receipts

Date	Brief Description of Items	Income	Principal

NOTE: Schedule A should reflect only those items received during administration that are not shown on the inventory. Classification of items as income or principal is to be in accordance with the provisions of the Florida Uniform Principal and Income Act, Chapter 738, Florida Statutes.

Entries involving the sale of assets or other adjustments to the carrying values of assets are to be shown on Schedule D, and not on Schedule A.

_____ ACCOUNTING OF PERSONAL REPRESENTATIVE,

ESTATE OF _____

From: _____, _____, Through: _____, _____

SCHEDULE B   Disbursements

Date   Brief Description of Items   Income   Principal

NOTE: Schedule B should reflect only those items paid out during the accounting period. Classification of disbursements as income or principal is to be in accordance with the provisions of the Florida Uniform Principal and Income Act, Chapter 738, Florida Statutes.

Entries involving the purchase of assets or adjustments to the carrying values of assets are to be shown on Schedule D, and not on Schedule B.

_____ ACCOUNTING OF PERSONAL REPRESENTATIVE,

ESTATE OF _____

Florida Probate Rules

From: _____, _____, Through: _____, _____

SCHEDULE C   Distributions

Date	Brief Description of Items	Income	Principal

NOTE: Schedule C should reflect only those items or amounts distributed to beneficiaries during the accounting period. Assets distributed should be shown at their inventory or adjusted carrying values. Classification of distributions as income or principal is to be in accordance with the provisions of the Florida Uniform Principal and Income Act, Chapter 738, Florida Statutes.

Entries involving adjustments to the carrying values of assets are to be shown on Schedule D, and not on Schedule C.

_____ ACCOUNTING OF PERSONAL REPRESENTATIVE,

ESTATE OF _____

From: _____, _____, Through: _____, _____

SCHEDULE D   Capital Transactions and Adjustments

(Does not include distributions. Distributions are shown on Schedule C.)

Date	Brief Description of Transactions	Net Gain	Net Loss

TOTAL NET GAINS AND LOSSES

NET GAIN OR (LOSS)

NOTE: Schedule D should reflect all purchases and sales of assets and any adjustments to the carrying values of any assets.

Entries reflecting sales should show the inventory or adjusted carrying values, the costs and expenses of the sale, and the net proceeds received. The net gain or loss should be extended in the appropriate column on the right side of Schedule D.

Entries reflecting purchases should reflect the purchase price, any expenses of purchase or other adjustments to the purchase price, and the total amount paid. Presumably no gain or loss would be shown for purchases.

Entries reflecting adjustments in capital assets should explain the change (such as a stock split) and the net gain or loss should be shown in the appropriate column on the right side of Schedule D.

The NET gain or loss should be entered in the Principal column of the Summary.

_____ ACCOUNTING OF PERSONAL REPRESENTATIVE,

ESTATE OF _____

From: _____, _____, Through: _____, _____

SCHEDULE E   Assets on Hand at Close of Accounting Period

(Indicate where held and legal description, certificate numbers or other identification.)

	Estimated Current Value	Carrying Value

ASSETS OTHER THAN CASH:

OTHER ASSETS TOTAL _____

CASH:

CASH TOTAL $

TOTAL ASSETS (must agree with the Total for Item VI on Summary)

NOTE: Schedule E should be a complete list of all assets on hand reflecting inventory values for each item, adjusted in accordance with any appropriate entries on Schedule D.

Current market values for any assets that are known to be different from the inventory or carrying values as of the close of the accounting period should be shown in the column marked "Current Value." The total inventory or adjusted carrying value (not Current Value) must agree with the Total for Item VI on Summary.

APPENDIX B

UNIFORM FIDUCIARY ACCOUNTING PRINCIPLES

I.   ACCOUNTS SHOULD BE STATED IN A MANNER THAT IS UNDERSTANDABLE BY PERSONS WHO ARE NOT FAMILIAR WITH PRACTICES AND TERMINOLOGY PECULIAR TO THE ADMINISTRATION OF ESTATES AND TRUSTS.

Commentary: In order for an account to fulfill its basic function of communication, it is essential that it be stated in a manner that recognizes that the interested parties are not usually familiar with fiduciary accounts. It is neither practical nor desirable to require that accounts be tailored to meet individual disabilities of particular parties but any account should be capable of being understood by a person of average intelligence, literate in English, and familiar with basic financial terms who has read it with care and attention.

Problems arising from terminology or style are usually a reflection of the fact that people who become versed in a particular form of practice tend to forget that terms which are familiar and useful to them may convey nothing to someone else or may even be affirmatively misleading. For example, the terms "debit" and "credit" are generally incomprehensible to people with no knowledge of bookkeeping and many people who are familiar with them in other contexts would assume that in the context of fiduciary accounting, the receipt of an item is a "credit" to the fund rather than a "debit" to the fiduciary.

While the need for concise presentation makes a certain amount of abbreviation both acceptable and necessary, uncommon abbreviation of matters essential to an understanding of the account should be avoided or explained.

No position is taken for or against the use of direct print-outs from machine accounting systems. The quality of the accounts produced by these systems varies widely in the extent to which they can be understood by persons who are not familiar with them. To endorse or object to a direct print-out because it is produced by machine from previously stored data would miss the essential point by focusing attention upon the manner of preparation rather than the product.

II.   A FIDUCIARY ACCOUNT SHALL BEGIN WITH A CONCISE SUMMARY OF ITS PURPOSE AND CONTENT.

Commentary: Very few people can be expected to pay much attention to a document unless they have some understanding of its general purpose and its significance to them. Even with such an understanding, impressions derived from the first page or two will often determine whether the rest is read. The use that is made of these pages is therefore of particular significance.

The cover page should disclose the nature and function of the account. While a complete explanation of the significance of the account and the effect of its presentation upon the rights of the parties is obviously impractical for inclusion at this point, there should be at least a brief statement identifying the fiduciary and the subject matter, noting the importance of examining the account and giving an address where more information can be obtained.

It is assumed that the parties would also have enough information from other sources to understand the nature of their relationship to the fund (e.g., residuary legatee, life tenant, remainderman), the function of the account, and the obligation of the fiduciary to supply further relevant information upon request. It is also assumed that notice will be given of any significant procedural considerations such as limitation on the time within which objections must be presented. This would normally be provided by prior or contemporaneous memoranda, correspondence, or discussions.

A summary of the account shall also be presented at the outset. This summary, organized as a table of contents, shall indicate the order of the details presented in the account and shall show separate totals for the aggregate of the assets on hand at the beginning of the accounting period; transactions during the period; and the assets remaining on hand at the end of the period. Each entry in the summary shall be supported by a schedule in the account that provides the details on which the summary is based.

III.   A FIDUCIARY ACCOUNT SHALL CONTAIN SUFFICIENT INFORMATION TO PUT THE INTERESTED PARTIES ON NOTICE AS TO ALL SIGNIFICANT TRANSACTIONS AFFECTING ADMINISTRATION DURING THE ACCOUNTING PERIOD.

Commentary: The presentation of the information account shall allow an interested party to follow the progress of the fiduciary's administration of assets during the accounting period.

An account is not complete if it does not itemize, or make reference to, assets on hand at the beginning of the accounting period.

Illustration:

3.1 The first account for a decedent's estate or a trust may detail the items received by the fiduciary and for which the fiduciary is responsib'e. It may refer to the total amount of an inventory filed elsewhere or assets described in a schedule attached to a trust agreement.

Instead of retyping the complete list of assets in the opening balance, the preparer may prefer to attach as an exhibit a copy of the inventory, closing balance from the last account, etc., as appropriate, or may refer to them if previously provided to the interested parties who will receive it.

Transactions shall be described in sufficient detail to give interested parties notice of their purpose and effect. It should be recognized that too much detail may be counterproductive to making the account understandable. In accounts covering long periods or dealing with extensive assets, it is usually desirable to consolidate information. For instance, where income from a number of securities is being accounted for over a long period of time, a statement of the total dividends received on each security with appropriate indication of changes in the number of shares held will be more readily understandable and easier to check for completeness than a chronological listing of all dividends received.

Although detail should generally be avoided for routine transactions, it will often be necessary to proper understanding of an event that is somewhat out of the ordinary.

Illustrations:

3.2 Extraordinary appraisal costs should be shown separately and explained.

3.3 Interest and penalties in connection with late filing of tax returns should be shown separately and explained.

3.4 An extraordinary allocation between principal and income such as apportionment of proceeds of property acquired on foreclosure should be separately stated and explained.

3.5 Computation of a formula marital deduction gift involving non-probate assets should be explained.

IV. A FIDUCIARY ACCOUNT SHALL CONTAIN TWO VALUES, THE ASSET ACQUISITION VALUE OR CARRYING VALUE, AND CURRENT VALUE.

Commentary: In order for transactions to be reported on a consistent basis, an appropriate carrying value for assets must be chosen and employed consistently.

The carrying value of an asset should reflect its value at the time it is acquired by the fiduciary (or a predecessor fiduciary). When such a value is not precisely determinable, the figure used should reflect a thoughtful decision by the fiduciary. For assets owned by a decedent, inventory values or estate tax values — generally reflective of date of death — would be appropriate. Assets received in kind by a trustee from a settlor of an inter vivos trust should be carried at their value at the time of receipt. For assets purchased during the administration of the fund, cost would normally be used. Use of Federal income tax basis for carrying value is acceptable when basis is reasonably representative of real values at the time of acquisition. Use of tax basis as a carrying value under other circumstances could be affirmatively misleading to beneficiaries and therefore is not appropriate.

In the Model Account, carrying value is referred to as "fiduciary acquisition value." The Model Account establishes the initial carrying value of assets as their value at date of death for inventoried assets, date of receipt for subsequent receipts, and cost for investments.

Carrying value would not normally be adjusted for depreciation.

Except for adjustments that occur normally under the accounting system in use, carrying values should generally be continued unchanged through successive accounts and assets should not be arbitrarily "written up" or "written down." In some circumstances, however, with proper disclosure and explanation, carrying value may be adjusted.

Illustrations:

4.1 Carrying values based on date of death may be adjusted to reflect changes on audit of estate or inheritance tax returns.

4.2 Where appropriate under applicable local law, a successor fiduciary may adjust the carrying value of assets to reflect values at the start of that fiduciary's administration.

4.3 Assets received in kind in satisfaction of a pecuniary legacy should be carried at the value used for purposes of distribution.

Though essential for accounting purposes, carrying values are commonly misunderstood by laypersons as being a representation of actual values. To avoid this, the account should include both current values and carrying values.

The value of assets at the beginning and ending of each accounting period is necessary information for the evaluation of investment performance. Therefore, the account should show, or make reference to, current values at the start of the period for all assets whose carrying values were established in a prior accounting period.

Illustrations:

4.4 The opening balance of the first account of a testamentary trustee will usually contain assets received in kind from the executor. Unless the carrying value was written up at the time of distribution (e.g., 4.2 or 4.3 supra) these assets will be carried at a value established during the executor's administration. The current value at the beginning of the accounting period should also be shown.

4.5 An executor's first account will normally carry assets at inventory (date of death) values or costs. No separate listing of current values at the beginning of the accounting period is necessary.

Current values should also be shown for all assets on hand at the close of the accounting period. The date on which current values are determined shall be stated and shall be the last day of the accounting period, or a date as close thereto as reasonably possible.

Current values should be shown in a column parallel to the column of carrying values. Both columns should be totalled.

In determining current values for assets for which there is no readily ascertainable current value, the source of the value stated in the account shall be explained. The fiduciary shall make a good faith effort to determine realistic values but should not be expected to incur expenses for appraisals or similar costs when there is no reason to expect that the resulting information will be of practical consequence to the administration of the estate or the protection of the interests of the parties.

Illustrations:

4.6 When an asset is held under circumstances that make it clear that it will not be sold (e.g., a residence held for use of a beneficiary) the fiduciary's estimate of value would be acceptable in lieu of an appraisal.

4.7 Considerations such as a pending tax audit or offer of the property for sale may indicate the advisability of not publishing the fiduciary's best estimate of value. In such circumstances, a statement that value was fixed by some method such as "per company books," "formula under buy-sell agreement," or "300% of assessed value" would be acceptable, but the fiduciary would be expected to provide further information to interested parties upon request.

V.   GAINS AND LOSSES INCURRED DURING THE ACCOUNTING PERIOD SHALL BE SHOWN SEPARATELY IN THE SAME SCHEDULE.

Commentary: Each transaction involving the sale or other disposition of securities during the accounting period shall be shown as a separate item in one combined schedule of the account indicating the transaction, date, explanation, and any gain or loss.

Although gains and losses from the sale of securities can be shown separately in accounts, the preferred method of presentation is to present this information in a single schedule. Such a presentation provides the most meaningful description of investment performance and will tend to clarify relationships between gains and losses that are deliberately realized at the same time.

VI.   THE ACCOUNT SHALL SHOW SIGNIFICANT TRANS-ACTIONS THAT DO NOT AFFECT THE AMOUNT FOR WHICH THE FIDUCIARY IS ACCOUNTABLE.

Commentary: Transactions such as the purchase of an investment, receipt of a stock split, or change of a corporate name do not alter the total fund for which a fiduciary is accountable but must be shown in order to permit analysis and an understanding of the administration of the fund. These can be best shown in information schedules.

One schedule should list all investments made during the accounting period. It should include those subsequently sold as well as those still on hand. Frequently the same money will be used for a series of investments. Therefore, the schedule should not be totalled in order to avoid giving an exaggerated idea of the size of the fund.

A second schedule (entitled "Changes in Investment Holdings" in the Model Account) should show all transactions affecting a particular security holding, such as purchase of additional shares, partial sales, stock splits, change of corporate name, divestment distributions, etc. This schedule, similar to a ledger account for each holding, will reconcile opening and closing entries for particular holdings, explain changes in carrying value, and avoid extensive searches through the account for information scattered among other schedules.

RULE 5.350.   CONTINUANCE OF UNINCORPORATED BUSINESS OR VENTURE

(a)   Separate Accounts and Reports. In the conduct of an unincorporated business or venture, the personal representative shall keep separate, full, and accurate accounts of all receipts and expenditures and make reports as the court may require.

(b)   Petition. If the personal representative determines it to be in the best interest of the estate to continue an unincorporated business or venture beyond the time authorized by statute or will, the personal representative shall file a verified petition which shall include:

(1)   a statement of the nature of that business or venture;

(2)   a schedule of specific assets and liabilities;

(3)   the reasons for continuation;

(4)   the proposed form and times of accounting for that business or venture;

(5)   the period for which the continuation is requested; and

(6)   any other information pertinent to the petition.

(c)   Order. If the continuation is authorized, the order shall state:

(1)   the period for which that business or venture is to continue;

(2)   the particular powers of the personal representative in the continuation of that business or venture; and

(3)   the form and frequency of accounting by that business or venture.

(d)   Petition by Interested Person. Any interested person, at any time, may petition the court for an order regarding the operation of, accounting for, or termination of an unincorporated business or venture, and the court shall enter an order thereon.

Florida Probate Rules

Committee Notes

Rule History

1975 Revision: New rule. § 733.612, Fla. Stat.

1984 Revision: Extensive changes in rule and title. Clarifies procedural steps to be taken by a personal representative who determines it to be in the best interest of an estate to continue any unincorporated business beyond the time authorized by statute. Information required to be filed in a verified petition is specified, and normal information to be included in a court order is listed. Other pertinent information under (b)(6) may include provisions for insurance of business or venture, proposed professionals to be used in connection with such activities, how the business or venture shall be managed, the person or persons proposed for managerial positions, a list of all other employees, agents, or independent contractors employed by or affiliated with the business or venture, and proposed compensation for all such management personnel, agents, employees, and independent contractors. Committee notes revised and expanded.

1988 Revision: Editorial change in caption of (b). Committee notes revised. Citation form changes in committee notes.

1992 Revision: Committee notes revised. Citation form changes in committee notes.

2012 Revision: Committee notes revised.

Statutory Reference

§ 733.612(22), Fla. Stat. Transactions authorized for the personal representative; exceptions.

Rule References

Fla. Prob. R. 5.020 Pleadings; verification; motions.
Fla. Prob. R. 5.040 Notice.
Fla. Prob. R. 5.041 Service of pleadings and documents.
Fla. Prob. R. 5.330 Execution by personal representative.
Fla. R. Jud. Admin. 2.516 Service of pleadings and documents.

RULE 5.355.   PROCEEDINGS FOR REVIEW OF EMPLOYMENT OF AGENTS AND COMPENSATION OF PERSONAL REPRESENTATIVES AND ESTATE EMPLOYEES

After notice to all interested persons and upon petition of an interested person bearing all or a part of the impact of the payment of compensation to the personal representative or any person employed by the personal representative, the propriety of the employment and the reasonableness of the compensation or payment may be reviewed by the court. The petition shall state the grounds on which it is based. The burden of proving the propriety of the employment and the reasonableness of the compensation shall be upon the personal representative and the person employed by the personal representative. Any person who is determined to have received excessive compensation from an estate may be ordered to make appropriate refunds.

Committee Notes

This rule represents a rule implementation of the procedure formerly found in section 733.6175, Florida Statutes. It is not intended to change the effect of the statute from which it was derived but has been reformatted to conform with the structure of these rules. It is not intended to create a new procedure or modify an existing procedure.

Rule History

1988 Revision: New rule.

1992 Revision: Editorial changes. Committee notes revised. Citation form changes in committee notes.

1996 Revision: Committee notes revised.

2003 Revision: Committee notes revised.

2007 Revision: Committee notes revised.

2012 Revision: Committee notes revised.

Statutory References

§ 731.201(23), Fla. Stat. General definitions.
§ 731.301, Fla. Stat. Notice.
§ 733.612(19), Fla. Stat. Transactions authorized for the personal representative; exceptions.
§ 733.617, Fla. Stat. Compensation of personal representative.
§ 733.6171, Fla. Stat. Compensation of attorney for the personal representative.
§ 733.6175, Fla. Stat. Proceedings for review of employment of agents and compensation of personal representatives and employees of estate.

Rule References

Fla. Prob. R. 5.040 Notice.
Fla. Prob. R. 5.041 Service of pleadings and documents.
Fla. R. Jud. Admin. 2.516 Service of pleadings and documents.

RULE 5.360.   ELECTIVE SHARE

(a)   **Election.** An election to take the elective share may be filed by the surviving spouse, or on behalf of the surviving spouse by an attorney-in-fact or guardian of the property of the surviving spouse.

(1)   **Election by Surviving Spouse.** An electing surviving spouse must file the election within the time required by law and promptly serve a copy of the election on the personal representative in the manner provided for service of formal notice.

(2)   **Election by Attorney-in-Fact or Guardian of the Property of Surviving Spouse.**

          (A)   **Petition for Approval.** Before filing the election, the attorney-in-fact or guardian of the property of the surviving spouse must petition the court having jurisdiction of the probate proceeding for approval to make the election. The petition for approval must allege the authority to act on behalf of the surviving spouse and facts supporting the election.

          (B)   **Notice of Petition.** Upon receipt of the petition, the personal representative must promptly serve a copy of the petition by formal notice on all interested persons.

          (C)   **Order Authorizing Election.** If the election is approved, the order must include a finding that the election is in the best interests of the surviving spouse during the spouse's probable lifetime.

          (D)   **Filing the Election.** Upon entry of an order authorizing the filing of an election, the attorney-in-fact or guardian of the property must file the election within the later of the time provided by law or 30 days from service of the order and promptly serve a copy of the election on the personal representative in the manner provided for service of formal notice.

      (b)   **Procedure for Election.**

          (1)   **Extension.** Within the period provided by law to make the election, the surviving spouse or an attorney-in-fact or guardian of the property of the surviving spouse may petition the court for an extension of time for making an election or for approval to make the election. After notice and hearing the court for good cause shown may extend the time for election. If the court grants the petition for an extension, the election must be filed within the time allowed by the extension.

          (2)   **Withdrawal of Election.** The surviving spouse, an attorney-in- fact, a guardian of the property of the surviving spouse, or the personal representative of the surviving spouse's estate may withdraw the election within the time provided by law.

          (3)   **Service of Notice.** Upon receipt of an election the personal representative must serve a notice of election within 20 days following service of the election, together with a copy of the election, on all interested persons in the manner provided for service of formal notice. The notice of election must indicate the names and addresses of the attorneys for the surviving spouse and the personal representative and must state that:

          (A)   persons receiving a notice of election may be required to contribute toward the satisfaction of the elective share;

          (B)   objections to the election must be served within 20 days after service of the copy of the notice of election; and

          (C)   if no objection to the election is timely served, an order determining the surviving spouse's entitlement to the elective share may be granted without further notice.

          (4)   **Objection to Election.** Within 20 days after service of the notice of election, an interested person may serve an objection to the election which must state with particularity the grounds on which the objection is based. The objecting party must serve copies of the objection on the surviving spouse and the personal representative. If an objection is served, the personal representative must promptly serve a copy of the objection on all other interested persons who have not previously been served with a copy of the objection.

(c) **Determination of Entitlement.**

(1) **No Objection Served.** If no objection to the election is timely served, the court must enter an order determining the spouse's entitlement to the elective share.

(2) **Objection Served.** If an objection to the election is timely served, the court must determine the surviving spouse's entitlement to the elective share after notice and hearing.

(d) **Procedure to Determine Amount of Elective Share and Contribution.**

(1) **Petition by Personal Representative.** After entry of the order determining the surviving spouse's entitlement to the elective share, the personal representative must file and serve a petition to determine the amount of the elective share. The petition must

(A) give the name and address of each direct recipient known to the personal representative;

(B) describe the proposed distribution of assets to satisfy the elective share, and the time and manner of distribution; and

(C) identify those direct recipients, if any, from whom a specified contribution will be required and state the amount of contribution sought from each.

(2) **Service of Inventory.** The inventory of the elective estate required by rule 5.340, together with the petition, must be served within 60 days after entry of the order determining entitlement to the elective share on all interested persons in the manner provided for service of formal notice.

(3) **Petition by Spouse.** If the personal representative does not file the petition to determine the amount of the elective share within 90 days from rendition of the order of entitlement, the electing spouse or the attorney-in-fact or the guardian of the property or personal representative of the electing spouse may file the petition specifying as particularly as is known the value of the elective share.

(4) **Objection to Amount of Elective Share.** Within 20 days after service of the petition to determine the amount of the elective share, an interested person may serve an objection to the amount of or distribution of assets to satisfy the elective share. The objection must state with particularity the grounds on which the objection is based. The objecting party must serve copies of the objection on the surviving spouse and the personal representative. If an objection is served, the personal representative must promptly serve a copy of the objection on all interested persons who have not previously been served.

(5)   Determination of Amount of Elective Share and Contribution.

(A)   No Objection Served. If no objection is timely served to the petition to determine the amount of the elective share, the court must enter an order on the petition.

(B)   Objection Served. If an objection is timely served to the petition to determine the amount of the elective share, the court must determine the amount of the elective share and contribution after notice and hearing.

(6)   Order Determining Amount of Elective Share and Contribution. The order must:

(A)   set forth the amount of the elective share;

(B)   identify the assets to be distributed to the surviving spouse in satisfaction of the elective share; and

(C)   if contribution is necessary, specify the amount of contribution for which each direct recipient is liable.

(e)   Relief from Duty to Enforce Contribution. A petition to relieve the personal representative from the duty to enforce contribution must state the grounds on which it is based and notice must be served on interested persons.

Committee Notes

The extensive rewrite of this rule in 2001 is intended to conform it with and provide procedures to accommodate amendments to Florida's elective share statutes, §§ 732.201 et seq., Fla. Stat. Proceedings to determine entitlement to elective share are not specific adversary proceedings under rule 5.025(a), but may be declared adversary at the option of the party. Proceedings to determine the amount of elective share and contribution are specific adversary proceedings under rule 5.025(a). Requirements for service are intended to be consistent with the requirements for formal notice. Rule 5.040. Service of process may be required to obtain personal jurisdiction over direct recipients who are not otherwise interested persons and who have not voluntarily submitted themselves to the jurisdiction of the court. Rule 5.040(a)(3)(C); ch. 48, Fla. Stat. Process and Service of Process; ch. 49, Fla. Stat., Constructive Service of Process. An inventory of the elective estate should be afforded the same confidentiality as other estate inventories. § 733.604(1) and (2), Fla. Stat. In fulfilling his or her obligations under this rule, a personal representative is not required to make impractical or extended searches for property entering into the elective estate and the identities of direct recipients. Preexisting rights to dower and curtesy formerly addressed in subdivision (e) of this rule are now governed by new rule 5.365.

Counsel's attention is directed to Fla. Ethics Opinion 76-16, dated April 4, 1977, for guidance regarding the duties of an attorney with respect to spousal rights.

Rule History

1984 Revision: Extensive changes. Clarifies information to be included in a petition for elective share filed by a personal representative and specifies information to be included in an order determining elective share.
Committee notes revised and expanded.

1988 Revision: Extensive changes. A new procedure has been added providing for optional service of a notice of election together with a copy of the election and a procedure to expose objections to and determine right to entitlement, separate from the pre-existing procedure of determination of amount and setting aside. Subdivisions (c) and (d) represent rule implementation of procedure in statute. Committee notes revised and expanded. Citation form changes in committee notes.

1992 Revision: Editorial change. Committee notes revised. Citation form changes in committee notes.

2001 Revision: Entire rule rewritten. Committee notes revised.

2003 Revision: Committee notes revised.

2005 Revision: Subdivision (a) amended to require service in the manner of formal notice of the notice of election. Subdivision (b)(3) amended to provide time period for personal representative to service notice of election on interested persons, and title revised. Subdivision (d)(2) amended to provide time limit and service requirement for elective estate inventory and petition for determination of amount of elective share. Committee notes revised.

2010 Cycle Report Revision: Committee notes revised.

2010 Out-of-Cycle Report Revision: Subdivision (a)(2) amended to conform to an amendment to § 732.2125, Florida Statutes.

2012 Revision: Committee notes revised.

Statutory References

§ 732.201, Fla. Stat. Right to elective share.
§ 732.2025, Fla. Stat. Definitions.
§ 732.2035, Fla. Stat. Property entering into elective estate.
§ 732.2045, Fla. Stat. Exclusions and overlapping application.
§ 732.2055, Fla. Stat. Valuation of the elective estate.
§ 732.2065, Fla. Stat. Amount of the elective share.
§ 732.2075, Fla. Stat. Sources from which elective share payable; abatement.
§ 732.2085, Fla. Stat. Liability of direct recipients and beneficiaries.
§ 732.2095, Fla. Stat. Valuation of property used to satisfy elective share.
§ 732.2125, Fla. Stat. Right of election; by whom exercisable.
§ 732.2135, Fla. Stat. Time of election; extensions; withdrawal.
§ 732.2145, Fla. Stat. Order of contribution; personal representative's duty to collect contribution.
§ 733.604, Fla. Stat. Inventories and accountings; public records exemptions.

Florida Probate Rules

Rule References

Fla. Prob. R. 5.025 Adversary proceedings.
Fla. Prob. R. 5.040 Notice.
Fla. Prob. R. 5.041 Service of pleadings and documents.
Fla. Prob. R. 5.340 Inventory.
Fla. R. Jud. Admin. 2.516 Service of pleadings and documents.
Fla. R. App. P. 9.020(h) Definitions.

RULE 5.365. PETITION FOR DOWER

A widow may file an extraordinary petition for assignment of dower. The petition shall be filed in the court of each county where the widow's husband had conveyed land in which the widow had not relinquished her right of dower before October 1, 1973. Formal notice shall be served on persons adversely affected. The proceedings shall be as similar as possible to those formerly existing for the ordinary assignment of dower.

Committee Notes

Rule History

2001 Revision: Derived from former rule 5.360(e).

Statutory Reference

§ 732.111, Fla. Stat. Dower and curtesy abolished.

RULE 5.370. SALES OF REAL PROPERTY WHERE NO POWER CONFERRED

(a) **Petition.** When authorization or confirmation of the sale of real property is required, the personal representative shall file a verified petition setting forth the reasons for the sale, a description of the real property sold or proposed to be sold, and the price and terms of the sale.

(b) **Order.** If the sale is authorized or confirmed, the order shall describe the real property. An order authorizing a sale may provide for the public or private sale of the real property described therein, in parcels or as a whole. An order authorizing a private sale shall specify the price and terms of the sale. An order authorizing a public sale shall specify the type of notice of sale to be given by the personal representative.

Committee Notes

Petitions under the rule are governed by section 733.610, Florida Statutes, under which sales are voidable by interested persons if there was a conflict of interest without full disclosure and consent, unless the will or contract entered into by the decedent authorized the transaction or it was approved by the court after notice to all interested persons, and by section 733.609, Florida Statutes, involving bad faith actions by the personal representative. Note provision for attorneys' fees.

Florida Probate Rules

Rule History

1984 Revision: Extensive changes. Notice of hearing on any petition concerning sale of real property is required by statute unless waived. The requirement to record a certified copy of the order approving sale of real estate in each county where the real property or any part thereof is situated has been deleted. Committee notes revised and expanded.

1988 Revision: Committee notes expanded. Citation form changes in committee notes.

1992 Revision: Committee notes revised. Citation form changes in committee notes.

1996 Revision: Editorial changes.

2012 Revision: Committee notes revised.

Statutory References

§ 733.609, Fla. Stat. Improper exercise of power; breach of fiduciary duty.
§ 733.610, Fla. Stat. Sale, encumbrance or transaction involving conflict of interest.
§ 733.613(1), Fla. Stat. Personal representative's right to sell real property.
§ 733.810, Fla. Stat. Distribution in kind; valuation.

Rule References

Fla. Prob. R. 5.020 Pleadings; verification; motions.
Fla. Prob. R. 5.040 Notice.
Fla. Prob. R. 5.041 Service of pleadings and documents.
Fla. Prob. R. 5.180 Waiver and consent.
Fla. R. Jud. Admin. 2.516 Service of pleadings and documents.

RULE 5.380. COMPULSORY PAYMENT OF DEVISES OR DISTRIBUTIVE INTERESTS

(a)　　**Petition.** A beneficiary may file a petition setting forth the facts that entitle the beneficiary to compel payment of devises or distributive interests stating that the property will not be required for the payment of debts, family allowance, spouse's elective share, estate and inheritance taxes, claims, charges, and expenses of administration, or for providing funds for contribution or enforcing equalization in case of advancements.

(b)　　**Order.** If the court finds that the property will not be required for the purposes set forth in subdivision (a), it may enter an order describing the property to be surrendered or delivered and compelling the personal representative, prior to the final settlement of the personal representative's accounts, to do one or more of the following:

(1)　　Pay all or any part of a devise in money.

(2)　　Deliver specific personal property within the personal representative's custody and control.

        (3)   Pay all or any part of a distributive interest in the personal estate of a decedent.

        (4)   Surrender real property.

    (c)   **Bond.** Before the entry of an order of partial distribution, the court may require the person entitled to distribution to give a bond with sureties as prescribed by law.

Committee Notes

Rule History

1984 Revision: Extensive changes. Committee notes revised.

1988 Revision: Editorial change in caption of (a). Citation form change in committee notes.

1992 Revision: Editorial changes. Committee notes revised. Citation form changes in committee notes.

2003 Revision: Committee notes revised.

2012 Revision: Committee notes revised.

Statutory References

§ 731.301, Fla. Stat. Notice.
§ 733.802, Fla. Stat. Proceedings for compulsory payment of devises or distributive interest.

Rule References

Fla. Prob. R. 5.020 Pleadings; verification; motions.
Fla. Prob. R. 5.040 Notice.
Fla. Prob. R. 5.041 Service of pleadings and documents.
Fla. R. Jud. Admin. 2.516 Service of pleadings and documents.

RULE 5.385.   DETERMINATION OF BENEFICIARIES AND SHARES

    (a)   **Beneficiaries and Shares.** If a personal representative or other interested person is in doubt or is unable to determine with certainty beneficiaries entitled to an estate or the shares of any beneficiary of an estate, or a beneficiary entitled to any asset or interest in an estate, the personal representative or other interested person may petition the court to determine beneficiaries.

    (b)   **Petition.** The petition shall include:

        (1)   the names, residences, and post office addresses of all persons who may have an interest, except creditors of the decedent, known to the petitioner or ascertainable by diligent search and inquiry;

(2)   a statement of the nature of the interest of each person;

(3)   designation of any person believed to be a minor or incapacitated, and whether any person so designated is under legal guardianship in this state;

(4)   a statement as to whether petitioner believes that there are, or may be, persons whose names are not known to petitioner who have claims against, or interest in, the estate as beneficiaries.

(c)   Order. After formal notice and hearing, the court shall enter an order determining the beneficiaries or the shares and amounts they are entitled to receive, or both.

Committee Notes

This rule represents a rule implementation of the procedure formerly found in section 733.105, Florida Statutes. It is not intended to change the effect of the statute from which it was derived but has been reformatted to conform with the structure of these rules. It is not intended to create a new procedure or modify an existing procedure.

Rule History

1988 Revision: New rule.

1992 Revision: Editorial changes. Committee notes revised. Citation form changes in committee notes.

2002 Revision: Subdivision (c) added to implement procedure formerly found in section 733.105(2), Florida Statutes. Committee notes revised.

2003 Revision: Change in subdivision (c) to replace "heirs or devisees" with "beneficiaries" to incorporate term used in section 733.105, Florida Statutes. Committee notes revised.

2007 Revision: Committee notes revised.

2012 Revision: Committee notes revised.

Statutory References

ch. 49, Fla. Stat. Constructive service of process.
§ 731.201(2), (23), Fla. Stat. General definitions.
§ 731.301, Fla. Stat. Notice.
§ 733.105, Fla. Stat. Determination of beneficiaries.

Rule References

Fla. Prob. R. 5.025 Adversary proceedings.
Fla. Prob. R. 5.040 Notice.
Fla. Prob. R. 5.041 Service of pleadings and documents.
Fla. Prob. R. 5.120 Administrator ad litem and guardian ad litem.
Fla. Prob. R. 5.205(a)(5) Filing evidence of death.

Fla. R. Jud. Admin. 2.516 Service of pleadings and documents.

RULE 5.386. ESCHEAT

(a) **Escheat Proceeding.** If it appears to the personal representative that an estate may escheat or there is doubt about the existence of any person entitled to the estate, the personal representative shall institute a proceeding to determine beneficiaries within 1 year after letters have been issued to the personal representative, and notice shall be served on the Department of Legal Affairs. If the personal representative fails to institute the proceeding within the time fixed, it may be instituted by the Department of Legal Affairs.

(b) **Court's Report.** On or before January 15 of each year, each court shall furnish to the Department of Legal Affairs a list of all estates being administered in which no person appears to be entitled to the property and the personal representative has not instituted a proceeding for the determination of beneficiaries.

(c) **Administration.** Except as herein provided, escheated estates shall be administered as other estates.

Committee Notes

This rule represents a rule implementation of the procedure formerly found in section 732.107, Florida Statutes. It is not intended to change the effect of the statute from which it was derived but has been reformatted to conform with the structure of these rules. It is not intended to create a new procedure or modify an existing procedure.

Rule History

1988 Revision: New rule.

1992 Revision: Editorial change. Committee notes revised. Citation form changes in committee notes.

2003 Revision: Committee notes revised.

2012 Revision: Committee notes revised.

Statutory References

§ 732.107, Fla. Stat. Escheat.
§ 733.105, Fla. Stat. Determination of beneficiaries.
§ 733.816, Fla. Stat. Disposition of unclaimed property held by personal representatives.

Rule References

Fla. Prob. R. 5.020 Pleadings; verification; motions.
Fla. Prob. R. 5.040 Notice.
Fla. Prob. R. 5.041 Service of pleadings and documents.
Fla. Prob. R. 5.042 Time.
Fla. Prob. R. 5.385 Determination of beneficiaries and shares.
Fla. R. Jud. Admin. 2.516 Service of pleadings and documents.

RULE 5.395. NOTICE OF FEDERAL ESTATE TAX RETURN

When a federal estate tax return is required, the personal representative shall file a notice stating the due date of the return. The notice shall be filed within 12 months from the date letters are issued and copies of the notice shall be served on interested persons. Whenever the due date is subsequently extended, similar notice shall be filed and served.

Committee Notes

The purpose of the rule is to require notification to the court and all interested persons that the time for closing the estate is extended when a federal estate tax return is required.

Rule History

1984 Revision: New rule.

1988 Revision: Citation form change in committee notes.

1992 Revision: Committee notes revised. Citation form changes in committee notes.

2003 Revision: Committee notes revised.

Rule Reference

Fla. Prob. R. 5.400 Distribution and discharge.

RULE 5.400. DISTRIBUTION AND DISCHARGE

(a) **Petition for Discharge; Final Accounting.** A personal representative who has completed administration except for distribution shall file a final accounting and a petition for discharge including a plan of distribution.

(b) **Contents.**

The petition for discharge shall contain a statement:

(1) that the personal representative has fully administered the estate;

(2) that all claims which were presented have been paid, settled, or otherwise disposed of;

(3) that the personal representative has paid or made provision for taxes and expenses of administration;

(4) showing the amount of compensation paid or to be paid to the personal representative, attorneys, accountants, appraisers, or other agents employed by the personal representative and the manner of determining that compensation;

(5)   showing a plan of distribution which shall include:

(A)   a schedule of all prior distributions;

(B)   the property remaining in the hands of the personal representative for distribution;

(C)   a schedule describing the proposed distribution of the remaining assets; and

(D)   the amount of funds retained by the personal representative to pay expenses that are incurred in the distribution of the remaining assets and termination of the estate administration;

(6)   that any objections to the accounting, the compensation paid or proposed to be paid, or the proposed distribution of assets must be filed within 30 days from the date of service of the last of the petition for discharge or final accounting; and also that within 90 days after filing of the objection, a notice of hearing thereon must be served or the objection is abandoned; and

(7)   that objections, if any, shall be in writing and shall state with particularity the item or items to which the objection is directed and the grounds on which the objection is based.

(c)   Closing Estate; Extension. The final accounting and petition for discharge shall be filed and served on interested persons within 12 months after issuance of letters for estates not required to file a federal estate tax return, otherwise within 12 months from the date the return is due, unless the time is extended by the court for cause shown after notice to interested persons. The petition to extend time shall state the status of the estate and the reason for the extension.

(d)   Distribution. The personal representative shall promptly distribute the estate property in accordance with the plan of distribution, unless objections are filed as provided in these rules.

(e)   Discharge. On receipt of evidence that the estate has been fully administered and properly distributed, the court shall enter an order discharging the personal representative and releasing the surety on any bond.

Committee Notes

The rule establishes a procedure for giving notice and serving the final accounting, petition for discharge, and plan of distribution to all interested persons prior to distribution and discharge. No distinction is made in plans of distribution which distribute estate property in kind among multiple residual beneficiaries proportionate to their respective interests and those which include equalizing adjustments in cash or property and which do not make prorated distribution. If disclosure of the compensation or disclosure of the manner of determining the compensation in the petition for discharge is to be waived, the form of waiver must conform to rule 5.180(b).

Rule History

1980 Revision: Change in prior (a)(6) to require that an objection set forth the basis on which it is being made.

1984 Revision: This rule has been substantially revised. Portions of the prior rule are now incorporated in rules 5.400 and 5.401. The committee has included the procedure for filing and serving of objections to the final accounting, petition for discharge, plan of distribution, or compensation in rule 5.401.

1988 Revision: Subdivision (b)(1) is deleted to avoid duplication with rule 5.346. Subdivision (c) is amended to add the 12-month time specification of section 733.901(1), Florida Statutes. Committee notes revised. Citation form changes in committee notes.

1992 Revision: Subdivision (b)(5)(D) is added. Editorial changes. Committee notes revised. Citation form changes in committee notes.

1996 Revision: Addition in (a)(4) of specific attorney fee compensation disclosure requirements found in § 733.6171(9), Florida Statutes, and expanded to cover all compensation. Committee notes revised.

2003 Revision: Committee notes revised.

2005 Revision: Subdivision (f) deleted to avoid duplication with rule 5.180.

2006 Revision: Committee notes revised.

2007 Revision: Committee notes revised.

2012 Revision: Committee notes revised.

Statutory References

§ 731.201(12), (23), Fla. Stat. General definitions.
§ 731.302, Fla. Stat. Waiver and consent by interested person.
§ 733.809, Fla. Stat. Right of retainer.
§ 733.810, Fla. Stat. Distribution in kind; valuation.
§ 733.811, Fla. Stat. Distribution; right or title of distributee.
§ 733.812, Fla. Stat. Improper distribution or payment; liability of distributee or payee.
§ 733.901, Fla. Stat. Final discharge.

Rule References

Fla. Prob. R. 5.020 Pleadings; verification; motions.
Fla. Prob. R. 5.040 Notice.
Fla. Prob. R. 5.041 Service of pleadings and documents.
Fla. Prob. R. 5.042 Time.
Fla. Prob. R. 5.180 Waiver and consent.
Fla. Prob. R. 5.330 Execution by personal representative.
Fla. Prob. R. 5.346 Fiduciary accounting.
Fla. Prob. R. 5.401 Objections to petition for discharge or final accounting.

Fla. R. Jud. Admin. 2.250(a)(1)(D) Time standards for trial and appellate courts and reporting requirements.

Fla. R. Jud. Admin. 2.516 Service of pleadings and documents.

RULE 5.401. OBJECTIONS TO PETITION FOR DISCHARGE OR FINAL ACCOUNTING

(a) Objections. An interested person may object to the petition for discharge or final accounting within 30 days after the service of the later of the petition or final accounting on that interested person.

(b) Contents. Written objections to the petition for discharge or final accounting must state with particularity the items to which the objections are directed and must state the grounds on which the objections are based.

(c) Service. Copies of the objections shall be served by the objector on the personal representative and interested persons not later than 30 days after the last date on which the petition for discharge or final accounting was served on the objector.

(d) Hearing on Objections. Any interested person may set a hearing on the objections. Notice of the hearing shall be given to all interested persons. If a notice of hearing on the objections is not served within 90 days of filing of the objections, the objections shall be deemed abandoned and the personal representative may make distribution as set forth in the plan of distribution.

(e) Order on Objections. The court shall sustain or overrule any objections to the petition for discharge and final accounting and shall determine a plan of distribution.

(f) Discharge. On receipt of evidence that the estate has been distributed according to the plan determined by the court and the claims of creditors have been paid or otherwise disposed of, the court shall enter an order discharging the personal representative and releasing the surety on any bond.

Committee Notes

Rule History

1984 Revision: New rule. Objections to the petition for discharge or final accounting were formerly under prior rule 5.400. Clarifies procedure for objections.

1988 Revision: Editorial changes in (a). Committee notes revised. Citation form changes in committee notes.

1992 Revision: Committee notes revised. Citation form changes in committee notes.

1996 Revision: Subdivision (d) amended to clarify that 90-day period pertains to service of hearing notice, not the actual hearing date.

2003 Revision: Committee notes revised.

2007 Revision: Committee notes revised.

2012 Revision: Committee notes revised.

Statutory References

§ 731.201(12), (23), Fla. Stat. General definitions.
§ 733.6175, Fla. Stat. Proceedings for review of employment of agents and compensation of personal representatives and employees of estate.
§ 733.901, Fla. Stat. Final discharge.

Rule References

Fla. Prob. R. 5.020 Pleadings; verification; motions.
Fla. Prob. R. 5.040 Notice.
Fla. Prob. R. 5.041 Service of pleadings and documents.
Fla. Prob. R. 5.042 Time.
Fla. Prob. R. 5.180 Waiver and consent.
Fla. Prob. R. 5.400 Distribution and discharge.
Fla. R. Jud. Admin. 2.516 Service of pleadings and documents.

RULE 5.402.   NOTICE OF LIEN ON PROTECTED HOMESTEAD

(a)   Filing. If the personal representative has recorded a notice of lien on protected homestead, the personal representative shall file a copy of the recorded notice in the probate proceeding.

(b)   Contents. The notice of lien shall contain:

(1)   the name and address of the personal representative and the personal representative's attorney;

(2)   the legal description of the real property;

(3)   to the extent known, the name and address of each person appearing to have an interest in the property; and

(4)   a statement that the personal representative has expended or is obligated to expend funds to preserve, maintain, insure, or protect the property and that the lien stands as security for recovery of those expenditures and obligations incurred, including fees and costs.

(c)   Service. A copy of the recorded notice of lien shall be served on interested persons in the manner provided for service of formal notice.

Committee Notes

Rule History

2005 Revision: New rule.

2012 Revision: Committee notes revised.

Statutory References

§ 733.608, Fla. Stat. General power of the personal representative.

Rule References

Fla. Prob. R. 5.040 Notice.
Fla. Prob. R. 5.041 Service of pleadings and documents.
Fla. Prob. R. 5.403 Proceedings to determine amount of lien on protected homestead.
Fla. Prob. R. 5.404 Notice of taking possession of protected homestead.
Fla. Prob. R. 5.405 Proceedings to determine protected homestead real property.
Fla. R. Jud. Admin. 2.516 Service of pleadings and documents.

RULE 5.403. PROCEEDINGS TO DETERMINE AMOUNT OF LIEN ON PROTECTED HOMESTEAD

(a)   Petition. A personal representative or interested person may file a petition to determine the amount of any lien on protected homestead.

(b)   Contents. The petition shall be verified by the petitioner and shall state:

(1)   the name and address of the personal representative and the personal representative's attorney;

(2)   the interest of the petitioner;

(3)   the legal description of the real property;

(4)   to the extent known, the name and address of each person appearing to have an interest in the property; and

(5)   to the extent known, the amounts paid or obligated to be paid by the personal representative to preserve, maintain, insure, or protect the protected homestead, including fees and costs.

(c)   Service. The petition shall be served on interested persons by formal notice.

Committee Notes

Rule History

2005 Revision: New rule.

2012 Revision: Committee notes revised.

Statutory References

§ 733.608, Fla. Stat. General power of the personal representative.

Rule References

Fla. Prob. R. 5.040 Notice.
Fla. Prob. R. 5.041 Service of pleadings and documents.
Fla. Prob. R. 5.402 Notice of lien on protected homestead.
Fla. Prob. R. 5.404 Notice of taking possession of protected homestead.
Fla. Prob. R. 5.405 Proceedings to determine protected homestead real property.
Fla. R. Jud. Admin. 2.516 Service of pleadings and documents.

RULE 5.404. NOTICE OF TAKING POSSESSION OF PROTECTED HOMESTEAD

(a) **Filing of Notice.** If a personal representative takes possession of what appears reasonably to be protected homestead pending a determination of its homestead status, the personal representative shall file a notice of that act.

(b) **Contents of Notice.** The notice shall contain:

(1) a legal description of the property;

(2) a statement of the limited purpose for preserving, insuring, and protecting it for the heirs or devisees pending a determination of the homestead status;

(3) the name and address of the personal representative and the personal representative's attorney;

(4) if known, the location, date, and time the petition to determine homestead status will be heard, and

(5) if the personal representative is in possession when the notice is filed, the date the personal representative took possession.

(c) **Service of Notice.** The notice shall be served in the manner provided for service of formal notice on interested persons and on any person in actual possession of the property.

Committee Notes

Rule History

2002 Revision: New rule.

2005 Revision: Term "devisees" substituted for "beneficiaries" in subdivision (b)(2) to clarify the status of persons interested in protected homestead. Committee notes revised.

Statutory References

§ 732.401, Fla. Stat. Descent of homestead.
§ 732.4015, Fla. Stat. Devise of homestead.
§ 733.608(2), Fla. Stat. General power of the personal representative.

Rule References

Fla. Prob. R. 5.402 Notice of lien on protected homestead.

Fla. Prob. R. 5.403 Proceedings to determine amount of lien on protected homestead.

Fla. Prob. R. 5.405 Proceedings to determine protected homestead real property.

RULE 5.405.   PROCEEDINGS TO DETERMINE PROTECTED HOMESTEAD REAL PROPERTY

(a)   **Petition.** An interested person may file a petition to determine protected homestead real property owned by the decedent.

(b)   **Contents.** The petition shall be verified by the petitioner and shall state:

(1)   the date of the decedent's death;

(2)   the county of the decedent's domicile at the time of death;

(3)   the name of the decedent's surviving spouse and the names and dates of birth of the decedent's surviving lineal descendants;

(4)   a legal description of the property owned by the decedent on which the decedent resided; and

(5)   any other facts in support of the petition.

(c)   **Order.** The court's order on the petition shall describe the real property and determine whether any of the real property constituted the protected homestead of the decedent. If the court determines that any of the real property was the protected homestead of the decedent, the order shall identify the person or persons entitled to the protected homestead real property and define the interest of each.

Committee Notes

This rule establishes the procedure by which the personal representative or any interested person may petition the court for a determination that certain real property constituted the decedent's protected homestead property, in accordance with article X, section 4 of the Florida Constitution. The jurisdiction of the court to determine constitutional protected homestead property was established by *In re Noble's Estate*, 73 So. 2d 873 (Fla. 1954).

Rule History

1984 Revision: New rule.

1988 Revision: Editorial change in (a). Subdivision (b)(4) amended to conform to constitutional change. Committee notes revised. Citation form change in committee notes.

1992 Revision: Editorial change. Committee notes revised. Citation form changes in committee notes.

1996 Revision: Subdivision (c) amended to require description of real property that is the subject of the petition, description of any homestead property, and definition of specific interests of persons entitled to homestead real property.

2002 Revision: Replaces "homestead" with "protected homestead" throughout to conform to addition of term in section 731.201(29), Florida Statutes. Committee notes revised.

2003 Revision: Committee notes revised.

2007 Revision: Committee notes revised.

2010 Revision: Committee notes revised.

2012 Revision: Committee notes revised.

Constitutional Reference

Art. X, § 4, Fla. Const.

Statutory References

§ 731.104, Fla. Stat. Verification of documents.
§ 731.201(33), Fla. Stat. General definitions.
§ 732.401, Fla. Stat. Descent of homestead.
§ 732.4015, Fla. Stat. Devise of homestead.
§ 733.607, Fla. Stat. Possession of estate.
§ 733.608, Fla. Stat. General power of the personal representative.

Rule References

Fla. Prob. R. 5.020 Pleadings; verification; motions.
Fla. Prob. R. 5.040 Notice.
Fla. Prob. R. 5.041 Service of pleadings and documents.
Fla. Prob. R. 5.205(a)(6) Filing evidence of death.
Fla. Prob. R. 5.340 Inventory.
Fla. Prob. R. 5.404 Notice of taking possession of protected homestead.
Fla. R. Jud. Admin. 2.516 Service of pleadings and documents.

RULE 5.406.   PROCEEDINGS TO DETERMINE EXEMPT PROPERTY

(a)   **Petition.** An interested person may file a petition to determine exempt property within the time allowed by law.

(b)   **Contents.** The petition shall be verified by the petitioner and shall:

(1)   describe the property and the basis on which it is claimed as exempt property; and

(2)   state the name and address of the decedent's surviving spouse or, if none, the names and addresses of decedent's children entitled by law to the exempt

property and the dates of birth of those who are minors.

(c) **Order.** The court shall determine each item of exempt property and its value, if necessary to determine its exempt status, and order the surrender of that property to the persons entitled to it.

Committee Notes

This rule establishes the procedure by which the personal representative or any interested person may petition the court for determination of exempt property in accordance with article X, section 4 of the Florida Constitution and section 732.402, Florida Statutes.

Section 732.402, Florida Statutes, specifies the time within which the petition to determine exempt property must be filed, within 4 months after the date of service of the notice of administration, unless extended as provided in the statute.

Rule History

1984 Revision: New rule.

1988 Revision: Subdivision (a) revised to reflect editorial changes and to require verification. Subdivision (b)(1) revised to require the basis for asserting exempt property status. Subdivision (b)(2) added the requirement of stating addresses of those entitled to exempt property. Subdivision (c) revised to reflect editorial changes and to require determination of the value of each item of exempt property. Committee notes revised.

1992 Revision: Committee notes revised. Citation form changes in committee notes.

1996 Revision: Editorial changes in rule to conform to similar language in rule 5.405. Committee notes revised.

2003 Revision: Committee notes revised.

2010 Revision: Subdivision (c) amended to limit the instances in which the value of the property claimed as exempt needs to be stated in the order.

2012 Revision: Committee notes revised.

Statutory References

§ 731.104, Fla. Stat. Verification of documents.
§ 732.402, Fla. Stat. Exempt property.

Rule References

Fla. Prob. R. 5.020 Pleadings; verification; motions.
Fla. Prob. R. 5.040 Notice.
Fla. Prob. R. 5.041 Service of pleadings and documents.
Fla. Prob. R. 5.042 Time.
Fla. Prob. R. 5.420 Disposition of personal property without administration.
Fla. R. Jud. Admin. 2.516 Service of pleadings and documents.

RULE 5.407. **PROCEEDINGS TO DETERMINE FAMILY ALLOWANCE**

(a) **Petition.** An interested person may file a petition to determine family allowance.

(b) **Contents.** The petition shall be verified by the petitioner and shall:

(1) state the names and addresses of the decedent's surviving spouse and the decedent's lineal heirs who were being supported by the decedent or who were entitled to be supported by the decedent at the time of the decedent's death, stating the dates of birth of those who are minors; and

(2) for each person for whom an allowance is sought, state the person's name and relationship to the decedent, the basis on which the allowance is claimed, and the amount sought.

(c) **Order.** The order shall identify the persons entitled to the allowance, the amount to which each is entitled, the method of payment, and to whom payment should be made.

Committee Notes

Rule History

2003 Revision: New rule.

2012 Revision: Editorial change in (b)(1) for gender neutrality. Committee notes revised.

Statutory References

§ 731.104, Fla. Stat. Verification of documents.
§ 732.403, Fla. Stat. Family allowance.

Rule References

Fla. Prob. R. 5.020 Pleadings; verification; motions.
Fla. Prob. R. 5.040 Notice.
Fla. Prob. R. 5.041 Service of pleadings and documents.
Fla. R. Jud. Admin. 2.516 Service of pleadings and documents.

RULE 5.420. **DISPOSITION OF PERSONAL PROPERTY WITHOUT ADMINISTRATION**

(a) **Application.** An interested person may request a disposition of the decedent's personal property without administration. An application signed by the applicant shall set forth:

(1) the description and value of the exempt property;

(2)   the description and value of the other assets of the decedent;

(3)   the amount of preferred funeral expenses and reasonable and necessary medical and hospital expenses for the last 60 days of the last illness together with accompanying statements or payment receipts; and

(4)   each requested payment or distribution of personal property.

(b)   Exempt Property. If the decedent's personal property includes exempt property, or property that can be determined to be exempt property, the application must also be signed by all persons entitled to the exempt property or by their representative.

(c)   Preparation. On request, the clerk shall assist the applicant in the preparation of the required writing.

(d)   Disposition. If the court is satisfied that disposition without administration is appropriate, the court may, without hearing, by letter or other writing authorize the payment, transfer, or disposition of the decedent's personal property to those persons entitled to it.

Committee Notes

Section 732.402, Florida Statutes, requires persons entitled to exempt property, which excludes property specifically or demonstratively devised, to file timely a petition to determine exempt property. Accordingly, disposition of personal property under this rule should not be granted if decedent's personal property includes exempt property without all persons entitled thereto agreeing to such disposition.

Rule History

1977 Revision: Permits the clerk to perform limited ministerial acts in the completion of the application.

1984 Revision: Editorial changes. Delineates the required contents of the application. Committee notes revised.

1988 Revision: Subdivision (a)(3) changed to require applicant to attach accompanying statements or payment receipts regarding priority expenses. Subdivision (b) added to require persons entitled to exempt property to agree to the proposed disposition. Committee notes expanded.

1992 Revision: Editorial change. Committee notes revised. Citation form changes in committee notes.

2003 Revision: Committee notes revised.

Statutory References

§ 732.402, Fla. Stat. Exempt property.
§ 735.301, Fla. Stat. Disposition without administration.

Florida Probate Rules

Rule Reference

Fla. Prob. R. 5.205(a)(4) Filing evidence of death.

RULE 5.430.   **RESIGNATION OF PERSONAL REPRESENTATIVE**

    (a)   **Resignation.** A personal representative may resign with court approval.

    (b)   **Petition for Resignation.** The personal representative seeking to resign shall file a petition for resignation. The petition shall be verified and shall state:

    (1)   the personal representative desires to resign and be relieved of all powers, duties, and obligations as personal representative;

    (2)   the status of the estate administration and that the interests of the estate will not be jeopardized if the resignation is accepted;

    (3)   whether a proceeding for accounting, surcharge, or indemnification or other proceeding against the resigning personal representative is pending; and

    (4)   whether the appointment of a successor fiduciary is necessary. If the petition nominates a successor fiduciary, it shall state the nominee's priority under the Florida Probate Code, if any, and that the nominee is qualified to serve under the laws of Florida.

    (c)   **Service.** The petition shall be served by formal notice on all interested persons and the personal representative's surety, if any.

    (d)   **Appointment of Successor.** Before accepting the resignation, the court shall determine the necessity for appointment of a successor fiduciary. If there is no joint personal representative serving, the court shall appoint a successor fiduciary.

    (e)   **Acceptance of Resignation.** The court may accept the resignation and revoke the letters of the resigning personal representative if the interests of the estate are not jeopardized. Acceptance of the resignation shall not exonerate the resigning personal representative or the resigning personal representative's surety from liability.

    (f)   **Delivery of Records and Property.** The resigning personal representative shall immediately upon acceptance of the resignation by the court deliver to the remaining personal representative or the successor fiduciary all of the records of the estate and all property of the estate, unless otherwise directed by the court.

    (g)   **Petition for Discharge; Accounting.** The resigning personal representative shall file an accounting and a petition for discharge within 30 days after the date that the letters of the resigning personal representative are revoked by the court. The petition for discharge shall be verified and shall state:

    (1)   that the letters of the resigning personal representative have been revoked;

(2)   that the resigning personal representative has surrendered all undistributed estate assets, records, documents, papers, and other property of or concerning the estate to the remaining personal representative or the successor fiduciary; and

(3)   the amount of compensation paid or to be paid the resigning personal representative and the attorney and other persons employed by the resigning personal representative.

(h)   Notice, Filing, and Objections to Accounting. Notice of, filing of, and objections to the accounting of the resigning personal representative shall be as provided in rule 5.345.

(i)   Notice of Filing and Objections to Petition for Discharge.

(1)   Notice of filing and a copy of the petition for discharge shall be served on all interested persons. The notice shall state that objections to the petition for discharge must be filed within 30 days after the later of service of the petition or service of the accounting on that interested person.

(2)   Any interested person may file an objection to the petition for discharge within 30 days after the later of service of the petition or service of the accounting on that interested person. Any objection not filed within such time shall be deemed abandoned. An objection shall be in writing and shall state with particularity the item or items to which the objection is directed and the grounds on which the objection is based.

(3)   The objecting party shall serve a copy of the objection on the resigning personal representative and other interested persons.

(4)   Any interested person may set a hearing on the objections. Notice of the hearing shall be given to the resigning personal representative and other interested persons.

(j)   Failure to File Accounting or Deliver Records or Property. The resigning personal representative shall be subject to contempt proceedings if the resigning personal representative fails to file an accounting or fails to deliver all property of the estate and all estate records under the control of the resigning personal representative to the remaining personal representative or the successor fiduciary within the time prescribed by this rule or by court order.

(k)   Discharge. The court shall enter an order discharging the resigning personal representative and releasing the surety on any bond after the court is satisfied that the resigning personal representative has delivered all records and property of the estate to the remaining personal representative or the successor fiduciary; that all objections, if any, to the accounting of the resigning personal representative have been withdrawn, abandoned, or judicially resolved; and that the liability of the resigning personal representative has been determined and satisfied.

Committee Notes

In the event of resignation of a personal representative, if a joint personal representative is not serving, the successor fiduciary must file an oath and designation of a successor resident agent.

This rule was revised to implement the revisions to the probate code that govern resignation of personal representative. The committee intended to separate the procedure with respect to resignation from removal because these proceedings may differ in practice.

Rule History

1975 Revision: The rule provides for the orderly succession of personal representatives in the event a personal representative resigns or is removed.

1977 Revision: Editorial change in committee note.

1988 Revision: Editorial changes; captions added to subdivisions. Committee notes revised. Citation form changes in committee notes.

1992 Revision: Editorial changes. Committee notes revised. Citation form changes in committee notes.

2003 Revision: Rule completely revised to comply with statutory changes. Committee notes revised.

2007 Revision: Committee notes revised.

2012 Revision: Committee notes revised.

Statutory References

§ 731.104, Fla. Stat. Verification of documents.
§ 731.201(23), Fla. Stat. General definitions.
§ 733.101, Fla. Stat. Venue of probate proceedings.
§ 733.502, Fla. Stat. Resignation of personal representative.
§ 733.503, Fla. Stat. Appointment of successor upon resignation.
§ 733.5035, Fla. Stat. Surrender of assets after resignation.
§ 733.5036, Fla. Stat. Accounting and discharge following resignation.

Rule References

Fla. Prob. R. 5.020 Pleadings; verification; motions.
Fla. Prob. R. 5.040 Notice.
Fla. Prob. R. 5.041 Service of pleadings and documents.
Fla. Prob. R. 5.180 Waiver and consent.
Fla. Prob. R. 5.310 Disqualification of personal representative; notification.
Fla. Prob. R. 5.330 Execution by personal representative.
Fla. Prob. R. 5.345 Accountings other than personal representatives' final accountings.
Fla. Prob. R. 5.346 Fiduciary accounting.
Fla. Prob. R. 5.401 Objections to petition for discharge or final accounting.
Fla. R. Jud. Admin. 2.516 Service of pleadings and documents

RULE 5.440. **PROCEEDINGS FOR REMOVAL OF PERSONAL REPRESENTATIVE**

(a) **Commencement of Proceeding.** The court on its own motion may remove, or any interested person by petition may commence a proceeding to remove, a personal representative. A petition for removal shall state the facts constituting the grounds upon which removal is sought, and shall be filed in the court having jurisdiction over the administration of the estate.

(b) **Accounting.** A removed personal representative shall file an accounting within 30 days after removal.

(c) **Delivery of Records and Property.** A removed personal representative shall, immediately after removal or within such time prescribed by court order, deliver to the remaining personal representative or to the successor fiduciary all of the records of the estate and all of the property of the estate.

(d) **Failure to File Accounting or Deliver Records and Property.** If a removed personal representative fails to file an accounting or fails to deliver all property of the estate and all estate records under the control of the removed personal representative to the remaining personal representative or to the successor fiduciary within the time prescribed by this rule or by court order, the removed personal representative shall be subject to contempt proceedings.

Committee Notes

The revision of subdivision (a) of this rule by the addition of its final phrase represents a rule implementation of the procedure found in section 733.505, Florida Statutes. It is not intended to change the effect of the statute from which it was derived but has been reformatted to conform with the structure of these rules. It is not intended to create a new procedure or modify an existing procedure.

Rule History

1980 Revision: Subdivision (a) amended to require formal notice to interested persons and to delete requirement that court give directions as to mode of notice. Surety authorized to petition for removal.

1984 Revision: Editorial changes. Provisions in prior rule for contempt have been deleted since the court has the inherent power to punish for contempt. Committee notes revised.

1988 Revision: Last phrase of (a) added to implement the procedure found in section 733.505, Florida Statutes. Subdivision (b) amended to parallel interim accounting rules. Deletes ability to extend time to file and adds reference to court power to punish for contempt. Committee notes expanded. Editorial changes. Citation form changes in committee notes.

1992 Revision: Editorial changes. Committee notes revised. Citation form changes in committee notes.

2002 Revision: Entire rule amended. Contents of accountings by removed fiduciaries are now governed by rule 5.346. Editorial changes in (a), (c), and (d). Committee notes revised.

2003 Revision: Committee notes revised.

2007 Revision: Committee notes revised.

2010 Revision: Editorial change in title to clarify scope of rule.

2012 Revision: Committee notes revised.

Statutory References

§ 731.201(23), Fla. Stat. General definitions.
§ 733.504, Fla. Stat. Removal of personal representative; causes of removal.
§ 733.505, Fla. Stat. Jurisdiction in removal proceedings.
§ 733.506, Fla. Stat. Proceedings for removal.
§ 733.5061, Fla. Stat. Appointment of successor upon removal.
§ 733.508, Fla. Stat. Accounting and discharge of removed personal representatives upon removal.
§ 733.509, Fla. Stat. Surrender of assets upon removal.

Rule References

Fla. Prob. R. 5.020 Pleadings; verification; motions.
Fla. Prob. R. 5.025 Adversary proceedings.
Fla. Prob. R. 5.040 Notice.
Fla. Prob. R. 5.041 Service of pleadings and documents.
Fla. Prob. R. 5.042 Time.
Fla. Prob. R. 5.150 Order requiring accounting.
Fla. Prob. R. 5.310 Disqualification of personal representative; notification.
Fla. Prob. R. 5.345 Accountings other than personal representatives' final accountings.
Fla. Prob. R. 5.346 Fiduciary accounting.
Fla. R. Jud. Admin. 2.516 Service of pleadings and documents.

RULE 5.460.   SUBSEQUENT ADMINISTRATION

(a)   Petition. If, after an estate is closed, additional property of the decedent is discovered or if further administration of the estate is required for any other reason, any interested person may file a petition for further administration of the estate. The petition shall be filed in the same probate file as the original administration.

(b)   Contents. The petition shall state:

(1)   the name, address, and interest of the petitioner in the estate;

(2)   the reason for further administration of the estate;

(3)   the description, approximate value, and location of any asset not included among the assets of the prior administration; and

        (4)   a statement of the relief sought.

       (c)   **Order.** The court shall enter such orders as appropriate. Unless required, the court need not revoke the order of discharge, reissue letters, or require bond.

Committee Notes

       This rule establishes a procedure for further administration after estate is closed, which may be summary in nature.

Rule History

       1984 Revision: Extensive changes. Committee notes revised.

       1992 Revision: Citation form change in committee notes.

       2003 Revision: Committee notes revised.

       2012 Revision: Committee notes revised.

Statutory Reference

       § 733.903, Fla. Stat. Subsequent administration.

Rule References

       Fla. Prob. R. 5.020 Pleadings; verification; motions.
       Fla. Prob. R. 5.040 Notice.
       Fla. Prob. R. 5.041 Service of pleadings and documents.
       Fla. R. Jud. Admin. 2.516 Service of pleadings and documents.

RULE 5.470.   ANCILLARY ADMINISTRATION

       (a)   **Petition.** The petition for ancillary letters shall include an authenticated copy of so much of the domiciliary proceedings as will show:

       (1)   for a testate estate the will, petition for probate, order admitting the will to probate, and authority of the personal representative; or

       (2)   for an intestate estate the petition for administration and authority of the personal representative to act.

       (b)   **Notice.** Before ancillary letters shall be issued to any person, formal notice shall be given to:

       (1)   all known persons qualified to act as ancillary personal representative and whose entitlement to preference of appointment is equal to or greater than petitioner's and who have not waived notice or joined in the petition; and

       (2)   all domiciliary personal representatives who have not waived notice or joined in the petition.

(c)   Probate of Will. On filing the authenticated copy of a will, the court shall determine whether the will complies with Florida law to entitle it to probate. If it does comply, the court shall admit the will to probate.

Committee Notes

Rule History

1975 Revision: The rule sets out the procedural requirements for issuance of ancillary letters.

1984 Revision: Editorial changes with addition of notice requirement in (b). Committee notes revised.

1988 Revision: Committee notes revised.

1992 Revision: Changed rule to require that notice be given to persons qualified to act as ancillary personal   representative whose entitlement to preference of appointment is equal to or greater than petitioner's and to all   domiciliary personal representatives prior to entry of an order admitting the will to probate. Committee notes   revised. Citation form changes in committee notes.

1996 Revision: The requirement that a filing of an authenticated copy of a will be a "probated" will is   removed from subdivision (c). There may be circumstances in which a will is on deposit or file in a foreign   jurisdiction but is not being offered for probate. That should not preclude an ancillary administration in Florida of   that estate. This change is not intended to allow an authenticated copy of any document other than an original   instrument to be filed under this rule and considered for probate.

2003 Revision: Committee notes revised.

2005 Revision: Committee notes revised.

2010 Revision: Committee notes revised.

2012 Revision: Committee notes revised.

Statutory References

§ 731.201(1), Fla. Stat. General definitions.
§ 733.212, Fla. Stat. Notice of administration; filing of objections.
§ 733.2121, Fla. Stat. Notice to creditors; filing of claims.
§ 734.102, Fla. Stat. Ancillary administration.
§ 734.1025, Fla. Stat. Nonresident decedent's testate estate with property not exceeding $50,000 in this   state; determination of claims.

Rule References

Fla. Prob. R. 5.020 Pleadings; verification; motions.
Fla. Prob. R. 5.040 Notice.
Fla. Prob. R. 5.041 Service of pleadings and documents.
Fla. Prob. R. 5.042 Time.

Fla. Prob. R. 5.065(b) Notice of civil action or ancillary administration.

Fla. Prob. R. 5.205(a)(2) Filing evidence of death.

Fla. Prob. R. 5.215 Authenticated copy of will.

Fla. Prob. R. 5.240 Notice of administration.

Fla. Prob. R. 5.241 Notice to creditors.

Fla. Prob. R. 5.475 Ancillary administration, short form.

Fed. R. Civ. P. 44(a) Proving an official record.

Fla. R. Jud. Admin. 2.516 Service of pleadings and documents.

RULE 5.475.   ANCILLARY ADMINISTRATION, SHORT FORM

(a)   Filing Requirements. The foreign personal representative of a testate estate that meets the requirements of section 734.1025, Florida Statutes, may file with the clerk in the county where any property is located an authenticated copy of so much of the transcript of the foreign proceedings as will show:

(1)   the probated will and all probated codicils of the decedent;

(2)   the order admitting them to probate;

(3)   the letters or their equivalent; and

(4)   the part of the record showing the names of the beneficiaries of the estate or an affidavit of the foreign personal representative reciting that the names are not shown or not fully disclosed by the foreign record and specifying the names.

On presentation of the foregoing, the court shall admit the will and any codicils to probate if they comply with section 732.502(1) or section 732.502(2), Florida Statutes.

(b)   Notice to Creditors. After complying with the foregoing requirements, the foreign personal representative may cause a notice to creditors to be published as required by these rules.

(c)   Claims Procedure. The procedure for filing or barring claims and objecting to them and for suing on them shall be the same as for other estates, except as provided in this rule.

(d)   Order. If no claims are filed against the estate within the time allowed, the court shall enter an order adjudging that notice to creditors has been duly published and proof thereof filed and that no claims have been filed against the estate or that all claims have been satisfied.

(e)   Notification of Claims Filed. If any claim is filed against the estate within the time allowed, the clerk shall send to the foreign personal representative a copy of the claim and a notice setting a date for a hearing to appoint an ancillary personal representative. At the hearing, the court shall appoint an ancillary personal representative according to the preferences as provided by law.

(f)   Objections to Claims. If an ancillary personal representative is appointed pursuant to this rule, the procedure for filing, objecting to, and suing on claims shall be the same as for other estates, except that the ancillary personal representative appointed shall have not less than 30 days from the date of appointment within which to object to any claim filed.

Committee Notes

This rule represents a rule implementation of the procedure found in section 734.1025, Florida Statutes. It is not intended to change the effect of the statute from which it was derived but has been reformatted to conform with the structure of these rules. It is not intended to create a new procedure or modify an existing procedure.

Rule History

1988 Revision: New rule.

1992 Revision: Editorial changes. Committee notes revised. Citation form changes in committee notes.

2003 Revision: Committee notes revised.

2005 Revision: Deletion of reference to intestate estates in subdivision (a) to conform to 2001 amendments to section 734.1025, Florida Statutes. Editorial changes throughout.

2012 Revision: Committee notes revised.

Statutory References

§ 733.2121, Fla. Stat. Notice to creditors; filing of claims.
§ 734.102, Fla. Stat. Ancillary administration.
§ 734.1025, Fla. Stat. Nonresident decedent's testate estate with property not exceeding $50,000 in this state; determination of claims.

Rule References

Fla. Prob. R. 5.020 Pleadings; verification; motions.
Fla. Prob. R. 5.040 Notice.
Fla. Prob. R. 5.041 Service of pleadings and documents.
Fla. Prob. R. 5.042 Time.
Fla. Prob. R. 5.065(b) Notice of civil action or ancillary administration.
Fla. Prob. R. 5.205(a)(2) Filing evidence of death.
Fla. Prob. R. 5.215 Authenticated copy of will.
Fla. Prob. R. 5.240 Notice of administration.
Fla. Prob. R. 5.241 Notice to creditors.
Fla. Prob. R. 5.470 Ancillary administration.
Fla. R. Jud. Admin. 2.516 Service of pleadings and documents.

RULE 5.490.   FORM AND MANNER OF PRESENTING CLAIM

(a)   **Form.** A creditor's statement of claim shall be verified and filed with the clerk and shall state:

(1)   the basis for the claim;

(2)   the amount claimed;

(3)   the name and address of the creditor;

(4)   the security for the claim, if any; and

(5)   whether the claim is currently due or involves an uncertainty and, if not due, then the due date and, if contingent or unliquidated, the nature of the uncertainty.

(b) **Copy.** At the time of filing the claim, the creditor shall also furnish the clerk with a copy thereof.

(c) **Mailing.** The clerk shall mail a copy of claims, noting the fact and date of mailing on the original, to the attorney for the personal representative unless all personal representatives file a notice directing that copies of claims be mailed to a designated personal representative or attorney of record. Absent designation, a copy of claims shall be mailed to the attorney for the personal representative named first in the letters of administration.

(d) **Validity of Claim.** Failure to deliver or receive a copy of the claim shall not affect the validity of the claim.

(e) **Amending Claims.** If a claim as filed is sufficient to notify interested persons of its substance but is otherwise defective as to form, the court may permit the claim to be amended at any time.

(f) **Service by Personal Representative.** If the personal representative files a claim individually, or in any other capacity creating a conflict of interest between the personal representative and any interested person, then at the time the claim is filed, the personal representative shall serve all interested persons with a copy of the claim and notice of the right to object to the claim. The notice shall state that an interested person may object to a claim as provided by law and rule 5.496. Service shall be either by informal notice or in the manner provided for service of formal notice. Service on one interested person by a chosen method shall not preclude service on another interested person by another method.

Committee Notes

Subdivision (e) of this rule represents a rule implementation of the procedure found in section 733.704, Florida Statutes. It is not intended to change the effect of the statute from which it was derived but has been reformatted to conform with the structure of these rules. It is not intended to create a new procedure or modify an existing procedure.

Rule History

1975 Revision: Sets forth the claims procedure to be followed and clarifies the matter of delivery of copies where there are multiple personal representatives or where the attorney of record desires to accept such delivery.

1984 Revision: Extensive editorial changes and requires furnishing of copy of claim to the attorney for the personal representative. Committee notes revised.

1988 Revision: Clarifies the matter of delivery of copies and directs the clerk to mail the same to the attorney for the personal representative unless designations are filed by all personal representatives to the contrary. Subdivision (e) added to implement the procedure found in section 733.704, Florida Statutes. Editorial changes. Committee notes expanded. Citation form change in committee notes.

1992 Revision: Committee notes revised. Citation form changes in committee notes. 1999 Revision: Reference to repealed rule deleted from committee notes. 2003 Revision: Committee notes revised.

2007 Revision: Editorial change in (a). New (f) added, providing procedure for notice when personal representative files a claim individually or otherwise has a conflict of interest with any interested person regarding a claim.

Statutory References

§ 731.104, Fla. Stat. Verification of documents.
§ 733.2121, Fla. Stat. Notice to creditors; filing of claims.
§ 733.702, Fla. Stat. Limitations on presentation of claims.
§ 733.703, Fla. Stat. Form and manner of presenting claim.
§ 733.704, Fla. Stat. Amendment of claims.
§ 733.708, Fla. Stat. Compromise.
§ 733.710, Fla. Stat. Limitations on claims against estates.
§ 734.102, Fla. Stat. Ancillary administration.

Rule References

Fla. Prob. R. 5.020 Pleadings; verification; motions.
Fla. Prob. R. 5.241 Notice to creditors.
Fla. Prob. R. 5.470 Ancillary administration.
Fla. Prob. R. 5.475 Ancillary administration, short form.
Fla. Prob. R. 5.530 Summary administration.

RULE 5.496.   **FORM AND MANNER OF OBJECTING TO CLAIM**

(a)   **Filing.** An objection to a claim, other than a personal representative's proof of claim, shall be in writing and filed on or before the expiration of 4 months from the first publication of notice to creditors or within 30 days from the timely filing or amendment of the claim, whichever occurs later.

(b)   **Service.** A personal representative or other interested person who files an objection to the claim shall serve a copy of the objection on the claimant. If the objection is filed by an interested person other than the personal representative, a copy of the objection shall also be served on the personal representative. Any objection shall include a certificate of service.

(c)   **Notice to Claimant.** An objection shall contain a statement that the claimant is limited to a period of 30 days from the date of service of an objection within which to bring an action as provided by law.

Florida Probate Rules

Committee Notes

This rule represents an implementation of the procedure found in section 733.705, Florida Statutes, and adds a requirement to furnish notice of the time limitation in which an independent action or declaratory action must be filed after objection to a claim.

Rule History

1992 Revision: New rule.

2003 Revision: Reference in (a) to notice of administration changed to notice to creditors. Committee notes revised.

2005 Revision: Removed provision for objections to personal representative's proof of claim, now addressed in rule 5.498, and subsequent subdivisions relettered. Reference to service on the claimant's attorney removed because service on the attorney is required by rule 5.041(b). Committee notes revised.

2007 Revision: Editorial change in (a). Second sentence of (b) added to specify that the objection must include a certificate of service.

2010 Revision: Subdivision (b) amended to delete the requirement to serve a copy of an objection to a claim within 10 days, and to clarify the requirement to include a certificate of service.

2012 Revision: Committee notes revised.

Statutory References

§ 731.201(4), Fla. Stat. General definitions.
§ 733.705, Fla. Stat. Payment of and objection to claims.

Rule References

Fla. Prob. R. 5.040 Notice.
Fla. Prob. R. 5.041 Service of pleadings and documents.
Fla. Prob. R. 5.498 Personal representative's proof of claim.
Fla. Prob. R. 5.499 Form and manner of objecting to personal representative's proof of claim. Fla. R. Jud. Admin. 2.516 Service of pleadings and documents.

RULE 5.498. **PERSONAL REPRESENTATIVE'S PROOF OF CLAIM**

    (a)   **Contents.** A personal representative's proof of claim shall state:

        (1)   the basis for each claim;

        (2)   the amount claimed;

        (3)   the name and address of the claimant;

        (4)   the security for the claim, if any;

(5)   whether the claim is matured, unmatured, contingent, or unliquidated;

(6)   whether the claim has been paid or is to be paid; and

(7)   that any objection to a claim listed as to be paid shall be filed no later than 4 months from first publication of the notice to creditors or 30 days from the date of the filing of the proof of claim, whichever occurs later.

(b)   **Service.** The proof of claim shall be served at the time of filing or promptly thereafter on all interested persons.

Committee Notes

This rule represents an implementation of the procedure found in section 733.703(2), Florida Statutes, with respect to a proof of claim filed by the personal representative.

Rule History

2005 Revision: New rule.

2007 Revision: Subdivision (b) amended to eliminate the need to serve claimants listed as paid on the proof of claim, and clarifying editorial change.

2012 Revision: Committee notes revised.

Statutory References

§ 733.703(2), Fla. Stat. Form and manner of presenting claim.
§ 733.705, Fla. Stat. Payment of and objection to claims.

Rule References

Fla. Prob. R. 5.041 Service of pleadings and documents.
Fla. Prob. R. 5.499 Form and manner of objecting to personal representative's proof of claim.
Fla. R. Jud. Admin. 2.516 Service of pleadings and documents.

RULE 5.499.   FORM AND MANNER OF OBJECTING TO PERSONAL REPRESENTATIVE'S PROOF OF CLAIM

(a)   **Filing.** An objection to a personal representative's proof of claim shall be in writing and filed on or before the expiration of 4 months from the first publication of notice to creditors or within 30 days from the timely filing of the proof of claim, whichever occurs later.

(b)   **Contents.** The objection shall identify the particular item or items to which objection is made. An objection to an item listed on the proof of claim as to be paid shall also contain a statement that the claimant is limited to a period of 30 days from the date of service of an objection within which to bring an independent action as provided by law.

(c)   **Items Listed as Paid.** If an objection is filed to an item listed on the proof of claim as paid, it shall not be necessary for the claimant to file an independent action as to that item. Liability as between estate and the personal representative individually for claims listed on the proof of claim as paid, or for claims treated as if they were listed on the proof of claim as paid, shall be determined in the estate administration, in a proceeding for accounting or surcharge, or in another appropriate proceeding, whether or not an objection has been filed.

(d)   **Items Paid Before Objection.** If an item listed as to be paid is paid by the personal representative prior to the filing of an objection as to that item, the item shall be treated as if it were listed on the proof of claim as paid.

(e)   **Service.** The objector shall serve a copy of the objection on the personal representative and, in the case of any objection to an item listed as to be paid, shall also serve a copy on that claimant within 10 days after the filing of the objection. In the case of an objection to an item listed as to be paid, the objection shall include a certificate of service.

Committee Notes

This rule represents an implementation of the procedure found in section 733.705, Florida Statutes, with   respect to a proof of claim filed by the personal representative. The rule recognizes the different treatment between   items listed on a proof of claim as having been paid versus items listed as to be paid. An objection to an item listed   as to be paid is treated in the same manner as a creditor's claim and there is a requirement to furnish notice of the   time limitation in which an independent action or declaratory action must be filed after objection to a claim.

Rule History

2005 Revision: New rule.

2007 Revision: Editorial change in (a). Extensive revisions to rest of rule to clarify the differences in procedure between items listed as paid and items listed as to be paid. Committee notes revised.

2012 Revision: Committee notes revised.

Statutory Reference

§ 733.705, Fla. Stat. Payment of and objection to claims.

Rule References

Fla. Prob. R. 5.040 Notice.
Fla. Prob. R. 5.041 Service of pleadings and documents.
Fla. Prob. R. 5.496 Form and manner of objecting to claim.
Fla. Prob. R. 5.498 Personal representative's proof of claim.
Fla. R. Jud. Admin. 2.516 Service of pleadings and documents.

RULE 5.510.   ESTABLISHMENT AND PROBATE OF LOST OR DESTROYED WILL

(a)   Proceeding. The establishment and probate of a lost or destroyed will shall be in one proceeding.

(b)   Petition. The petition, in addition to reciting information required under these rules for petition for administration, shall include a statement of the facts constituting grounds on which relief is sought, and a statement of the contents of the will or, if available, a copy of the will.

(c)   Testimony. The testimony of each witness in the proceeding shall be reduced to writing and filed and may be used as evidence in any contest of the will if the witness has died or moved from the state.

(d)   Notice. No lost or destroyed will shall be admitted to probate unless formal notice has been given to those who, but for the will, would be entitled to the property thereby devised.

(e)   Order. The order admitting the will to probate shall state in full its terms and provisions.

Committee Notes

This rule represents a rule implementation of the procedure formerly found in section 733.207, Florida Statutes. It is not intended to change the effect of the statute from which it was derived but has been reformatted to conform with the structure of these rules. It is not intended to create a new procedure or modify an existing procedure.

Rule History

1977 Revision: Editorial change in subdivision (c) of prior rule.

1984 Revision: Extensive changes. Committee notes revised.

1988 Revision: Rule rewritten to conform to statute. Committee notes expanded. Citation form change in committee notes.

1992 Revision: Committee notes revised. Citation form change in committee notes.

2002 Revision: Subdivision (d) added to implement procedure formerly found in section 733.207(3), Florida Statutes. Committee notes revised.

2003 Revision: Committee notes revised.

2012 Revision: Committee notes revised.

Statutory Reference

§ 733.207, Fla. Stat. Establishment and probate of lost or destroyed will.

Rule References

Fla. Prob. R. 5.020 Pleadings; verification; motions.
Fla. Prob. R. 5.025 Adversary proceedings.
Fla. Prob. R. 5.040 Notice.
Fla. Prob. R. 5.041 Service of pleadings and documents.
Fla. Prob. R. 5.042 Time.
Fla. Prob. R. 5.200 Petition for administration.
Fla. R. Jud. Admin. 2.516 Service of pleadings and documents.

RULE 5.530.   SUMMARY ADMINISTRATION

(a)   **Petition.** The petition shall be verified as required by law and shall contain:

(1)   a statement of the interest of each petitioner, each petitioner's name and address, and the name and office address of each petitioner's attorney;

(2)   the name and last known address of the decedent, last 4 digits of the decedent's social security number,   date and place of death of the decedent, and state and county of the decedent's domicile;

(3)   so far as is known, the names and addresses of the surviving spouse, if any, and the beneficiaries and their relationship to the decedent and the date of birth of any who are minors;

(4)   a statement showing venue;

(5)   a statement whether domiciliary or principal proceedings are pending in another state or country, if known, and the name and address of the foreign personal representative and the court issuing letters;

(6)   a statement that the decedent's will, if any, does not direct administration as required by chapter 733, Florida Statutes;

(7)   a statement that the value of the entire estate subject to administration in this state, less the value of property exempt from the claims of creditors, does not exceed $75,000 or that the decedent has been dead for more than 2 years;

(8)   a description of all assets in the estate and the estimated value of each, and a separate description of any protected homestead and exempt property;

(9)   a statement either that all creditors' claims are barred or that a diligent search and reasonable inquiry for any known or reasonably ascertainable creditors has been made and one of the following:

(A)   A statement that the estate is not indebted.

(B)   The name and address of each creditor, the nature of the debt, the amount of the debt and whether the amount is estimated or exact, and when the debt is due. If provision for payment of the debt has been made other than for full payment in the proposed order of distribution, the following information shall be shown:

(i)   The name of the person who will pay the debt.

(ii)   The creditor's written consent for substitution or assumption of the debt by another person

(iii)   The amount to be paid if the debt has been compromised.

(iv)   The terms for payment and any limitations on the liability of the person paying the debt;

(10)   in an intestate estate, a statement that after the exercise of reasonable diligence each petitioner is unaware of any unrevoked wills or codicils;

(11)   in a testate estate, a statement identifying all unrevoked wills and codicils being presented for probate, and a statement that each petitioner is unaware of any other unrevoked will or codicil; and

(12)   a schedule of proposed distribution of all probate assets and the person to whom each asset is to be distributed.

(b)   Service. The joinder in, or consent to, a petition for summary administration is not required of a beneficiary who will receive full distributive share under the proposed distribution. Any beneficiary and any known or reasonably ascertainable creditor not joining or consenting shall receive formal notice of the petition.

(c)   Testate Estate. In a testate estate, on the filing of the petition for summary administration, the decedent's will shall be proved and admitted to probate.

(d)   Order. If the court determines that the decedent's estate qualifies for summary administration, it shall enter an order distributing the probate assets and specifically designating the person to whom each asset is to be distributed.

Committee Notes

Verification and service of a petition for summary administration are governed by rules 5.020, 5.040, and 5.41. Section 735.206(2), Florida Statutes, relating to diligent search for, and service of the petition for summary administration on, reasonably ascertainable creditors is substantive. Nothing in this rule is intended to change the effect of the statutory amendments.

Rule History

1977 Revision: Changes to conform to 1975 statutory revision. Established the requirements of a petition for summary administration and provided for the hearing thereon and the entry of the order of distribution of the assets.

1984 Revision: Extensive revisions and editorial changes. Committee notes revised.

Florida Probate Rules

1988 Revision: Editorial change in caption of (a). Committee notes revised.

1992 Revision: Editorial changes. Committee notes revised. Citation form changes in committee notes.

2002 Revision: Replaces "homestead" with "protected homestead" in (a)(2) to conform to addition of term in section 731.201(29), Florida Statutes. Committee notes revised.

2003 Revision: Committee notes revised.

2005 Revision: Subdivision (a)(3) amended to include requirements of section 735.206(2), Florida Statutes.

2007 Revision: Rule substantially rewritten to require petition to include essentially the same information required to be stated in a petition for administration and to require the petitioners to specify facts showing they are entitled to summary administration. New subdivision (b) added to provide for formal notice of the petition, and subsequent subdivisions relettered.

2011 Revision: Subdivision (a)(2) amended to limit listing of decedent's social security number to last four digits.

2012 Revision: Committee notes revised.

Statutory References

§ 731.104, Fla. Stat. Verification of documents.
§§ 735.201–735.2063, Fla. Stat. Summary administration.

Rule References

Fla. Prob. R. 5.020 Pleadings; verification; motions.
Fla. Prob. R. 5.040 Notice.
Fla. Prob. R. 5.041 Service of pleadings and documents.
Fla. Prob. R. 5.205(a)(3) Filing evidence of death.
Fla. R. Jud. Admin. 2.516 Service of pleadings and documents.

PART III — GUARDIANSHIP

RULE 5.540.   HEARINGS

(a)   Application. All hearings under chapter 744 and under section 393.12, Florida Statutes, shall be open unless the alleged incapacitated person, adjudicated ward, or person alleged to have a developmental disability elects to have the hearing closed.

(b)   Election. An election to close a hearing may be made before the hearing by filing a written notice. Subject to the court's approval, an election to close or reopen a hearing may be made at any time during the hearing by oral or written motion.

Committee Notes

This rule permits an alleged incapacitated person, adjudicated ward, or person alleged to have a developmental disability to elect to have all hearings open or closed at any time by oral or written election.

Rule History

1991 Revision: New rule.

1992 Revision: Committee notes revised.

2008 Revision: Subdivision (a) amended to include persons with a developmental disability. Committee notes revised.

Statutory References

§ 393.12, Fla. Stat. Capacity; appointment of guardian advocate.
§ 744.1095, Fla. Stat. Hearings.
§ 744.3085, Fla. Stat. Guardian advocates.

Rule Reference

Fla. Prob. R. 5.541 Recording of hearings.

RULE 5.541.   RECORDING OF HEARINGS

Electronic or stenographic recordings shall be made of all hearings on the:

(a)   adjudication of incapacity;

(b)   appointment of a guardian;

(c)   modification, termination, or revocation of the adjudication of incapacity;

(d)   restoration of capacity; or

(e)   restoration of rights.

Committee Notes

This rule represents a rule implementation of the procedure found in sections 744.109 and 744.3031, Florida Statutes. It is not intended to change the effect of the statutes from which it is derived, or to create a new procedure or modify an existing procedure.

Rule History

1991 Revision: New rule.

1992 Revision: Editorial changes. Committee notes revised. Citation form change in committee notes.

2003 Revision: Committee notes revised.

2008 Revision: New subdivision (e) added for proceedings involving guardian advocates. Committee notes revised

Statutory References

§ 393.12, Fla. Stat. Capacity; appointment of guardian advocate.
§ 744.109, Fla. Stat. Records.
§ 744.3031, Fla. Stat. Emergency temporary guardianship.
§ 744.3085, Fla. Stat. Guardian advocates.
§ 744.3371, Fla. Stat. Notice of petition for appointment of guardian and hearing.

RULE 5.550. PETITION TO DETERMINE INCAPACITY

(a) **Contents.** The petition to determine incapacity shall be verified by the petitioner and shall state:

(1) the name, age, and present address of the petitioner and the petitioner's relationship to the alleged incapacitated person;

(2) the name, age, county of residence, and present address of the alleged incapacitated person, and specify the primary language spoken by the alleged incapacitated person, if known;

(3) that the petitioner believes the alleged incapacitated person to be incapacitated, the facts on which such belief is based, and the names and addresses of all persons known to the petitioner who have knowledge of such facts through personal observation;

(4) the name and address of the alleged incapacitated person's attending or family physician, if known;

(5) which rights the alleged incapacitated person is incapable of exercising to the best of the petitioner's knowledge; and, if the petitioner has insufficient experience to make that judgment, the petitioner shall so indicate;

(6) whether plenary or limited guardianship is sought for the alleged incapacitated person; and

(7) the names, relationships, and addresses of the next of kin of the alleged incapacitated person, specifying the dates of birth of any who are minors, to the extent known to the petitioner.

(b) **Notice.**

(1) **Contents.** The notice of filing the petition to determine incapacity shall state:

(A) the time and place of the hearing to inquire into the capacity of the alleged incapacitated person;

(B)   that an attorney has been appointed to represent such person; and

(C)   that if the court determines that such person is incapable of exercising any of the rights enumerated in the petition a guardian may be appointed.

(2)   **Service on Alleged Incapacitated Person.** The notice and a copy of the petition to determine incapacity shall be personally served by an elisor appointed by the court, who may be the court appointed counsel for the alleged incapacitated person. The elisor shall read the notice to the alleged incapacitated person, but need not read the petition. A return of service shall be filed by the elisor certifying that the notice and petition have been served on and the notice read to the alleged incapacitated person. No responsive pleading is required and no default may be entered for failure to file a responsive pleading. The allegations of the petition are deemed denied.

(3)   **Service on Others.** A copy of the petition and the notice shall also be served on counsel for the alleged incapacitated person, and on all next of kin.

(c)   **Verified Statement.** An interested person may file a verified statement that shall state:

(1)   that he or she has a good faith belief that the alleged incapacitated person's trust, trust amendment, or durable power of attorney is invalid; and

(2)   facts constituting a reasonable basis for that belief.

(d)   **Order.** When an order determines that a person is incapable of exercising delegable rights, it shall specify whether there is an alternative to guardianship that will sufficiently address the problems of the incapacitated person.

Committee Notes

Rule History

1980 Revision: Implements 1979 amendments to section 744.331, Florida Statutes.

1984 Revision: Change in title of rule. Editorial changes and adds a provision for service of petition. Committee notes revised.

1988 Revision: Committee notes revised. Citation form changes in committee notes.

1989 Revision by Ad Hoc Committee: The committee realized that formal notice as defined in rule 5.040(a)(1) requires the recipient of notice to file a responsive pleading within 20 days after the service of the notice. The committee believed that to impose such a requirement on the alleged incapacitated person would contravene the legislative intent of the 1989 revisions to chapter 744, Florida Statutes. The committee observed that the time required for appointment of mandatory appointed counsel might render a responsive pleading within 20 days impossible for the alleged incapacitated person. The committee concluded that, procedurally, notice upon the alleged incapacitated person should occur in the same manner as formal notice in rule 5.040, but the required response under that rule should not be imposed upon the alleged incapacitated person.

1991 Revision: Implements 1989 amendments to sections 744.3201 and 744.331, Florida Statutes, and 1990 technical amendments.

1992 Revision: Citation form changes in committee notes.

2006 Revision: Subdivisions (c) and (d) added to incorporate 2006 amendment to section 744.441 and creation of section 744.462, Florida Statutes. Committee notes revised.

Statutory References

§ 744.3201, Fla. Stat. Petition to determine incapacity.
§ 744.331, Fla. Stat. Procedures to determine incapacity.
§ 744.3371, Fla. Stat. Notice of petition for appointment of guardian and hearing.
§ 744.441(11), Fla. Stat. Powers of guardian upon court approval.
§ 744.462, Fla. Stat. Determination regarding alternatives to guardianship.

Rule References

Fla. Prob. R. 5.020 Pleadings; verification; motions.
Fla. Prob. R. 5.040(a)(3) Notice.
Fla. Prob. R. 5.800(a) Application of revised chapter 744 to existing guardianships.

RULE 5.552.   VOLUNTARY GUARDIANSHIP OF PROPERTY

(a)   Petition for Appointment of Guardian. The petition for voluntary guardianship shall be verified by the petitioner and shall state:

(1)   the facts to establish venue;

(2)   the petitioner's residence and post office address;

(3)   that the petitioner although mentally competent is incapable of the care, custody, and management of the petitioner's estate by reason of age or physical infirmity, and is voluntarily petitioning to have a guardian of the petitioner's property appointed;

(4)   whether the guardianship shall apply to all of the petitioner's property or less than all of the petitioner's property; and if less than all of the petitioner's property, the specific property to which the guardianship is to apply;

(5)   the name and residence and post office address of any proposed guardian;

(6)   that the proposed guardian is qualified to serve or that a willing and qualified proposed guardian has not been located; and

(7)   the names and post office addresses of persons to whom the petitioner requests that notice of the hearing for the appointment of the guardian, and any petition for authority to act, be given.

(b) **Certificate of Licensed Physician.** The petition shall be accompanied by a certificate of a licensed physician as required by law.

(c) **Notice of Hearing.** Notice of hearing on the petition for appointment, and any petition for authority to act, shall be given to the ward and any person to whom the ward requests notice be given, which request can be made in the petition for appointment or a subsequent written request for notice signed by the ward.

(d) **Annual Report.** The annual report shall be accompanied by a certificate from a licensed physician as required by law.

(e) **Termination.** The ward may terminate a voluntary guardianship by filing a notice of termination. Copies of the notice shall be served on all interested persons. The guardian shall file a petition for discharge in accordance with these rules.

Committee Notes

Rule History

2003 Revision: New rule.

2006 Revision: New (d) added to incorporate 2006 amendment to section 744.341, Florida Statutes, requiring inclusion of physician's certificate in annual report, and subsequent subdivision relettered. Committee notes revised.

Statutory Reference

§ 744.341, Fla. Stat. Voluntary guardianship.

Rule Reference

Fla. Prob. R. 5.680 Termination of guardianship.
Fla. Prob. R. 5.695 Annual guardianship report.

RULE 5.555. GUARDIANSHIPS OF MINORS

(a) **Application.** This rule shall apply to any guardianship for a minor.

(b) **Petition to Determine Incapacity.** No petition to determine incapacity need be filed.

(c) **Petition for Appointment of Guardian.** The petition shall be verified by the petitioner and shall state:

(1) the facts to establish venue;

(2) the petitioner's residence and post office address;

(3) the name, age, and residence and post office address of the minor;

(4)   the names and addresses of the parents of the minor and if none, the next of kin known to the petitioner;

(5)   the name and residence and post office address of the proposed guardian, and that the proposed guardian is qualified to serve; or, that a willing and qualified guardian has not been located;

(6)   the proposed guardian's relationship to and any previous association with the minor;

(7)   the reasons why the proposed guardian should be appointed; and

(8)   the nature and value of the property subject to the guardianship.

(d)   Notice. Formal notice of the petition for appointment of guardian shall be served on any parent who is not a petitioner or, if there is no parent, on the persons with whom the minor resides and on such other persons as the court may direct.

(e)   Initial and Annual Guardianship Reports.

(1)   The initial guardianship report shall consist only of the verified inventory. The annual guardianship report shall consist only of the annual accounting.

(2)   The guardian shall file an initial and annual guardianship plan as required by law.

(3)   Unless otherwise ordered by the court or required by law, the guardian need not serve a copy of the initial guardianship report and the annual guardianship reports on the ward.

(f)   Inspection of Inventory or Accounting. Unless otherwise ordered by the court for good cause shown, any inventory, amended or supplementary inventory, or accounting is subject to inspection only by the clerk, the ward or the ward's attorney, and the guardian or the guardian's attorney.

Committee Notes

The provisions of chapter 744, Florida Statutes, and the guardianship rules enacted in 1989 leave some uncertainty with respect to the procedural requirements in guardianships for minors who are not incapacitated persons. This rule is intended to address only certain procedures with respect to the establishment and administration of guardianships over minors. The committee believes that certain provisions of the guardianship law and rules apply to both guardianships of minors as well as guardianships of incapacitated persons and no change has been suggested with respect to such rules. Because no adjudication of a minor is required by statute, it is contemplated that appointment of a guardian for a minor may be accomplished without a hearing. Initial and annual guardianship reports for minors have been simplified where all assets are on deposit with a designated financial institution under applicable Florida law.

Rule History

1991 Revision: New rule adopted to apply to guardianships over minors who are not incapacitated persons.

1992 Revision: Committee notes revised. Citation form changes in committee notes.

1996 Revision: Committee notes revised.

2000 Revision: Deletes requirement in subdivision (c) to report social security number of proposed guardian.

2003 Revision: Deletes requirement in subdivision (c) to report social security number of minor. Committee notes revised.

2006 Revision: Subdivision (e)(2) amended to conform to requirement in sections 744.362(1) and 744.3675, Florida Statutes, to file initial and annual guardianship plans. Subdivision (e)(3) amended to eliminate requirement of service on ward unless ordered by court or required by statute.

Statutory References

§ 69.031, Fla. Stat. Designated financial institutions for assets in hands of guardians, curators, administrators, trustees, receivers, or other officers.
§ 744.3021, Fla. Stat. Guardians of minors.
§ 744.334, Fla. Stat. Petition for appointment of guardian or professional guardian; contents.
§ 744.3371(2), Fla. Stat. Notice of petition for appointment of guardian and hearing.
§ 744.342, Fla. Stat. Minors; guardianship.
§ 744.362, Fla. Stat. Initial guardianship report.
§ 744.363, Fla. Stat. Initial guardianship plan.
§ 744.365, Fla. Stat. Verified inventory.
§ 744.367, Fla. Stat. Duty to file annual guardianship report.
§ 744.3675, Fla. Stat. Annual guardianship plan.
§ 744.3678, Fla. Stat. Annual accounting.
§ 744.3679, Fla. Stat. Simplified accounting procedures in certain cases.

Rule References

Fla. Prob. R. 5.040 Notice.
Fla. Prob. R. 5.541 Recording of hearings.
Fla. Prob. R. 5.560 Petition for appointment of guardian of an incapacitated person.
Fla. Prob. R. 5.620 Inventory.
Fla. Prob. R. 5.636 Settlement of minors' claims.
Fla. Prob. R. 5.690 Initial guardianship report.

**RULE 5.560.   PETITION FOR APPOINTMENT OF GUARDIAN
OF AN INCAPACITATED PERSON**

    (a)   **Contents.** The petition shall be verified by the petitioner and shall state:

     (1)   the facts to establish venue;

     (2)   the petitioner's residence and post office address;

     (3)   the name, age, and residence and post office address of the alleged incapacitated person;

     (4)   the nature of the incapacity, the extent of guardianship, either limited or plenary, requested for the alleged incapacitated person, and the nature and value of property subject to the guardianship;

     (5)   the names and addresses of the next of kin of the alleged incapacitated person known to the petitioner;

     (6)   the name and residence and post office address of the proposed guardian, and that the proposed guardian is qualified to serve, or that a willing and qualified guardian has not been located;

     (7)   the proposed guardian's relationship to and any previous association with the alleged incapacitated person;

     (8)   the reasons why the proposed guardian should be appointed;

     (9)   whether there are alternatives to guardianship known to the petitioner that may sufficiently address the problems of the alleged incapacitated person in whole or in part; and

     (10)   if the proposed guardian is a professional guardian, a statement that the proposed guardian has complied with the registration requirements of section 744.1083, Florida Statutes.

(b) **Notice.** Notice of filing the petition for appointment of guardian may be served as a part of the notice of filing the petition to determine incapacity, but shall be served a reasonable time before the hearing on the petition or other pleading seeking appointment of a guardian.

(c) **Service on Public Guardian.** If the petitioner requests appointment of the public guardian, a copy of the petition and the notice shall be served on the public guardian.

Committee Notes

Rule History

1975 Revision: Substantially the same as section 744.334, Florida Statutes, expanded to include provisions of section 744.302, Florida Statutes, and section 744.312, Florida Statutes, by reference.

1977 Revision: Change in committee notes to conform to statutory renumbering.

1980 Revision: Implements 1979 amendment to section 744.334, Florida Statutes.

1984 Revision: Combines rule 5.560 and part of prior rule 5.570. Editorial changes and committee notes revised.

1988 Revision: Editorial changes. Committee notes revised. Citation form changes in committee notes.

1989 Revision by Ad Hoc Committee: Subdivision (a)(4) of the former rule has been deleted altogether because the date and court of adjudication will probably not be known at the time of filing the petition for the appointment since petition for appointment will henceforth be filed contemporaneously with the petition to determine incapacity.

1991 Revision: Implements 1989 amendments to sections 744.334 and 744.331(1), Florida Statutes, and 1990 technical amendments. Subdivision (c)(1) deleted because rule 5.555(d) addresses service on parents.

1992 Revision: Citation form changes in committee notes.

1996 Revision: Deletes requirement in subdivision (a) to report social security number of alleged incapacitated person. Adds provision to subdivision (b) for notice before hearing when petition is not served simultaneously with petition to determine incapacity.

2000 Revision: Deletes requirement in subdivision (a) to report social security number of proposed guardian.

2003 Revision: Committee notes revised.

2006 Revision: New (a)(9) added to incorporate 2006 passage of section 744.462, Florida Statutes. Subdivision (a)(10) added to implement section 744.1083, Florida Statutes. Committee notes revised.

Statutory References

§ 744.1083, Fla. Stat. Professional guardian registration.
§ 744.309, Fla. Stat. Who may be appointed guardian of a resident ward.
§ 744.312, Fla. Stat. Considerations in appointment of guardian.
§ 744.331, Fla. Stat. Procedures to determine incapacity.
§ 744.334, Fla. Stat. Petition for appointment of guardian or professional guardian; contents.
§ 744.3371(1), Fla. Stat. Notice of petition for appointment of guardian and hearing.
§ 744.341, Fla. Stat. Voluntary guardianship.
§ 744.344, Fla. Stat. Order of appointment.
§ 744.462, Fla. Stat. Determination regarding alternatives to guardianship.
§ 744.703, Fla. Stat. Office of public guardian; appointment, notification.

Rule References

Fla. Prob. R. 5.020 Pleadings; verification; motions.
Fla. Prob. R. 5.040 Notice.
Fla. Prob. R. 5.550 Petition to determine incapacity.

RULE 5.590.   **APPLICATION FOR APPOINTMENT AS GUARDIAN; DISCLOSURE STATEMENT; FILING**

(a)   **Individual Applicants.**

(1)   The application for appointment shall contain:

(A)   the applicant's qualifications to serve as a guardian; and

(B)   the names of all wards for whom the applicant is then acting as guardian, the court file number and circuit court in which each case is pending, and a statement as to whether the applicant is acting as a limited or plenary guardian of the person or property, or both, of each ward.

(2)   The application for appointment shall be filed and served a reasonable time before the hearing on the appointment of a guardian.

(b)   **Nonprofit Corporate Guardians.**

(1)   No application for appointment shall be required of a nonprofit corporate guardian.

(2)   A disclosure statement shall contain:

(A)   the corporation's qualifications to serve as a guardian; and

(B)   the names of all wards for whom the corporation is then acting as guardian, the court file number and circuit court in which each case is pending, and a statement as to whether the corporation is acting as a limited or plenary guardian of the person or property, or both, of each ward.

(3)   The disclosure statement of a nonprofit corporate guardian shall be filed quarterly with the clerk of the court for each circuit in which the corporation has been appointed, or is seeking appointment, as guardian.

(c)   **For Profit Corporations and Associations.** No application for appointment or disclosure statement shall be required of any for profit corporation or association authorized to exercise fiduciary powers under Florida law.

(d)   **Public Guardians.** No application for appointment or disclosure statement shall be required of a public guardian.

Committee Notes

Rule History

1988 Revision: Prior rule deleted; text of rule moved to rule 5.650.

1989 Revision: Rule reactivated with different title and text.

1991 Revision: Implements 1989 and 1990 amendments to section 744.3125, Florida Statutes.

1992 Revision: Citation form change in committee notes.

1996 Revision: Adds filing and service provisions consistent with rule 5.560. Corrects reference to corporations qualified to exercise fiduciary powers. Editorial changes. Adds statutory references.

2003 Revision: Committee notes revised.

2006 Revision: Committee notes revised.

2008 Revision: Committee notes revised.

Statutory References

§ 393.063(17), Fla. Stat. Definitions.
§ 393.12, Fla. Stat. Capacity; appointment of guardian advocate.
§ 744.102(4), (9), (11), (14), (22) Fla. Stat. Definitions.
§ 744.3085, Fla. Stat. Guardian advocates.
§ 744.309, Fla. Stat. Who may be appointed guardian of a resident ward.
§ 744.3125, Fla. Stat. Application for appointment.
§ 744.331(1), Fla. Stat. Procedures to determine incapacity.
§ 744.3371, Fla. Stat. Notice of petition for appointment of guardian and hearing.

RULE 5.600.   OATH

Every guardian or emergency temporary guardian shall take an oath to perform faithfully the duties of guardian or emergency temporary guardian before exercising such authority. The oath may be incorporated in the petition for appointment of guardian, or petition for appointment of emergency temporary guardian, if verified by the prospective guardian.

Committee Notes

Rule History

1977 Revision: Change in committee notes to conform to statutory renumbering. Rule permits oath of guardian to be incorporated in petition for appointment and in designation of resident agent.

1984 Revision: Editorial change and deletes genders.

1989 Revision: Prior rule adopted as temporary emergency rule.

1991 Revision: Permits oath to be incorporated in application for appointment of guardian, adds reference to temporary emergency guardian, and makes editorial change.

1992 Revision: Editorial changes.

2008 Revision: Committee notes revised.

Statutory References

§ 393.12, Fla. Stat. Capacity; appointment of guardian advocate.
§ 744.347, Fla. Stat. Oath of guardian.

RULE 5.610.   EXECUTION BY GUARDIAN

The guardian shall sign the:

(a)   initial guardianship plan;

(b)   inventory, amended inventory, or supplemental inventory;

(c)   annual guardianship plan;

(d)   annual accounting;

(e)   guardian's petition for court approval required by law;

(f)   petition for discharge;

(g)   final report; and

(h)   resignation of guardian.

Committee Notes

Rule History

1975 Revision: Rule lists what guardian shall sign and includes any petition for court approval required by   section 744.441, Florida Statutes. The rule requires that the guardian have actual knowledge of the more important   steps and acts of administration.

1977 Revision: Change in statutory reference in rule and in committee note to conform to statutory renumbering.

1988 Revision: Editorial changes. Committee notes revised. Citation form changes in rule and committee notes.

1989 Revision: Prior rule deleted and replaced by temporary emergency rule.

1991 Revision: Changes to conform to 1989 and 1990 revisions to guardianship law. Adds additional   documents to be signed by the guardian. Statutory references added.

2003 Revision: Committee notes revised.

2008 Revision: Committee notes revised.

Statutory References

§ 393.12, Fla. Stat. Capacity; appointment of guardian advocate.

§ 744.362, Fla. Stat. Initial guardianship report.

§ 744.363, Fla. Stat. Initial guardianship plan.

§ 744.365, Fla. Stat. Verified inventory.

§ 744.367, Fla. Stat. Duty to file annual guardianship report.

§ 744.3675, Fla. Stat. Annual guardianship plan.

§ 744.3678, Fla. Stat. Annual accounting.

§ 744.387, Fla. Stat. Settlement of claims.

§ 744.441, Fla. Stat. Powers of guardian upon court approval.

§ 744.446, Fla. Stat. Conflicts of interest; prohibited activities; court approval; breach of fiduciary duty.

§ 744.447, Fla. Stat. Petition for authorization to act.

§ 744.451, Fla. Stat. Order.

§ 744.467, Fla. Stat. Resignation of guardian.

§ 744.511, Fla. Stat. Accounting upon removal.

§ 744.521, Fla. Stat. Termination of guardianship.

§ 744.524, Fla. Stat. Termination of guardianship on change of domicile of resident ward.

§ 744.527(1), Fla. Stat. Final reports and application for discharge; hearing.

§ 744.534, Fla. Stat. Disposition of unclaimed funds held by guardian.

RULE 5.620.   INVENTORY

(a)   Inventory. Within 60 days after issuance of letters, the guardian of the property shall file a verified inventory as required by law. All property not in the guardian's possession as of the date the inventory is filed shall be so identified.

(b)   Amended or Supplemental Inventory. If the guardian of the property learns of any property not included in the inventory, or learns that the description in the inventory is inaccurate, the guardian shall, within 30 days of this discovery, file a verified amended or supplemental inventory showing the change.

(c)   Substantiating Papers. Unless ordered by the court, the guardian need not file the papers substantiating the inventory. Upon reasonable written request, the guardian of the property shall make the substantiating papers available for examination to those persons entitled to receive or inspect the inventory.

(d)   Safe-Deposit Box Inventory. If the ward has a safe-deposit box, a copy of the safe-deposit box inventory shall be filed as part of the verified inventory.

(e)   Guardian Advocates. This rule shall apply to a guardian advocate to the extent that the guardian advocate was granted authority over the property of the person with a developmental disability.

Committee Notes

Rule History

1977 Revision: Change in committee notes to conform to statutory renumbering.

1984 Revision: Change to require inventory to be filed within 60 days after issuance of letters, rather than after appointment. Committee notes revised.

1988 Revision: Editorial changes. Committee notes revised. Citation form change in committee notes.

1989 Revision: Prior rule deleted and replaced by temporary emergency rule.

1991 Revision: Former rule 5.620(b) has been deleted as partly substantive and addressed in section 744.381, Florida Statutes, and the procedural part is unnecessary.

The committee recognizes the conflict between this rule and section 744.362, Florida Statutes, which requires the filing of the initial guardianship report (which includes the inventory) within 60 days after appointment. The committee believes this provision, which attempts to regulate when a paper must be filed with the court, is procedural and that a guardian may not receive letters of guardianship empowering the guardian to act contemporaneously with the appointment. Therefore, the issuance of letters is a more practical time from which to measure the beginning of the time period for the accomplishment of this act.

1992 Revision: Citation form changes in committee notes.

2005 Revision: Editorial changes in (d).

2007 Revision: Committee notes revised.

2008 Revision: Adds reference to guardian advocate in new (e). Committee notes revised.

2012 Revision: Committee notes revised.

Statutory References

§ 393.12, Fla. Stat. Capacity; appointment of guardian advocate.
§ 744.362, Fla. Stat. Initial guardianship report.
§ 744.365, Fla. Stat. Verified inventory.
§ 744.3701, Fla. Stat. Inspection of report.
§ 744.381, Fla. Stat. Appraisals.
§ 744.384, Fla. Stat. Subsequently discovered or acquired property.

Rule References

Fla. Prob. R. 5.020 Pleadings; verification; motions.
Fla. Prob. R. 5.041 Service of pleadings and documents.
Fla. Prob. R. 5.060 Request for notices and copies of pleadings.
Fla. Prob. R. 5.610 Execution by guardian.
Fla. Prob. R. 5.649 Guardian advocate.
Fla. Prob. R. 5.690 Initial guardianship report.
Fla. Prob. R. 5.700 Objection to guardianship reports.
Fla. R. Jud. Admin. 2.516 Service of pleadings and documents.

RULE 5.625.   NOTICE OF COMPLETION OF GUARDIAN EDUCATION REQUIREMENTS

(a)   Filing. Unless the guardian education requirement is waived by the court, each guardian, other than a professional guardian, shall file with the court within 4 months after the issuance of letters of guardianship or letters of guardian advocacy a notice of completion of guardian education requirements.

    (b)   **Content.** The notice shall state:

          (1)   that the guardian has completed the required number of hours of course instruction and training covering the legal duties and responsibilities of a guardian, the rights of a ward, the availability of local resources to aid a ward, and the preparation of habilitation plans and annual guardianship reports, including accountings;

          (2)   the date the course was completed;

          (3)   the name of the course completed; and

          (4)   the name of the entity or instructor that taught the course.

    (c)   **Verification.** The notice shall be verified by the guardian.

Committee Notes

Rule History

2005 Revision: New rule.

2006 Revision: Subdivision (a) amended to conform to 2006 amendment to section 744.3145(4), Florida Statutes.

2008 Revision: Adds reference in (a) to guardian advocacy. Committee notes revised.

Statutory References

§ 393.12, Fla. Stat. Capacity; appointment of guardian advocate.
§ 744.3145, Fla. Stat. Guardian education requirements.

RULE 5.630.   **PETITION FOR APPROVAL OF ACTS**

    (a)   **Contents.** When authorization or confirmation of any act of the guardian is required, application shall be made by verified petition stating the facts showing:

          (1)   the expediency or necessity for the action;

          (2)   a description of any property involved;

          (3)   the price and terms of any sale, mortgage, or other contract;

          (4)   whether the ward has been adjudicated incapacitated to act with respect to the rights to be exercised;

          (5)   whether the action requested conforms to the guardianship plan; and

Florida Probate Rules

(6)   the basis for the relief sought.

(b)   Notice. No notice of a petition to authorize sale of perishable personal property or of property rapidly deteriorating shall be required. Notice of a petition to perform any other act requiring a court order shall be given to the ward, to the next of kin, if any, and to those persons who have filed requests for notices and copies of pleadings.

(c)   Order.

(1)   If the act is authorized or confirmed, the order shall describe the permitted act and authorize the guardian to perform it or confirm its performance.

(2)   If a sale or mortgage is authorized or confirmed, the order shall describe the property. If a sale is to be private, the order shall specify the price and the terms of the sale. If a sale is to be public, the order shall state that the sale shall be made to the highest bidder and that the court reserves the right to reject all bids.

(3)   If the guardian is authorized to bring an action to contest the validity of all or part of a revocable trust, the order shall contain a finding that the action appears to be in the ward's best interests during the ward's probable lifetime. If the guardian is not authorized to bring such an action, the order shall contain a finding concerning the continued need for a guardian and the extent of the need for delegation of the ward's rights.

Committee Notes

Rule History

1975 Revision: Substantially the same as sections 744.503, 744.447, and 744.451, Florida Statutes, with editorial changes.

1977 Revision: Change in statutory reference in rule and in committee note to conform to statutory renumbering.

1980 Revision: Implements 1979 amendment to section 744.447(2), Florida Statutes.

1988 Revision: Editorial changes; captions added to subdivisions. Committee notes revised. Citation form changes in rule and committee notes.

1989 Revision: Prior rule deleted and replaced by temporary emergency rule.

1991 Revision: Changes to conform to 1989 revised guardianship law.

1992 Revision: Committee notes revised. Citation form changes in committee notes.

2006 Revision: New (a)(6) added to incorporate 2006 amendment to section 744.441, Florida Statutes. New (c)(3) added to reflect passage of 2006 amendment to section 737.2065, Florida Statutes. Committee notes revised.

2007 Revision: Committee notes revised.

2008 Revision: Committee notes revised.

2012 Revision: Committee notes revised.

Statutory References

§ 393.12, Fla. Stat. Capacity; appointment of guardian advocate.
§ 736.0207, Fla. Stat. Trust contests.
§ 744.3215, Fla. Stat. Rights of persons determined incapacitated.
§ 744.441, Fla. Stat. Powers of guardian upon court approval.
§ 744.447, Fla. Stat. Petition for authorization to act.
§ 744.451, Fla. Stat. Order.

Rule References

Fla. Prob. R. 5.020 Pleadings; verification; motions.
Fla. Prob. R. 5.025 Adversary proceedings.
Fla. Prob. R. 5.040 Notice.
Fla. Prob. R. 5.041 Service of pleadings and documents.
Fla. Prob. R. 5.060 Request for notices and copies of pleadings.
Fla. Prob. R. 5.610 Execution by guardian.
Fla. Prob. R. 5.636 Settlement of minors' claims.
Fla. Prob. R. 5.649 Guardian advocate.
Fla. R. Jud. Admin. 2.516 Service of pleadings and documents.

RULE 5.635. PETITION FOR EXTRAORDINARY AUTHORITY

(a) **Contents.** When authorization for extraordinary authority is sought as permitted by law, application shall be made by verified petition stating:

(1) the petitioner's interest in the proceeding;

(2) the specific authority requested; and

(3) the facts constituting the basis for the relief sought and that the authority being requested is in the best interest of the ward.

(b) **Notice.**

(1) The petition shall be served by formal notice. For good cause shown, the court may shorten the time for response to the formal notice and may set an expedited hearing.

(2) The petition shall be served on the guardian of the person, if the guardian is not the petitioner, the ward, the next of kin, if any, those interested persons who have filed requests for notices and copies of pleadings, and such other persons as the court may direct.

(c) **Hearing.** The hearing shall be at a time and place that will enable the ward to express the ward's views to the court.

Florida Probate Rules

Committee Notes

Rule History

1991 Revision: New rule.

1992 Revision: Committee notes revised.

2008 Revision: Committee notes revised.

Statutory References

§ 393.12, Fla. Stat. Capacity; appointment of guardian advocate.
§ 744.3215(4), Fla. Stat. Rights of persons determined incapacitated.
§ 744.3725, Fla. Stat. Procedure for extraordinary authority.

RULE 5.636.   SETTLEMENT OF MINORS' CLAIMS

(a)   Time of Settlement. Claims on behalf of minors may be settled either before or after an action is filed.

(b)   Petition. The petition for approval of a settlement shall contain:

(1)   the name, residence address, and date of birth of the minor;

(2)   the name and address of any guardian appointed for the minor;

(3)   the name and residence address of the natural guardians or other persons having legal custody of the minor;

(4)   a statement disclosing the interests of any natural or court-appointed guardian whose interest may be in conflict with that of the minor;

(5)   a description of the cause of action in which the minor's interest arises;

(6)   a summary of the terms of the proposed settlement; and

(7)   copies of all agreements, releases, or other documents to be executed on behalf of the minor.

(c)   Notice. Notice of the petition shall be given to the court-appointed guardians for the minor, to the natural guardians or other persons with legal custody of the minor, to the minor if age 14 or older, and to the minor's next of kin if required by the court.

(d)   Guardian Ad Litem. The court shall appoint a guardian ad litem on behalf of a minor, without bond or notice, with respect to any proposed settlement that exceeds $50,000 and affects the interests of the minor, if:

(1)   there is no court-appointed guardian of the minor;

(2)   the court-appointed guardian may have an interest adverse to

the minor; or

> (3)   the court determines that representation of the minor's interest is otherwise inadequate.

> **(e)   Valuation of Proposed Settlement.** A proposed settlement is deemed to exceed $50,000 if the gross amount payable exceeds $50,000, without reduction to reflect present value or fees and costs.

> **(f)   Report.** A guardian ad litem appointed with respect to a proposed settlement affecting the interests of a minor shall, not later than 5 days prior to the hearing on a petition for order authorizing settlement, file and serve a report indicating the guardian ad litem's determination regarding whether the proposed settlement will be in the best interest of the minor. The report shall include:

> (1)   a statement of the facts of the minor's claim and the terms of the proposed settlement, including any benefits to any persons or parties with related claims;

> (2)   a list of the persons interviewed and documents reviewed by the guardian ad litem in evaluating the minor's claim and proposed settlement; and

> (3)   the guardian ad litem's analysis of whether the proposed settlement will be in the best interest of the minor.

> A copy of the report shall be served on those persons on whom service is required in subdivision (c) of this rule.

Committee Notes

When a civil action is pending, the petition for approval of settlement should be filed in that civil action. In all other circumstances, the petition for approval of settlement should be filed in the same court and assigned to a judge who would preside over a petition for appointment of guardian of a minor.

The total settlement to be considered under subdivisions (d) and (e) is not limited to the amounts received only by the minor, but includes all settlement payments or proceeds received by all parties to the claim or action. For example, the proposed settlement may have a gross value of $60,000, with $30,000 payable to the minor and $30,000 payable to another party. In that instance the total proposed settlement exceeds $50,000. Further, the "gross amount payable" under subdivision (e) is the total sum payable, without reducing the settlement amount by fees and costs that might be paid from the proceeds of the settlement. For example, if the proposed settlement is $60,000 but $20,000 of that sum will be paid to the attorneys representing the minor's interest in the action, the "gross amount payable" still exceeds $50,000. Likewise, the "gross amount payable" cannot be reduced to reflect the present value   of the proposed settlement on behalf of the minor.

Rule History

1992 Revision: New rule.

2003 Revision: Committee notes revised.

Florida Probate Rules

2006 Revision: Amended to reflect 2006 passage of new section 744.3025, Claims of Minors, increasing dollar figure from $25,000 to $50,000 as threshold amount requiring appointment of guardian ad litem if interests of minor are not otherwise adequately represented. Committee notes revised.

Statutory References

§ 744.3025, Fla. Stat. Claims of minors.
§ 744.387, Fla. Stat. Settlement of claims.
§ 744.391, Fla. Stat. Actions by and against guardian or ward.
§ 744.441, Fla. Stat. Powers of guardian upon court approval.
§ 744.446, Fla. Stat. Conflicts of interest; prohibited activities; court approval; breach of fiduciary duty.
§ 744.447, Fla. Stat. Petition for authorization to act.
§ 768.23, Fla. Stat. Protection of minors and incompetents.
§ 768.25, Fla. Stat. Court approval of settlements.

Rule References

Fla. Prob. R. 5.040 Notice.
Fla. Prob. R. 5.042 Time.
Fla. Prob. R. 5.120 Administrator ad litem and guardian ad litem.
Fla. Prob. R. 5.610 Execution by guardian.
Fla. Prob. R. 5.630 Petition for approval of acts.

RULE 5.640.   CONTINUANCE OF UNINCORPORATED BUSINESS OR VENTURE OF WARD

(a)   Continuance of Business. When the ward is adjudicated incapacitated while engaged in any unincorporated business or venture, or the court finds that a person with a developmental disability lacks capacity to manage an unincorporated business or venture, the court may authorize the guardian to continue the business or venture for a reasonable time under the supervision of the court.

(b)   Petition. Before an order is made under subdivision (a), the guardian shall file a verified petition, alleging sufficient facts to make it appear that it is in the best interest of the ward's estate to continue the business or venture.

(c)   Order. The order authorizing the continuance of the business or venture may empower the guardian to make contracts necessary to conduct the business or venture and to incur debts and pay out money in the proper conduct of the business or venture. The net profits only of the business or venture are to be added to the assets of the ward's estate.

(d)   Accounts and Reports. In the conduct of the business or venture, the guardian shall keep full and accurate accounts of all receipts and expenditures and make reports as the court requires.

(e)   Discontinuance of Business. Any person interested in the ward's estate may at any time petition the court for an order requiring the guardian to discontinue and to wind up the business or venture, and the court, after notice to the guardian, shall enter such order thereon as is in the best interest of the ward's estate.

Florida Probate Rules

Committee Notes

Rule History

1975 Revision: Implements section 744.441(16), Florida Statutes. The rule is patterned after rule 5.350 pertaining to the continuation of a business of a decedent by a personal representative.

1977 Revision: No change in rule. Change in committee note to conform to statutory renumbering.

1988 Revision: Change in title of rule; captions added to subdivisions. Committee notes revised. Citation form changes in committee notes.

1989 Revision: Prior rule deleted and replaced by temporary emergency rule.

1991 Revision: Editorial changes in (a), (b), and (e).

1992 Revision: Citation form changes in committee notes.

2008 Revision: Subdivision (a) amended to include persons with a developmental disability. Committee notes revised.

Statutory References

§ 393.12, Fla. Stat. Capacity; appointment of guardian advocate.
§ 744.3085, Fla. Stat. Guardian advocates.
§ 744.441(13), Fla. Stat. Powers of guardian upon court approval.
§ 744.447, Fla. Stat. Petition for authorization to act.

Rule Reference

Fla. Prob. R. 5.350 Continuance of unincorporated business or venture.

RULE 5.645. MANAGEMENT OF PROPERTY OF NONRESIDENT WARD BY FOREIGN GUARDIAN

(a)   Petition. A guardian of the property of a nonresident ward, duly appointed by a court of another state, territory, or country, who desires to manage any part or all of the property of the ward located in this state, may file a verified petition for authority to manage the property. The petition shall state:

(1)   the circumstances of the guardian's appointment;

(2)   a description of the property and its estimated value; and

(3)   the indebtedness, if any, existing against the ward in this state.

(b)   Designation of Resident Agent. The guardian shall designate a resident agent as required by these rules.

(c)   Oath. The guardian shall file an oath as required by these rules.

(d) **Filing of Authenticated Copies.** The guardian shall file authenticated copies of:

      (1) letters of guardianship or other authority to act as guardian; and

      (2) bond or other security, if any.

(e) **Order.** The court shall determine if the foreign bond or other security is sufficient to guarantee the faithful management of the ward's property in this state. The court may require a new guardian's bond in this state in an amount it deems necessary. The order shall authorize the guardian to manage the property and shall specifically describe the property.

Committee Notes

Rule History

2007 Revision: New rule.

Statutory References

§ 744.306, Fla. Stat. Foreign guardians.
§ 744.307, Fla. Stat. Foreign guardian may manage the property of nonresident ward.

Rule References

Fla. Prob. R. 5.110 Address designation for personal representative or guardian; designation of resident agent and acceptance.
Fla. Prob. R. 5.600 Oath.

RULE 5.646. STANDBY GUARDIANS

(a) **Petition for Appointment of Standby Guardian for Minor.**

      (1) **Contents.** A minor's guardian or the natural guardians of a minor may petition for the appointment of a standby guardian of the person or property of the minor. The petition shall be verified by the petitioner and shall state:

          (A) the facts to establish venue;

          (B) the petitioner's residence and post office address;

          (C) the name, age, and residence and post office address of the minor;

          (D) the names and addresses of the parents of the minor and, if none, the next of kin known to the petitioner;

          (E) the name and residence and post office address of

the proposed standby guardian, and that the proposed standby guardian is qualified to serve;

(F)   the proposed standby guardian's relationship to and any previous association with the minor;

(G)   the reasons why the proposed standby guardian should be appointed; and

(H)   the nature and value of the property subject to the guardianship.

(2)   Notice and Waiver of Notice. Notice of the hearing on the petition must be served on the parents, natural or adoptive, of the minor and on any guardian for the minor. Notice may be waived by those required to receive notice or by the court for good cause.

(b)   Petition for Appointment of Standby Guardian for Incapacitated Person.

(1)   Contents. A currently serving guardian may petition for the appointment of a standby guardian of the person or property of an incapacitated person. The petition shall be verified by the petitioner and shall state:

(A)   the petitioner's residence and post office address;

(B)   the name, age, and residence and post office address of the incapacitated person;

(C)   the nature of the incapacity, the extent of guardianship, either limited or plenary, and the nature and value of property subject to the guardianship;

(D)   the names and addresses of the next of kin of the incapacitated person known to the petitioner;

(E)   the name and residence and post office address of the proposed standby guardian, and that the proposed standby guardian is qualified to serve;

(F)   the proposed standby guardian's relationship to and any previous association with the incapacitated person; and

(G)   the reasons why the proposed standby guardian should be appointed.

(2)   Notice. Notice of the hearing on the petition must be served on the incapacitated person's next of kin.

(c)   Petition for Confirmation.

(1)   Contents. A standby guardian, not later than 20 days after the assumption of duties as guardian, shall petition for confirmation of appointment. The petition shall be verified by the petitioner and shall state:

    (A)   the petitioner's residence and post office address;

    (B)   the name, age, and residence and post office address of the incapacitated person or minor;

    (C)   the nature of the incapacity, the extent of guardianship, either limited or plenary, and the nature and value of property subject to the guardianship;

    (D)   the names and addresses of the next of kin of the incapacitated person or minor known to the petitioner;

    (E)   the name and residence and post office address of the proposed guardian, and that the proposed guardian is qualified to serve;

    (F)   the proposed guardian's relationship to and any previous association with the incapacitated person or minor;

    (G)   the reasons why appointment of the proposed guardian should be confirmed; and

    (H)   if the proposed guardian is a professional guardian, a statement that the proposed guardian has complied with the educational requirements of section 744.1083, Florida Statutes.

    (2)   **Service.** The petition for confirmation and notice of hearing shall be served on the incapacitated person's next of kin a reasonable time before the hearing on the petition or other pleading seeking confirmation of the guardian.

Committee Notes

The standby guardian must file an oath pursuant to rule 5.600 before commencing the exercise of authority as guardian. Prior to appointment, the standby guardian must file an application pursuant to rule 5.590.

Section 393.12(10), Florida Statutes, provides that a guardian advocate shall have all of the duties, responsibilities, and powers of a guardian under Chapter 744, Florida Statutes. However, section 744.304 authorizes the appointment of a standby guardian only for a minor or incapacitated person.

Rule History

2006 Revision: New rule.

2008 Revision: Committee notes revised.

Statutory Reference

§ 744.304, Fla. Stat. Standby guardianship.

Rule References

Fla. Prob. R. 5.590 Application for appointment as guardian; disclosure statement; filing. Fla. Prob. R. 5.600 Oath.

RULE 5.647.   SURROGATE GUARDIAN

(a)   Petition for Designation of Surrogate Guardian. A guardian may file a petition to designate a surrogate guardian to exercise the powers of the guardian if the guardian is unavailable to act. The surrogate must be a professional guardian. The petition shall state:

(1)   the name and business address of the surrogate guardian;

(2)   the requested duration of the appointment; and

(3)   the powers to be exercised by the surrogate guardian.

(b)   Service. The petition for appointment of a surrogate guardian shall be served on all interested persons and the ward, unless the ward is a minor.

(c)   Oath. The surrogate guardian must file with the court an oath swearing or affirming that the surrogate guardian will faithfully perform the duties delegated.

(d)   Termination. Prior to the expiration of the period granted by court order, the guardian may terminate the authority of the surrogate guardian by filing a written notice of the termination with the court and serving it on the surrogate guardian.

Committee Notes

Rule History

2006 Revision: New rule.

2008 Revision: Committee notes revised.

Statutory References

§ 393.12, Fla. Stat. Capacity; appointment of guardian advocate.
§ 744.442, Fla. Stat. Delegation of authority.

RULE 5.648.   EMERGENCY TEMPORARY GUARDIAN

(a)   Petition for Appointment of Emergency Temporary Guardian. Prior to appointment of a guardian but after a petition for determination of incapacity has been filed, the alleged incapacitated person or any adult interested in the welfare of that person may petition for the appointment of an emergency temporary guardian of the person or property. The petition shall be verified and shall state:

(1)   the petitioner's residence and post office address;

(2)   the name, age, and residence and post office address of the

alleged incapacitated person;

        (3)   that there appears to be imminent danger that the physical or mental health or safety of the alleged incapacitated person will be seriously impaired or that the alleged incapacitated person's property is in danger of being wasted, misappropriated, or lost unless immediate action is taken;

        (4)   the nature of the emergency and the reason immediate action must be taken;

        (5)   the extent of the emergency temporary guardianship, either limited or plenary, requested for the alleged incapacitated person, and, if known, the nature and value of the property to be subject to the emergency temporary guardianship;

        (6)   the names and addresses of the next of kin of the alleged incapacitated person known to the petitioner;

        (7)   the name and residence and post office address of the proposed emergency temporary guardian, and that the proposed emergency temporary guardian is qualified to serve, or that a willing and qualified emergency temporary guardian has not been located, and;

        (8)   the proposed emergency temporary guardian's relationship to or any previous association with the alleged incapacitated person.

    (b)   **Notice.** Unless the court orders otherwise, notice of filing of the petition for appointment of an emergency temporary guardian and any hearing on the petition shall be served before the hearing on the petition on the alleged incapacitated person and on the alleged incapacitated person's attorney.

    (c)   **Service on Public Guardian.** If the petitioner requests appointment of the public guardian as emergency temporary guardian, a copy of the petition and notice shall be served on the public guardian.

    (d)   **Order.** The order appointing the emergency temporary guardian shall specify the powers and duties of the emergency temporary guardian.

    (e)   **Extension of Authority.** Prior to the expiration of the authority of the emergency temporary guardian, any interested person may file a verified petition for extension of authority of the emergency temporary guardian. The petition must show that the conditions that warranted the initial appointment of the emergency temporary guardian still exist. The petition shall be served on the ward's attorney and on the emergency guardian.

    (f)   **Final Report.** An emergency temporary guardian shall file a final report no later than 30 days after the expiration of the emergency temporary guardianship. A copy of the final report shall be served on the successor guardian, if any, the ward, and the ward's attorney. With approval of the court, service on the ward may be accomplished by serving the attorney for the ward.

        (1)   If the emergency temporary guardian is a guardian of the property, the final report shall consist of a verified inventory of the ward's property as of the date letters of emergency temporary guardianship were issued, a final accounting that gives

a full and correct account of the receipts and disbursements of all the ward's property over which the guardian had control, and a statement of the property on hand at the end of the emergency temporary guardianship.

(2) If the emergency temporary guardian is a guardian of the person, the final report shall summarize the activities of the guardian with regard to residential placement, medical condition, mental health and rehabilitative services, and the social condition of the ward to the extent of the authority granted to the emergency temporary guardian.

(3) If the emergency temporary guardian becomes the successor guardian of the property or person of the ward, the final report must satisfy the requirements of, and shall serve as, the initial report of the guardian of the property or person of the ward, as the case may be, as set forth in rule 5.690.

Committee Notes

Rule History

2007 Revision: New rule.

Statutory References

§ 744.3031, Fla. Stat. Emergency temporary guardianship.
§ 744.344(4), Fla. Stat. Order of appointment.

Rule References

Fla. Prob. R. 5.600 Oath.

Fla. Prob. R. 5.690 Initial guardianship report.

RULE 5.649. GUARDIAN ADVOCATE

(a) **Petition for Appointment of Guardian Advocate.** A petition to appoint a guardian advocate for a person with a developmental disability may be executed by an adult person who is a resident of this state. The petition must be verified by the petitioner and must state:

(1) the name, age, and present address of the petitioner and the petitioner's relationship to the person with a developmental disability;

(2) the name, age, county of residence, and present address of the person with a developmental disability;

(3) that the petitioner believes that the person needs a guardian advocate and the factual information on which such belief is based;

(4) the exact areas in which the person lacks the ability to make informed decisions about the person's care and treatment services or to meet the essential requirements for the person's physical health or safety;

(5)   the legal disabilities to which the person is subject;

(6)   the name of the proposed guardian advocate, the relationship of that person to the person with a developmental disability, the relationship of the proposed guardian advocate with the providers of health care services, residential services, or other services to the person with developmental disabilities, and the reason why this person should be appointed. If a willing and qualified guardian advocate cannot be located, the petition shall so state; and

(7)   whether the petitioner has knowledge, information, or belief that the person with a developmental disability has executed an advance directive under chapter 765, Florida Statutes, or a durable power of attorney under chapter 709, Florida Statutes.

(b)   Notice.

(1)   Notice of the filing of the petition must be given to the person with a developmental disability, both verbally and in writing, in the language of the person and in English. Notice must also be given to the person with a developmental disability's next of kin, any designated health care surrogate, an attorney-in-fact designated in a durable power of attorney, and such other persons as the court may direct. A copy of the petition to appoint a guardian advocate must be served with the notice.

(2)   The notice must state that a hearing will be held to inquire into the capacity of the person with a developmental disability to exercise the rights enumerated in the petition. The notice must also state the date of the hearing on the petition.

(3)   The notice must state that the person with a developmental disability has the right to be represented by counsel of the person's own choice and that if the person cannot afford an attorney, the court shall appoint one.

(c)   Counsel. Within 3 days after a petition has been filed, the court shall appoint an attorney to represent a person with a developmental disability who is the subject of a petition to appoint a guardian advocate. The person with a developmental disability may substitute his or her own attorney for the attorney appointed by the court.

(d)   Order. If the court finds the person with a developmental disability requires the appointment of a guardian advocate, the order appointing the guardian advocate shall contain findings of facts and conclusions of law, including:

(1)   the nature and scope of the person's inability to make decisions;

(2)   the exact areas in which the individual lacks ability to make informed decisions about care and treatment services or to meet the essential requirements for the individual's physical health and safety;

(3)   if the person has executed an advance directive or durable power of attorney, a determination as to whether the documents sufficiently address the needs of the person and a finding that the advance directive or durable power of attorney does not provide an alternative to the appointment of a guardian advocate that sufficiently addresses the needs of the person with a developmental disability;

(4)   if a durable power of attorney exists, the powers of the attorney- in-fact, if any, that are suspended and granted to the guardian advocate;

(5)   if an advance directive exists and the court determines that the appointment of a guardian advocate is necessary, the authority, if any, the guardian advocate shall exercise over the health care surrogate;

(6)   the specific legal disabilities to which the person with a developmental disability is subject;

(7)   the name of the person selected as guardian advocate; and

(8)   the powers, duties, and responsibilities of the guardian advocate, including bonding of the guardian advocate as provided by law.

Committee Notes

Rule History

2008 Revision: New rule.

Statutory References

§ 393.063(9), Fla. Stat. Definitions.
§ 393.12, Fla. Stat. Capacity; appointment of guardian advocate.
§ 709.08, Fla. Stat. Durable power of attorney.
§ 765.101, Fla. Stat. Definitions.
§ 765.104, Fla. Stat. Amendment or revocation.
§ 765.202, Fla. Stat. Designation of a health care surrogate.
§ 765.204, Fla. Stat. Capacity of principal; procedure.
§ 765.205(3), Fla. Stat. Responsibility of the surrogate.
§ 765.302, Fla. Stat. Procedure for making a living will; notice to physician.
§ 765.401, Fla. Stat. The proxy.

Rule References

Fla. Prob. R. 5.020 Pleadings; verification; motions.
Fla. Prob. R. 5.540 Hearings.
Fla. Prob. R. 5.681 Restoration of rights of person with developmental disability.

RULE 5.650.   **RESIGNATION OR DISQUALIFICATION OF GUARDIAN; APPOINTMENT OF SUCCESSOR**

(a)   **Resignation and Petition for Discharge.** A guardian seeking to resign shall file a resignation and petition for discharge.

(b)   **Contents.** The resignation and petition for discharge shall state:

(1)   that the guardian wishes to resign and be relieved of all duties as guardian:

(2)   the amount of compensation to be paid to the guardian and to the attorneys, accountants, or other agents employed by the guardian; and

(3)   the names and addresses of the successor guardian and the successor guardian's attorney, or that a successor guardian has not yet been appointed or duly qualified.

(c)   **Final Report.** A resigning guardian of the property shall file a final report showing receipts, disbursements, amounts reserved for unpaid and anticipated costs and fees, and other relevant financial information from the date of the previous annual accounting, and a list of assets to be turned over to the successor guardian.

(d)   **Notice.** A notice shall be served stating that:

(1)   any objection shall be in writing and shall state with particularity each item to which the objection is directed and the grounds on which the objection is based;

(2)   any objection to the resignation, petition for discharge, or final report shall be filed within 30 days from the date of service of the petition for discharge; and

(3)   within 90 days after filing of the objection, a notice of hearing thereon shall be served or the objection is abandoned.

(e)   **Service.** A copy of the resignation, petition for discharge, final report, and notice of resignation and petition for discharge shall be served on the ward, any surety on the guardian's bond, any successor guardian, and such other persons as the court may direct.

(f)   **Objections.** Objections shall be in the form and be filed within the time set forth in the notice of resignation and petition for discharge. A copy of the objections shall be served by the objector on the ward, all guardians, any surety on the guardian's bond, and any successor guardian.

(g)   **Disposition of Objections.** Any interested person may set a hearing on the objections. Notice of the hearing shall be served on the guardian, the successor guardian, if any, and any other interested persons. If a notice of hearing on the objections is not served within 90 days of filing of the objections, the objections will be deemed abandoned.

(h)   **Discharge.** The guardian's resignation shall not be accepted and the guardian shall not be discharged until all objections have been withdrawn, abandoned, or judicially resolved and a successor guardian has been appointed and duly qualified. After all objections have been withdrawn, abandoned, or judicially resolved, if the court is satisfied that the resigning guardian has faithfully discharged the duties of the guardianship and the interests of the ward are protected, and the resigning guardian of the property has delivered the assets of the ward, all guardianship records, and all money due to the ward from the guardian to the remaining or successor guardian, the court shall enter an order accepting resignation of guardian and granting discharge.

(i)   **Disqualification.** Any guardian who is improperly appointed, or who becomes disqualified to act after appointment, shall immediately file a resignation and petition for discharge and proceed in accordance with this rule.

(j) **Nonresident Guardians.** Nonresident guardians appointed before October 1, 1989, shall not be automatically disqualified to serve and shall not be required to resign and initiate their own removal.

(k) **Guardian Advocates.** This rule shall apply to guardian advocates, except that a final report shall be required of a guardian advocate only if the guardian advocate's authority included the management of the property of the person with a developmental disability.

Committee Notes

Rule History

1975 Revision: Substantially the same as sections 744.467 and 744.471, Florida Statutes, with editorial changes

1977 Revision: No change in rule. Change in committee note to conform to statutory renumbering.

1988 Revision: Editorial changes in (a). Text of rule 5.590 inserted in (b). Editorial change in (c). Captions added to subdivisions. Committee notes revised. Citation form changes in committee notes.

1989 Revision: Prior rule deleted and replaced by temporary emergency rule.

1991 Revision: Substantial revision of entire rule to harmonize with procedure for termination of guardianship under rules 5.670 and 5.680. Subdivision (k) transferred from temporary emergency rule 5.800.

1992 Revision: Committee notes revised. Citation form changes in committee notes.

2007 Revision: Subdivision (i) deleted because right of waiver is substantive. Subsequent subdivisions relettered.

2008 Revision: Subdivision (k) added to include guardian advocates. Committee notes revised.

2012 Revision: Committee notes revised.

Statutory References

§ 393.12, Fla. Stat. Capacity; appointment of guardian advocate.

§ 744.102(11), Fla. Stat. Definitions.

§ 744.3085, Fla. Stat. Guardian advocates.

§ 744.467, Fla. Stat. Resignation of guardian.

§ 744.471, Fla. Stat. Appointment of successor.

Rule References

Fla. Prob. R. 5.040 Notice.
Fla. Prob. R. 5.041 Service of pleadings and documents.
Fla. Prob. R. 5.180 Waiver and consent.
Fla. Prob. R. 5.610 Execution by guardian.
Fla. Prob. R. 5.649 Guardian advocate.
Fla. Prob. R. 5.681 Restoration of rights of person with developmental disability.
Fla. R. Jud. Admin. 2.516 Service of pleadings and documents.

RULE 5.660.   PROCEEDINGS FOR REMOVAL OF GUARDIAN

(a)   Notice. Proceedings for removal of a guardian may be instituted by a court, by any surety or other interested person, or by the ward, and formal notice of the petition for removal of a guardian shall be served on all guardians, other interested persons, next of kin, and the ward. The pleading shall state with particularity the reasons why the guardian should be removed.

(b)   Accounting. A removed guardian shall file with the court an accounting for the guardianship within 20 days after the guardian's removal. A copy of the accounting shall be served on the successor guardian and the ward, unless the ward is a minor.

(c)   Transfer of Property and Records. The removed guardian (or the guardian's heirs, personal representative, or surety) shall turn over all the property of the ward in the removed guardian's control and all guardianship records to the duly qualified successor. The successor guardian shall, or the ward may, demand of the removed guardian (or the guardian's heirs, personal representative, or surety) all of those items.

(d)   Failure to Comply. If a removed guardian fails to file a true, complete, and final accounting for the guardianship or to turn over to the successor all property of the ward in the removed guardian's control and all guardianship records, the court shall issue a show-cause order.

(e)   Guardian Advocates. Subdivisions (b) through (d) of this rule shall apply to guardian advocates only to the extent that the guardian advocate was granted authority over the property of the person with a developmental disability.

Committee Notes

Rule History

1977 Revision: No change in rule. Change in committee notes to conform to statutory renumbering.

1980 Revision: Subdivision (a) amended to specifically authorize any guardian or next of kin to file the petition and to require formal notice in conformity with rule 5.630(b).

1984 Revision: Subdivision (b) amended to conform to statute. Editorial changes and committee notes revised.

1988 Revision: Subdivision (a) rewritten for clarity. Language in (b) deleted as surplusage. Editorial change in caption of (c). Committee notes revised. Citation form change in committee notes.

1989 Revision: Prior rule deleted and replaced by temporary emergency rule.

1991 Revision: Subdivision (a) amended to require that the petition allege specific reasons why the guardian should be removed and to require service of the petition on the ward. Otherwise, editorial changes in all subdivisions.

1992 Revision: Citation form changes in committee notes.

2006 Revision: Requirement in (b) to serve minors deleted to conform to 2006 amendment to section 744.511, Florida Statutes.

2008 Revision: Subdivision (e) added to include guardian advocates. Committee notes revised.

2012 Revision: Committee notes revised.

Statutory References

§ 393.12, Fla. Stat. Capacity; appointment of guardian advocate.
§ 744.3085, Fla. Stat. Guardian advocates.
§ 744.474, Fla. Stat. Reasons for removal of guardian.
§ 744.477, Fla. Stat. Proceedings for removal of a guardian.
§ 744.511, Fla. Stat. Accounting upon removal.
§ 744.514, Fla. Stat. Surrender of property upon removal.
§ 744.517, Fla. Stat. Proceedings for contempt.

Rule References

Fla. Prob. R. 5.025 Adversary proceedings.
Fla. Prob. R. 5.040 Notice.
Fla. Prob. R. 5.041(b) Service of pleadings and documents.
Fla. Prob. R. 5.649 Guardian advocate.
Fla. R. Jud. Admin. 2.516 Service of pleadings and documents.

RULE 5.670. TERMINATION OF GUARDIANSHIP ON CHANGE OF DOMICILE OF RESIDENT WARD

(a) **Petition for Discharge.** The Florida guardian may file a petition for discharge when the domicile of a resident ward has changed to a foreign jurisdiction, the foreign court having jurisdiction over the ward at the ward's new domicile has appointed a foreign guardian, and the foreign guardian has qualified and posted a bond in the amount required by the foreign court.

(b) **Contents of Petition.** The petition for discharge shall state:

(1) that the grounds set forth in subdivision (a) have occurred;

(2) that the guardian has fully administered the Florida guardianship; and

(3)   the amount of compensation to be paid to the guardian and to the attorneys, accountants, or other agents employed by the guardian.

(c)   **Final Report.** The Florida guardian of the property shall file a final report showing receipts, disbursements, amounts reserved for unpaid and anticipated costs and fees, and other relevant financial information from the date of the previous annual accounting, and a list of the assets to be turned over to the foreign guardian.

(d)   **Notice.** The Florida guardian of the property shall publish a notice as required by law, which shall state:

(1)   the name of the ward;

(2)   the file number of the guardianship;

(3)   the designation and address of the court;

(4)   the name and address of the guardian and the guardian's attorney;

(5)   the name and address of the foreign guardian and the foreign guardian's attorney, if any;

(6)   the date of first publication;

(7)   that a petition for discharge has been filed upon the grounds of change of domicile of the ward;

(8)   the date the guardian will apply for discharge;

(9)   that the jurisdiction of the ward will be transferred to the foreign jurisdiction;

(10)   that any objection shall be in writing and shall state with particularity each item to which the objection is directed and the grounds on which the objection is based;

(11)   that any objection to the final report or the petition for discharge shall be filed within the later of 30 days from the date of service of the petition for discharge or the date of first publication of the notice; and

(12)   that within 90 days after filing of the objection, a notice of hearing thereon shall be served or the objection is abandoned.

(e)   **Service.** A copy of the petition for discharge and of the notice of petition for discharge shall be served on the foreign guardian and such other persons as the court may direct.

(f)   **Objections.** Objections shall be in the form and be filed within the time set forth in the notice of petition for discharge. A copy of the objections shall be served by the objector on the Florida guardian and the foreign guardian.

(g) **Disposition of Objections.** Any interested person may set a hearing on the objections. Notice of the hearing shall be served on the Florida guardian, the foreign guardian, and any other interested persons. If a notice of hearing on the objections is not served within 90 days of filing of the objections, the objections will be deemed abandoned.

(h) **Discharge.** The Florida guardian may not be discharged until all objections have been withdrawn, abandoned, or judicially resolved. After all objections have been withdrawn, abandoned, or judicially resolved, if the court is satisfied that the Florida guardian has faithfully discharged the duties of the guardianship and the interests of the ward are protected, and the Florida guardian of the property has delivered the assets of the ward to the foreign guardian, the court shall enter an order of discharge.

Committee Notes

Rule History

1977 Revision: Change in committee notes to conform to statutory renumbering.

1984 Revision: Adds 30-day requirement for filing objections. Editorial changes and committee notes revised.

1988 Revision: Editorial change in (c). First and last sentences of (d) deleted and clarifying word added.

1989 Revision: Prior rule adopted as temporary emergency rule.

1991 Revision: Substantial revision of entire rule to harmonize with procedure for discharge of guardian under rule 5.680 and to conform to section 744.524, Florida Statutes.

1992 Revision: Committee notes revised. Citation form changes in committee notes.

2007 Revision: Subdivision (i) deleted because right of waiver is substantive. Committee notes revised.

2008 Revision: Committee notes revised.

2012 Revision: Committee notes revised.

Statutory References

§ 393.12, Fla. Stat. Capacity; appointment of guardian advocate.
§ 744.102(8), (9), Fla. Stat. Definitions.
§ 744.201, Fla. Stat. Domicile of ward.
§ 744.202, Fla. Stat. Venue.
§ 744.2025, Fla. Stat. Change of ward's residence.
§ 744.524, Fla. Stat. Termination of guardianship on change of domicile of resident ward.
§ 744.531, Fla. Stat. Order of discharge.

Rule References

Fla. Prob. R. 5.041 Service of pleadings and documents.
Fla. Prob. R. 5.180 Waiver and consent.
Fla. Prob. R. 5.610 Execution by guardian.
Fla. Prob. R. 5.680 Termination of guardianship.
Fla. R. Jud. Admin. 2.516 Service of pleadings and documents.

RULE 5.680.   TERMINATION OF GUARDIANSHIP

(a)   **Petition for Discharge.** When the ward has become sui juris, has terminated a voluntary guardianship, has been restored to capacity, has had all rights restored, or has died, or when the guardian has been unable to locate the ward after diligent search, or, for a guardian of the property, when the property subject to the guardianship has been exhausted, the guardian shall file a petition for discharge. A guardian of the person is discharged without further proceeding upon filing a certified copy of the ward's death certificate.

(b)   **Contents of Petition.** The petition for discharge shall state:

(1)   the reason for termination of the guardianship;

(2)   that the guardian has fully administered the guardianship; and

(3)   the amount of unpaid and anticipated costs and fees to be paid to the guardian and to the attorneys, accountants, or other agents employed by the guardian.

(c)   **Final Report.** The guardian of the property shall promptly file a final report. If the ward has died, the guardian must file the report no later than 45 days after he or she has been served with letters of administration, letters of curatorship, or an order of summary administration. The report shall show receipts, disbursements, amounts reserved for unpaid and anticipated disbursements, costs, and fees, including the amounts set forth in subdivision (b)(3), and other relevant financial information from the date of the previous annual accounting, and a list of the assets to be turned over to the person entitled to them.

(d)   **Notice.** A notice shall be served stating:

(1)   that any objection shall be in writing and shall state with particularity each item to which the objection is directed and the grounds on which the objection is based;

(2)   that any objection to the final report or the petition for discharge shall be filed within 30 days from the date of service of the petition for discharge; and

(3)   that within 90 days after filing of the objection, a notice of hearing thereon shall be served or the objection is abandoned.

(e)   **Service.** The guardian applying for discharge shall serve a copy of the petition for discharge and final report on the ward, on the personal representative of a deceased ward, or if there are no assets justifying qualification of a personal representative for the estate of a deceased ward, on the known next of kin of the deceased ward, or such other persons as the court may direct; provided however, that a guardian of the property who is subsequently appointed personal representative shall serve a copy of the petition for discharge and final report on all beneficiaries of the ward's estate.

(f) **Objections.** All persons served shall have 30 days to file objections to the petition for discharge and final report. The objections shall state with particularity the items to which the objections are directed and shall state the grounds on which the objections are based. Copies of the objections shall be served by the objector on the guardian. Any interested person may set a hearing on the objections. Notice of the hearing shall be served on the guardian and any other interested persons. If a notice of hearing on the objections is not served within 90 days of filing of the objections, the objections will be deemed abandoned. The guardian may not be discharged until all objections have been withdrawn, abandoned, or judicially resolved, and the petition for discharge of the guardian is granted by the court.

(g) **Discharge.** The guardian may not be discharged until all objections are withdrawn, abandoned, or judicially resolved. After all objections are withdrawn, abandoned, or judicially resolved, and if it appears that the guardian has paid all amounts reserved to the persons entitled to them and has made full and complete distribution of the ward's assets to the persons entitled to them and has otherwise faithfully discharged the duties of the guardian, the court shall grant the petition for discharge and enter an order of discharge. If objections are filed and are not withdrawn, abandoned, or judicially resolved, the court shall conduct a hearing in the same manner as for a hearing on objections to annual guardianship plans. After hearing, if the court is satisfied that the guardian has faithfully discharged the duties of the guardianship and the interests of the ward are protected, and the guardian has rendered a complete and accurate final report and has delivered the assets of the ward to the person entitled to them, the court shall enter an order of discharge.

Committee Notes

Rule History

1975 Revision: Implements sections 744.527 and 744.531, Florida Statutes, and also requires the guardian applying for discharge to do so by filing a petition for discharge and provides the procedure pertaining thereto.

1977 Revision: No change in rule. Change in committee note to conform to statutory renumbering.

1988 Revision: Captions added to subdivisions. Committee notes revised. Citation form changes in committee notes.

1989 Revision: Prior rule deleted and replaced by temporary emergency rule.

1991 Revision: Substantial revision of entire rule to harmonize with procedure for discharge of personal representatives under rules 5.400 and 5.401.

1992 Revision: Committee notes revised. Citation form changes in committee notes.

1996 Revision: Editorial changes to clarify that all anticipated costs and fees should be shown on final report and thereafter paid prior to transfer of assets and discharge of guardian.

2003 Revision: Subdivision (a) amended to reflect addition of rule 5.552 dealing with voluntary guardianship of property. Committee notes revised.

2006 Revision: Subdivision (c) amended to conform to 2006 amendments to section 744.527, Florida Statutes. Subdivision (h) deleted as unnecessary because substantive right of waiver is provided by section 731.302, Florida Statutes.

2008 Revision: Reference to restoration of rights added in subdivision (a). Committee notes revised.

2012 Revision: Committee notes revised.

Statutory References

§ 393.12, Fla. Stat. Capacity; appointment of guardian advocate.
§ 744.521, Fla. Stat. Termination of guardianship.
§ 744.527, Fla. Stat. Final reports and application for discharge; hearing.
§ 744.528, Fla. Stat. Discharge of guardian named as personal representative.
§ 744.531, Fla. Stat. Order of discharge.
§ 744.534, Fla. Stat. Disposition of unclaimed funds held by guardian.

Rule References

Fla. Prob. R. 5.040 Notice.
Fla. Prob. R. 5.041 Service of pleadings and documents.
Fla. Prob. R. 5.180 Waiver and consent.
Fla. Prob. R. 5.552 Voluntary guardianship of property.
Fla. Prob. R. 5.610 Execution by guardian.
Fla. Prob. R. 5.681 Restoration of rights of person with developmental disability.
Fla. R. Jud. Admin. 2.516 Service of pleadings and documents.

RULE 5.681. RESTORATION OF RIGHTS OF PERSON WITH DEVELOPMENTAL DISABILITY

(a)   Contents of Petition. A petition for restoration of rights of a person with a developmental disability shall contain:

(1)   facts that support the suggestion that restoration is feasible and would not pose a detriment to the health or welfare of the ward; and

(2)   a statement that the person with a developmental disability is capable of exercising some or all of the rights that were granted to the guardian advocate.

(b)   Counsel. Within 3 days after filing the petition, counsel shall be appointed for the person for whom a guardian advocate has been appointed as provided by law.

(c)   Notice. Upon the appointment of counsel, the clerk shall immediately send notice of the filing of the petition, together with a copy of the petition, to the person for whom a guardian advocate was appointed, the person's guardian advocate, the person's attorney, and any other interested person as directed by the court. The notice must contain a statement that all objections to the petition must be filed within 20 days after service of the notice. Formal notice shall be served on the guardian advocate. Informal notice may be served on the other persons. The clerk shall file proof of service. Notice need not be served on the petitioner.

(d) **Objections.** Any objection shall be in writing and shall state with particularity each item to which the objection is directed and the grounds on which the objection is based. The objector shall serve a copy of the objection on the person with the developmental disability, the person's attorney, the person's guardian advocate, and any other interested persons as directed by the court.

(e) **Order.**

(1) **With Hearing.** The court shall enter an order denying the petition or restoring all or some of the rights that were granted to the guardian advocate. If only some rights are restored to the person with a developmental disability, the order must state which rights are restored and amend the letters of guardian advocacy accordingly.

(2) **Without Hearing.** If the petitioner has attached evidence supporting the petition and if no objection is filed, the court may restore all or some of the person's rights that were granted to a guardian advocate.

(f) **Amended Plan.** Within 60 days after the order restoring rights is entered, the guardian advocate shall file an amended plan. A copy of the amended plan and accounting shall be served on the person with a developmental disability and the person's attorney.

Committee Notes

Rule History

2008 Revision: New rule.

Statutory References

§ 393.063(9), Fla. Stat. Definitions.
§ 393.12, Fla. Stat. Capacity; appointment of guardian advocate.
§ 709.08, Fla. Stat. Durable power of attorney.
§ 765.101, Fla. Stat. Definitions.
§ 765.104, Fla. Stat. Amendment or revocation.
§ 765.202, Fla. Stat. Designation of a health care surrogate.
§ 765.204, Fla. Stat. Capacity of principal; procedure.
§ 765.205(3), Fla. Stat. Responsibility of the surrogate.
§ 765.302, Fla. Stat. Procedure for making a living will; notice to physician.
§ 765.401, Fla. Stat. The proxy.

Rule References

Fla. Prob. R. 5.020 Pleadings; verification; motions.
Fla. Prob. R. 5.540 Hearings.

Fla. Prob. R. 5.541 Recording of hearings.
Fla. Prob. R. 5.680 Termination of guardianship.

RULE 5.685. DETERMINATION REGARDING ALTERNATIVES TO GUARDIANSHIP

(a) Reporting by Guardian. The guardian shall promptly file a report attaching a copy of a final order or judgment that determines the validity of a ward's durable power of attorney, trust, or trust amendment.

(b) Petition. At any time after the appointment of a guardian, the guardian, the ward, the ward's attorney, if any, or any other interested person may file a verified petition stating that there is an alternative to guardianship that will sufficiently address the problems of the ward.

(c) Contents of Petition. The petition to determine alternatives to guardianship shall state:

(1) the petitioner's interest in the proceeding; and

(2) the facts constituting the basis for the relief sought and that the proposed alternative to guardianship will sufficiently address the problems of the ward and is in the ward's best interest.

(d) Service. The petition shall be served on the guardian, the ward, the ward's attorney, if any, those interested persons who have filed requests for notices and copies of pleadings, and such other persons as the court may direct.

(e) Order. The order shall specify whether there is an alternative to guardianship that will sufficiently address the problems of the ward, the continued need for a guardian, and the extent of the need for delegation of the ward's rights.

Committee Notes

Rule History

2006 Revision: New rule.

Statutory References

§ 744.331, Fla. Stat. Procedures to determine incapacity.
§ 744.462, Fla. Stat. Determination regarding alternatives to guardianship.

RULE 5.690. INITIAL GUARDIANSHIP REPORT

(a) Contents and Filing. An initial guardianship report shall be filed within 60 days after the issuance of letters of guardianship. The guardian of the property shall file the initial guardianship report consisting of the verified inventory. The guardian of the person shall file the initial guardianship report consisting of the guardianship plan.

(b) Service. Copies of the initial guardianship report shall be served on the ward, unless the ward is a minor under the age of 14 years or is totally incapacitated, and the attorney for the ward, if any. With approval of the court, service on the ward may be accomplished by serving the attorney for the ward.

Committee Notes

The committee recognizes the conflict between this rule and section 744.362, Florida Statutes, which requires the filing of the initial guardianship report (which includes the inventory) within 60 days after appointment. The committee believes this provision, which attempts to regulate when a paper must be filed with the court, is procedural and that a guardian may not receive letters of guardianship empowering the guardian to act contemporaneously with the appointment. Therefore, the issuance of letters is a more practical time from which to measure the beginning of the time period for the accomplishment of this act.

In the event the guardian of the property and the guardian of the person are not the same entity or person, they shall make a good faith effort to jointly file the initial guardianship report.

Rule History

1991 Revision: New rule.

1992 Revision: Addition of phrase in subdivision (b) to conform to 1992 amendment to section 744.362(1), Florida Statutes. Citation form changes in committee notes.

2012 Revision: Committee notes revised.

Statutory References

§ 744.362, Fla. Stat. Initial guardianship report.
§ 744.363, Fla. Stat. Initial guardianship plan.
§ 744.365, Fla. Stat. Verified inventory.
§ 744.3701, Fla. Stat. Inspection of report.
§ 744.384, Fla. Stat. Subsequently discovered or acquired property.

Rule References

Fla. Prob. R. 5.020 Pleadings; verification; motions.
Fla. Prob. R. 5.041 Service of pleadings and documents.
Fla. Prob. R. 5.060 Request for notices and copies of pleadings.
Fla. Prob. R. 5.180 Waiver and consent.
Fla. Prob. R. 5.610 Execution by guardian.
Fla. Prob. R. 5.620 Inventory.
Fla. Prob. R. 5.700 Objection to guardianship reports.
Fla. R. Jud. Admin. 2.516 Service of pleadings and documents.

RULE 5.695.   ANNUAL GUARDIANSHIP REPORT

(a)   **Contents and Filing.**

(1)   **Guardian of the Person.** Unless the court requires reporting

on a calendar year basis, the guardian of the person shall file an annual guardianship plan within 90 days after the last day of the anniversary month in which the letters of guardianship were issued. The plan shall be for the year ending on the last day of such anniversary month. If the court requires reporting on a calendar year basis, the guardianship plan shall be filed on or before April 1 of each year.

(2) **Guardian of the Property.** Unless the court requires or authorizes reporting on a fiscal year basis, the guardian of the property shall file an annual accounting on or before April 1 of each year. The annual accounting shall cover the preceding annual accounting period. If the court requires or authorizes reporting on a fiscal year basis, the annual accounting shall be filed on or before the first day of the fourth month after the end of the fiscal year.

(b) **Service.** Copies of the annual plan and accounting shall be served on the ward, unless the ward is a minor or is totally incapacitated, and the attorney for the ward, if any. With the approval of the court, service on the ward may be accomplished by serving the attorney for the ward. The guardian shall serve copies on such other persons as the court may direct.

Committee Notes

The annual guardianship report consists of the annual plan for the guardian of the person and the annual accounting for the guardian of the property.

For annual guardianship reports regarding minors, see rule 5.555.

With approval of the court, service on the ward may be accomplished by service on the attorney for the ward, if any. The committee was concerned that actual service on a ward of the accounting or guardianship plan may give uninterested persons access to financial or personal information to the detriment of the ward. The committee believes that under such circumstances, the guardian of the property could seek an order under section 744.371(5), Florida Statutes, even if the ward's circumstances were set out in detail in a pleading other than the annual guardianship report. Such court order may be sought in appropriate circumstances at the time of the initial hearing to determine incapacity.

Rule History

1975 Revision: Substantially the same as section 744.427(1), (2), and (4), Florida Statutes, and section 744.437, Florida Statutes, with editorial changes and providing for the waiving, by a ward who has become sui juris or by the personal representative of a deceased ward, of the filing of an annual accounting. The rule requires the guardian of the property of a ward to appear before the court at the time he files his annual accounting or at such time the court shall determine in order that the court may inquire as to any matter relating to the physical and financial well-being of the ward. This appears to be in conflict with section 744.437, Florida Statutes, which refers to "every guardian" but in the same sentence it refers to "at the time the guardian files his annual return" and only the guardian of the property is required to file an annual accounting.

1977 Revision: No change in rule. Change in committee note to conform to statutory renumbering.

1980 Revision: Subdivision (e) amended to avoid conflict with statutory changes in section 744.437, Florida Statutes (1979).

1988 Revision: Matter in (b) deleted; covered in sections 744.427(2) and 744.434, Florida Statutes. Subdivision (c) deleted; covered in section 744.427(4), Florida Statutes. Captions added to subdivisions. Committee notes revised. Citation form changes in committee notes.

1989 Revision: Prior rule deleted and replaced by temporary emergency rule.

1991 Revision: Substantial changes and rule renumbered.

1992 Revision: Addition of language in subdivisions (a)(1) and (a)(2) to implement 1992 amendments to sections 744.367(1) and (2), Florida Statutes. Committee notes revised. Citation form changes in committee notes.

2006 Revision: Requirement in (b) to serve minors age 14 and above deleted to conform to amendment to section 744.367(3), Florida Statutes. Committee notes revised.

2012 Revision: Committee notes revised.

Statutory References

§ 744.367, Fla. Stat. Duty to file annual guardianship report.
§ 744.3675, Fla. Stat. Annual guardianship plan.
§ 744.3678, Fla. Stat. Annual accounting.
§ 744.3685, Fla. Stat. Order requiring guardianship report; contempt.
§ 744.3701, Fla. Stat. Inspection of report.
§ 744.371, Fla. Stat. Relief to be granted.
§ 744.3735, Fla. Stat. Annual appearance of the guardian.

Rule References

Fla. Prob. R. 5.020 Pleadings; verification; motions.
Fla. Prob. R. 5.041 Service of pleadings and documents.
Fla. Prob. R. 5.060 Request for notices and copies of pleadings.
Fla. Prob. R. 5.180 Waiver and consent.
Fla. Prob. R. 5.552 Voluntary guardianship of property.
Fla. Prob. R. 5.555 Guardianships of minors.
Fla. Prob. R. 5.610 Execution by guardian.
Fla. Prob. R. 5.700 Objection to guardianship reports.
Fla. Prob. R. 5.800(b) Application of revised chapter 744 to existing guardianships.
Fla. R. Jud. Admin. 2.516 Service of pleadings and documents.

RULE 5.696.   ANNUAL ACCOUNTING

(a)   Contents and Filing. The guardian of the property shall file an annual accounting as required by law. The annual accounting shall include:

(1)   a full and correct account of the receipts and disbursements of all of the ward's property over which the guardian has control and a statement of the ward's property on hand at the end of the accounting period; and

(2)   a copy of the statements of all of the ward's cash accounts as of the end of the accounting period from each institution where the cash is deposited.

(b)   Substantiating Papers. Unless otherwise ordered by the court, the guardian need not file the papers substantiating the annual accounting. Upon reasonable written request, the guardian of the property shall make the substantiating papers available for examination to persons entitled to receive or inspect the annual accounting.

(c)   Interim Inspection of Records. Upon reasonable written request and notice, the guardian of the property shall make all material financial records pertaining to the guardianship available for inspections to those persons entitled to receive or inspect the annual accounting.

Committee Notes

Rule History

1991 Revision: New rule.

1992 Revision: Citation form changes in committee notes.

2010 Revision: Editorial change in (b) to delete redundant language.

2012 Revision: Committee notes revised.

Statutory References

§ 744.367, Fla. Stat. Duty to file annual guardianship report.
§ 744.3678, Fla. Stat. Annual accounting.
§ 744.3701, Fla. Stat. Inspection of report.
§ 744.3735, Fla. Stat. Annual appearance of the guardian.

Rule References

Fla. Prob. R. 5.020 Pleadings; verification; motions.
Fla. Prob. R. 5.041 Service of pleadings and documents.
Fla. Prob. R. 5.060 Request for notices and copies of pleadings.
Fla. Prob. R. 5.610 Execution by guardian.
Fla. Prob. R. 5.695 Annual guardianship report.
Fla. Prob. R. 5.700 Objection to guardianship reports.
Fla. R. Jud. Admin. 2.516 Service of pleadings and documents.

RULE 5.697.   MAGISTRATES' REVIEW OF GUARDIANSHIP INVENTORIES, ACCOUNTINGS, AND PLANS

(a)   General Magistrates. The court may appoint general magistrates to review guardianship inventories, accountings, and plans. General magistrates shall be members of The Florida Bar and shall continue in office until removed by the court. The order appointing a general magistrate shall be recorded. Each general magistrate shall take the oath required of officers of the court by the Florida Constitution. The oath shall be recorded before the magistrate begins to act.

(b) **Special Magistrates.** In connection with the court's review of guardianship inventories, accountings, and plans, the court may appoint members of The Florida Bar as special magistrates for any particular service required by the court. Special magistrates shall be governed by all laws and rules relating to general magistrates except special magistrates shall not be required to take an oath unless specifically required by the court. For good cause shown, the court may appoint a person other than a member of The Florida Bar as a special magistrate.

(c) **General Powers and Duties.** Every magistrate shall act under the direction of the court. Process issued by a magistrate shall be directed as provided by law. All grounds for disqualification of a judge shall apply to magistrates.

(d) **Hearings.** Hearings before any magistrate may be held in the county where the action is pending, or at any other place by order of the court for the convenience of the witnesses or the parties. A magistrate shall give notice of hearings to all parties. If any party fails to appear, the magistrate may proceed ex parte or may continue the hearing to a future day, with notice to the absent party. The magistrate shall proceed with reasonable diligence and the least practicable delay. Any party may apply to the court for an order directing the magistrate to accelerate the proceedings and to make a report promptly. Evidence shall be taken in writing or by electronic recording by the magistrate or by some other person under the magistrate's authority in the magistrate's presence and shall be filed with the magistrate's report. The magistrate may examine and take testimony from the parties and their witnesses under oath, on all matters authorized by the court for review by the magistrate and may require production of all books, papers, writings, vouchers, and other documents applicable to those matters. The magistrate shall admit only evidence that would be admissible in court. The magistrate may take all actions concerning evidence that may be taken by the court.

(e) **Magistrate's Report.** The magistrate's report shall contain a description of the matters considered and the magistrate's conclusions and any recommendations. No part of any statement of facts, account, charge, deposition, examination, or answer used before the magistrate shall be recited. The magistrate shall be required to file a report only if a hearing is held pursuant to subdivision (d) of this rule or if specifically directed to do so by the court.

(f) **Filing Report; Service; Exceptions.** The magistrate shall file a report with the court and serve copies on the parties. The parties may serve exceptions to the report within 10 days from the date the report is served on them. If no exceptions are timely filed, the court shall take appropriate action on the report. All timely filed exceptions shall be heard by the court on reasonable notice by any party.

Committee Notes

Rule History

1991 Revision: This is a new rule, patterned after Florida Rule of Civil Procedure 1.490.

1992 Revision: Editorial change. Citation form change in committee notes.

2004 Revision: Change in nomenclature from "master" to "magistrate" to track similar change in the Florida Statutes.

2007 Revision: Title of rule and subdivisions (a) and (b) amended to include inventories. "Shall" substituted for "may" in last sentence of subdivision (f). Committee notes revised.

Statutory Reference

§ 744.369(2), Fla. Stat. Judicial review of guardianship reports.

Rule References

Fla. Prob. R. 5.095 General and special magistrates.
Fla. R. Civ. P. 1.490 Magistrates.

RULE 5.700.   OBJECTION TO GUARDIANSHIP REPORTS

(a)   **Objections.** The ward, or any other interested person, may file an objection to any part of a guardianship report within the time provided by law.

(b)   **Contents.** Any objection shall be in writing and shall state with particularity each item to which the objection is directed and the grounds on which the objection is based.

(c)   **Service.** The objector shall serve a copy of the objection on each guardian and on any other person as directed by the court.

Committee Notes

Rule History

1975 Revision: Substantially the same as section 744.427(3), (5), and (6), Florida Statutes, with editorial changes.

1977 Revision: No change in rule. Change in committee note to conform to statutory renumbering.

1988 Revision: Captions added to subdivisions. Committee notes revised. Citation form change in committee notes.

1989 Revision: Prior rule deleted and replaced by temporary emergency rule.

1991 Revision: Revised to conform with new statutory requirements.

1992 Revision: Citation form changes in committee notes.

2008 Revision: Committee notes revised.

2012 Revision: Committee notes revised.

Statutory References

§ 393.12, Fla. Stat. Capacity; appointment of guardian advocate.

§ 744.362, Fla. Stat. Initial guardianship report.
§ 744.363, Fla. Stat. Initial guardianship plan.
§ 744.365, Fla. Stat. Verified inventory.
§ 744.367, Fla. Stat. Duty to file annual guardianship report.
§ 744.3675, Fla. Stat. Annual guardianship plan.
§ 744.3678, Fla. Stat. Annual accounting.

Rule References

Fla. Prob. R. 5.020 Pleadings; verification; motions.
Fla. Prob. R. 5.041 Service of pleadings and documents.
Fla. Prob. R. 5.060 Request for notices and copies of pleadings.
Fla. Prob. R. 5.180 Waiver and consent.
Fla. Prob. R. 5.610 Execution by guardian.
Fla. R. Jud. Admin. 2.516 Service of pleadings and documents.

RULE 5.705.   **PETITION FOR INTERIM JUDICIAL REVIEW**

(a)   **Contents.** A petition for interim judicial review shall be verified, state the petitioner's interest in the proceeding, state with particularity the manner in which the guardian's action or proposed action does not comply with or exceeds the guardian's authority under the guardian plan, and state why the action or proposed action of the guardian is not in the best interest of the ward.

(b)   **Service.** The petition shall be served by formal notice.

(c)   **Hearing.** The petitioner or any interested person may set the matter for hearing.

(d)   **Expedited Proceedings.** For good cause shown, the court may shorten the time for response to the formal notice and may set an expedited hearing.

Committee Notes

Rule History

1991 Revision: New rule.

2000 Revision: Subdivision (d) added to permit expedited proceedings.

2008 Revision: Committee notes revised.
Statutory References

§ 393.12, Fla. Stat. Capacity; appointment of guardian advocate.
§ 744.3715, Fla. Stat. Petition for interim judicial review.

RULE 5.710.   **REPORTS OF PUBLIC GUARDIAN**

The public guardian, as the guardian of a ward, shall file:

(a)   an initial report as required by law;

(b)   annual guardianship reports, which shall include the dates of quarterly visits to the ward, as required by law;

(c)   a report within 6 months of his or her appointment as guardian of a ward, which shall also be filed with the executive director of the Statewide Public Guardianship Office, stating:

(1)   the public guardian's efforts to locate a family member or friend, other person, bank, or corporation to act as guardian of the ward; and

(2)   the ward's potential to be restored to capacity;

(d)   an annual report, filed with the Statewide Public Guardianship Office, by September 1 for the preceding fiscal year, on the operations of the office of public guardian; and

(e)   a report of an independent audit by a qualified certified public accountant, to be filed with the Statewide Public Guardianship Office every 2 years.

Committee Notes

Rule History

1987 Revision: This is a new rule and was promulgated to establish procedures to accommodate the Public Guardian Act. See § 744.701, et seq., Fla. Stat. See also Fla. Prob. R. 5.560.

1989 Revision: Prior rule adopted as temporary emergency rule.

1991 Revision: Editorial changes.

1992 Revision: Citation form changes in committee notes.

 2007 Revision: Rule extensively amended to specify reports a public guardian is required to file.

2010 Revision: Editorial change in (e).

Statutory Reference

§§ 744.701-744.709, Fla. Stat. Public Guardianship Act.

Rule Reference

Fla. Prob. R. 5.560 Petition for appointment of guardian of an incapacitated person.

RULE 5.720.   COURT MONITOR

(a)   Appointment. Upon motion or inquiry by any interested person or upon its own motion, the court may appoint a court monitor in any proceeding over which it has jurisdiction.

(b) **Order of Appointment.** The order of appointment shall state the name, address, and phone number of the monitor and shall set forth the matters to be investigated. The order may authorize the monitor to investigate, seek information, examine documents, or interview the ward. The order of appointment shall be served upon the guardian, the ward, and such other persons as the court may determine.

(c) **Report.** The monitor shall file a verified written report with the court setting forth the monitor's findings. The report shall be served on the guardian, the ward, and such other persons as the court may determine.

(d) **Protection of Ward.** If it appears from the monitor's report that further action by the court to protect the interests of the ward is necessary, the court shall, after a hearing with notice, enter any order necessary to protect the ward or the ward's property, including amending the plan, requiring an accounting, ordering production of assets, or initiating proceedings to remove a guardian. Notice of the hearing shall be served on the guardian, the ward, and such other persons as the court may determine.

Committee Notes

This rule applies to the non-emergency appointment of court monitors.

Rule History

2006 Revision: New rule.

2008 Revision: Editorial change in (d). Committee notes revised.

Statutory References

§ 393.12, Fla. Stat. Capacity; appointment of guardian advocate.
§ 744.107, Fla. Stat. Court monitors.
§ 744.3701, Fla. Stat. Inspection of report.

RULE 5.725. **EMERGENCY COURT MONITOR**

(a) **Appointment.** Upon motion or inquiry by any interested person or upon its own motion, the court may appoint a court monitor on an emergency basis without notice in any proceeding over which it has jurisdiction.

(b) **Order of Appointment.** The order of appointment shall specifically find that there appears to be imminent danger that the physical or mental health or safety of the ward will be seriously impaired or that the ward's property is in danger of being wasted, misappropriated, or lost unless immediate action is taken. The scope of the matters to be investigated and the powers and duties of the monitor must be specifically enumerated in the order.

(c) **Duration of Authority.** The authority of a monitor expires 60 days after the date of appointment or upon a finding of no probable cause, whichever occurs first. The court may enter an order extending the authority of the monitor for an additional 30 days upon a showing that an emergency condition still exists.

(d) **Report.** Within 15 days after the entry of an order of appointment, the monitor shall file a verified written report setting forth the monitor's findings and recommendations. The report may be supported by documents or other evidence. The time for filing the report may be extended by the court for good cause.

(e) **Review.** Upon review of the report, the court shall enter an order determining whether there is probable cause to take further action to protect the person or property of the ward.

(1) If the court finds no probable cause, the court shall enter an order finding no probable cause and discharging the monitor.

(2) If the court finds probable cause, the court shall enter an order directed to the respondent stating the essential facts constituting the conduct charged and requiring the respondent to appear before the court to show cause why the court should not take further action. The order shall specify the time and place of the hearing with a reasonable time to allow for the preparation of a defense after service of the order. A copy of the order to show cause together with the order of appointment and report of the monitor shall be served upon the guardian, the ward, the ward's attorney, if any, and the respondent.

(f) **Protecting Ward.** If at any time prior to the hearing on the order to show cause the court enters a temporary injunction, a restraining order, an order freezing assets, an order suspending the guardian or appointing a guardian ad litem, or any other order to protect the physical or mental health, safety, or property of the ward, the order or injunction shall be served on the guardian, the ward, the ward's attorney, if any, and such other persons as the court may determine.

Committee Notes

Rule History

2006 Revision: New rule.

2008 Revision: Committee notes revised.

2010 Revision: Editorial change in (c).

Statutory References

§ 393.12, Fla. Stat. Capacity; appointment of guardian advocate.
§ 744.1075, Fla. Stat. Emergency court monitor.

RULE 5.800. **APPLICATION OF REVISED CHAPTER 744 TO EXISTING GUARDIANSHIPS**

(a) **Prior Adjudication of Incompetency.** When an adjudication of incompetency has taken place under chapter 744, Florida Statutes, before October 1, 1989, no readjudication of incapacity shall be required.

(b) **Annual Guardianship Reports.** Guardians appointed before October 1, 1989, shall file annual guardianship reports as required by law.

Committee Notes

Rule History

1989 Revision by Ad Hoc Committee: The committee adopted a position that guardians appointed before the effective date of the 1989 revisions to chapter 744, Florida Statutes, should comply with all sections of the law that apply to future acts of the guardian. For example, all guardians will in the future file annual reports and will be responsible for the continuing well-being of their wards. The committee recognized a distinction between those actions that will necessarily occur on a continuing basis throughout the guardianship and those actions that happen at a particular moment in time but are not necessarily ongoing duties. There are two and only two specific examples to which the statutory reforms would not apply retrospectively if the above distinction is adopted. First, the initial adjudication of incapacity occurs only once in any guardianship. Although guardianships are reevaluated annually, the statute does not contemplate a complete readjudication procedure every year. Therefore, the committee concluded that the initial adjudicatory hearing need not be repeated for wards adjudicated incompetent before October 1, 1989. Second, as concerns nonresident guardians appointed before October 1, 1989, normally, a guardian is appointed only once at the beginning of the guardianship. While these nonresident guardians would be expected to obey all provisions of the law prospectively, they would not be required to initiate their own removal.

1991 Revision: Editorial changes in first sentence of (a), and rest of subdivision deleted as unnecessary. Subdivision (b) has been transferred to rule 5.650. Date reference no longer required in (c), and modified to make filing requirement of preexisting guardianships consistent with the current statutory provisions.

1992 Revision: Citation form changes in committee notes.

Statutory References

§ 744.367, Fla. Stat. Duty to file annual guardianship report.
§ 744.3675, Fla. Stat. Annual guardianship plan.
§ 744.3678, Fla. Stat. Annual accounting.

Rule References

Fla. Prob. R. 5.695 Annual guardianship report.
Fla. Prob. R. 5.696 Annual accounting.

PART IV — EXPEDITED JUDICIAL INTERVENTION CONCERNING MEDICAL TREATMENT PROCEDURES

RULE 5.900.   EXPEDITED JUDICIAL INTERVENTION CONCERNING MEDICAL TREATMENT PROCEDURES

(a)   **Petition.** Any proceeding for expedited judicial intervention concerning medical treatment procedures may be brought by any interested adult person and shall be commenced by the filing of a verified petition which states:

(1)   the name and address of the petitioner;

(2)   the name and location of the person who is the subject of the

petition (hereinafter referred to as the "patient");

      (3)   the relationship of the petitioner to the patient;

      (4)   the names, relationship to the patient, and addresses if known to the petitioner, of:

      (A)   the patient's spouse and adult children;

      (B)   the patient's parents (if the patient is a minor);

      (C)   if none of the above, the patient's next of kin;

      (D)   any guardian and any court-appointed health care decision-maker;

      (E)   any person designated by the patient in a living will or other document to exercise the patient's health care decision in the event of the patient's incapacity;

      (F)   the administrator of the hospital, nursing home, or other facility where the patient is located;

      (G)   the patient's principal treating physician and other physicians known to have provided any medical opinion or advice about any condition of the patient relevant to this petition; and

      (H)   all other persons the petitioner believes may have information concerning the expressed wishes of the patient; and

      (5)   facts sufficient to establish the need for the relief requested, including, but not limited to, facts to support the allegation that the patient lacks the capacity to make the requisite medical treatment decision.

      (b)   **Supporting Documentation.** Any affidavits and supporting documentation, including any living will or designation of health care decision- maker, shall be attached to the petition.

      (c)   **Notice.** Unless waived by the court, notice of the petition and the preliminary hearing shall be served on the following persons who have not joined in the petition or otherwise consented to the proceedings:

      (1)   the patient;

      (2)   the patient's spouse and the patient's parents, if the patient is a minor;

      (3)   the patient's adult children;

      (4)   any guardian and any court-appointed health care decision-maker;

(5)   any person designated by the patient in a living will or other document to exercise the patient's health care decision in the event of the patient's incapacity;

(6)   the administrator of the hospital, nursing home, or other facility where the patient is located;

(7)   the patient's principal treating physician and other physicians believed to have provided any medical opinion or advice about any condition of the patient relevant to this petition;

(8)   all other persons the petitioner believes may have information concerning the expressed wishes of the patient; and

(9)   such other persons as the court may direct.

(d)   Hearing. A preliminary hearing on the petition shall be held within 72 hours after the filing of the petition. At that time the court shall review the petition and supporting documentation. In its discretion the court shall either:

(1)   rule on the relief requested immediately after the preliminary hearing; or

(2)   conduct an evidentiary hearing not later than 4 days after the preliminary hearing and rule on the relief requested immediately after the evidentiary hearing.

Committee Notes

This rule was submitted by the committee in response to the request contained in footnote 17 of *In re Guardianship of Browning*, 568 So.2d 4 (Fla. 1990). See also *Cruzan by Cruzan v. Director*, Missouri Department of Health, 497 U.S. 261, 110 S.Ct. 2841, 111 L. Ed.2d 224 (1990).

The promulgation of this rule is not intended to imply that judicial intervention is required to terminate life- prolonging procedures.

Practitioners should note that the criteria and standards of proof contained in Browning differ from the criteria and standards of proof presently existing in chapter 765, Florida Statutes.

Rule History

1991 Revision: New rule.

1992 Revision: This rule was created on an emergency basis and on further review, the committee decided it needed to clarify that the petition should include an allegation that the patient lacks capacity to make the requisite medical treatment decision, and that the patient should receive notice of the petition and hearing. Committee notes revised. Citation form changes in committee notes.

2008 Revision: Committee notes revised.

Constitutional Reference

Art. I, § 23, Fla. Const.

Statutory References

§ 393.12, Fla. Stat. Capacity; appointment of guardian advocate.
§ 709.08, Fla. Stat. Durable power of attorney.
§ 731.302, Fla. Stat. Waiver and consent by interested person.
§ 744.102, Fla. Stat. Definitions.
§ 744.104, Fla. Stat. Verification of documents.
§ 744.3115, Fla. Stat. Advance directives for health care.
ch. 765, Fla. Stat. Health care advance directives.

Rule References

Fla. Prob. R. 5.020 Pleadings; verification; motions.
Fla. Prob. R. 5.040 Notice.

End of Florida Probate Rules

Florida Probate Code

Florida Probate Code

TITLE XLII
ESTATES AND TRUSTS

CHAPTER 731
PROBATE CODE: GENERAL PROVISIONS

PART I
SHORT TITLE; CONSTRUCTION

731.005 Short title.—Chapters 731-735 shall be known and may be cited as the Florida Probate Code and referred to as the "code."

History.—s. 1, ch. 74-106; s. 1, ch. 75-220; s. 4, ch. 2001-226.

731.011 Determination of substantive rights; procedures.—The code became effective on January 1, 1976. The substantive rights of all persons that vested prior to January 1, 1976, shall be determined as provided in former chapters 731-737 and 744-746. The procedures for the enforcement of vested substantive rights shall be as provided in the Florida Probate Rules.

History.—s. 4, ch. 74-106; ss. 2, 113, ch. 75-220; s. 5, ch. 2001-226.

731.102 Construction against implied repeal.—This code is intended as unified coverage of its subject matter. No part of it shall be impliedly repealed by subsequent legislation if that construction can reasonably be avoided.

History.—s. 1, ch. 74-106; s. 2, ch. 75-220.

731.103 Evidence as to death or status.—In proceedings under this code and under chapter 736, the following additional rules relating to determination of death and status are applicable:

(1)   An authenticated copy of a death certificate issued by an official or agency of the place where the death purportedly occurred is prima facie proof of the fact, place, date, and time of death and the identity of the decedent.

(2)   A copy of any record or report of a governmental agency, domestic or foreign, that a person is alive, missing, detained, or, from the facts related, presumed dead is prima facie evidence of the status and of the dates, circumstances, and places disclosed by the record or report.

(3)   A person who is absent from the place of his or her last known domicile for a continuous period of 5 years and whose absence is not satisfactorily explained after diligent search and inquiry is presumed to be dead. The person's death is presumed to have occurred at the end of the period unless there is evidence establishing that death occurred earlier. Evidence showing that the absent person was exposed to a specific peril of death may be a sufficient basis for the court determining at any time after such exposure that he or she died less than 5 years after the date on which his or her absence commenced. A petition for this determination shall be filed in the county in Florida where the decedent maintained his or her domicile or in any county of this state if the decedent was not a resident of Florida at the time his or her absence commenced.

(4)   This section does not preclude the establishment of death by direct or circumstantial evidence prior to expiration of the 5-year time period set forth in subsection (3).

History.—s. 1, ch. 74-106; s. 2, ch. 75-220; s. 946, ch. 97-102; s. 1, ch. 2003-154; s. 27, ch. 2006-217.

Note.—Created from former s. 734.34.

731.1035 Applicable rules of evidence.—In proceedings under this code, the rules of evidence in civil actions are applicable unless specifically changed by the code.

History.—s. 28, ch. 2006-217.

731.104 Verification of documents.—When verification of a document is required in this code or by rule, the document filed shall include an oath or affirmation as provided in the Florida Probate Rules. Any person who willfully includes a false statement in the document shall be guilty of perjury.

History.—s. 1, ch. 74-106; s. 2, ch. 75-220; s. 6, ch. 2001-226.

731.105 In rem proceeding.—Probate proceedings are in rem proceedings.

History.—s. 3, ch. 75-220.

731.106 Assets of nondomiciliaries.—

(1)   A debt in favor of a nondomiciliary, other than one evidenced by investment or commercial paper or other instrument, is located in the county where the debtor resides or, if the debtor is not an individual, at the place where the debtor has its principal office. Commercial paper, investment paper, and other instruments are located where the instrument is at the time of death.

(2)   When a nonresident decedent, whether or not a citizen of the United States, provides by will that the testamentary disposition of tangible or intangible personal property having a situs within this state, or of real property in this state, shall be construed and regulated by the laws of this state, the validity and effect of the dispositions shall be determined by Florida law. The court may, and in the case of a decedent who was at the time of death a resident of a foreign country the court shall, direct the personal representative appointed in this state to make distribution directly to those designated by the decedent's will as beneficiaries of the tangible or intangible property or to the persons entitled to receive the decedent's personal estate under the laws of the decedent's domicile.

History.—s. 3, ch. 75-220; s. 1, ch. 77-174; s. 947, ch. 97-102; s. 7, ch. 2001-226.

731.109 Seal of the court.—For the purposes of this code, the seal of the clerk of the circuit court is the seal of the court.

History.—s. 3, ch. 75-220.

731.110 Caveat; proceedings.—

(1)   Any interested person who is apprehensive that an estate, either testate or intestate, will be administered or that a will may be admitted to probate without that person's knowledge may file a caveat with the court. The caveat of the interested person, other than a creditor, may be filed before or after the death of the person for whom the estate will be, or is being, administered. The caveat of a creditor may be filed only after the person's death.

(2)   If the caveator is a nonresident and is not represented by an attorney admitted to practice in this state who has signed the caveat, the caveator must designate some person residing in the county in which the caveat is filed as the agent of the caveator, upon whom service may be made; however, if the caveator is represented by an attorney admitted to practice in this state who has signed the caveat, it is not necessary to designate a resident agent.

(3)   If a caveat has been filed by an interested person other than a creditor, the court may not admit a will of the decedent to probate or appoint a personal representative until formal notice of the petition for administration has been served on the caveator or the caveator's designated agent and the caveator has had the opportunity to participate in proceedings on the petition, as provided by the Florida Probate Rules. This subsection does not require a caveator to be served with formal notice of its own petition for administration.

(4)   A caveat filed before the death of the person for whom the estate will be administered expires 2 years after filing.

History.—s. 3, ch. 75-220; s. 2, ch. 77-87; s. 1, ch. 85-79; s. 2, ch. 92-200; s. 948, ch. 97-102; s. 9, ch. 2001-226; s. 2, ch. 2007-74; s. 3, ch. 2010-132; s. 5, ch. 2013-172.

731.155 Applicability.—This act shall take effect January 1, 2002. The substantive rights of all persons that have vested prior to January 1, 2002, shall be determined as provided in former chapters 63, 215, 409, 660, and 731-737 as they existed prior to January 1, 2002. The procedures for the enforcement of substantive rights which have vested prior to January 1, 2002, shall be as provided in this act, except that any Family Administration filed before January 1, 2002, may be completed as a Family Administration.

History.—s. 195, ch. 2001-226.

PART II
DEFINITIONS

731.201 General definitions.—Subject to additional definitions in subsequent chapters that are applicable to specific chapters or parts, and unless the context otherwise requires, in this code, in s. 409.9101, and in chapters 736, 738, 739, and 744, the term:

(1)   "Authenticated," when referring to copies of documents or judicial proceedings required to be filed with the court under this code, means a certified copy or a copy authenticated according to the Federal Rules of Civil Procedure.

(2)   "Beneficiary" means heir at law in an intestate estate and devisee in a testate estate. The term "beneficiary" does not apply to an heir at law or a devisee after that

person's interest in the estate has been satisfied. In the case of a devise to an existing trust or trustee, or to a trust or trustee described by will, the trustee is a beneficiary of the estate. Except as otherwise provided in this subsection, the beneficiary of the trust is not a beneficiary of the estate of which that trust or the trustee of that trust is a beneficiary. However, if each trustee is also a personal representative of the estate, each qualified beneficiary of the trust as defined in s. 736.0103 shall be regarded as a beneficiary of the estate.

(3)   "Child" includes a person entitled to take as a child under this code by intestate succession from the parent whose relationship is involved, and excludes any person who is only a stepchild, a foster child, a grandchild, or a more remote descendant.

(4)   "Claim" means a liability of the decedent, whether arising in contract, tort, or otherwise, and funeral expense. The term does not include an expense of administration or estate, inheritance, succession, or other death taxes.

(5)   "Clerk" means the clerk or deputy clerk of the court.

(6)   "Collateral heir" means an heir who is related to the decedent through a common ancestor but who is not an ancestor or descendant of the decedent.

(7)   "Court" means the circuit court.

(8)   "Curator" means a person appointed by the court to take charge of the estate of a decedent until letters are issued.

(9)   "Descendant" means a person in any generational level down the applicable individual's descending line and includes children, grandchildren, and more remote descendants. The term "descendant" is synonymous with the terms "lineal descendant" and "issue" but excludes collateral heirs.

(10)   "Devise," when used as a noun, means a testamentary disposition of real or personal property and, when used as a verb, means to dispose of real or personal property by will or trust. The term includes "gift," "give," "bequeath," "bequest," and "legacy." A devise is subject to charges for debts, expenses, and taxes as provided in this code, the will, or the trust.

(11)   "Devisee" means a person designated in a will or trust to receive a devise. Except as otherwise provided in this subsection, in the case of a devise to an existing trust or trustee, or to a trust or trustee of a trust described by will, the trust or trustee, rather than the beneficiaries of the trust, is the devisee. However, if each trustee is also a personal representative of the estate, each qualified beneficiary of the trust as defined in s. 736.0103 shall be regarded as a devisee.

(12)   "Distributee" means a person who has received estate property from a personal representative or other fiduciary other than as a creditor or purchaser. A testamentary trustee is a distributee only to the extent of distributed assets or increments to them remaining in the trustee's hands. A beneficiary of a testamentary trust to whom the trustee has distributed property received from a personal representative is a distributee. For purposes of this provision, "testamentary trustee" includes a trustee to whom assets are transferred by will, to the extent of the devised assets.

(13)   "Domicile" means a person's usual place of dwelling and shall be synonymous with residence.

(14)   "Estate" means the property of a decedent that is the subject of administration.

(15)   "Exempt property" means the property of a decedent's estate which is described in s. 732.402.

(16)   "File" means to file with the court or clerk.

(17)   "Foreign personal representative" means a personal representative of another state or a foreign country.

(18)   "Formal notice" means a form of notice that is described in and served by a method of service provided under rule 5.040(a) of the Florida Probate Rules.

(19)   "Grantor" means one who creates or adds to a trust and includes "settlor" or "trustor" and a testator who creates or adds to a trust.

(20)   "Heirs" or "heirs at law" means those persons, including the surviving spouse, who are entitled under the statutes of intestate succession to the property of a decedent.

(21)   "Incapacitated" means a judicial determination that a person lacks the capacity to manage at least some of the person's property or to meet at least some of the person's essential health and safety requirements. A minor shall be treated as being incapacitated.

(22)   "Informal notice" or "notice" means a method of service for pleadings or papers as provided under rule 5.040(b) of the Florida Probate Rules.

(23)   "Interested person" means any person who may reasonably be expected to be affected by the outcome of the particular proceeding involved. In any proceeding affecting the estate or the rights of a beneficiary in the estate, the personal representative of the estate shall be deemed to be an interested person. In any proceeding affecting the expenses of the administration and obligations of a decedent's estate, or any claims described in s. 733.702(1), the trustee of a trust described in s. 733.707(3) is an interested person in the administration of the grantor's estate. The term does not include a beneficiary who has received complete distribution. The meaning, as it relates to particular persons, may vary from time to time and must be determined according to the particular purpose of, and matter involved in, any proceedings.

(24)   "Letters" means authority granted by the court to the personal representative to act on behalf of the estate of the decedent and refers to what has been known as letters testamentary and letters of administration. All letters shall be designated "letters of administration."

(25)   "Minor" means a person under 18 years of age whose disabilities have not been removed by marriage or otherwise.

(26)   "Other state" means any state of the United States other than Florida

and includes the District of Columbia, the Commonwealth of Puerto Rico, and any territory or possession subject to the legislative authority of the United States.

(27)   "Parent" excludes any person who is only a stepparent, foster parent, or grandparent.

(28)   "Personal representative" means the fiduciary appointed by the court to administer the estate and refers to what has been known as an administrator, administrator cum testamento annexo, administrator de bonis non, ancillary administrator, ancillary executor, or executor.

(29)   "Petition" means a written request to the court for an order.

(30)   "Power of appointment" means an authority, other than as an incident of the beneficial ownership of property, to designate recipients of beneficial interests in property.

(31)   "Probate of will" means all steps necessary to establish the validity of a will and to admit a will to probate.

(32)   "Property" means both real and personal property or any interest in it and anything that may be the subject of ownership.

(33)   "Protected homestead" means the property described in s. 4(a)(1), Art. X of the State Constitution on which at the death of the owner the exemption inures to the owner's surviving spouse or heirs under s. 4(b), Art. X of the State Constitution. For purposes of the code, real property owned in tenancy by the entireties or in joint tenancy with rights of survivorship is not protected homestead.

(34)   "Residence" means a person's place of dwelling.

(35)   "Residuary devise" means a devise of the assets of the estate which remain after the provision for any devise which is to be satisfied by reference to a specific property or type of property, fund, sum, or statutory amount. If the will contains no devise which is to be satisfied by reference to a specific property or type of property, fund, sum, or statutory amount, "residuary devise" or "residue" means a devise of all assets remaining after satisfying the obligations of the estate.

(36)   "Security" means a security as defined in s. 517.021.

(37)   "Security interest" means a security interest as defined in s. 671.201.

(38)   "Trust" means an express trust, private or charitable, with additions to it, wherever and however created. It also includes a trust created or determined by a judgment or decree under which the trust is to be administered in the manner of an express trust. "Trust" excludes other constructive trusts, and it excludes resulting trusts; conservatorships; custodial arrangements pursuant to the Florida Uniform Transfers to Minors Act; business trusts providing for certificates to be issued to beneficiaries; common trust funds; land trusts under s. 689.071, except to the extent provided in s. 689.071(7); trusts created by the form of the account or by the deposit agreement at a financial institution; voting trusts; security arrangements; liquidation trusts; trusts for the primary purpose of paying debts, dividends, interest, salaries, wages, profits, pensions, or employee

benefits of any kind; and any arrangement under which a person is nominee or escrowee for another.

(39)   "Trustee" includes an original, additional, surviving, or successor trustee, whether or not appointed or confirmed by court.

(40)   "Will" means an instrument, including a codicil, executed by a person in the manner prescribed by this code, which disposes of the person's property on or after his or her death and includes an instrument which merely appoints a personal representative or revokes or revises another will.

History.—s. 1, ch. 74-106; s. 4, ch. 75-220; s. 1, ch. 77-174; s. 2, ch. 85-79; s. 66, ch. 87-226; s. 1, ch. 88-340; s. 7, ch. 93-257; s. 6, ch. 95-401; s. 949, ch. 97-102; s. 52, ch. 98-421; s. 11, ch. 2001-226; s. 106, ch. 2002-1; s. 2, ch. 2003-154; s. 2, ch. 2005-108; s. 29, ch. 2006-217; s. 3, ch. 2007-74; s. 8, ch. 2007-153; s. 1, ch. 2009-115; s. 4, ch. 2010-132; s. 1, ch. 2012-109; s. 16, ch. 2013-172.

Note.—Created from former s. 731.03.

PART III
NOTICE AND REPRESENTATION

731.301 Notice.—

(1)   If notice to an interested person of a petition or other proceeding is required, the notice shall be given to the interested person or that person's attorney as provided in the code or the Florida Probate Rules.

(2)   In a probate proceeding, formal notice is sufficient to acquire jurisdiction over the person receiving formal notice to the extent of the person's interest in the estate or in the decedent's protected homestead.

(3)   Persons given proper notice of a proceeding are bound by all orders entered in that proceeding.

History.—s. 1, ch. 74-106; s. 5, ch. 75-220; s. 3, ch. 77-87; s. 1, ch. 77-174; s. 1, ch. 93-257; s. 64, ch. 95-211; s. 950, ch. 97-102; s. 12, ch. 2001-226; s. 5, ch. 2010-132.

Note.—Created from former s. 732.28.

731.302 Waiver and consent by interested person.—Subsequent to the filing of a petition for administration, an interested person, including a guardian ad litem, administrator ad litem, guardian of the property, personal representative, trustee, or other fiduciary, or a sole holder or all coholders of a power of revocation or a power of appointment, may waive, to the extent of that person's interest or the interest which that person represents, subject to the provisions of ss. 731.303 and 733.604, any right or notice or the filing of any document, exhibit, or schedule required to be filed and may consent to any action or proceeding which may be required or permitted by this code.

History.—s. 1, ch. 74-106; s. 6, ch. 75-220; s. 4, ch. 77-87; s. 267, ch. 79-400; s. 3, ch. 84-106; s. 25, ch. 2003-154.

Florida Probate Code

Note.—Created from former s. 732.28.

731.303 Representation.—In the administration of or in judicial proceedings involving estates of decedents, the following apply:

(1)   Persons are bound by orders binding others in the following cases:

(a)   1.   Orders binding the sole holder or all coholders of a power of revocation or a general, special, or limited power of appointment, including one in the form of a power of amendment or revocation to the extent that the power has not become unexercisable in fact, bind all persons to the extent that their interests, as persons who may take by virtue of the exercise or nonexercise of the power, are subject to the power.

2.   Subparagraph 1. does not apply to:

a.   Any matter determined by the court to involve fraud or bad faith by the trustee;

b.   A power of a trustee to distribute trust property; or

c.   A power of appointment held by a person while the person is the sole trustee.

(b)   To the extent there is no conflict of interest between them or among the persons represented:

1.   Orders binding a guardian of the property bind the ward.

2.   Orders binding a trustee bind beneficiaries of the trust in proceedings to probate a will, in establishing or adding to a trust, in reviewing the acts or accounts of a prior fiduciary, and in proceedings involving creditors or other third parties. However, for purposes of this section, a conflict of interest shall be deemed to exist when each trustee of a trust that is a beneficiary of the estate is also a personal representative of the estate.

3.   Orders binding a personal representative bind persons interested in the undistributed assets of a decedent's estate, in actions or proceedings by or against the estate.

(c)   An unborn or unascertained person, or a minor or any other person under a legal disability, who is not otherwise represented is bound by an order to the extent that person's interest is represented by another party having the same or greater quality of interest in the proceeding.

(2)   Orders binding a guardian of the person shall not bind the ward.

(3)   In proceedings involving the administration of estates, notice is required as follows:

(a)   Notice as prescribed by law shall be given to every interested person, or to one who can bind the interested person as described in paragraph (1)(a) or paragraph (1)(b). Notice may be given both to the interested person and to another who can bind him or her.

(b)   Notice is given to unborn or unascertained persons who are not represented pursuant to paragraph (1)(a) or paragraph (1)(b) by giving notice to all known persons whose interests in the proceedings are the same as, or of a greater quality than, those of the unborn or unascertained persons.

(4)   If the court determines that representation of the interest would otherwise be inadequate, the court may, at any time, appoint a guardian ad litem to represent the interests of an incapacitated person, an unborn or unascertained person, a minor or any other person otherwise under a legal disability, or a person whose identity or address is unknown. If not precluded by conflict of interest, a guardian ad litem may be appointed to represent several persons or interests.

(5)   The holder of a power of appointment over property not held in trust may represent and bind persons whose interests, as permissible appointees, takers in default, or otherwise, are subject to the power. Representation under this subsection does not apply to:

(a)   Any matter determined by the court to involve fraud or bad faith by the trustee;

(b)   A power of a trustee to distribute trust property; or

(c)   A power of appointment held by a person while the person is the sole trustee.

History.—s. 1, ch. 74-106; s. 7, ch. 75-220; s. 5, ch. 77-87; s. 1, ch. 77-174; s. 1, ch. 88-217; s. 3, ch. 92-200; s. 951, ch. 97-102; s. 13, ch. 2001-226; s. 3, ch. 2002-82; s. 3, ch. 2003-154; s. 30, ch. 2006-217; s. 9, ch. 2007-153.

731.401   Arbitration of disputes.—

(1)   A provision in a will or trust requiring the arbitration of disputes, other than disputes of the validity of all or a part of a will or trust, between or among the beneficiaries and a fiduciary under the will or trust, or any combination of such persons or entities, is enforceable.

(2)   Unless otherwise specified in the will or trust, a will or trust provision requiring arbitration shall be presumed to require binding arbitration under chapter 682, the Revised Florida Arbitration Code. If an arbitration enforceable under this section is governed under chapter 682, the arbitration provision in the will or trust shall be treated as an agreement for the purposes of applying chapter 682.

History.—s. 4, ch. 2007-74; s. 37, ch. 2013-232.

Florida Probate Code

732.101 Intestate estate.—

(1)   Any part of the estate of a decedent not effectively disposed of by will passes to the decedent's heirs as prescribed in the following sections of this code.

(2)   The decedent's death is the event that vests the heirs' right to the decedent's intestate property.

History.—s. 1, ch. 74-106; s. 8, ch. 75-220; s. 14, ch. 2001-226.

Note.—Created from former s. 731.23.

732.102 Spouse's share of intestate estate.—The intestate share of the surviving spouse is:

(1)   If there is no surviving descendant of the decedent, the entire intestate estate.

(2)   If the decedent is survived by one or more descendants, all of whom are also descendants of the surviving spouse, and the surviving spouse has no other descendant, the entire intestate estate.

(3)   If there are one or more surviving descendants of the decedent who are not lineal descendants of the surviving spouse, one-half of the intestate estate.

(4)   If there are one or more surviving descendants of the decedent, all of whom are also descendants of the surviving spouse, and the surviving spouse has one or more descendants who are not descendants of the decedent, one-half of the intestate estate.

History.—s. 1, ch. 74-106; s. 8, ch. 75-220; s. 15, ch. 2001-226; s. 5, ch. 2007-74; s. 2, ch. 2011-183.

Note.—Created from former s. 731.23.

732.103 Share of other heirs.—The part of the intestate estate not passing to the surviving spouse under s. 732.102, or the entire intestate estate if there is no surviving spouse, descends as follows:

(1)   To the descendants of the decedent.

(2)   If there is no descendant, to the decedent's father and mother equally, or to the survivor of them.

(3)   If there is none of the foregoing, to the decedent's brothers and sisters and the descendants of deceased brothers and sisters.

(4)   If there is none of the foregoing, the estate shall be divided, one-half of which shall go to the decedent's paternal, and the other half to the decedent's maternal, kindred in the following order:

(a)   To the grandfather and grandmother equally, or to the survivor of them.

(b)   If there is no grandfather or grandmother, to uncles and aunts and descendants of deceased uncles and aunts of the decedent.

(c)   If there is either no paternal kindred or no maternal kindred, the estate shall go to the other kindred who survive, in the order stated above.

(5)   If there is no kindred of either part, the whole of the property shall go to the kindred of the last deceased spouse of the decedent as if the deceased spouse had survived the decedent and then died intestate entitled to the estate.

(6)   If none of the foregoing, and if any of the descendants of the decedent's great-grandparents were Holocaust victims as defined in s. 626.9543(3)(a), including such victims in countries cooperating with the discriminatory policies of Nazi Germany, then to the descendants of the great-grandparents. The court shall allow any such descendant to meet a reasonable, not unduly restrictive, standard of proof to substantiate his or her lineage. This subsection only applies to escheated property and shall cease to be effective for proceedings filed after December 31, 2004.

History.—s. 1, ch. 74-106; s. 8, ch. 75-220; s. 1, ch. 77-174; s. 16, ch. 2001-226; s. 145, ch. 2004-390; s. 102, ch. 2006-1; s. 6, ch. 2007-74.

Note.—Created from former s. 731.23.

732.104 Inheritance per stirpes.—Descent shall be per stirpes, whether to descendants or to collateral heirs.

History.—s. 1, ch. 74-106; s. 9, ch. 75-220; s. 7, ch. 2007-74.

Note.—Created from former s. 731.25.

732.105 Half blood.—When property descends to the collateral kindred of the intestate and part of the collateral kindred are of the whole blood to the intestate and the other part of the half blood, those of the half blood shall inherit only half as much as those of the whole blood; but if all are of the half blood they shall have whole parts.

History.—s. 1, ch. 74-106; s. 10, ch. 75-220.

Note.—Created from former s. 731.24.

732.106 Afterborn heirs.—Heirs of the decedent conceived before his or her death, but born thereafter, inherit intestate property as if they had been born in the decedent's lifetime.

History.—s. 1, ch. 74-106; s. 10, ch. 75-220; s. 6, ch. 77-87; s. 952, ch. 97-102.

Note.—Created from former s. 731.11.

Florida Probate Code

732.107 Escheat.—

(1)   When a person dies leaving an estate without being survived by any person entitled to a part of it, that part shall escheat to the state.

(2)   Property that escheats shall be sold as provided in the Florida Probate Rules and the proceeds paid to the Chief Financial Officer of the state and deposited in the State School Fund.

(3)   At any time within 10 years after the payment to the Chief Financial Officer, a person claiming to be entitled to the proceeds may reopen the administration to assert entitlement to the proceeds. If no claim is timely asserted, the state's rights to the proceeds shall become absolute.

(4)   The Department of Legal Affairs shall represent the state in all proceedings concerning escheated estates.

(5)   (a)   If a person entitled to the proceeds assigns the rights to receive payment to an attorney, Florida-certified public accountant, or private investigative agency which is duly licensed to do business in this state pursuant to a written agreement with that person, the Department of Financial Services is authorized to make distribution in accordance with the assignment.

(b)   Payments made to an attorney, Florida-certified public accountant, or private investigative agency shall be promptly deposited into a trust or escrow account which is regularly maintained by the attorney, Florida-certified public accountant, or private investigative agency in a financial institution authorized to accept such deposits and located in this state.

(c)   Distribution by the attorney, Florida-certified public accountant, or private investigative agency to the person entitled to the proceeds shall be made within 10 days following final credit of the deposit into the trust or escrow account at the financial institution, unless a party to the agreement protests the distribution in writing before it is made.

(d)   The department shall not be civilly or criminally liable for any proceeds distributed pursuant to this subsection, provided such distribution is made in good faith.

History.—s. 1, ch. 74-106; s. 10, ch. 75-220; s. 4, ch. 89-291; s. 9, ch. 89-299; s. 953, ch. 97-102; s. 32, ch. 2001-36; s. 17, ch. 2001-226; s. 1896, ch. 2003-261.

Note.—Created from former s. 731.33.

732.108 Adopted persons and persons born out of wedlock.—

(1)   For the purpose of intestate succession by or from an adopted person, the adopted person is a descendant of the adopting parent and is one of the natural kindred of all members of the adopting parent's family, and is not a descendant of his or her natural parents, nor is he or she one of the kindred of any member of the natural parent's family or any prior adoptive parent's family, except that:

        (a)   Adoption of a child by the spouse of a natural parent has no effect on the relationship between the child and the natural parent or the natural parent's family.

        (b)   Adoption of a child by a natural parent's spouse who married the natural parent after the death of the other natural parent has no effect on the relationship between the child and the family of the deceased natural parent.

        (c)   Adoption of a child by a close relative, as defined in s. 63.172(2), has no effect on the relationship between the child and the families of the deceased natural parents.

        (2)   For the purpose of intestate succession in cases not covered by subsection (1), a person born out of wedlock is a descendant of his or her mother and is one of the natural kindred of all members of the mother's family. The person is also a descendant of his or her father and is one of the natural kindred of all members of the father's family, if:

        (a)   The natural parents participated in a marriage ceremony before or after the birth of the person born out of wedlock, even though the attempted marriage is void.

        (b)   The paternity of the father is established by an adjudication before or after the death of the father. Chapter 95 shall not apply in determining heirs in a probate proceeding under this paragraph.

        (c)   The paternity of the father is acknowledged in writing by the father.

History.—s. 1, ch. 74-106; s. 11, ch. 75-220; s. 7, ch. 77-87; s. 1, ch. 77-174; s. 2, ch. 87-27; s. 954, ch. 97-102; s. 8, ch. 2007-74; s. 2, ch. 2009-115.

Note.—Created from former ss. 731.29, 731.30.

732.1081 Termination of parental rights.—For the purpose of intestate succession by a natural or adoptive parent, a natural or adoptive parent is barred from inheriting from or through a child if the natural or adoptive parent's parental rights were terminated pursuant to chapter 39 prior to the death of the child, and the natural or adoptive parent shall be treated as if the parent predeceased the child.

History.—s. 4, ch. 2012-109.

732.109 Debts to decedent.—A debt owed to the decedent shall not be charged against the intestate share of any person except the debtor. If the debtor does not survive the decedent, the debt shall not be taken into account in computing the intestate share of the debtor's heirs.

History.—s. 1, ch. 74-106; s. 11, ch. 75-220.

Note.—Created from former s. 736.01.

Florida Probate Code

732.1101 Aliens.—Aliens shall have the same rights of inheritance as citizens.

History.—s. 1, ch. 74-106; s. 113, ch. 75-220; s. 955, ch. 97-102; s. 18, ch. 2001-226.

Note.—Created from former s. 731.28.

732.111 Dower and curtesy abolished.—Dower and curtesy are abolished.

History.—s. 1, ch. 74-106; s. 113, ch. 75-220.

PART II
ELECTIVE SHARE OF SURVIVING SPOUSE; RIGHTS IN COMMUNITY PROPERTY

732.201 Right to elective share.—The surviving spouse of a person who dies domiciled in Florida has the right to a share of the elective estate of the decedent as provided in this part, to be designated the elective share.

History.—s. 1, ch. 74-106; s. 13, ch. 75-220; s. 1, ch. 99-343.

Note.—Created from former s. 731.34.

732.2025 Definitions.—As used in ss. 732.2025-732.2155, the term:

(1)   "Direct recipient" means the decedent's probate estate and any other person who receives property included in the elective estate by transfer from the decedent, including transfers described in s. 732.2035(8), by right of survivorship, or by beneficiary designation under a governing instrument. For this purpose, a beneficiary of an insurance policy on the decedent's life, the net cash surrender value of which is included in the elective estate, is treated as having received property included in the elective estate. In the case of property held in trust, "direct recipient" includes the trustee but excludes the beneficiaries of the trust.

(2)   "Elective share trust" means a trust under which:

(a)   The surviving spouse is entitled for life to the use of the property or to all of the income payable at least as often as annually;

(b)   The surviving spouse has the right under the terms of the trust or state law to require the trustee either to make the property productive or to convert it within a reasonable time; and

(c)   During the spouse's life, no person other than the spouse has the power to distribute income or principal to anyone other than the spouse.
As used in this subsection, the term "income" has the same meaning as that provided in s. 643(b) of the Internal Revenue Code, as amended, and regulations adopted under that section.

(3)   "General power of appointment" means a power of appointment under which the holder of the power, whether or not the holder has the capacity to exercise it, has the power to create a present or future interest in the holder, the holder's estate, or the creditors of either. The term includes a power to consume or invade the principal of a trust, but only if the power is not limited by an ascertainable standard relating to the holder's

health, education, support, or maintenance.

(4) "Governing instrument" means a deed; will; trust; insurance or annuity policy; account with payable-on-death designation; security registered in beneficiary form (TOD); pension, profit-sharing, retirement, or similar benefit plan; an instrument creating or exercising a power of appointment or a power of attorney; or a dispositive, appointive, or nominative instrument of any similar type.

(5) "Payor" means an insurer, business entity, employer, government, governmental agency or subdivision, or any other person, other than the decedent's personal representative or a trustee of a trust created by the decedent, authorized or obligated by law or a governing instrument to make payments.

(6) "Person" includes an individual, trust, estate, partnership, association, company, or corporation.

(7) "Probate estate" means all property wherever located that is subject to estate administration in any state of the United States or in the District of Columbia.

(8) "Qualifying special needs trust" or "supplemental needs trust" means a trust established for an ill or disabled surviving spouse with court approval before or after a decedent's death, if, commencing on the decedent's death:

(a) The income and principal are distributable to or for the benefit of the spouse for life in the discretion of one or more trustees less than half of whom are ineligible family trustees. For purposes of this paragraph, ineligible family trustees include the decedent's grandparents and any descendants of the decedent's grandparents who are not also descendants of the surviving spouse; and

(b) During the spouse's life, no person other than the spouse has the power to distribute income or principal to anyone other than the spouse.
The requirement for court approval shall not apply if the aggregate value of all property in all qualifying special needs trusts for the spouse is less than $100,000. For purposes of this subsection, value is determined on the "applicable valuation date" as defined in s. 732.2095(1)(a).

(9) "Revocable trust" means a trust that is includable in the elective estate under s. 732.2035(4).

(10) "Transfer in satisfaction of the elective share" means an irrevocable transfer by the decedent during life to an elective share trust.

(11) "Transfer tax value" means the value the interest would have for purposes of the United States estate and gift tax laws if it passed without consideration to an unrelated person on the applicable valuation date.

History.—s. 2, ch. 99-343; s. 19, ch. 2001-226; s. 2, ch. 2002-82; s. 151, ch. 2004-5; s. 9, ch. 2007-74; s. 3, ch. 2009-115.

732.2035 Property entering into elective estate.—Except as provided in s. 732.2045, the elective estate consists of the sum of the values as determined under s. 732.2055 of the following property interests:

Florida Probate Code

(1)   The decedent's probate estate.

(2)   The decedent's ownership interest in accounts or securities registered in "Pay On Death," "Transfer On Death," "In Trust For," or coownership with right of survivorship form. For this purpose, "decedent's ownership interest" means, in the case of accounts or securities held in tenancy by the entirety, one-half of the value of the account or security, and in all other cases, that portion of the accounts or securities which the decedent had, immediately before death, the right to withdraw or use without the duty to account to any person.

(3)   The decedent's fractional interest in property, other than property described in subsection (2) or subsection (7), held by the decedent in joint tenancy with right of survivorship or in tenancy by the entirety. For this purpose, "decedent's fractional interest in property" means the value of the property divided by the number of tenants.

(4)   That portion of property, other than property described in subsection (2), transferred by the decedent to the extent that at the time of the decedent's death the transfer was revocable by the decedent alone or in conjunction with any other person. This subsection does not apply to a transfer that is revocable by the decedent only with the consent of all persons having a beneficial interest in the property.

(5)   (a)   That portion of property, other than property described in subsection (3), subsection (4), or subsection (7), transferred by the decedent to the extent that at the time of the decedent's death:

1.   The decedent possessed the right to, or in fact enjoyed the possession or use of, the income or principal of the property; or

2.   The principal of the property could, in the discretion of any person other than the spouse of the decedent, be distributed or appointed to or for the benefit of the decedent.
In the application of this subsection, a right to payments under a commercial or private annuity, an annuity trust, a unitrust, or a similar arrangement shall be treated as a right to that portion of the income of the property necessary to equal the annuity, unitrust, or other payment.

(b)   The amount included under this subsection is:

1.   With respect to subparagraph (a)1., the value of the portion of the property to which the decedent's right or enjoyment related, to the extent the portion passed to or for the benefit of any person other than the decedent's probate estate; and

2.   With respect to subparagraph (a)2., the value of the portion subject to the discretion, to the extent the portion passed to or for the benefit of any person other than the decedent's probate estate.

(c)   This subsection does not apply to any property if the decedent's only interests in the property are that:

1.   The property could be distributed to or for the

benefit of the decedent only with the consent of all persons having a beneficial interest in the property; or

2. The income or principal of the property could be distributed to or for the benefit of the decedent only through the exercise or in default of an exercise of a general power of appointment held by any person other than the decedent; or

3. The income or principal of the property is or could be distributed in satisfaction of the decedent's obligation of support; or

4. The decedent had a contingent right to receive principal, other than at the discretion of any person, which contingency was beyond the control of the decedent and which had not in fact occurred at the decedent's death.

(6) The decedent's beneficial interest in the net cash surrender value immediately before death of any policy of insurance on the decedent's life.

(7) The value of amounts payable to or for the benefit of any person by reason of surviving the decedent under any public or private pension, retirement, or deferred compensation plan, or any similar arrangement, other than benefits payable under the federal Railroad Retirement Act or the federal Social Security System. In the case of a defined contribution plan as defined in s. 414(i) of the Internal Revenue Code of 1986, as amended, this subsection shall not apply to the excess of the proceeds of any insurance policy on the decedent's life over the net cash surrender value of the policy immediately before the decedent's death.

(8) Property that was transferred during the 1-year period preceding the decedent's death as a result of a transfer by the decedent if the transfer was either of the following types:

(a) Any property transferred as a result of the termination of a right or interest in, or power over, property that would have been included in the elective estate under subsection (4) or subsection (5) if the right, interest, or power had not terminated until the decedent's death.

(b) Any transfer of property to the extent not otherwise included in the elective estate, made to or for the benefit of any person, except:

1. Any transfer of property for medical or educational expenses to the extent it qualifies for exclusion from the United States gift tax under s. 2503(e) of the Internal Revenue Code, as amended; and

2. After the application of subparagraph 1., the first annual exclusion amount of property transferred to or for the benefit of each donee during the 1-year period, but only to the extent the transfer qualifies for exclusion from the United States gift tax under s. 2503(b) or (c) of the Internal Revenue Code, as amended. For purposes of this subparagraph, the term "annual exclusion amount" means the amount of one annual exclusion under s. 2503(b) or (c) of the Internal Revenue Code, as amended.

(c) Except as provided in paragraph (d), for purposes of this subsection:

1.   A "termination" with respect to a right or interest in property occurs when the decedent transfers or relinquishes the right or interest, and, with respect to a power over property, a termination occurs when the power terminates by exercise, release, lapse, default, or otherwise.

2.   A distribution from a trust the income or principal of which is subject to subsection (4), subsection (5), or subsection (9) shall be treated as a transfer of property by the decedent and not as a termination of a right or interest in, or a power over, property.

(d)   Notwithstanding anything in paragraph (c) to the contrary:

1.   A "termination" with respect to a right or interest in property does not occur when the right or interest terminates by the terms of the governing instrument unless the termination is determined by reference to the death of the decedent and the court finds that a principal purpose for the terms of the instrument relating to the termination was avoidance of the elective share.

2.   A distribution from a trust is not subject to this subsection if the distribution is required by the terms of the governing instrument unless the event triggering the distribution is determined by reference to the death of the decedent and the court finds that a principal purpose of the terms of the governing instrument relating to the distribution is avoidance of the elective share.

(9)   Property transferred in satisfaction of the elective share.

History.—s. 15, ch. 75-220; s. 3, ch. 99-343; s. 20, ch. 2001-226; s. 10, ch. 2007-74.

Note.—Former s. 732.206.

732.2045 Exclusions and overlapping application.—

(1)   EXCLUSIONS.—Section 732.2035 does not apply to:

(a)   Except as provided in s. 732.2155(4), any transfer of property by the decedent to the extent the transfer is irrevocable before the effective date of this subsection or after that date but before the date of the decedent's marriage to the surviving spouse.

(b)   Any transfer of property by the decedent to the extent the decedent received adequate consideration in money or money's worth for the transfer.

(c)   Any transfer of property by the decedent made with the written consent of the decedent's spouse. For this purpose, spousal consent to split-gift treatment under the United States gift tax laws does not constitute written consent to the transfer by the decedent.

(d)   The proceeds of any policy of insurance on the decedent's life in excess of the net cash surrender value of the policy whether payable to the decedent's estate, a trust, or in any other manner.

(e)   Any policy of insurance on the decedent's life maintained pursuant to a court order.

(f)   The decedent's one-half of the property to which ss. 732.216-732.228, or any similar provisions of law of another state, apply and real property that is community property under the laws of the jurisdiction where it is located.

(g)   Property held in a qualifying special needs trust on the date of the decedent's death.

(h)   Property included in the gross estate of the decedent for federal estate tax purposes solely because the decedent possessed a general power of appointment.

(i)   Property which constitutes the protected homestead of the decedent whether held by the decedent or by a trust at the decedent's death.

(2)   OVERLAPPING APPLICATION.—If s. 732.2035(1) and any other subsection of s. 732.2035 apply to the same property interest, the amount included in the elective estate under other subsections is reduced by the amount included under subsection (1). In all other cases, if more than one subsection of s. 732.2035 applies to a property interest, only the subsection resulting in the largest elective estate shall apply.

History.—s. 4, ch. 99-343; s. 21, ch. 2001-226; s. 4, ch. 2009-115.

732.2055 Valuation of the elective estate.—For purposes of s. 732.2035, "value" means:

(1)   In the case of any policy of insurance on the decedent's life includable under s. 732.2035(4), (5), or (6), the net cash surrender value of the policy immediately before the decedent's death.

(2)   In the case of any policy of insurance on the decedent's life includable under s. 732.2035(8), the net cash surrender value of the policy on the date of the termination or transfer.

(3)   In the case of amounts includable under s. 732.2035(7), the transfer tax value of the amounts on the date of the decedent's death.

(4)   In the case of other property included under s. 732.2035(8), the fair market value of the property on the date of the termination or transfer, computed after deducting any mortgages, liens, or security interests on the property as of that date.

(5)   In the case of all other property, the fair market value of the property on the date of the decedent's death, computed after deducting from the total value of the property:

(a)   All claims paid or payable from the elective estate; and

(b)   To the extent they are not deducted under paragraph (a), all mortgages, liens, or security interests on the property.

History.—s. 5, ch. 99-343; s. 22, ch. 2001-226.

732.2065 Amount of the elective share.—The elective share is an amount equal to 30 percent of the elective estate.

History.—s. 15, ch. 75-220; s. 1, ch. 81-27; s. 6, ch. 99-343.

Note.—Former s. 732.207.

732.2075 Sources from which elective share payable; abatement.—

(1)   Unless otherwise provided in the decedent's will or, in the absence of a provision in the decedent's will, in a trust referred to in the decedent's will, the following are applied first to satisfy the elective share:

(a)   Property interests included in the elective estate that pass or have passed to or for the benefit of the surviving spouse, including interests that are contingent upon making the election, but only to the extent that such contingent interests do not diminish other property interests that would be applied to satisfy the elective share in the absence of the contingent interests.

(b)   To the extent paid to or for the benefit of the surviving spouse, amounts payable under any plan or arrangement described in s. 732.2035(7).

(c)   To the extent paid to or for the benefit of the surviving spouse, the decedent's one-half of any property described in s. 732.2045(1)(f).

(d)   To the extent paid to or for the benefit of the surviving spouse, the proceeds of any term or other policy of insurance on the decedent's life if, at the time of decedent's death, the policy was owned by any person other than the surviving spouse.

(e)   Property held for the benefit of the surviving spouse in a qualifying special needs trust.

(f)   Property interests that would have satisfied the elective share under any preceding paragraph of this subsection but were disclaimed.

(2)   If, after the application of subsection (1), the elective share is not fully satisfied, the unsatisfied balance shall be allocated entirely to one class of direct recipients of the remaining elective estate and apportioned among those recipients, and if the elective share amount is not fully satisfied, to the next class of direct recipients, in the following order of priority, until the elective share amount is satisfied:

(a)   Class 1.—The decedent's probate estate and revocable trusts.

(b)   Class 2.—Recipients of property interests, other than protected charitable interests, included in the elective estate under s. 732.2035(2), (3), or (6) and, to the extent the decedent had at the time of death the power to designate the recipient of the property, property interests, other than protected charitable interests, included under s. 732.2035(5) and (7).

(c)   Class 3.—Recipients of all other property interests, other than protected charitable interests, included in the elective estate.

For purposes of this subsection, a protected charitable interest is any interest for which a charitable deduction with respect to the transfer of the property was allowed or allowable to the decedent or the decedent's spouse under the United States gift or income tax laws.

(3)   If, after the application of subsections (1) and (2), the elective share amount is not fully satisfied, the additional amount due to the surviving spouse shall be determined and satisfied as follows:

(a)   The remaining unsatisfied balance shall be satisfied from property described in paragraphs (1)(a) and (b) which passes or which has passed in a trust in which the surviving spouse has a beneficial interest, other than an elective share trust or a qualified special needs trust.

(b)   In determining the amount of the remaining unsatisfied balance, the effect, if any, of any change caused by the operation of this subsection in the value of the spouse's beneficial interests in property described in paragraphs (1)(a) and (b) shall be taken into account, including, if necessary, further recalculations of the value of those beneficial interests.

(c)   If there is more than one trust to which this subsection could apply, unless otherwise provided in the decedent's will or, in the absence of a provision in the decedent's will, in a trust referred to in the decedent's will, the unsatisfied balance shall be apportioned pro rata to all such trusts in proportion to the value, as determined under s. 732.2095(2)(d), of the surviving spouse's beneficial interests in the trusts.

(4)   If, after the application of subsections (1), (2), and (3), the elective share is not fully satisfied, any remaining unsatisfied balance shall be satisfied from direct recipients of protected charitable lead interests, but only to the extent and at such times that contribution is permitted without disqualifying the charitable interest in that property for a deduction under the United States gift tax laws. For purposes of this subsection, a protected charitable lead interest is a protected charitable interest as defined in subsection (2) in which one or more deductible interests in charity precede some other nondeductible interest or interests in the property.

(5)   The contribution required of the decedent's probate estate and revocable trusts may be made in cash or in kind. In the application of this subsection, subsections (6) and (7) are to be applied to charge contribution for the elective share to the beneficiaries of the probate estate and revocable trusts as if all beneficiaries were taking under a common governing instrument.

(6)   Unless otherwise provided in the decedent's will or, in the absence of a provision in the decedent's will, in a trust referred to in the decedent's will, any amount to be satisfied from the decedent's probate estate, other than from property passing to an inter vivos trust, shall be paid from the assets of the probate estate in the order prescribed in s. 733.805.

(7)   Unless otherwise provided in the trust instrument or, in the decedent's will if there is no provision in the trust instrument, any amount to be satisfied from trust property shall be paid from the assets of the trust in the order provided for claims under s. 736.05053(2) and (3). A direction in the decedent's will is effective only for revocable trusts.

History.—s. 15, ch. 75-220; s. 7, ch. 99-343; s. 23, ch. 2001-226; s. 4, ch. 2002-82; s. 31, ch. 2006-217; s. 11, ch. 2007-74; s. 5, ch. 2009-115.

Note.—Former s. 732.209.

732.2085 Liability of direct recipients and beneficiaries.—

(1)   Only direct recipients of property included in the elective estate and the beneficiaries of the decedent's probate estate or of any trust that is a direct recipient, are liable to contribute toward satisfaction of the elective share.

(a)   Within each of the classes described in s. 732.2075(2)(b) and (c), each direct recipient is liable in an amount equal to the value, as determined under s. 732.2055, of the proportional part of the liability for all members of the class.

(b)   Trust and probate estate beneficiaries who receive a distribution of principal after the decedent's death are liable in an amount equal to the value of the principal distributed to them multiplied by the contribution percentage of the distributing trust or estate. For this purpose, "contribution percentage" means the remaining unsatisfied balance of the trust or estate at the time of the distribution divided by the value of the trust or estate as determined under s. 732.2055. "Remaining unsatisfied balance" means the amount of liability initially apportioned to the trust or estate reduced by amounts or property previously contributed by any person in satisfaction of that liability.

(2)   In lieu of paying the amount for which they are liable, beneficiaries who have received a distribution of property included in the elective estate and direct recipients other than the decedent's probate estate or revocable trusts, may:

(a)   Contribute a proportional part of all property received; or

(b)   With respect to any property interest received before the date of the court's order of contribution:

1.   Contribute all of the property; or

2.   If the property has been sold or exchanged prior to the date on which the spouse's election is filed, pay an amount equal to the value of the property, less reasonable costs of sale, on the date it was sold or exchanged.
In the application of paragraph (a), the "proportional part of all property received" is determined separately for each class of priority under s. 732.2075(2).

(3)   If a person pays the value of the property on the date of a sale or exchange or contributes all of the property received, as provided in paragraph (2)(b):

(a)   No further contribution toward satisfaction of the elective share shall be required with respect to that property.

(b)   Any unsatisfied contribution is treated as additional unsatisfied balance and reapportioned to other recipients as provided in s. 732.2075 and this section.

(4)   If any part of s. 732.2035 or s. 732.2075 is preempted by federal law

with respect to a payment, an item of property, or any other benefit included in the elective estate, a person who, not for value, receives the payment, item of property, or any other benefit is obligated to return the payment, item of property, or benefit, or is personally liable for the amount of the payment or the value of that item of property or benefit, as provided in ss. 732.2035 and 732.2075, to the person who would have been entitled to it were that section or part of that section not preempted.

History.—s. 8, ch. 99-343; s. 24, ch. 2001-226; s. 6, ch. 2009-115.

732.2095 Valuation of property used to satisfy elective share.—

(1)　　DEFINITIONS.—As used in this section, the term:

(a)　　"Applicable valuation date" means:

1.　　In the case of transfers in satisfaction of the elective share, the date of the decedent's death.

2.　　In the case of property held in a qualifying special needs trust on the date of the decedent's death, the date of the decedent's death.

3.　　In the case of other property irrevocably transferred to or for the benefit of the surviving spouse during the decedent's life, the date of the transfer.

4.　　In the case of property distributed to the surviving spouse by the personal representative, the date of distribution.

5.　　Except as provided in subparagraphs 1., 2., and 3., in the case of property passing in trust for the surviving spouse, the date or dates the trust is funded in satisfaction of the elective share.

6.　　In the case of property described in s. 732.2035(2) or (3), the date of the decedent's death.

7.　　In the case of proceeds of any policy of insurance payable to the surviving spouse, the date of the decedent's death.

8.　　In the case of amounts payable to the surviving spouse under any plan or arrangement described in s. 732.2035(7), the date of the decedent's death.

9.　　In all other cases, the date of the decedent's death or the date the surviving spouse first comes into possession of the property, whichever occurs later.

(b)　　"Qualifying power of appointment" means a general power of appointment that is exercisable alone and in all events by the decedent's spouse in favor of the spouse or the spouse's estate. For this purpose, a general power to appoint by will is a qualifying power of appointment if the power may be exercised by the spouse in favor of the spouse's estate without the consent of any other person.

(c)　　　"Qualifying invasion power" means a power held by the surviving spouse or the trustee of an elective share trust to invade trust principal for the health, support, and maintenance of the spouse. The power may, but need not, provide that the other resources of the spouse are to be taken into account in any exercise of the power.

(2)　　　Except as provided in this subsection, the value of property for purposes of s. 732.2075 is the fair market value of the property on the applicable valuation date.

(a)　　　If the surviving spouse has a life interest in property not in trust that entitles the spouse to the use of the property for life, the value of the spouse's interest is one-half of the value of the property on the applicable valuation date.

(b)　　　If the surviving spouse has an interest in a trust, or portion of a trust, which meets the requirements of an elective share trust, the value of the spouse's interest is a percentage of the value of the principal of the trust, or trust portion, on the applicable valuation date as follows:

1.　　　One hundred percent if the trust instrument includes both a qualifying invasion power and a qualifying power of appointment.

2.　　　Eighty percent if the trust instrument includes a qualifying invasion power but no qualifying power of appointment.

3.　　　Fifty percent in all other cases.

(c)　　　If the surviving spouse is a beneficiary of a trust, or portion of a trust, which meets the requirements of a qualifying special needs trust, the value of the principal of the trust, or trust portion, on the applicable valuation date.

(d)　　　If the surviving spouse has an interest in a trust that does not meet the requirements of either an elective share trust or a qualifying special needs trust, the value of the spouse's interest is the transfer tax value of the interest on the applicable valuation date; however, the aggregate value of all of the spouse's interests in the trust shall not exceed one-half of the value of the trust principal on the applicable valuation date.

(e)　　　In the case of any policy of insurance on the decedent's life the proceeds of which are payable outright or to a trust described in paragraph (b), paragraph (c), or paragraph (d), the value of the policy for purposes of s. 732.2075 and paragraphs (b), (c), and (d) is the net proceeds.

(f)　　　In the case of a right to one or more payments from an annuity or under a similar contractual arrangement or under any plan or arrangement described in s. 732.2035(7), the value of the right to payments for purposes of s. 732.2075 and paragraphs (b), (c), and (d) is the transfer tax value of the right on the applicable valuation date.

History.—s. 9, ch. 99-343; s. 25, ch. 2001-226.

732.2105 Effect of election on other interests.—The elective share shall be in addition to homestead, exempt property, and allowances as provided in part IV.

History.—s. 15, ch. 75-220; s. 10, ch. 99-343; s. 26, ch. 2001-226.

Note.—Former s. 732.208.

732.2115 Protection of payors and other third parties.—Although a property interest is included in the decedent's elective estate under s. 732.2035(2)-(8), a payor or other third party is not liable for paying, distributing, or transferring the property to a beneficiary designated in a governing instrument, or for taking any other action in good faith reliance on the validity of a governing instrument.

History.—s. 11, ch. 99-343.

732.2125 Right of election; by whom exercisable.—The right of election may be exercised:

    (1)   By the surviving spouse.

    (2)   With approval of the court having jurisdiction of the probate proceeding by an attorney in fact or a guardian of the property of the surviving spouse. Before approving the election, the court shall determine that the election is in the best interests of the surviving spouse during the spouse's probable lifetime.

History.—s. 15, ch. 75-220; s. 12, ch. 99-343; s. 27, ch. 2001-226; s. 6, ch. 2010-132.

Note.—Former s. 732.210.

732.2135 Time of election; extensions; withdrawal.—

    (1)   Except as provided in subsection (2), the election must be filed on or before the earlier of the date that is 6 months after the date of service of a copy of the notice of administration on the surviving spouse, or an attorney in fact or guardian of the property of the surviving spouse, or the date that is 2 years after the date of the decedent's death.

    (2)   Within the period provided in subsection (1), the surviving spouse or an attorney in fact or guardian of the property of the surviving spouse may petition the court for an extension of time for making an election. For good cause shown, the court may extend the time for election. If the court grants the petition for an extension, the election must be filed within the time allowed by the extension.

    (3)   The surviving spouse or an attorney in fact, guardian of the property, or personal representative of the surviving spouse may withdraw an election at any time within 8 months after the decedent's death and before the court's order of contribution.

    (4)   A petition for an extension of the time for making the election or for approval to make the election shall toll the time for making the election.

    (5)   If the court determines that an election is made or pursued in bad faith, the court may assess attorney's fees and costs against the surviving spouse or the surviving spouse's estate.

History.—s. 15, ch. 75-220; s. 13, ch. 99-343; s. 28, ch. 2001-226; s. 4, ch. 2006-134; s. 7, ch. 2009-115.

Note.—Former s. 732.212.

732.2145 Order of contribution; personal representative's duty to collect contribution.—

(1)   The court shall determine the elective share and contribution. Contributions shall bear interest at the statutory rate beginning 90 days after the order of contribution. The order is prima facie correct in proceedings in any court or jurisdiction.

(2)   Except as provided in subsection (3), the personal representative shall collect contribution from the recipients of the elective estate as provided in the court's order of contribution.

(a)   If property within the possession or control of the personal representative is distributable to a beneficiary or trustee who is required to contribute in satisfaction of the elective share, the personal representative shall withhold from the distribution the contribution required of the beneficiary or trustee.

(b)   If, after the order of contribution, the personal representative brings an action to collect contribution from property not within the personal representative's control, the judgment shall include the personal representative's costs and reasonable attorney's fees. The personal representative is not required to seek collection of any portion of the elective share from property not within the personal representative's control until after the entry of the order of contribution.

(3)   A personal representative who has the duty under this section of enforcing contribution may be relieved of that duty by an order of the court finding that it is impracticable to enforce contribution in view of the improbability of obtaining a judgment or the improbability of collection under any judgment that might be obtained, or otherwise. The personal representative shall not be liable for failure to attempt collection if the attempt would have been economically impracticable.

(4)   Nothing in this section limits the independent right of the surviving spouse to collect the elective share as provided in the order of contribution, and that right is hereby conferred. If the surviving spouse brings an action to enforce the order, the judgment shall include the surviving spouse's costs and reasonable attorney's fees.

History.—s. 14, ch. 99-343; s. 29, ch. 2001-226.

732.2155 Effective date; effect of prior waivers; transition rules.—

(1)   Sections 732.201-732.2155 are effective on October 1, 1999, for all decedents dying on or after October 1, 2001. The law in effect prior to October 1, 1999, applies to decedents dying before October 1, 2001.

(2)   Nothing in ss. 732.201-732.2155 modifies or applies to the rights of spouses under chapter 61.

(3)   A waiver of elective share rights before the effective date of this section which is otherwise in compliance with the requirements of s. 732.702 is a waiver of all rights under ss. 732.201-732.2145.

(4)   Notwithstanding anything in s. 732.2045(1)(a) to the contrary, any trust created by the decedent before the effective date of ss. 732.201-732.2145 that meets the requirements of an elective share trust is treated as if the decedent created the trust after the effective date of these sections and in satisfaction of the elective share.

(5)   Sections 732.201-732.2155 do not affect any interest in contracts entered into for adequate consideration in money or money's worth before October 1, 1999, to the extent that the contract was irrevocable at all times from October 1, 1999, until the date of the decedent's death.

(6)   Sections 732.201-732.2155 do not affect any interest in property held, as of the decedent's death, in a trust, whether revocable or irrevocable, if:

(a)   The property was an asset of the trust at all times between October 1, 1999, and the date of the decedent's death;

(b)   The decedent was not married to the decedent's surviving spouse when the property was transferred to the trust; and

(c)   The property was a nonmarital asset as defined in s. 61.075 immediately prior to the decedent's death.

History.—s. 15, ch. 99-343; s. 30, ch. 2001-226.

732.216 Short title.—Sections 732.216-732.228 may be cited as the "Florida Uniform Disposition of Community Property Rights at Death Act."

History.—s. 4, ch. 92-200.

732.217 Application.—Sections 732.216-732.228 apply to the disposition at death of the following property acquired by a married person:

(1)   Personal property, wherever located, which:

(a)   Was acquired as, or became and remained, community property under the laws of another jurisdiction;

(b)   Was acquired with the rents, issues, or income of, or the proceeds from, or in exchange for, community property; or

(c)   Is traceable to that community property.

(2)   Real property, except real property held as tenants by the entirety, which is located in this state, and which:

(a)   Was acquired with the rents, issues, or income of, the proceeds from, or in exchange for, property acquired as, or which became and remained, community property under the laws of another jurisdiction; or

(b)   Is traceable to that community property.

History.—s. 5, ch. 92-200; s. 4, ch. 2003-154.

732.218 Rebuttable presumptions.—In determining whether ss. 732.216-732.228 apply to specific property, the following rebuttable presumptions apply:

(1)   Property acquired during marriage by a spouse of that marriage while domiciled in a jurisdiction under whose laws property could then be acquired as community property is presumed to have been acquired as, or to have become and remained, property to which these sections apply.

(2)   Real property located in this state, other than homestead and real property held as tenants by the entirety, and personal property wherever located acquired by a married person while domiciled in a jurisdiction under whose laws property could not then be acquired as community property and title to which was taken in a form which created rights of survivorship are presumed to be property to which these sections do not apply.

History.—s. 6, ch. 92-200; s. 31, ch. 2001-226.

732.219 Disposition upon death.—Upon the death of a married person, one-half of the property to which ss. 732.216-732.228 apply is the property of the surviving spouse and is not subject to testamentary disposition by the decedent or distribution under the laws of succession of this state. One-half of that property is the property of the decedent and is subject to testamentary disposition or distribution under the laws of succession of this state. The decedent's one-half of that property is not in the elective estate.

History.—s. 7, ch. 92-200; s. 32, ch. 2001-226; s. 107, ch. 2002-1.

732.221 Perfection of title of personal representative or beneficiary.—If the title to any property to which ss. 732.216-732.228 apply is held by the surviving spouse at the time of the decedent's death, the personal representative or a beneficiary of the decedent may institute an action to perfect title to the property. The personal representative has no duty to discover whether any property held by the surviving spouse is property to which ss. 732.216-732.228 apply, unless a written demand is made by a beneficiary within 3 months after service of a copy of the notice of administration on the beneficiary or by a creditor within 3 months after the first publication of the notice to creditors.

History.—s. 8, ch. 92-200; s. 33, ch. 2001-226.

732.222 Purchaser for value or lender.—

(1)   If a surviving spouse has apparent title to property to which ss. 732.216-732.228 apply, a purchaser for value or a lender taking a security interest in the property takes the interest in the property free of any rights of the personal representative or a beneficiary of the decedent.

(2)   If a personal representative or a beneficiary of the decedent has apparent title to property to which ss. 732.216-732.228 apply, a purchaser for value or a lender taking a security interest in the property takes that interest in the property free of any rights of the surviving spouse.

(3)   A purchaser for value or a lender need not inquire whether a vendor or borrower acted properly.

(4)   The proceeds of a sale or creation of a security interest must be treated as the property transferred to the purchaser for value or a lender.

History.—s. 9, ch. 92-200; s. 956, ch. 97-102; s. 34, ch. 2001-226.

732.223 Perfection of title of surviving spouse.—If the title to any property to which ss. 732.216-732.228 apply was held by the decedent at the time of the decedent's death, title of the surviving spouse may be perfected by an order of the probate court or by execution of an instrument by the personal representative or the beneficiaries of the decedent with the approval of the probate court. The probate court in which the decedent's estate is being administered has no duty to discover whether property held by the decedent is property to which ss. 732.216-732.228 apply. The personal representative has no duty to discover whether property held by the decedent is property to which ss. 732.216-732.228 apply unless a written demand is made by the surviving spouse or the spouse's successor in interest within 3 months after service of a copy of the notice of administration on the surviving spouse or the spouse's successor in interest.

History.—s. 10, ch. 92-200; s. 957, ch. 97-102; s. 35, ch. 2001-226.

732.224 Creditor's rights.—Sections 732.216-732.228 do not affect rights of creditors with respect to property to which ss. 732.216-732.228 apply.

History.—s. 11, ch. 92-200.

732.225 Acts of married persons.—Sections 732.216-732.228 do not prevent married persons from severing or altering their interests in property to which these sections apply. The reinvestment of any property to which these sections apply in real property located in this state which is or becomes homestead property creates a conclusive presumption that the spouses have agreed to terminate the community property attribute of the property reinvested.

History.—s. 12, ch. 92-200.

732.226 Limitations on testamentary disposition.—Sections 732.216-732.228 do not authorize a person to dispose of property by will if it is held under limitations imposed by law preventing testamentary disposition by that person.

History.—s. 13, ch. 92-200.

732.227 Homestead defined.—For purposes of ss. 732.216-732.228, the term "homestead" refers only to property the descent and devise of which is restricted by s. 4(c), Art. X of the State Constitution.

History.—s. 14, ch. 92-200.

732.228 Uniformity of application and construction.—Sections 732.216-732.228 are to be so applied and construed as to effectuate their general purpose to make uniform the law with respect to the subject of these sections among those states which enact them.

History.—s. 15, ch. 92-200.

Florida Probate Code

732.301 Pretermitted spouse.—When a person marries after making a will and the spouse survives the testator, the surviving spouse shall receive a share in the estate of the testator equal in value to that which the surviving spouse would have received if the testator had died intestate, unless:

(1) Provision has been made for, or waived by, the spouse by prenuptial or postnuptial agreement;

(2) The spouse is provided for in the will; or

(3) The will discloses an intention not to make provision for the spouse.
The share of the estate that is assigned to the pretermitted spouse shall be obtained in accordance with s. 733.805.

History.—s. 1, ch. 74-106; s. 16, ch. 75-220; s. 9, ch. 77-87.

Note.—Created from former s. 731.10.

732.302 Pretermitted children.—When a testator omits to provide by will for any of his or her children born or adopted after making the will and the child has not received a part of the testator's property equivalent to a child's part by way of advancement, the child shall receive a share of the estate equal in value to that which the child would have received if the testator had died intestate, unless:

(1) It appears from the will that the omission was intentional; or

(2) The testator had one or more children when the will was executed and devised substantially all the estate to the other parent of the pretermitted child and that other parent survived the testator and is entitled to take under the will.
The share of the estate that is assigned to the pretermitted child shall be obtained in accordance with s. 733.805.

History.—s. 1, ch. 74-106; s. 16, ch. 75-220; s. 958, ch. 97-102; s 36, ch. 2001-226.

Note.—Created from former s. 731.11.

732.401 Descent of homestead.—

(1) If not devised as authorized by law and the constitution, the homestead shall descend in the same manner as other intestate property; but if the decedent is survived by a spouse and one or more descendants, the surviving spouse shall take a life estate in the homestead, with a vested remainder to the descendants in being at the time of the decedent's death per stirpes.

(2) In lieu of a life estate under subsection (1), the surviving spouse may elect to take an undivided one-half interest in the homestead as a tenant in common, with

the remaining undivided one-half interest vesting in the decedent's descendants in being at the time of the decedent's death, per stirpes.

      (a)   The right of election may be exercised:

          1.   By the surviving spouse; or

          2.   With the approval of a court having jurisdiction of the real property, by an attorney in fact or guardian of the property of the surviving spouse. Before approving the election, the court shall determine that the election is in the best interests of the surviving spouse during the spouse's probable lifetime.

      (b)   The election must be made within 6 months after the decedent's death and during the surviving spouse's lifetime. The time for making the election may not be extended except as provided in paragraph (c).

      (c)   A petition by an attorney in fact or by a guardian of the property of the surviving spouse for approval to make the election must be filed within 6 months after the decedent's death and during the surviving spouse's lifetime. If the petition is timely filed, the time for making the election shall be extended for at least 30 days after the rendition of the order allowing the election.

      (d)   Once made, the election is irrevocable.

      (e)   The election shall be made by filing a notice of election containing the legal description of the homestead property for recording in the official record books of the county or counties where the homestead property is located. The notice must be in substantially the following form:

ELECTION OF SURVIVING SPOUSE TO TAKE A ONE-HALF INTEREST OF DECEDENT'S INTEREST IN HOMESTEAD PROPERTY

STATE OF

COUNTY OF

1.   The decedent,   , died on   . On the date of the decedent's death, The decedent was married to   , who survived the decedent.

2.   At the time of the decedent's death, the decedent owned an interest in real property that the affiant believes to be homestead property described in s. 4, Article X of the State Constitution, which real property being in   County, Florida, and described as:

      (description of homestead property)   .

3.   Affiant elects to take one-half of decedent's interest in the homestead as a tenant in common in lieu of a life estate.

4.   If affiant is not the surviving spouse, affiant is the surviving spouse's attorney in fact or guardian of the property, and an order has been rendered by a court having jurisdiction of the real property authorizing the undersigned to make this election.

Florida Probate Code

(Affiant)

Sworn to (or affirmed) and subscribed before me this   day of   (month) ,
            (year)   , by   (affiant)

(Signature of Notary Public-State of Florida)

(Print, Type, or Stamp Commissioned Name of Notary Public)

Personally Known OR Produced Identification

(Type of Identification Produced)

(3)   Unless and until an election is made under subsection (2), expenses relating to the ownership of the homestead shall be allocated between the surviving spouse, as life tenant, and the decedent's descendants, as remaindermen, in accordance with chapter 738. If an election is made, expenses relating to the ownership of the homestead shall be allocated between the surviving spouse and the descendants as tenants in common in proportion to their respective shares, effective as of the date the election is filed for recording.

(4)   If the surviving spouse's life estate created in subsection (1) is disclaimed pursuant to chapter 739, the interests of the decedent's descendants may not be divested.

(5)   This section does not apply to property that the decedent owned in tenancy by the entireties or in joint tenancy with rights of survivorship.

History.—s. 1, ch. 74-106; s. 17, ch. 75-220; s. 37, ch. 2001-226; s. 12, ch. 2007-74; s. 7, ch. 2010-132; s. 3, ch. 2012-109.

Note.—Created from former s. 731.27.

732.4015 Devise of homestead.—

(1)   As provided by the Florida Constitution, the homestead shall not be subject to devise if the owner is survived by a spouse or a minor child or minor children, except that the homestead may be devised to the owner's spouse if there is no minor child or minor children.

(2)   For the purposes of subsection (1), the term:

(a)   "Owner" includes the grantor of a trust described in s. 733.707(3) that is evidenced by a written instrument which is in existence at the time of the grantor's death as if the interest held in trust was owned by the grantor.

(b)   "Devise" includes a disposition by trust of that portion of the trust estate which, if titled in the name of the grantor of the trust, would be the grantor's homestead.

(3)   If an interest in homestead has been devised to the surviving spouse as authorized by law and the constitution, and the surviving spouse's interest is disclaimed, the

disclaimed interest shall pass in accordance with chapter 739.

History.—s. 1, ch. 74-106; ss. 18, 30, ch. 75-220; s. 16, ch. 92-200; s. 959, ch. 97-102; s. 38, ch. 2001-226; s. 13, ch. 2007-74; s. 8, ch. 2010-132.

732.4017 Inter vivos transfer of homestead property.—

(1)   If the owner of homestead property transfers an interest in that property, including a transfer in trust, with or without consideration, to one or more persons during the owner's lifetime, the transfer is not a devise for purposes of s. 731.201(10) or s. 732.4015, and the interest transferred does not descend as provided in s. 732.401 if the transferor fails to retain a power, held in any capacity, acting alone or in conjunction with any other person, to revoke or revest that interest in the transferor.

(2)   As used in this section, the term "transfer in trust" refers to a trust under which the transferor of the homestead property, alone or in conjunction with another person, does not possess a right of revocation as that term is defined in s. 733.707(3)(e). A power possessed by the transferor which is exercisable during the transferor's lifetime to alter the beneficial use and enjoyment of the interest within a class of beneficiaries identified only in the trust instrument is not a right of revocation if the power may not be exercised in favor of the transferor, the transferor's creditors, the transferor's estate, or the creditors of the transferor's estate or exercised to discharge the transferor's legal obligations. This subsection does not create an inference that a power not described in this subsection is a power to revoke or revest an interest in the transferor.

(3)   The transfer of an interest in homestead property described in subsection (1) may not be treated as a devise of that interest even if:

(a)   The transferor retains a separate legal or equitable interest in the homestead property, directly or indirectly through a trust or other arrangement such as a term of years, life estate, reversion, possibility of reverter, or fractional fee interest;

(b)   The interest transferred does not become a possessory interest until a date certain or upon a specified event, the occurrence or nonoccurrence of which does not constitute a power held by the transferor to revoke or revest the interest in the transferor, including, without limitation, the death of the transferor; or

(c)   The interest transferred is subject to divestment, expiration, or lapse upon a date certain or upon a specified event, the occurrence or nonoccurrence of which does not constitute a power held by the transferor to revoke or revest the interest in the transferor, including, without limitation, survival of the transferor.

(4)   It is the intent of the Legislature that this section clarify existing law.

History.—s. 9, ch. 2010-132.

732.402   Exempt property.—

(1)   If a decedent was domiciled in this state at the time of death, the surviving spouse, or, if there is no surviving spouse, the children of the decedent shall have the right to a share of the estate of the decedent as provided in this section, to be designated "exempt property."

(2)   Exempt property shall consist of:

(a)   Household furniture, furnishings, and appliances in the decedent's usual place of abode up to a net value of $20,000 as of the date of death.

(b)   Two motor vehicles as defined in s. 316.003(21), which do not, individually as to either such motor vehicle, have a gross vehicle weight in excess of 15,000 pounds, held in the decedent's name and regularly used by the decedent or members of the decedent's immediate family as their personal motor vehicles.

(c)   All qualified tuition programs authorized by s. 529 of the Internal Revenue Code of 1986, as amended, including, but not limited to, the Florida Prepaid College Trust Fund advance payment contracts under s. 1009.98 and the Florida Prepaid College Trust Fund participation agreements under s. 1009.981.

(d)   All benefits paid pursuant to s. 112.1915.

(3)   Exempt property shall be exempt from all claims against the estate except perfected security interests thereon.

(4)   Exempt property shall be in addition to protected homestead, statutory entitlements, and property passing under the decedent's will or by intestate succession.

(5)   Property specifically or demonstratively devised by the decedent's will to any devisee shall not be included in exempt property. However, persons to whom property has been specifically or demonstratively devised and who would otherwise be entitled to it as exempt property under this section may have the court determine the property to be exempt from claims, except for perfected security interests thereon, after complying with the provisions of subsection (6).

(6)   Persons entitled to exempt property shall be deemed to have waived their rights under this section unless a petition for determination of exempt property is filed by or on behalf of the persons entitled to the exempt property on or before the later of the date that is 4 months after the date of service of the notice of administration or the date that is 40 days after the date of termination of any proceeding involving the construction, admission to probate, or validity of the will or involving any other matter affecting any part of the estate subject to this section.

(7)   Property determined as exempt under this section shall be excluded from the value of the estate before residuary, intestate, or pretermitted or elective shares are determined.

History.—s. 1, ch. 74-106; s. 19, ch. 75-220; s. 10, ch. 77-87; s. 1, ch. 77-174; s. 1, ch. 81-238; s. 3, ch. 85-79; s. 67, ch. 87-226; s. 51, ch. 98-421; s. 3, ch. 99-220; s. 3, ch. 2001-180; s. 39, ch. 2001-226; s. 1036, ch. 2002-387; s. 5, ch. 2006-134; s. 5, ch. 2006-303; s. 8, ch. 2009-115.

Note.—Section 8, ch. 85-79, provides in pertinent part that with respect to s. 3, ch. 85-79, "the substantive rights of all persons which have vested prior to October 1, 1985, shall be determined as provided in s. 732.402, Florida Statutes, 1983."

Florida Probate Code

Note.—Created from former s. 734.08.

732.403 Family allowance.—In addition to protected homestead and statutory entitlements, if the decedent was domiciled in Florida at the time of death, the surviving spouse and the decedent's lineal heirs the decedent was supporting or was obligated to support are entitled to a reasonable allowance in money out of the estate for their maintenance during administration. The court may order this allowance to be paid as a lump sum or in periodic installments. The allowance shall not exceed a total of $18,000. It shall be paid to the surviving spouse, if living, for the use of the spouse and dependent lineal heirs. If the surviving spouse is not living, it shall be paid to the lineal heirs or to the persons having their care and custody. If any lineal heir is not living with the surviving spouse, the allowance may be made partly to the lineal heir or guardian or other person having the heir's care and custody and partly to the surviving spouse, as the needs of the dependent heir and the surviving spouse appear. The family allowance is not chargeable against any benefit or share otherwise passing to the surviving spouse or to the dependent lineal heirs, unless the will otherwise provides. The death of any person entitled to a family allowance terminates the right to that part of the allowance not paid. For purposes of this section, the term "lineal heir" or "lineal heirs" means lineal ascendants and lineal descendants of the decedent.

History.—s. 1, ch. 74-106; s. 19, ch. 75-220; s. 960, ch. 97-102; s. 40, ch. 2001-226.

Note.—Created from former s. 733.20.

PART V
WILLS

732.501 Who may make a will.—Any person who is of sound mind and who is either 18 or more years of age or an emancipated minor may make a will.

History.—s. 1, ch. 74-106; s. 113, ch. 75-220; s. 41, ch. 2001-226.

Note.—Created from former s. 731.04.

732.502 Execution of wills.—Every will must be in writing and executed as follows:

(1) (a) Testator's signature.—

1. The testator must sign the will at the end; or

2. The testator's name must be subscribed at the end of the will by some other person in the testator's presence and by the testator's direction.

(b) Witnesses.—The testator's:

1. Signing, or

2. Acknowledgment:

a. That he or she has previously signed the will, or

    b.   That another person has subscribed the
testator's name to it,
must be in the presence of at least two attesting witnesses.

    (c)   Witnesses' signatures.—The attesting witnesses must sign the
will in the presence of the testator and in the presence of each other.

    (2)   Any will, other than a holographic or nuncupative will, executed by a
nonresident of Florida, either before or after this law takes effect, is valid as a will in this
state if valid under the laws of the state or country where the will was executed. A will in
the testator's handwriting that has been executed in accordance with subsection (1) shall not
be considered a holographic will.

    (3)   Any will executed as a military testamentary instrument in accordance
with 10 U.S.C. s. 1044d, Chapter 53, by a person who is eligible for military legal
assistance is valid as a will in this state.

    (4)   No particular form of words is necessary to the validity of a will if it is
executed with the formalities required by law.

    (5)   A codicil shall be executed with the same formalities as a will.

History.—s. 1, ch. 74-106; s. 21, ch. 75-220; s. 11, ch. 77-87; s. 961, ch. 97-102; s. 42, ch.
2001-226; s. 5, ch. 2003-154.

Note.—Created from former s. 731.07.

732.503 Self-proof of will.—

    (1)   A will or codicil executed in conformity with s. 732.502 may be made
self-proved at the time of its execution or at any subsequent date by the acknowledgment of
it by the testator and the affidavits of the witnesses, made before an officer authorized to
administer oaths and evidenced by the officer's certificate attached to or following the will,
in substantially the following form:

STATE OF FLORIDA

COUNTY OF

I,   , declare to the officer taking my acknowledgment of this instrument,
and to the subscribing witnesses, that I signed this instrument as my will.

Testator

We,   and   , have been sworn by the officer signing below, and
declare to that officer on our oaths that the testator declared the instrument to be the
testator's will and signed it in our presence and that we each signed the instrument as a
witness in the presence of the testator and of each other.

Witness

Witness

Acknowledged and subscribed before me by the testator, (type or print testator's name), who is personally known to me or who has produced (state type of identification—see s. 117.05(5)(b)2.) as identification, and sworn to and subscribed before me by the witnesses, (type or print name of first witness) who is personally known to me or who has produced (state type of identification—see s. 117.05(5)(b)2.) as identification and (type or print name of second witness) who is personally known to me or who has produced (state type of identification—see s. 117.05(5)(b)2.) as identification, and subscribed by me in the presence of the testator and the subscribing witnesses, all on (date).

(Signature of Officer)

(Print, type, or stamp commissioned name and affix official seal)

(2)   A will or codicil made self-proved under former law, or executed in another state and made self-proved under the laws of that state, shall be considered as self-proved under this section.

History.—s. 1, ch. 74-106; s. 21, ch. 75-220; s. 12, ch. 77-87; s. 8, ch. 93-62; s. 962, ch. 97-102; s. 18, ch. 98-246; s. 43, ch. 2001-226.

Note.—Created from former s. 731.071.

732.504 Who may witness.—

(1)   Any person competent to be a witness may act as a witness to a will.

(2)   A will or codicil, or any part of either, is not invalid because the will or codicil is signed by an interested witness.

History.—s. 1, ch. 74-106; s. 22, ch. 75-220; s. 1, ch. 77-174; s. 268, ch. 79-400.

732.505 Revocation by writing.—A will or codicil, or any part of either, is revoked:

(1)   By a subsequent inconsistent will or codicil, even though the subsequent inconsistent will or codicil does not expressly revoke all previous wills or codicils, but the revocation extends only so far as the inconsistency.

(2)   By a subsequent will, codicil, or other writing executed with the same formalities required for the execution of wills declaring the revocation.

History.—s. 1, ch. 74-106; s. 23, ch. 75-220; s. 13, ch. 77-87; s. 269, ch. 79-400; s. 44, ch. 2001-226.

Note.—Created from former ss. 731.12, 731.13.

732.506 Revocation by act.—A will or codicil is revoked by the testator, or some other person in the testator's presence and at the testator's direction, by burning, tearing, canceling, defacing, obliterating, or destroying it with the intent, and for the purpose, of revocation.

History.—s. 1, ch. 74-106; s. 23, ch. 75-220; s. 963, ch. 97-102.

Note.—Created from former s. 731.14.

732.507 Effect of subsequent marriage, birth, adoption, or dissolution of marriage.—

(1) Neither subsequent marriage, birth, nor adoption of descendants shall revoke the prior will of any person, but the pretermitted child or spouse shall inherit as set forth in ss. 732.301 and 732.302, regardless of the prior will.

(2) Any provision of a will executed by a married person that affects the spouse of that person shall become void upon the divorce of that person or upon the dissolution or annulment of the marriage. After the dissolution, divorce, or annulment, the will shall be administered and construed as if the former spouse had died at the time of the dissolution, divorce, or annulment of the marriage, unless the will or the dissolution or divorce judgment expressly provides otherwise.

History.—s. 1, ch. 74-106; s. 113, ch. 75-220; s. 3, ch. 90-23; s. 45, ch. 2001-226; s. 14, ch. 2007-74.

Note.—Created from former ss. 731.10, 731.101, 731.11.

732.508 Revival by revocation.—

(1) The revocation by the testator of a will that revokes a former will shall not revive the former will, even though the former will is in existence at the date of the revocation of the subsequent will.

(2) The revocation of a codicil to a will does not revoke the will, and, in the absence of evidence to the contrary, it shall be presumed that in revoking the codicil the testator intended to reinstate the provisions of a will or codicil that were changed or revoked by the revoked codicil, as if the revoked codicil had never been executed.

History.—s. 1, ch. 74-106; s. 25, ch. 75-220.

Note.—Created from former s. 731.15.

732.509 Revocation of codicil.—The revocation of a will revokes all codicils to that will.

History.—s. 1, ch. 74-106; s. 113, ch. 75-220.

Note.—Created from former s. 731.16.

732.5105 Republication of wills by codicil.—The execution of a codicil referring to a previous will has the effect of republishing the will as modified by the codicil.

History.—s. 1, ch. 74-106; s. 113, ch. 75-220.

Note.—Created from former s. 731.17.

732.511 Republication of wills by reexecution.—If a will has been revoked or if it is invalid for any other reason, it may be republished and made valid by its reexecution or the execution of a codicil republishing it with the formalities required by this law for the execution of wills.

History.—s. 1, ch. 74-106; s. 113, ch. 75-220.

Note.—Created from former s. 731.18.

732.512 Incorporation by reference.—

(1)   A writing in existence when a will is executed may be incorporated by reference if the language of the will manifests this intent and describes the writing sufficiently to permit its identification.

(2)   A will may dispose of property by reference to acts and events which have significance apart from their effect upon the dispositions made by the will, whether they occur before or after the execution of the will or before or after the testator's death. The execution or revocation of a will or trust by another person is such an event.

History.—s. 1, ch. 74-106; s. 27, ch. 75-220.

732.513 Devises to trustee.—

(1)   A valid devise may be made to the trustee of a trust that is evidenced by a written instrument in existence at the time of making the will, or by a written instrument subscribed concurrently with making of the will, if the written instrument is identified in the will.

(2)   The devise shall not be invalid for any or all of the following reasons:

(a)   Because the trust is amendable or revocable, or both, by any person.

(b)   Because the trust has been amended or revoked in part after execution of the will or a codicil to it.

(c)   Because the only res of the trust is the possible expectancy of receiving, as a named beneficiary, a devise under a will or death benefits as described in s. 733.808, and even though the testator or other person has reserved any or all rights of ownership in the death benefit policy, contract, or plan, including the right to change the beneficiary.

(d)   Because of any of the provisions of s. 689.075.

(3)   The devise shall dispose of property under the terms of the instrument that created the trust as previously or subsequently amended.

(4)   An entire revocation of the trust by an instrument in writing before the testator's death shall invalidate the devise or bequest.

Florida Probate Code

(5)   Unless the will provides otherwise, the property devised shall not be held under a testamentary trust of the testator but shall become a part of the principal of the trust to which it is devised.

History.—s. 1, ch. 74-106; s. 3, ch. 75-74; s. 113, ch. 75-220; s. 2, ch. 88-340; s. 46, ch. 2001-226; s. 32, ch. 2006-217.

Note.—Created from former s. 736.17.

732.514 Vesting of devises.—The death of the testator is the event that vests the right to devises unless the testator in the will has provided that some other event must happen before a devise vests.

History.—s. 1, ch. 74-106; ss. 28, 113, ch. 75-220; s. 964, ch. 97-102; s. 47, ch. 2001-226.

Note.—Created from former ss. 731.21 and 733.102.

732.515 Separate writing identifying devises of tangible property.—A written statement or list referred to in the decedent's will shall dispose of items of tangible personal property, other than property used in trade or business, not otherwise specifically disposed of by the will. To be admissible under this section as evidence of the intended disposition, the writing must be signed by the testator and must describe the items and the devisees with reasonable certainty. The writing may be prepared before or after the execution of the will. It may be altered by the testator after its preparation. It may be a writing that has no significance apart from its effect upon the dispositions made by the will. If more than one otherwise effective writing exists, then, to the extent of any conflict among the writings, the provisions of the most recent writing revoke the inconsistent provisions of each prior writing.

History.—s. 1, ch. 74-106; s. 29, ch. 75-220; s. 48, ch. 2001-226.

732.5165 Effect of fraud, duress, mistake, and undue influence.—A will is void if the execution is procured by fraud, duress, mistake, or undue influence. Any part of the will is void if so procured, but the remainder of the will not so procured shall be valid if it is not invalid for other reasons. If the revocation of a will, or any part thereof, is procured by fraud, duress, mistake, or undue influence, such revocation is void.

History.—s. 31, ch. 75-220; s. 6, ch. 2011-183.

732.517 Penalty clause for contest.—A provision in a will purporting to penalize any interested person for contesting the will or instituting other proceedings relating to the estate is unenforceable.

History.—s. 1, ch. 74-106; s. 113, ch. 75-220.

732.518 Will contests.—An action to contest the validity of all or part of a will or the revocation of all or part of a will may not be commenced before the death of the testator.

History.—s. 17, ch. 92-200; s. 7, ch. 2011-183.

Florida Probate Code

732.6005 Rules of construction and intention.—

(1)   The intention of the testator as expressed in the will controls the legal effect of the testator's dispositions. The rules of construction expressed in this part shall apply unless a contrary intention is indicated by the will.

(2)   Subject to the foregoing, a will is construed to pass all property which the testator owns at death, including property acquired after the execution of the will.

History.—s. 1, ch. 74-106; ss. 33, 35, ch. 75-220; s. 965, ch. 97-102; s. 49, ch. 2001-226.

Note.—Created from former ss. 732.41 and 732.602.

732.601   Simultaneous Death Law.—Unless a contrary intention appears in the governing instrument:

(1)   When title to property or its devolution depends on priority of death and there is insufficient evidence that the persons have died otherwise than simultaneously, the property of each person shall be disposed of as if that person survived.

(2)   When two or more beneficiaries are designated to take successively by reason of survivorship under another person's disposition of property and there is insufficient evidence that the beneficiaries died otherwise than simultaneously, the property thus disposed of shall be divided into as many equal parts as there are successive beneficiaries and the parts shall be distributed to those who would have taken if each designated beneficiary had survived.

(3)   When there is insufficient evidence that two joint tenants or tenants by the entirety died otherwise than simultaneously, the property so held shall be distributed one-half as if one had survived and one-half as if the other had survived. If there are more than two joint tenants and all of them so died, the property thus distributed shall be in the proportion that one bears to the number of joint tenants.

(4)   When the insured and the beneficiary in a policy of life or accident insurance have died and there is insufficient evidence that they died otherwise than simultaneously, the proceeds of the policy shall be distributed as if the insured had survived the beneficiary.

History.—s. 1, ch. 74-106; s. 34, ch. 75-220; s. 966, ch. 97-102; s. 50, ch. 2001-226.

Note.—Created from former s. 736.05.

732.603   Antilapse; deceased devisee; class gifts.—

(1)   Unless a contrary intent appears in the will, if a devisee who is a grandparent, or a descendant of a grandparent, of the testator:

(a)   Is dead at the time of the execution of the will;

(b)   Fails to survive the testator; or

(c)   Is required by the will or by operation of law to be treated as having predeceased the testator,

a substitute gift is created in the devisee's surviving descendants who take per stirpes the property to which the devisee would have been entitled had the devisee survived the testator.

(2)   When a power of appointment is exercised by will, unless a contrary intent appears in the document creating the power of appointment or in the testator's will, if an appointee who is a grandparent, or a descendant of a grandparent, of the donor of the power:

(a)   Is dead at the time of the execution of the will or the creation of the power;

(b)   Fails to survive the testator; or

(c)   Is required by the will, the document creating the power, or by operation of law to be treated as having predeceased the testator,

a substitute gift is created in the appointee's surviving descendants who take per stirpes the property to which the appointee would have been entitled had the appointee survived the testator. Unless the language creating a power of appointment expressly excludes the substitution of the descendants of an object of a power for the object, a surviving descendant of a deceased object of a power of appointment may be substituted for the object whether or not the descendant is an object of the power.

(3)   In the application of this section:

(a)   Words of survivorship in a devise or appointment to an individual, such as "if he survives me," or to "my surviving children," are a sufficient indication of an intent contrary to the application of subsections (1) and (2). Words of survivorship used by the donor of the power in a power to appoint to an individual, such as the term "if he survives the donee," or in a power to appoint to the donee's "then surviving children," are a sufficient indication of an intent contrary to the application of subsection (2).

(b)   The term:

1.   "Appointment" includes an alternative appointment and an appointment in the form of a class gift.

2.   "Appointee" includes:

a.   A class member if the appointment is in the form of a class gift.

b.   An individual or class member who was deceased at the time the testator executed his or her will as well as an individual or class member who was then living but who failed to survive the testator.

3.   "Devise" also includes an alternative devise and a devise in the form of a class gift.

4.   "Devisee" also includes:

a.   A class member if the devise is in the form of a class gift.

b.   An individual or class member who was deceased at the time the testator executed his or her will as well as an individual or class member who was then living but who failed to survive the testator.

(4)   This section applies only to outright devises and appointments. Devises and appointments in trust, including to a testamentary trust, are subject to s. 736.1106.

History.—s. 1, ch. 74-106; s. 36, ch. 75-220; s. 967, ch. 97-102; s. 51, ch. 2001-226; s. 6, ch. 2003-154; s. 33, ch. 2006-217.

Note.—Created from former s. 731.20.

732.604 Failure of testamentary provision.—

(1)   Except as provided in s. 732.603, if a devise other than a residuary devise fails for any reason, it becomes a part of the residue.

(2)   Except as provided in s. 732.603, if the residue is devised to two or more persons, the share of a residuary devisee that fails for any reason passes to the other residuary devisee, or to the other residuary devisees in proportion to the interests of each in the remaining part of the residue.

History.—s. 1, ch. 74-106; s. 113, ch. 75-220; s. 968, ch. 97-102; s. 52, ch. 2001-226; s. 29, ch. 2003-154; s. 34, ch. 2006-217.

732.605 Change in securities; accessions; nonademption.—

(1)   If the testator intended a specific devise of certain securities rather than their equivalent value, the specific devisee is entitled only to:

(a)   As much of the devised securities as is a part of the estate at the time of the testator's death.

(b)   Any additional or other securities of the same entity owned by the testator because of action initiated by the entity, excluding any acquired by exercise of purchase options.

(c)   Securities of another entity owned by the testator as a result of a merger, consolidation, reorganization, or other similar action initiated by the entity.

(d)   Securities of the same entity acquired as a result of a plan of reinvestment.

Florida Probate Code

(2)   Distributions before death with respect to a specifically devised security, whether in cash or otherwise, which are not provided for in subsection (1) are not part of the specific devise.

History.—s. 1, ch. 74-106; s. 113, ch. 75-220; s. 53, ch. 2001-226.

732.606 Nonademption of specific devises in certain cases; sale by guardian of the property; unpaid proceeds of sale, condemnation, or insurance.—

(1)   If specifically devised property is sold by a guardian of the property or if a condemnation award or insurance proceeds are paid to a guardian of the property, the specific devisee has the right to a general pecuniary devise equal to the net sale price, the condemnation award, or the insurance proceeds. This subsection does not apply if, subsequent to the sale, condemnation, or casualty, it is adjudicated that the disability of the testator has ceased and the testator survives the adjudication by 1 year. The right of the specific devisee under this subsection is reduced by any right described in subsection (2).

(2)   A specific devisee has the right to the remaining specifically devised property and:

(a)   Any balance of the purchase price owing from a purchaser to the testator at death because of sale of the property plus any security interest.

(b)   Any amount of a condemnation award for the taking of the property unpaid at death.

(c)   Any proceeds unpaid at death on fire or casualty insurance on the property.

(d)   Property owned by the testator at death as a result of foreclosure, or obtained instead of foreclosure, of the security for the specifically devised obligation.

History.—s. 1, ch. 74-106; s. 38, ch. 75-220; s. 969, ch. 97-102; s. 54, ch. 2001-226.

732.607 Exercise of power of appointment.—A general residuary clause in a will, or a will making general disposition of all the testator's property, does not exercise a power of appointment held by the testator unless specific reference is made to the power or there is some other indication of intent to include the property subject to the power.

History.—s. 1, ch. 74-106; s. 38, ch. 75-220.

732.608 Construction of terms.—The laws used to determine paternity and relationships for the purposes of intestate succession apply when determining whether class gift terminology and terms of relationship include adopted persons and persons born out of wedlock.

History.—s. 1, ch. 74-106; s. 38, ch. 75-220; s. 10, ch. 2010-132.

732.609 Ademption by satisfaction.—Property that a testator gave to a person in the testator's lifetime is treated as a satisfaction of a devise to that person, in whole or in part, only if the will provides for deduction of the lifetime gift, the testator declares in a contemporaneous writing that the gift is to be deducted from the devise or is in satisfaction of the devise, or the devisee acknowledges in writing that the gift is in satisfaction. For purposes of part satisfaction, property given during the testator's lifetime is valued at the time the devisee came into possession or enjoyment of the property or at the time of the death of the testator, whichever occurs first.

History.—s. 1, ch. 74-106; s. 38, ch. 75-220.

732.611 Devises to multigeneration classes to be per stirpes.—Unless the will provides otherwise, all devises to descendants, issue, and other multigeneration classes shall be per stirpes.

History.—s. 1, ch. 74-106; s. 38, ch. 75-220; s. 35, ch. 2006-217.

732.615 Reformation to correct mistakes.—Upon application of any interested person, the court may reform the terms of a will, even if unambiguous, to conform the terms to the testator's intent if it is proved by clear and convincing evidence that both the accomplishment of the testator's intent and the terms of the will were affected by a mistake of fact or law, whether in expression or inducement. In determining the testator's original intent, the court may consider evidence relevant to the testator's intent even though the evidence contradicts an apparent plain meaning of the will.

History.—s. 3, ch. 2011-183.

732.616 Modification to achieve testator's tax objectives.—Upon application of any interested person, to achieve the testator's tax objectives the court may modify the terms of a will in a manner that is not contrary to the testator's probable intent. The court may provide that the modification has retroactive effect.

History.—s. 4, ch. 2011-183.

PART VII
CONTRACTUAL ARRANGEMENTS RELATING TO DEATH

732.701 Agreements concerning succession.—

(1)   No agreement to make a will, to give a devise, not to revoke a will, not to revoke a devise, not to make a will, or not to make a devise shall be binding or enforceable unless the agreement is in writing and signed by the agreeing party in the presence of two attesting witnesses. Such an agreement executed by a nonresident of Florida, either before or after this law takes effect, is valid in this state if valid when executed under the laws of the state or country where the agreement was executed, whether or not the agreeing party is a Florida resident at the time of death.

(2)   The execution of a joint will or mutual wills neither creates a presumption of a contract to make a will nor creates a presumption of a contract not to revoke the will or wills.

History.—s. 1, ch. 74-106; s. 39, ch. 75-220; s. 55, ch. 2001-226.

Note.—Created from former s. 731.051.

Florida Probate Code

732.702 Waiver of spousal rights.—

(1)   The rights of a surviving spouse to an elective share, intestate share, pretermitted share, homestead, exempt property, family allowance, and preference in appointment as personal representative of an intestate estate or any of those rights, may be waived, wholly or partly, before or after marriage, by a written contract, agreement, or waiver, signed by the waiving party in the presence of two subscribing witnesses. The requirement of witnesses shall be applicable only to contracts, agreements, or waivers signed by Florida residents after the effective date of this law. Any contract, agreement, or waiver executed by a nonresident of Florida, either before or after this law takes effect, is valid in this state if valid when executed under the laws of the state or country where it was executed, whether or not he or she is a Florida resident at the time of death. Unless the waiver provides to the contrary, a waiver of "all rights," or equivalent language, in the property or estate of a present or prospective spouse, or a complete property settlement entered into after, or in anticipation of, separation, dissolution of marriage, or divorce, is a waiver of all rights to elective share, intestate share, pretermitted share, homestead, exempt property, family allowance, and preference in appointment as personal representative of an intestate estate, by the waiving party in the property of the other and a renunciation by the waiving party of all benefits that would otherwise pass to the waiving party from the other by intestate succession or by the provisions of any will executed before the written contract, agreement, or waiver.

(2)   Each spouse shall make a fair disclosure to the other of that spouse's estate if the agreement, contract, or waiver is executed after marriage. No disclosure shall be required for an agreement, contract, or waiver executed before marriage.

(3)   No consideration other than the execution of the agreement, contract, or waiver shall be necessary to its validity, whether executed before or after marriage.

History.—s. 1, ch. 74-106; s. 39, ch. 75-220; s. 14, ch. 77-87; s. 56, ch. 2001-226.

732.703 Effect of divorce, dissolution, or invalidity of marriage on disposition of certain assets at death.—

(1)   As used in this section, unless the context requires otherwise, the term:

(a)   "Asset," when not modified by other words or phrases, means an asset described in subsection (3), except as provided in paragraph (4)(j).

(b)   "Beneficiary" means any person designated in a governing instrument to receive an interest in an asset upon the death of the decedent.

(c)   "Death certificate" means a certified copy of a death certificate issued by an official or agency for the place where the decedent's death occurred.

(d)   "Employee benefit plan" means any funded or unfunded plan, program, or fund established by an employer to provide an employee's beneficiaries with benefits that may be payable on the employee's death.

(e)   "Governing instrument" means any writing or contract governing the disposition of all or any part of an asset upon the death of the decedent.

(f)   "Payor" means any person obligated to make payment of the decedent's interest in an asset upon the death of the decedent, and any other person who is in control or possession of an asset.

(g)   "Primary beneficiary" means a beneficiary designated under the governing instrument to receive an interest in an asset upon the death of the decedent who is not a secondary beneficiary. A person who receives an interest in the asset upon the death of the decedent due to the death of another beneficiary prior to the decedent's death is also a primary beneficiary.

(h)   "Secondary beneficiary" means a beneficiary designated under the governing instrument who will receive an interest in an asset if the designation of the primary beneficiary is revoked or otherwise cannot be given effect.

(2)   A designation made by or on behalf of the decedent providing for the payment or transfer at death of an interest in an asset to or for the benefit of the decedent's former spouse is void as of the time the decedent's marriage was judicially dissolved or declared invalid by court order prior to the decedent's death, if the designation was made prior to the dissolution or court order. The decedent's interest in the asset shall pass as if the decedent's former spouse predeceased the decedent. An individual retirement account described in s. 408 or s. 408A of the Internal Revenue Code of 1986, or an employee benefit plan, may not be treated as a trust for purposes of this section.

(3)   Subsection (2) applies to the following assets in which a resident of this state has an interest at the time of the resident's death:

(a)   A life insurance policy, qualified annuity, or other similar tax-deferred contract held within an employee benefit plan.

(b)   An employee benefit plan.

(c)   An individual retirement account described in s. 408 or s. 408A of the Internal Revenue Code of 1986, including an individual retirement annuity described in s. 408(b) of the Internal Revenue Code of 1986.

(d)   A payable-on-death account.

(e)   A security or other account registered in a transfer-on-death form.

(f)   A life insurance policy, annuity, or other similar contract that is not held within an employee benefit plan or a tax-qualified retirement account.

(4)   Subsection (2) does not apply:

(a)   To the extent that controlling federal law provides otherwise;

(b)   If the governing instrument is signed by the decedent, or on behalf of the decedent, after the order of dissolution or order declaring the marriage invalid and such governing instrument expressly provides that benefits will be payable to the decedent's former spouse;

(c)   To the extent a will or trust governs the disposition of the assets and s. 732.507(2) or s. 736.1105 applies;

(d)   If the order of dissolution or order declaring the marriage invalid requires that the decedent acquire or maintain the asset for the benefit of a former spouse or children of the marriage, payable upon the death of the decedent either outright or in trust, only if other assets of the decedent fulfilling such a requirement for the benefit of the former spouse or children of the marriage do not exist upon the death of the decedent;

(e)   If, under the terms of the order of dissolution or order declaring the marriage invalid, the decedent could not have unilaterally terminated or modified the ownership of the asset, or its disposition upon the death of the decedent;

(f)   If the designation of the decedent's former spouse as a beneficiary is irrevocable under applicable law;

(g)   If the governing instrument is governed by the laws of a state other than this state;

(h)   To an asset held in two or more names as to which the death of one coowner vests ownership of the asset in the surviving coowner or coowners;

(i)   If the decedent remarries the person whose interest would otherwise have been revoked under this section and the decedent and that person are married to one another at the time of the decedent's death; or

(j)   To state-administered retirement plans under chapter 121.

(5)   In the case of an asset described in paragraph (3)(a), paragraph (3)(b), or paragraph (3)(c), unless payment or transfer would violate a court order directed to, and served as required by law on, the payor:

(a)   If the governing instrument does not explicitly specify the relationship of the beneficiary to the decedent or if the governing instrument explicitly provides that the beneficiary is not the decedent's spouse, the payor is not liable for making any payment on account of, or transferring any interest in, the asset to the beneficiary.

(b)   As to any portion of the asset required by the governing instrument to be paid after the decedent's death to a primary beneficiary explicitly designated in the governing instrument as the decedent's spouse:

1.   If the death certificate states that the decedent was married at the time of his or her death to that spouse, the payor is not liable for making a payment on account of, or for transferring an interest in, that portion of the asset to such primary beneficiary.

2.   If the death certificate states that the decedent was not married at the time of his or her death, or if the death certificate states that the decedent was married to a person other than the spouse designated as the primary beneficiary at the time of his or her death, the payor is not liable for making a payment on account of, or for transferring an interest in, that portion of the asset to a secondary beneficiary under the governing instrument.

           3.   If the death certificate is silent as to the decedent's marital status at the time of his or her death, the payor is not liable for making a payment on account of, or for transferring an interest in, that portion of the asset to the primary beneficiary upon delivery to the payor of an affidavit validly executed by the primary beneficiary in substantially the following form:

STATE OF

COUNTY OF

Before me, the undersigned authority, personally appeared   (type   or   print Affiant's name)   ("Affiant"), who swore or affirmed that:

1.   (Type or print name of Decedent)   ("Decedent")   died   on   (type or print the date of the Decedent's death)   .

2.   Affiant is a "primary beneficiary" as that term is defined in Section 732.703, Florida Statutes. Affiant and Decedent were married on   (type or print the date of marriage), and were legally married to one another on the date of the Decedent's death.

    (Affiant)

Sworn to or affirmed before me by the affiant who is personally known to me or who has produced (state type of identification)   as identification this   day of   (month)   ,....(year)....

    (Signature of Officer)

    (Print, Type, or Stamp Commissioned name of Notary Public)

           4.   If the death certificate is silent as to the decedent's marital status at the time of his or her death, the payor is not liable for making a payment on account of, or for transferring an interest in, that portion of the asset to the secondary beneficiary upon delivery to the payor of an affidavit validly executed by the secondary beneficiary affidavit in substantially the following form:

STATE OF

COUNTY OF

Before me, the undersigned authority, personally appeared (type or print Affiant's name) ("Affiant"), who swore or affirmed that:

1.   (Type or print name of Decedent)   ("Decedent")   died   on   (type or print the date of the Decedent's death)   .

2.   Affiant is a "secondary beneficiary" as that term is defined in Section 732.703, Florida Statutes. On the date of the Decedent's death, the Decedent was not legally married to the spouse designated as the "primary beneficiary" as that term is defined in Section 732.703, Florida Statutes.

Sworn to or affirmed before me by the affiant who is personally known to me or who has

produced (state type of identification)   as identification this   day of   (month) ,
(year)   .

(Signature of Officer)

(Print, Type, or Stamp Commissioned name of Notary Public)

(6)   In the case of an asset described in paragraph (3)(d), paragraph (3)(e), or paragraph (3)(f), the payor is not liable for making any payment on account of, or transferring any interest in, the asset to any beneficiary.

(7)   Subsections (5) and (6) apply notwithstanding the payor's knowledge that the person to whom the asset is transferred is different from the person who would own the interest pursuant to subsection (2).

(8)   This section does not affect the ownership of an interest in an asset as between the former spouse and any other person entitled to such interest by operation of this section, the rights of any purchaser for value of any such interest, the rights of any creditor of the former spouse or any other person entitled to such interest, or the rights and duties of any insurance company, financial institution, trustee, administrator, or other third party.

(9)   This section applies to all designations made by or on behalf of decedents dying on or after July 1, 2012, regardless of when the designation was made.

History.—s. 1, ch. 2012-148; s. 6, ch. 2013-172.

PART VIII
GENERAL PROVISIONS

732.802   Killer not entitled to receive property or other benefits by reason of victim's death.—

(1)   A surviving person who unlawfully and intentionally kills or participates in procuring the death of the decedent is not entitled to any benefits under the will or under the Florida Probate Code, and the estate of the decedent passes as if the killer had predeceased the decedent. Property appointed by the will of the decedent to or for the benefit of the killer passes as if the killer had predeceased the decedent.

(2)   Any joint tenant who unlawfully and intentionally kills another joint tenant thereby effects a severance of the interest of the decedent so that the share of the decedent passes as the decedent's property and the killer has no rights by survivorship. This provision applies to joint tenancies with right of survivorship and tenancies by the entirety in real and personal property; joint and multiple-party accounts in banks, savings and loan associations, credit unions, and other institutions; and any other form of coownership with survivorship incidents.

(3)   A named beneficiary of a bond, life insurance policy, or other contractual arrangement who unlawfully and intentionally kills the principal obligee or the person upon whose life the policy is issued is not entitled to any benefit under the bond, policy, or other contractual arrangement; and it becomes payable as though the killer had predeceased the decedent.

(4)   Any other acquisition of property or interest by the killer, including a life estate in homestead property, shall be treated in accordance with the principles of this section.

(5)   A final judgment of conviction of murder in any degree is conclusive for purposes of this section. In the absence of a conviction of murder in any degree, the court may determine by the greater weight of the evidence whether the killing was unlawful and intentional for purposes of this section.

(6)   This section does not affect the rights of any person who, before rights under this section have been adjudicated, purchases from the killer for value and without notice property which the killer would have acquired except for this section, but the killer is liable for the amount of the proceeds or the value of the property. Any insurance company, bank, or other obligor making payment according to the terms of its policy or obligation is not liable by reason of this section unless prior to payment it has received at its home office or principal address written notice of a claim under this section.

History.—s. 1, ch. 74-106; s. 113, ch. 75-220; s. 1, ch. 82-71.

Note.—Created from former s. 731.31.

732.804 Provisions relating to disposition of the body.—Before issuance of letters, any person may carry out written instructions of the decedent relating to the decedent's body and funeral and burial arrangements. The fact that cremation occurred pursuant to a written direction signed by the decedent that the body be cremated is a complete defense to a cause of action against any person acting or relying on that direction.

History.—s. 1, ch. 74-106; s. 43, ch. 75-220; s. 971, ch. 97-102; s. 58, ch. 2001-226.

732.805 Spousal rights procured by fraud, duress, or undue influence.—

(1)   A surviving spouse who is found to have procured a marriage to the decedent by fraud, duress, or undue influence is not entitled to any of the following rights or benefits that inure solely by virtue of the marriage or the person's status as surviving spouse of the decedent unless the decedent and the surviving spouse voluntarily cohabited as husband and wife with full knowledge of the facts constituting the fraud, duress, or undue influence or both spouses otherwise subsequently ratified the marriage:

(a)   Any rights or benefits under the Florida Probate Code, including, but not limited to, entitlement to elective share or family allowance; preference in appointment as personal representative; inheritance by intestacy, homestead, or exempt property; or inheritance as a pretermitted spouse.

(b)   Any rights or benefits under a bond, life insurance policy, or other contractual arrangement if the decedent is the principal obligee or the person upon whose life the policy is issued, unless the surviving spouse is provided for by name, whether or not designated as the spouse, in the bond, life insurance policy, or other contractual arrangement.

(c)   Any rights or benefits under a will, trust, or power of appointment, unless the surviving spouse is provided for by name, whether or not designated as the spouse, in the will, trust, or power of appointment.

(d) Any immunity from the presumption of undue influence that a surviving spouse may have under state law.

(2) Any of the rights or benefits listed in paragraphs (1)(a)-(c) which would have passed solely by virtue of the marriage to a surviving spouse who is found to have procured the marriage by fraud, duress, or undue influence shall pass as if the spouse had predeceased the decedent.

(3) A challenge to a surviving spouse's rights under this section may be maintained as a defense, objection, or cause of action by any interested person after the death of the decedent in any proceeding in which the fact of marriage may be directly or indirectly material.

(4) The contestant has the burden of establishing, by a preponderance of the evidence, that the marriage was procured by fraud, duress, or undue influence. If ratification of the marriage is raised as a defense, the surviving spouse has the burden of establishing, by a preponderance of the evidence, the subsequent ratification by both spouses.

(5) In all actions brought under this section, the court shall award taxable costs as in chancery actions, including attorney's fees. When awarding taxable costs and attorney's fees, the court may direct payment from a party's interest, if any, in the estate, or enter a judgment that may be satisfied from other property of the party, or both.

(6) An insurance company, financial institution, or other obligor making payment according to the terms of its policy or obligation is not liable by reason of this section unless, before payment, it received written notice of a claim pursuant to this section.

(a) The notice required by this subsection must be in writing and must be accomplished in a manner reasonably suitable under the circumstances and likely to result in receipt of the notice. Permissible methods of notice include first-class mail, personal delivery, delivery to the person's last known place of residence or place of business, or a properly directed facsimile or other electronic message.

(b) To be effective, notice to a financial institution or insurance company must contain the name, address, and the taxpayer identification number, or the account or policy number, of the principal obligee or person whose life is insured and shall be directed to an officer or a manager of the financial institution or insurance company in this state. If the financial institution or insurance company has no offices in this state, the notice shall be directed to the principal office of the financial institution or insurance company.

(c) Notice shall be effective when given, except that notice to a financial institution or insurance company is not effective until 5 business days after being given.

(7) The rights and remedies granted in this section are in addition to any other rights or remedies a person may have at law or equity.

(8) Unless sooner barred by adjudication, estoppel, or a provision of the Florida Probate Code or Florida Probate Rules, an interested person is barred from bringing

an action under this section unless the action is commenced within 4 years after the decedent's date of death. A cause of action under this section accrues on the decedent's date of death.

History.—s. 11, ch. 2010-132.

732.806 Gifts to lawyers and other disqualified persons.—

(1)   Any part of a written instrument which makes a gift to a lawyer or a person related to the lawyer is void if the lawyer prepared or supervised the execution of the written instrument, or solicited the gift, unless the lawyer or other recipient of the gift is related to the person making the gift.

(2)   This section is not applicable to a provision in a written instrument appointing a lawyer, or a person related to the lawyer, as a fiduciary.

(3)   A provision in a written instrument purporting to waive the application of this section is unenforceable.

(4)   If property distributed in kind, or a security interest in that property, is acquired by a purchaser or lender for value from a person who has received a gift in violation of this section, the purchaser or lender takes title free of any claims arising under this section and incurs no personal liability by reason of this section, whether or not the gift is void under this section.

(5)   In all actions brought under this section, the court must award taxable costs as in chancery actions, including attorney fees. When awarding taxable costs and attorney fees under this section, the court may direct payment from a party's interest in the estate or trust, or enter a judgment that may be satisfied from other property of the party, or both. Attorney fees and costs may not be awarded against a party who, in good faith, initiates an action under this section to declare a gift void.

(6)   If a part of a written instrument is invalid by reason of this section, the invalid part is severable and may not affect any other part of the written instrument which can be given effect, including a term that makes an alternate or substitute gift. In the case of a power of appointment, this section does not affect the power to appoint in favor of persons other than the lawyer or a person related to the lawyer.

(7)   For purposes of this section:

(a)   A lawyer is deemed to have prepared, or supervised the execution of, a written instrument if the preparation, or supervision of the execution, of the written instrument was performed by an employee or lawyer employed by the same firm as the lawyer.

(b)   A person is "related" to an individual if, at the time the lawyer prepared or supervised the execution of the written instrument or solicited the gift, the person is:

1.   A spouse of the individual;

2.   A lineal ascendant or descendant of the individual;

231

3.   A sibling of the individual;

4.   A relative of the individual or of the individual's spouse with whom the lawyer maintains a close, familial relationship;

5.   A spouse of a person described in subparagraph 2., subparagraph 3., or subparagraph 4.; or

6.   A person who cohabitates with the individual.

(c)   The term "written instrument" includes, but is not limited to, a will, a trust, a deed, a document exercising a power of appointment, or a beneficiary designation under a life insurance contract or any other contractual arrangement that creates an ownership interest or permits the naming of a beneficiary.

(d)   The term "gift" includes an inter vivos gift, a testamentary transfer of real or personal property or any interest therein, and the power to make such a transfer regardless of whether the gift is outright or in trust; regardless of when the transfer is to take effect; and regardless of whether the power is held in a fiduciary or nonfiduciary capacity.

(8)   The rights and remedies granted in this section are in addition to any other rights or remedies a person may have at law or in equity.

History.—s. 7, ch. 2013-172.

PART IX
PRODUCTION OF WILLS

732.901   Production of wills.—

(1)   The custodian of a will must deposit the will with the clerk of the court having venue of the estate of the decedent within 10 days after receiving information that the testator is dead. The custodian must supply the testator's date of death or the last four digits of the testator's social security number to the clerk upon deposit.

(2)   Upon petition and notice, the custodian of any will may be compelled to produce and deposit the will. All costs, damages, and a reasonable attorney's fee shall be adjudged to petitioner against the delinquent custodian if the court finds that the custodian had no just or reasonable cause for failing to deposit the will.

(3)   An original will submitted to the clerk with a petition or other pleading is deemed to have been deposited with the clerk.

(4)   Upon receipt, the clerk shall retain and preserve the original will in its original form for at least 20 years. If the probate of a will is initiated, the original will may be maintained by the clerk with the other pleadings during the pendency of the proceedings, but the will must at all times be retained in its original form for the remainder of the 20-year period whether or not the will is admitted to probate or the proceedings are terminated. Transforming and storing a will on film, microfilm, magnetic, electronic, optical, or other substitute media or recording a will onto an electronic recordkeeping system, whether or not

in accordance with the standards adopted by the Supreme Court of Florida, or permanently recording a will does not eliminate the requirement to preserve the original will.

(5)   For purposes of this section, the term "will" includes a separate writing as described in s. 732.515.

History.—s. 1, ch. 74-106; s. 44, ch. 75-220; s. 18, ch. 92-200; s. 972, ch. 97-102; s. 59, ch. 2001-226; s. 8, ch. 2013-172.

Note.—Created from former s. 732.22.

Florida Probate Code

PART I
GENERAL PROVISIONS

733.101 Venue of probate proceedings.—

(1)   The venue for probate of wills and granting letters shall be:

(a)   In the county in this state where the decedent was domiciled.

(b)   If the decedent had no domicile in this state, then in any county where the decedent's property is located.

(c)   If the decedent had no domicile in this state and possessed no property in this state, then in the county where any debtor of the decedent resides.

(2)   For the purpose of this section, a married woman whose husband is an alien or a nonresident of Florida may establish or designate a separate domicile in this state.

(3)   Whenever a proceeding is filed laying venue in an improper county, the court may transfer the action in the same manner as provided in the Florida Rules of Civil Procedure. Any action taken by the court or the parties before the transfer is not affected by the improper venue.

History.—s. 1, ch. 74-106; s. 46, ch. 75-220; s. 981, ch. 97-102; s. 78, ch. 2001-226.

Note.—Created from former s. 732.06.

733.103 Effect of probate.—

(1)   Until admitted to probate in this state or in the state where the decedent was domiciled, the will shall be ineffective to prove title to, or the right to possession of, property of the testator.

(2)   In any collateral action or proceeding relating to devised property, the probate of a will in Florida shall be conclusive of its due execution; that it was executed by a competent testator, free of fraud, duress, mistake, and undue influence; and that the will was unrevoked on the testator's death.

History.—s. 1, ch. 74-106; s. 48, ch. 75-220; s. 17, ch. 77-87; s. 1, ch. 77-174; s. 79, ch. 2001-226.

Note.—Created from former s. 732.26.

733.104 Suspension of statutes of limitation in favor of the personal representative.—

(1)   If a person entitled to bring an action dies before the expiration of the time limited for the commencement of the action and the cause of action survives, the action may be commenced by that person's personal representative before the later of the expiration of the time limited for the commencement of the action or 12 months after the

234

decedent's death.

(2)   If a person against whom a cause of action exists dies before the expiration of the time limited for commencement of the action and the cause of action survives, if a claim is timely filed, the expiration of the time limited for commencement of the action shall not apply.

History.—s. 1, ch. 74-106; s. 48, ch. 75-220; s. 1, ch. 77-174; s. 982, ch. 97-102; s. 80, ch. 2001-226.

Note.—Created from former s. 734.27.

733.105 Determination of beneficiaries.—

(1)   When property passes by intestate succession or the will is unclear and there is doubt about:

(a)   Who is entitled to receive any part of the property, or

(b)   The shares and amounts that any person is entitled to receive, any interested person may petition the court to determine beneficiaries or their shares.

(2)   Any personal representative who makes distribution or takes any other action pursuant to an order determining beneficiaries shall be fully protected.

(3)   A separate civil action to determine beneficiaries may be brought when an estate has not been administered.

History.—s. 1, ch. 74-106; s. 48, ch. 75-220; s. 226, ch. 77-104; s. 1, ch. 77-174; s. 983, ch. 97-102; s. 81, ch. 2001-226.

Note.—Created from former s. 734.25.

733.1051 Limited judicial construction of will with federal tax provisions.—

(1)   Upon the application of a personal representative or a person who is or may be a beneficiary who is affected by the outcome of the construction, a court at any time may construe the terms of a will to define the respective shares or determine beneficiaries, in accordance with the intention of a testator, if a disposition occurs during the applicable period and the will contains a provision that:

(a)   Includes a disposition formula referring to the terms "unified credit," "estate tax exemption," "applicable exemption amount," "applicable credit amount," "applicable exclusion amount," "generation-skipping transfer tax exemption," "GST exemption," "marital deduction," "maximum marital deduction," "unlimited marital deduction," or "maximum charitable deduction";

(b)   Measures a share of an estate based on the amount that may pass free of federal estate tax or the amount that may pass free of federal generation-skipping transfer tax;

(c)   Otherwise makes a disposition referring to a charitable deduction, marital deduction, or another provision of federal estate tax or generation-skipping transfer tax law; or

      (d)   Appears to be intended to reduce or minimize the federal estate tax or generation-skipping transfer tax.

      (2)   For purposes of this section:

      (a)   The term "applicable period" means a period beginning January 1, 2010, and ending on the end of the day on the earlier of December 31, 2010, or the day before the date that an act becomes law that repeals or otherwise modifies or has the effect of repealing or modifying s. 901 of the Economic Growth and Tax Relief Reconciliation Act of 2001.

      (b)   A "disposition occurs" when the testator dies.

      (3)   In construing the will, the court shall consider the terms and purposes of the will, the facts and circumstances surrounding the creation of the will, and the testator's probable intent. In determining the testator's probable intent, the court may consider evidence relevant to the testator's intent even though the evidence contradicts an apparent plain meaning of the will.

      (4)   This section does not apply to a disposition that is specifically conditioned upon no federal estate or generation-skipping transfer tax being imposed.

      (5)   (a)   Unless otherwise ordered by the court, during the applicable period and without court order, the personal representative administering a will containing one or more provisions described in subsection (1) may:

      1.   Delay or refrain from making any distribution.

      2.   Incur and pay fees and costs reasonably necessary to determine its duties and obligations, including compliance with provisions of existing and reasonably anticipated future federal tax laws.

      3.   Establish and maintain reserves for the payment of these fees and costs and federal taxes.

      (b)   The personal representative shall not be liable for its actions as provided in this subsection made or taken in good faith.

      (6)   The provisions of this section are in addition to, and not in derogation of, rights under the common law to construe a will.

      (7)   This section is remedial in nature and intended to provide a new or modified legal remedy. This section shall operate retroactively to January 1, 2010.

History.—s. 12, ch. 2010-132.

733.106 Costs and attorney's fees.—

      (1)   In all probate proceedings costs may be awarded as in chancery actions.

(2)   A person nominated as personal representative, or any proponent of a will if the person so nominated does not act within a reasonable time, if in good faith justified in offering the will in due form for probate, shall receive costs and attorney's fees from the estate even though probate is denied or revoked.

(3)   Any attorney who has rendered services to an estate may be awarded reasonable compensation from the estate.

(4)   When costs and attorney's fees are to be paid from the estate, the court may direct from what part of the estate they shall be paid.

History.—s. 1, ch. 74-106; s. 49, ch. 75-220; s. 984, ch. 97-102; s. 82, ch. 2001-226.

Note.—Created from former s. 732.14.

733.1061 Fees and costs; will reformation and modification.—

(1)   In a proceeding arising under s. 732.615 or s. 732.616, the court shall award taxable costs as in chancery actions, including attorney's fees and guardian ad litem fees.

(2)   When awarding taxable costs, including attorney's fees and guardian ad litem fees, under this section, the court in its discretion may direct payment from a party's interest, if any, in the estate or enter a judgment which may be satisfied from other property of the party, or both.

History.—s. 5, ch. 2011-183.

733.107 Burden of proof in contests; presumption of undue influence.—

(1)   In all proceedings contesting the validity of a will, the burden shall be upon the proponent of the will to establish prima facie its formal execution and attestation. A self-proving affidavit executed in accordance with s. 732.503 or an oath of an attesting witness executed as required in s. 733.201(2) is admissible and establishes prima facie the formal execution and attestation of the will. Thereafter, the contestant shall have the burden of establishing the grounds on which the probate of the will is opposed or revocation is sought.

(2)   The presumption of undue influence implements public policy against abuse of fiduciary or confidential relationships and is therefore a presumption shifting the burden of proof under ss. 90.301-90.304.

History.—s. 1, ch. 74-106; s. 50, ch. 75-220; s. 83, ch. 2001-226; s. 5, ch. 2002-82; s. 13, ch. 2010-132.

Note.—Created from former s. 732.31.

733.109 Revocation of probate.—

(1)   A proceeding to revoke the probate of a will shall be brought in the court having jurisdiction over the administration. Any interested person, including a

beneficiary under a prior will, unless barred under s. 733.212 or s. 733.2123, may commence the proceeding before final discharge of the personal representative.

(2)   Pending the determination of any petition for revocation of probate, the personal representative shall proceed with the administration of the estate as if no revocation proceeding had been commenced, except that no distribution may be made to beneficiaries in contravention of the rights of those who, but for the will, would be entitled to the property disposed of.

(3)   Revocation of probate of a will shall not affect or impair the title to property purchased in good faith for value from the personal representative prior to an order of revocation.

History.—s. 1, ch. 74-106; s. 50, ch. 75-220; s. 18, ch. 77-87; s. 227, ch. 77-104; s. 84, ch. 2001-226.

Note.—Created from former s. 732.30.

PART II
COMMENCING ADMINISTRATION

733.201   Proof of wills.—

(1)   Self-proved wills executed in accordance with this code may be admitted to probate without further proof.

(2)   A will may be admitted to probate upon the oath of any attesting witness taken before any circuit judge, commissioner appointed by the court, or clerk.

(3)   If it appears to the court that the attesting witnesses cannot be found or that they have become incapacitated after the execution of the will or their testimony cannot be obtained within a reasonable time, a will may be admitted to probate upon the oath of the personal representative nominated by the will as provided in subsection (2), whether or not the nominated personal representative is interested in the estate, or upon the oath of any person having no interest in the estate under the will stating that the person believes the writing exhibited to be the true last will of the decedent.

History.—s. 1, ch. 74-106; s. 51, ch. 75-220; s. 985, ch. 97-102; s. 85, ch. 2001-226; s. 9, ch. 2009-115.

Note.—Created from former s. 732.24.

733.202   Petition.—Any interested person may petition for administration.

History.—s. 1, ch. 74-106; s. 52, ch. 75-220; s. 19, ch. 77-87; s. 19, ch. 92-200; s. 986, ch. 97-102; s. 86, ch. 2001-226.

Note.—Created from former s. 732.43.

733.204   Probate of a will written in a foreign language.—

(1)   No will written in a foreign language shall be admitted to probate unless

Florida Probate Code

it is accompanied by a true and complete English translation.

(2)   No personal representative who complies in good faith with the English translation of the will as established by the court shall be liable for doing so.

History.—s. 1, ch. 74-106; s. 54, ch. 75-220; s. 1, ch. 77-174; s. 88, ch. 2001-226.

Note.—Created from former s. 732.34.

733.205 Probate of notarial will.—

(1)   When a copy of a notarial will in the possession of a notary entitled to its custody in a foreign state or country, the laws of which state or country require that the will remain in the custody of the notary, duly authenticated by the notary, whose official position, signature, and seal of office are further authenticated by an American consul, vice consul, or other American consular officer within whose jurisdiction the notary is a resident, or whose official position, signature, and seal of office have been authenticated according to the requirements of the Hague Convention of 1961, is presented to the court, it may be admitted to probate if the original could have been admitted to probate in this state.

(2)   The duly authenticated copy shall be prima facie evidence of its purported execution and of the facts stated in the certificate in compliance with subsection (1).

(3)   Any interested person may oppose the probate of such a notarial will or may petition for revocation of probate of such a notarial will, as in the original probate of a will in this state.

History.—s. 1, ch. 74-106; s. 55, ch. 75-220; s. 89, ch. 2001-226; s. 7, ch. 2003-154.

Note.—Created from former s. 732.37.

733.206 Probate of will of resident after foreign probate.—

(1)   If a will of any person who dies a resident of this state is admitted to probate in any other state or country through inadvertence, error, or omission before probate in this state, the will may be admitted to probate in this state if the original could have been admitted to probate in this state.

(2)   An authenticated copy of the will, foreign proof of the will, the foreign order of probate, and any letters issued shall be filed instead of the original will and shall be prima facie evidence of its execution and admission to foreign probate.

(3)   Any interested person may oppose the probate of the will or may petition for revocation of the probate of the will, as in the original probate of a will in this state.

History.—s. 1, ch. 74-106; s. 56, ch. 75-220; s. 90, ch. 2001-226.

Note.—Created from former s. 732.35.

733.207 Establishment and probate of lost or destroyed will.—Any interested person may establish the full and precise terms of a lost or destroyed will and offer the will for probate. The specific content of the will must be proved by the testimony of two disinterested witnesses, or, if a correct copy is provided, it shall be proved by one disinterested witness.

History.—s. 1, ch. 74-106; s. 57, ch. 75-220; s. 91, ch. 2001-226.

Note.—Created from former s. 732.27.

733.208 Discovery of later will.—On the discovery of a later will or codicil, any interested person may petition to revoke the probate of the earlier will or to probate the later will or codicil. No will or codicil may be offered after the testate or intestate estate has been completely administered and the personal representative discharged.

History.—s. 1, ch. 74-106; s. 58, ch. 75-220; s. 92, ch. 2001-226.

Note.—Created from former s. 732.32.

733.209 Estates of missing persons.—Any interested person may petition to administer the estate of a missing person; however, no personal representative shall be appointed until the court determines the missing person is dead.

History.—s. 1, ch. 74-106; s. 93, ch. 2001-226.

Note.—Created from former s. 732.53.

733.212 Notice of administration; filing of objections.—

(1)   The personal representative shall promptly serve a copy of the notice of administration on the following persons who are known to the personal representative:

(a)   The decedent's surviving spouse;

(b)   Beneficiaries;

(c)   The trustee of any trust described in s. 733.707(3) and each qualified beneficiary of the trust as defined in s. 736.0103, if each trustee is also a personal representative of the estate; and

(d)   Persons who may be entitled to exempt property
in the manner provided for service of formal notice, unless served under s. 733.2123. The personal representative may similarly serve a copy of the notice on any devisees under a known prior will or heirs or others who claim or may claim an interest in the estate.

(2)   The notice shall state:

(a)   The name of the decedent, the file number of the estate, the designation and address of the court in which the proceedings are pending, whether the estate is testate or intestate, and, if testate, the date of the will and any codicils.

(b)   The name and address of the personal representative and the name and address of the personal representative's attorney, and that the fiduciary lawyer-client privilege in s. 90.5021 applies with respect to the personal representative and any attorney employed by the personal representative.

(c)   That any interested person on whom a copy of the notice of administration is served must file on or before the date that is 3 months after the date of service of a copy of the notice of administration on that person any objection that challenges the validity of the will, the qualifications of the personal representative, the venue, or the jurisdiction of the court.

(d)   That persons who may be entitled to exempt property under s. 732.402 will be deemed to have waived their rights to claim that property as exempt property unless a petition for determination of exempt property is filed by such persons or on their behalf on or before the later of the date that is 4 months after the date of service of a copy of the notice of administration on such persons or the date that is 40 days after the date of termination of any proceeding involving the construction, admission to probate, or validity of the will or involving any other matter affecting any part of the exempt property.

(e)   That an election to take an elective share must be filed on or before the earlier of the date that is 6 months after the date of service of a copy of the notice of administration on the surviving spouse, or an attorney in fact or a guardian of the property of the surviving spouse, or the date that is 2 years after the date of the decedent's death.

(3)   Any interested person on whom a copy of the notice of administration is served must object to the validity of the will, the qualifications of the personal representative, the venue, or the jurisdiction of the court by filing a petition or other pleading requesting relief in accordance with the Florida Probate Rules on or before the date that is 3 months after the date of service of a copy of the notice of administration on the objecting person, or those objections are forever barred.

(4)   The appointment of a personal representative or a successor personal representative shall not extend or renew the period for filing objections under this section, unless a new will or codicil is admitted.

(5)   The personal representative is not individually liable to any person for giving notice under this section, regardless of whether it is later determined that notice was not required by this section. The service of notice in accordance with this section shall not be construed as conferring any right.

(6)   If the personal representative in good faith fails to give notice required by this section, the personal representative is not liable to any person for the failure. Liability, if any, for the failure is on the estate.

(7)   If a will or codicil is subsequently admitted to probate, the personal representative shall promptly serve a copy of a new notice of administration as required for an initial will admission.

(8)   For the purpose of determining deadlines established by reference to the date of service of a copy of the notice of administration in cases in which such service has been waived, service shall be deemed to occur on the date the waiver is filed.

History.—s. 1, ch. 74-106; s. 60, ch. 75-220; s. 227, ch. 77-104; s. 3, ch. 88-340; s. 2, ch.

Florida Probate Code

89-340; s. 2, ch. 90-23; s. 8, ch. 93-257; s. 7, ch. 95-401; s. 191, ch. 99-397; s. 94, ch. 2001-226; s. 8, ch. 2003-154; s. 6, ch. 2006-134; s. 36, ch. 2006-217; s. 8, ch. 2011-183; s. 17, ch. 2013-172.

Note.—Created from former s. 732.28.

733.2121 Notice to creditors; filing of claims.—

(1) Unless creditors' claims are otherwise barred by s. 733.710, the personal representative shall promptly publish a notice to creditors. The notice shall contain the name of the decedent, the file number of the estate, the designation and address of the court in which the proceedings are pending, the name and address of the personal representative, the name and address of the personal representative's attorney, and the date of first publication. The notice shall state that creditors must file claims against the estate with the court during the time periods set forth in s. 733.702, or be forever barred.

(2) Publication shall be once a week for 2 consecutive weeks, in a newspaper published in the county where the estate is administered or, if there is no newspaper published in the county, in a newspaper of general circulation in that county.

(3) (a) The personal representative shall promptly make a diligent search to determine the names and addresses of creditors of the decedent who are reasonably ascertainable, even if the claims are unmatured, contingent, or unliquidated, and shall promptly serve a copy of the notice on those creditors. Impracticable and extended searches are not required. Service is not required on any creditor who has filed a claim as provided in this part, whose claim has been paid in full, or whose claim is listed in a personal representative's timely filed proof of claim.

(b) The personal representative is not individually liable to any person for giving notice under this section, even if it is later determined that notice was not required. The service of notice to creditors in accordance with this section shall not be construed as admitting the validity or enforceability of a claim.

(c) If the personal representative in good faith fails to give notice required by this section, the personal representative is not liable to any person for the failure. Liability, if any, for the failure is on the estate.

(d) If a decedent at the time of death was 55 years of age or older, the personal representative shall promptly serve a copy of the notice to creditors and provide a copy of the death certificate on the Agency for Health Care Administration within 3 months after the first publication of the notice to creditors, unless the agency has already filed a statement of claim in the estate proceedings.

(e) If the Department of Revenue has not previously been served with a copy of the notice to creditors, then service of the inventory on the Department of Revenue shall be the equivalent of service of a copy of the notice to creditors.

(4) Claims are barred as provided in ss. 733.702 and 733.710.

History.—s. 95, ch. 2001-226; s. 9, ch. 2003-154; s. 4, ch. 2005-140.

733.2123 Adjudication before issuance of letters.—A petitioner may serve formal notice of the petition for administration on interested persons. A person who is served with such notice before the issuance of letters or who has waived notice may not challenge the validity of the will, testacy of the decedent, qualifications of the personal representative, venue, or jurisdiction of the court, except in the proceedings before issuance of letters.

History.—s. 60, ch. 75-220; s. 2, ch. 81-27; s. 987, ch. 97-102; s. 96, ch. 2001-226; s. 14, ch. 2010-132.

733.213 Probate as prerequisite to judicial construction of will.—A will may not be construed until it has been admitted to probate.

History.—s. 1, ch. 74-106; s. 61, ch. 75-220; s. 97, ch. 2001-226.

Note.—Created from former s. 732.42.

PART III
PREFERENCE IN APPOINTMENT AND QUALIFICATIONS OF PERSONAL REPRESENTATIVE

733.301 Preference in appointment of personal representative.—

(1)   In granting letters of administration, the following order of preference shall be observed:

(a)   In testate estates:

1.   The personal representative, or his or her successor, nominated by the will or pursuant to a power conferred in the will.

2.   The person selected by a majority in interest of the persons entitled to the estate.

3.   A devisee under the will. If more than one devisee applies, the court may select the one best qualified.

(b)   In intestate estates:

1.   The surviving spouse.

2.   The person selected by a majority in interest of the heirs.

3.   The heir nearest in degree. If more than one applies, the court may select the one best qualified.

(2)   A guardian of the property of a ward who if competent would be entitled to appointment as, or to select, the personal representative may exercise the right to select the personal representative.

(3)   In either a testate or an intestate estate, if no application is made by any of the persons described in subsection (1), the court shall appoint a capable person; but no person may be appointed under this subsection:

(a)   Who works for, or holds public office under, the court.

(b)   Who is employed by, or holds office under, any judge exercising probate jurisdiction.

(4)   After letters have been granted in either a testate or an intestate estate, if a person who was entitled to, and has not waived, preference over the person appointed at the time of the appointment and on whom formal notice was not served seeks the appointment, the letters granted may be revoked and the person entitled to preference may have letters granted after formal notice and hearing.

(5)   After letters have been granted in either a testate or an intestate estate, if any will is subsequently admitted to probate, the letters shall be revoked and new letters granted.

History.—s. 1, ch. 74-106; s. 62, ch. 75-220; s. 21, ch. 77-87; s. 1, ch. 77-174; s. 988, ch. 97-102; s. 98, ch. 2001-226.

Note.—Created from former s. 732.44.

733.302 Who may be appointed personal representative.—Subject to the limitations in this part, any person who is sui juris and is a resident of Florida at the time of the death of the person whose estate is to be administered is qualified to act as personal representative in Florida.

History.—s. 1, ch. 74-106; s. 63, ch. 75-220; s. 5, ch. 79-343; s. 989, ch. 97-102; s. 99, ch. 2001-226.

Note.—Created from former s. 732.45.

733.303 Persons not qualified.—

(1)   A person is not qualified to act as a personal representative if the person:

(a)   Has been convicted of a felony.

(b)   Is mentally or physically unable to perform the duties.

(c)   Is under the age of 18 years.

(2)   If the person named as personal representative in the will is not qualified, letters shall be granted as provided in s. 733.301.

History.—s. 1, ch. 74-106; s. 63, ch. 75-220; s. 22, ch. 77-87; s. 990, ch. 97-102.

Note.—Created from former s. 732.46.

733.304 Nonresidents.—A person who is not domiciled in the state cannot qualify as personal representative unless the person is:

(1)   A legally adopted child or adoptive parent of the decedent;

(2)   Related by lineal consanguinity to the decedent;

(3)   A spouse or a brother, sister, uncle, aunt, nephew, or niece of the decedent, or someone related by lineal consanguinity to any such person; or

(4)   The spouse of a person otherwise qualified under this section.

History.—s. 1, ch. 74-106; s. 63, ch. 75-220; s. 6, ch. 79-343.

Note.—Created from former s. 732.47.

733.305 Trust companies and other corporations and associations.—

(1)   All trust companies incorporated under the laws of Florida, all state banking corporations and state savings associations authorized and qualified to exercise fiduciary powers in Florida, and all national banking associations and federal savings and loan associations authorized and qualified to exercise fiduciary powers in Florida shall be entitled to act as personal representatives and curators of estates.

(2)   When a qualified corporation has been named as a personal representative in a will and subsequently transfers its business and assets to, consolidates or merges with, or is in any manner provided by law succeeded by, another qualified corporation, on the death of the testator, the successor corporation may qualify as personal representative unless the will provides otherwise.

(3)   A corporation authorized and qualified to act as a personal representative as a result of merger or consolidation shall succeed to the rights and duties of all predecessor corporations as the personal representative of estates upon filing proof in the court, and without a new appointment. A purchase of substantially all the assets and the assumption of substantially all the liabilities shall be deemed a merger for the purpose of this section.

History.—s. 1, ch. 74-106; s. 63, ch. 75-220; s. 1, ch. 77-174; s. 3, ch. 81-27; s. 100, ch. 2001-226.

Note.—Created from former s. 732.49.

733.306 Effect of appointment of debtor.—The appointment of a debtor as personal representative shall not extinguish the debt due the decedent.

History.—s. 1, ch. 74-106; s. 63, ch. 75-220; s. 101, ch. 2001-226.

Note.—Created from former s. 732.51.

733.307 Succession of administration.—The personal representative of the estate of a deceased personal representative is not authorized to administer the estate of the first decedent. On the death of a sole or surviving personal representative, the court shall appoint a successor personal representative to complete the administration of the estate.

History.—s. 1, ch. 74-106; s. 64, ch. 75-220; s. 102, ch. 2001-226.

Note.—Created from former s. 732.52.

733.308 Administrator ad litem.—When an estate must be represented and the personal representative is unable to do so, the court shall appoint an administrator ad litem without bond to represent the estate in that proceeding. The fact that the personal representative is seeking reimbursement for claims against the decedent does not require appointment of an administrator ad litem.

History.—s. 1, ch. 74-106; s. 65, ch. 75-220; s. 103, ch. 2001-226.

Note.—Created from former s. 732.55.

733.309 Executor de son tort.—No person shall be liable to a creditor of a decedent as executor de son tort, but any person taking, converting, or intermeddling with the property of a decedent shall be liable to the personal representative or curator, when appointed, for the value of all the property so taken or converted and for all damages to the estate caused by the wrongful action. This section shall not be construed to prevent a creditor of a decedent from suing anyone in possession of property fraudulently conveyed by the decedent to set aside the fraudulent conveyance.

History.—s. 1, ch. 74-106; s. 65, ch. 75-220; s. 991, ch. 97-102; s. 104, ch. 2001-226.

733.3101 Personal representative not qualified.—Any time a personal representative knows or should have known that he or she would not be qualified for appointment if application for appointment were then made, the personal representative shall promptly file and serve a notice setting forth the reasons. A personal representative who fails to comply with this section shall be personally liable for costs, including attorney's fees, incurred in any removal proceeding, if the personal representative is removed. This liability shall be cumulative to any other provided by law.

History.—s. 105, ch. 2001-226.

PART IV
FIDUCIARY BONDS

733.402 Bond of fiduciary; when required; form.—

(1) Unless the bond requirement has been waived by the will or by the court, every fiduciary to whom letters are granted shall execute and file a bond with surety, as defined in s. 45.011, to be approved by the clerk without a service fee. The bond shall be payable to the Governor and the Governor's successors in office, conditioned on the performance of all duties as personal representative according to law. The bond must be joint and several.

(2) No bond shall be void or invalid because of an informality in it or an informality or illegality in the appointment of the fiduciary. The bond shall have the same force as if the appointment had been legally made and the bond executed in proper form.

(3) The requirements of this section shall not apply to banks and trust companies authorized by law to act as personal representative.

(4)   On petition by any interested person or on the court's own motion, the court may waive the requirement of filing a bond, require a bond, increase or decrease the bond, or require additional surety.

History.—s. 1, ch. 74-106; s. 67, ch. 75-220; s. 24, ch. 77-87; s. 1, ch. 77-174; s. 992, ch. 97-102; s. 107, ch. 2001-226.

Note.—Created from former s. 732.61.

733.403 Amount of bond.—All bonds required by this part shall be in the penal sum that the court deems sufficient after consideration of the gross value of the estate, the relationship of the personal representative to the beneficiaries, exempt property and any family allowance, the type and nature of assets, known creditors, and liens and encumbrances on the assets.

History.—s. 1, ch. 74-106; s. 67, ch. 75-220; s. 108, ch. 2001-226.

Note.—Created from former ss. 732.63, 732.64, 732.66.

733.404 Liability of surety.—No surety for any personal representative or curator shall be charged beyond the value of the assets of an estate because of any omission or mistake in pleading or of false pleading of the personal representative or curator.

History.—s. 1, ch. 74-106; s. 68, ch. 75-220; s. 109, ch. 2001-226.

Note.—Created from former s. 732.65.

733.405 Release of surety.—

(1)   Subject to the limitations of this section, on the petition of any interested person, the surety is entitled to be released from liability for the future acts and omissions of the fiduciary.

(2)   Pending the hearing of the petition, the court may restrain the fiduciary from acting, except to preserve the estate.

(3)   On hearing, the court shall enter an order prescribing the amount of the new bond for the fiduciary and the date when the bond shall be filed. If the fiduciary fails to give the new bond, the fiduciary shall be removed at once, and further proceedings shall be had as in cases of removal.

(4)   The original surety shall remain liable in accordance with the terms of its original bond for all acts and omissions of the fiduciary that occur prior to the approval of the new surety and filing and approval of the bond. The new surety shall be liable on its bond only after the filing and approval of the new bond.

History.—s. 1, ch. 74-106; s. 68, ch. 75-220; s. 993, ch. 97-102; s. 110, ch. 2001-226.

Note.—Created from former s. 732.68.

733.406 Bond premium allowable as expense of administration.—A personal representative or other fiduciary required to give bond shall pay the reasonable premium as an expense of administration.

History.—s. 613, ch. 59-205; s. 3, ch. 76-168; s. 1, ch. 77-457; ss. 2, 3, ch. 81-318; ss. 253, 566, ch. 82-243; s. 994, ch. 97-102; s. 111, ch. 2001-226.

Note.—Former s. 627.753.

PART V
CURATORS; RESIGNATION AND REMOVAL OF PERSONAL REPRESENTATIVES

733.501 Curators.—

(1)   When it is necessary, the court may appoint a curator after formal notice to the person apparently entitled to letters of administration. The curator may be authorized to perform any duty or function of a personal representative. If there is great danger that any of the decedent's property is likely to be wasted, destroyed, or removed beyond the jurisdiction of the court and if the appointment of a curator would be delayed by giving notice, the court may appoint a curator without giving notice.

(2)   Bond shall be required of the curator as the court deems necessary. No bond shall be required of banks and trust companies as curators.

(3)   Curators shall be allowed reasonable compensation for their services, and the court may consider the provisions of s. 733.617.

(4)   Curators shall be subject to removal and surcharge.

History.—s. 1, ch. 74-106; s. 69, ch. 75-220; s. 1, ch. 77-174; s. 995, ch. 97-102; s. 112, ch. 2001-226; s. 108, ch. 2002-1.

Note.—Created from former s. 732.21.

733.502 Resignation of personal representative.—A personal representative may resign. After notice to all interested persons, the court may accept the resignation and then revoke the letters of the resigning personal representative if the interests of the estate are not jeopardized by the resignation. The acceptance of the resignation shall not exonerate the personal representative or the surety from liability.

History.—s. 1, ch. 74-106; s. 69, ch. 75-220; s. 25, ch. 77-87; s. 996, ch. 97-102; s. 113, ch. 2001-226.

Note.—Created from former s. 734.09.

733.503 Appointment of successor upon resignation.—When the personal representative's resignation is accepted, the court shall appoint a personal representative or shall appoint a curator to serve until a successor personal representative is appointed.

History.—s. 1, ch. 74-106; s. 69, ch. 75-220; s. 997, ch. 97-102; s. 114, ch. 2001-226.

Note.—Created from former s. 734.10.

733.5035 Surrender of assets after resignation.—When the resignation has been accepted by the court, all estate assets, records, documents, papers, and other property of or concerning the estate in the resigning personal representative's possession or control shall immediately be surrendered to the successor fiduciary. The court may establish the conditions and specify the assets and records, if any, that the resigning personal representative may retain until the final accounting of the resigning personal representative has been approved.

History.—s. 115, ch. 2001-226.

733.5036 Accounting and discharge following resignation.—

(1)   A resigning personal representative shall file and serve a final accounting of the personal representative's administration.

(2)   After determination and satisfaction of the liability, if any, of the resigning personal representative, after compensation of the personal representative and the attorney and other persons employed by the personal representative, and upon receipt of evidence that undistributed estate assets have been delivered to the successor fiduciary, the personal representative shall be discharged, the bond released, and the surety discharged.

History.—s. 116, ch. 2001-226.

733.504 Removal of personal representative; causes for removal.—A personal representative may be removed and the letters revoked for any of the following causes, and the removal shall be in addition to any penalties prescribed by law:

(1)   Adjudication that the personal representative is incapacitated.

(2)   Physical or mental incapacity rendering the personal representative incapable of the discharge of his or her duties.

(3)   Failure to comply with any order of the court, unless the order has been superseded on appeal.

(4)   Failure to account for the sale of property or to produce and exhibit the assets of the estate when so required.

(5)   Wasting or maladministration of the estate.

(6)   Failure to give bond or security for any purpose.

(7)   Conviction of a felony.

(8)   Insolvency of, or the appointment of a receiver or liquidator for, any corporate personal representative.

(9)   Holding or acquiring conflicting or adverse interests against the estate that will or may interfere with the administration of the estate as a whole. This cause of removal shall not apply to the surviving spouse because of the exercise of the right to the elective share, family allowance, or exemptions, as provided elsewhere in this code.

(10)   Revocation of the probate of the decedent's will that authorized or

designated the appointment of the personal representative.

(11)   Removal of domicile from Florida, if domicile was a requirement of initial appointment.

(12)   The personal representative would not now be entitled to appointment.

History.—s. 1, ch. 74-106; s. 69, ch. 75-220; s. 1, ch. 77-174; s. 998, ch. 97-102; s. 117, ch. 2001-226; s. 10, ch. 2009-115.

Note.—Created from former s. 734.11.

733.505 Jurisdiction in removal proceedings.—A petition for removal shall be filed in the court having jurisdiction of the administration.

History.—s. 1, ch. 74-106; s. 118, ch. 2001-226.

Note.—Created from former s. 734.12.

733.506 Proceedings for removal.—Proceedings for removal of a personal representative may be commenced by the court or upon the petition of an interested person. The court shall revoke the letters of a removed personal representative. The removal of a personal representative shall not exonerate the removed personal representative or the removed personal representative's surety from any liability.

History.—s. 1, ch. 74-106; s. 71, ch. 75-220; s. 119, ch. 2001-226.

Note.—Created from former s. 734.13.

733.5061 Appointment of successor upon removal.—When a personal representative is removed, the court shall appoint a personal representative or shall appoint a curator to serve until a successor personal representative is appointed.

History.—s. 120, ch. 2001-226.

733.508 Accounting and discharge of removed personal representatives upon removal.—

(1)   A removed personal representative shall file and serve a final accounting of that personal representative's administration.

(2)   After determination and satisfaction of the liability, if any, of the removed personal representative, after compensation of that personal representative and the attorney and other persons employed by that personal representative, and upon receipt of evidence that the estate assets have been delivered to the successor fiduciary, the removed personal representative shall be discharged, the bond released, and the surety discharged.

History.—s. 1, ch. 74-106; s. 999, ch. 97-102; s. 122, ch. 2001-226.

Note.—Created from former s. 734.15.

733.509 Surrender of assets upon removal.—Upon entry of an order removing a personal representative, the removed personal representative shall immediately deliver all estate assets, records, documents, papers, and other property of or concerning the estate in the removed personal representative's possession or control to the remaining personal representative or successor fiduciary.

History.—s. 1, ch. 74-106; s. 73, ch. 75-220; s. 123, ch. 2001-226.

Note.—Created from former s. 734.16.

PART VI
DUTIES AND POWERS OF PERSONAL REPRESENTATIVE

733.601 Time of accrual of duties and powers.—The duties and powers of a personal representative commence upon appointment. The powers of a personal representative relate back in time to give acts by the person appointed, occurring before appointment and beneficial to the estate, the same effect as those occurring after appointment. A personal representative may ratify and accept acts on behalf of the estate done by others when the acts would have been proper for a personal representative.

History.—s. 1, ch. 74-106; s. 74, ch. 75-220; s. 1000, ch. 97-102; s. 124, ch. 2001-226.

733.602 General duties.—

(1) A personal representative is a fiduciary who shall observe the standards of care applicable to trustees. A personal representative is under a duty to settle and distribute the estate of the decedent in accordance with the terms of the decedent's will and this code as expeditiously and efficiently as is consistent with the best interests of the estate. A personal representative shall use the authority conferred by this code, the authority in the will, if any, and the authority of any order of the court, for the best interests of interested persons, including creditors.

(2) A personal representative shall not be liable for any act of administration or distribution if the act was authorized at the time. Subject to other obligations of administration, a probated will is authority to administer and distribute the estate according to its terms. An order of appointment of a personal representative is authority to distribute apparently intestate assets to the heirs of the decedent if, at the time of distribution, the personal representative is not aware of a proceeding challenging intestacy or a proceeding questioning the appointment or fitness to continue. Nothing in this section affects the duty of the personal representative to administer and distribute the estate in accordance with the rights of interested persons.

History.—s. 1, ch. 74-106; s. 74, ch. 75-220; s. 27, ch. 77-87; s. 1, ch. 77-174; s. 270, ch. 79-400; s. 3, ch. 89-340; s. 1001, ch. 97-102; s. 125, ch. 2001-226; s. 37, ch. 2006-217; s. 11, ch. 2009-115.

733.603 Personal representative to proceed without court order.—A personal representative shall proceed expeditiously with the settlement and distribution of a decedent's estate and, except as otherwise specified by this code or ordered by the court, shall do so without adjudication, order, or direction of the court. A personal representative may invoke the jurisdiction of the court to resolve questions concerning the estate or its administration.

Florida Probate Code

History.—s. 1, ch. 74-106; s. 1002, ch. 97-102; s. 126, ch. 2001-226.

733.604 Inventories and accountings; public records exemptions.—

(1)(a)　Unless an inventory has been previously filed, a personal representative shall file a verified inventory of property of the estate, listing it with reasonable detail and including for each listed item its estimated fair market value at the date of the decedent's death.

(b)1.　Any inventory of an estate, whether initial, amended, or supplementary, filed with the clerk of the court in conjunction with the administration of an estate is confidential and exempt from s. 119.07(1) and s. 24(a), Art. I of the State Constitution.

2.　Any inventory of an elective estate, whether initial, amended, or supplementary, filed with the clerk of the court in conjunction with an election made in accordance with part II of chapter 732 is confidential and exempt from s. 119.07(1) and s. 24(a), Art. I of the State Constitution.

3.　Any accounting, whether interim, final, amended, or supplementary, filed in an estate proceeding is confidential and exempt from s. 119.07(1) and s. 24(a), Art. I of the State Constitution.

4.　Any inventory or accounting made confidential and exempt by subparagraph 1., subparagraph 2., or subparagraph 3. shall be disclosed by the custodian for inspection or copying:

a.　To the personal representative;

b.　To the personal representative's attorney;

c.　To an interested person as defined in s. 731.201; or

d.　By court order upon a showing of good cause.

5.　These exemptions apply to any inventory or accounting filed before, on, or after July 1, 2009.

6.　This paragraph is subject to the Open Government Sunset Review Act in accordance with s. 119.15 and shall stand repealed on October 2, 2014, unless reviewed and saved from repeal through reenactment by the Legislature.

(2)　If the personal representative learns of any property not included in the original inventory, or learns that the estimated value or description indicated in the original inventory for any item is erroneous or misleading, the personal representative shall file a verified amended or supplementary inventory showing any new items and their estimated value at the date of the decedent's death, or the revised estimated value or description.

(3)　Upon written request to the personal representative, a beneficiary shall be furnished a written explanation of how the inventory value for an asset was determined, or, if an appraisal was obtained, a copy of the appraisal, as follows:

(a)   To a residuary beneficiary or heir in an intestate estate, regarding all inventoried assets.

(b)   To any other beneficiary, regarding all assets distributed or proposed to be distributed to that beneficiary.

The personal representative must notify each beneficiary of that beneficiary's rights under this subsection. Neither a request nor the failure to request information under this subsection affects any rights of a beneficiary in subsequent proceedings concerning any accounting of the personal representative or the propriety of any action of the personal representative.

History.—s. 1, ch. 74-106; s. 76, ch. 75-220; s. 1, ch. 80-127; s. 4, ch. 84-106; s. 1, ch. 85-72; s. 29, ch. 85-342; s. 68, ch. 87-226; s. 28, ch. 95-401; s. 1003, ch. 97-102; s. 13, ch. 97-240; s. 127, ch. 2001-226; s. 1, ch. 2009-230.

Note.—Created from former s. 733.03.

733.6065 Opening safe-deposit box.—

(1)   Subject to the provisions of s. 655.936(2), the initial opening of a safe-deposit box that is leased or coleased by the decedent shall be conducted in the presence of any two of the following persons: an employee of the institution where the box is located, the personal representative, or the personal representative's attorney of record. Each person who is present must verify the contents of the box by signing a copy of the inventory under penalties of perjury. The personal representative shall file the safe-deposit box inventory, together with a copy of the box entry record from a date which is 6 months prior to the date of death to the date of inventory, with the court within 10 days after the box is opened. Unless otherwise ordered by the court, this inventory and the attached box entry record is subject to inspection only by persons entitled to inspect an inventory under s. 733.604(1). The personal representative may remove the contents of the box.

(2)   The right to open and examine the contents of a safe-deposit box leased by a decedent, or any documents delivered by a decedent for safekeeping, and to receive items as provided for in s. 655.935 is separate from the rights provided for in subsection (1).

History.—s. 129, ch. 2001-226; s. 7, ch. 2006-134; s. 71, ch. 2006-213.

733.607 Possession of estate.—

(1)   Except as otherwise provided by a decedent's will, every personal representative has a right to, and shall take possession or control of, the decedent's property, except the protected homestead, but any real property or tangible personal property may be left with, or surrendered to, the person presumptively entitled to it unless possession of the property by the personal representative will be necessary for purposes of administration. The request by a personal representative for delivery of any property possessed by a beneficiary is conclusive evidence that the possession of the property by the personal representative is necessary for the purposes of administration, in any action against the beneficiary for possession of it. The personal representative shall take all steps reasonably necessary for the management, protection, and preservation of the estate until distribution and may maintain an action to recover possession of property or to determine the title to it.

(2)   If, after providing for statutory entitlements and all devises other than residuary devises, the assets of the decedent's estate are insufficient to pay the expenses of the administration and obligations of the decedent's estate, the personal representative is entitled to payment from the trustee of a trust described in s. 733.707(3), in the amount the personal representative certifies in writing to be required to satisfy the insufficiency, subject to the exclusions and preferences under s. 736.05053. The provisions of s. 733.805 shall apply in determining the amount of any payment required by this section.

History.—s. 1, ch. 74-106; s. 28, ch. 77-87; s. 9, ch. 93-257; s. 9, ch. 95-401; s. 1005, ch. 97-102; s. 130, ch. 2001-226; s. 1, ch. 2010-122.

Note.—Created from former s. 733.01.

733.608   General power of the personal representative.—

(1)   All real and personal property of the decedent, except the protected homestead, within this state and the rents, income, issues, and profits from it shall be assets in the hands of the personal representative:

(a)   For the payment of devises, family allowance, elective share, estate and inheritance taxes, claims, charges, and expenses of the administration and obligations of the decedent's estate.

(b)   To enforce contribution and equalize advancement.

(c)   For distribution.

(2)   If property that reasonably appears to the personal representative to be protected homestead is not occupied by a person who appears to have an interest in the property, the personal representative is authorized, but not required, to take possession of that property for the limited purpose of preserving, insuring, and protecting it for the person having an interest in the property, pending a determination of its homestead status. If the personal representative takes possession of that property, any rents and revenues may be collected by the personal representative for the account of the heir or devisee, but the personal representative shall have no duty to rent or otherwise make the property productive.

(3)   If the personal representative expends funds or incurs obligations to preserve, maintain, insure, or protect the property referenced in subsection (2), the personal representative shall be entitled to a lien on that property and its revenues to secure repayment of those expenditures and obligations incurred. These expenditures and obligations incurred, including, but not limited to, fees and costs, shall constitute a debt owed to the personal representative that is charged against and which may be secured by a lien on the protected homestead, as provided in this section. The debt shall include any amounts paid for these purposes after the decedent's death and prior to the personal representative's appointment to the extent later ratified by the personal representative in the court proceeding provided for in this section.

(a)   On the petition of the personal representative or any interested person, the court having jurisdiction of the administration of the decedent's estate shall adjudicate the amount of the debt after formal notice to the persons appearing to have an interest in the property.

       (b)   The persons having an interest in the protected homestead shall have no personal liability for the repayment of the above noted debt. The personal representative may enforce payment of the debt through any of the following methods:

       1.   By foreclosure of the lien as provided in this section;

       2.   By offset of the debt against any other property in the personal representative's possession that otherwise would be distributable to any person having an interest in the protected homestead, but only to the extent of the fraction of the total debt owed to the personal representative the numerator of which is the value of that person's interest in the protected homestead and the denominator of which is the total value of the protected homestead; or

       3.   By offset of the debt against the revenues from the protected homestead received by the personal representative.

       (4)   The personal representative's lien shall attach to the property and take priority as of the date and time a notice of that lien is recorded in the official records of the county where that property is located, and the lien may secure expenditures and obligations incurred, including, but not limited to, fees and costs made before or after recording the notice. The notice of lien may be recorded before adjudicating the amount of the debt. The notice of lien shall also be filed in the probate proceeding, but failure to do so does not affect the validity of the lien. A copy of the notice of lien shall be served in the manner provided for service of formal notice upon each person appearing to have an interest in the property. The notice of lien must state:

       (a)   The name and address of the personal representative and the personal representative's attorney;

       (b)   The legal description of the property;

       (c)   The name of the decedent and also, to the extent known to the personal representative, the name and address of each person appearing to have an interest in the property; and

       (d)   That the personal representative has expended or is obligated to expend funds to preserve, maintain, insure, and protect the property and that the lien stands as security for recovery of those expenditures and obligations incurred, including, but not limited to, fees and costs.
Substantial compliance with the foregoing provisions renders the notice in comportment with this section.

       (5)   The lien shall terminate upon the earliest of:

       (a)   Recording a satisfaction or release signed by the personal representative in the official records of the county where the property is located;

       (b)   The discharge of the personal representative when the estate administration is complete;

(c)   One year from the recording of the lien in the official records unless a proceeding to determine the debt or enforce the lien has been filed; or

(d)   The entry of an order releasing the lien.

(6)   Within 14 days after receipt of the written request of any interested person, the personal representative shall deliver to the requesting person at a place designated in the written request an estoppel letter setting forth the unpaid balance of the debt secured by the lien referred to in this section. After complete satisfaction of the debt secured by the lien, the personal representative shall record within 30 days after complete payment, a satisfaction of the lien in the official records of the county where the property is located. If a judicial proceeding is necessary to compel compliance with the provisions of this subsection, the prevailing party shall be entitled to an award of attorney's fees and costs.

(7)   The lien created by this section may be foreclosed in the manner of foreclosing a mortgage under the provisions of chapter 702.

(8)   In any action for enforcement of the debt described in this section, the court shall award taxable costs as in chancery actions, including reasonable attorney's fees.

(9)   A personal representative entitled to recover a debt for expenditures and obligations incurred, including, but not limited to, fees and costs, under this section may be relieved of the duty to enforce collection by an order of the court finding:

(a)   That the estimated court costs and attorney's fees in collecting the debt will approximate or exceed the amount of the recovery; or

(b)   That it is impracticable to enforce collection in view of the improbability of collection.

(10)   A personal representative shall not be liable for failure to attempt to enforce collection of the debt if the personal representative reasonably believes it would have been economically impracticable.

(11)   The personal representative shall not be liable for failure to take possession of the protected homestead or to expend funds on its behalf. In the event that the property is determined by the court not to be protected homestead, subsections (2)-(10) shall not apply and any liens previously filed shall be deemed released upon recording of the order in the official records of the county where the property is located.

(12)   Upon the petition of an interested party to accommodate a sale or the encumbrance of the protected homestead, the court may transfer the lien provided for in this section from the property to the proceeds of the sale or encumbrance by requiring the deposit of the proceeds into a restricted account subject to the lien. The court shall have continuing jurisdiction over the funds deposited. The transferred lien shall attach only to the amount asserted by the personal representative, and any proceeds in excess of that amount shall not be subject to the lien or otherwise restricted under this section. Alternatively, the personal representative and the apparent owners of the protected homestead may agree to retain in escrow the amount demanded as reimbursement by the personal representative, to be held there under the continuing jurisdiction of the court pending a final determination of

the amount properly reimbursable to the personal representative under this section.

(13)   This act shall apply to estates of decedents dying after the date on which this act becomes a law.

History.—s. 1, ch. 74-106; s. 29, ch. 77-87; s. 131, ch. 2001-226; s. 10, ch. 2003-154; s. 15, ch. 2010-132.

Note.—Created from former s. 733.01(1).

733.609   Improper exercise of power; breach of fiduciary duty.—

(1)   A personal representative's fiduciary duty is the same as the fiduciary duty of a trustee of an express trust, and a personal representative is liable to interested persons for damage or loss resulting from the breach of this duty. In all actions for breach of fiduciary duty or challenging the exercise of or failure to exercise a personal representative's powers, the court shall award taxable costs as in chancery actions, including attorney's fees.

(2)   When awarding taxable costs, including attorney's fees, under this section, the court in its discretion may direct payment from a party's interest, if any, in the estate or enter a judgment which may be satisfied from other property of the party, or both.

(3)   This section shall apply to all proceedings commenced hereunder after the effective date, without regard to the date of the decedent's death.

History.—s. 1, ch. 74-106; s. 78, ch. 75-220; s. 1006, ch. 97-102; s. 132, ch. 2001-226; s. 11, ch. 2003-154.

733.610   Sale, encumbrance, or transaction involving conflict of interest.—Any sale or encumbrance to the personal representative or the personal representative's spouse, agent, or attorney, or any corporation or trust in which the personal representative has a substantial beneficial interest, or any transaction that is affected by a conflict of interest on the part of the personal representative, is voidable by any interested person except one who has consented after fair disclosure, unless:

(1)   The will or a contract entered into by the decedent expressly authorized the transaction; or

(2)   The transaction is approved by the court after notice to interested persons.

History.—s. 1, ch. 74-106; s. 78, ch. 75-220; s. 1007, ch. 97-102; s. 133, ch. 2001-226.

733.611   Persons dealing with the personal representative; protection.—Except as provided in s. 733.613(1), a person who in good faith either assists or deals for value with a personal representative is protected as if the personal representative acted properly. The fact that a person knowingly deals with the personal representative does not require the person to inquire into the authority of the personal representative. A person is not bound to see to the proper application of estate assets paid or delivered to the personal representative. This protection extends to instances in which a procedural irregularity or jurisdictional defect occurred in proceedings leading to the issuance of letters, including a case in which the alleged decedent is alive. This protection is in addition to any protection afforded by comparable provisions of the laws relating to commercial transactions and laws simplifying transfers of securities by fiduciaries.

History.—s. 1, ch. 74-106; s. 78, ch. 75-220; s. 30, ch. 77-87; s. 1, ch. 77-174; s. 1008, ch. 97-102; s. 134, ch. 2001-226.

733.612 Transactions authorized for the personal representative; exceptions.—Except as otherwise provided by the will or court order, and subject to the priorities stated in s. 733.805, without court order, a personal representative, acting reasonably for the benefit of the interested persons, may properly:

(1)   Retain assets owned by the decedent, pending distribution or liquidation, including those in which the personal representative is personally interested or that are otherwise improper for fiduciary investments.

(2)   Perform or compromise, or, when proper, refuse to perform, the decedent's contracts. In performing the decedent's enforceable contracts to convey or lease real property, among other possible courses of action, the personal representative may:

(a)   Convey the real property for cash payment of all sums remaining due or for the purchaser's note for the sum remaining due, secured by a mortgage on the property.

(b)   Deliver a deed in escrow, with directions that the proceeds, when paid in accordance with the escrow agreement, be paid as provided in the escrow agreement.

(3)   Receive assets from fiduciaries or other sources.

(4)   Invest funds as provided in ss. 518.10-518.14, considering the amount to be invested, liquidity needs of the estate, and the time until distribution will be made.

(5)   Acquire or dispose of an asset, excluding real property in this or another state, for cash or on credit and at public or private sale, and manage, develop, improve, exchange, partition, or change the character of an estate asset.

(6)   Make ordinary or extraordinary repairs or alterations in buildings or other structures; demolish improvements; or erect new party walls or buildings.

(7)   Enter into a lease, as lessor or lessee, for a term within, or extending beyond, the period of administration, with or without an option to renew.

(8)   Enter into a lease or arrangement for exploration and removal of minerals or other natural resources or enter into a pooling or unitization agreement.

(9)   Abandon property when it is valueless or so encumbered, or in a condition, that it is of no benefit to the estate.

(10)   Vote, or refrain from voting, stocks or other securities in person or by general or limited proxy.

(11)   Pay calls, assessments, and other sums chargeable or accruing against, or on account of, securities, unless barred by the provisions relating to claims.

(12)   Hold property in the name of a nominee or in other form without disclosure of the interest of the estate, but the personal representative is liable for any act of the nominee in connection with the property so held.

(13)   Insure the assets of the estate against damage or loss and insure against personal and fiduciary liability to third persons.

(14)   Borrow money, with or without security, to be repaid from the estate assets or otherwise, other than real property, and advance money for the protection of the estate.

(15)   Extend, renew, or in any manner modify any obligation owing to the estate. If the personal representative holds a mortgage, security interest, or other lien upon property of another person, he or she may accept a conveyance or transfer of encumbered assets from the owner in satisfaction of the indebtedness secured by its lien instead of foreclosure.

(16)   Pay taxes, assessments, and other expenses incident to the administration of the estate.

(17)   Sell or exercise stock subscription or conversion rights or consent, directly or through a committee or other agent, to the reorganization, consolidation, merger, dissolution, or liquidation of a corporation or other business enterprise.

(18)   Allocate items of income or expense to either estate income or principal, as permitted or provided by law.

(19)   Employ persons, including, but not limited to, attorneys, accountants, auditors, appraisers, investment advisers, and others, even if they are one and the same as the personal representative or are associated with the personal representative, to advise or assist the personal representative in the performance of administrative duties; act upon the recommendations of those employed persons without independent investigation; and, instead of acting personally, employ one or more agents to perform any act of administration, whether or not discretionary. Any fees and compensation paid to a person who is the same as, associated with, or employed by, the personal representative shall be taken into consideration in determining the personal representative's compensation.

(20)   Prosecute or defend claims or proceedings in any jurisdiction for the protection of the estate and of the personal representative.

(21)   Sell, mortgage, or lease any personal property of the estate or any interest in it for cash, credit, or for part cash or part credit, and with or without security for the unpaid balance.

(22)   Continue any unincorporated business or venture in which the decedent was engaged at the time of death:

(a)   In the same business form for a period of not more than 4 months from the date of appointment, if continuation is a reasonable means of preserving the value of the business, including good will.

(b)   In the same business form for any additional period of time that may be approved by court order.

(23)   Provide for exoneration of the personal representative from personal liability in any contract entered into on behalf of the estate.

(24)   Satisfy and settle claims and distribute the estate as provided in this code.

(25)   Enter into agreements with the proper officer or department head, commissioner, or agent of any department of the government of the United States, waiving the statute of limitations concerning the assessment and collection of any federal tax or any deficiency in a federal tax.

(26)   Make partial distribution to the beneficiaries of any part of the estate not necessary to satisfy claims, expenses of administration, taxes, family allowance, exempt property, and an elective share, in accordance with the decedent's will or as authorized by operation of law.

(27)   Execute any instruments necessary in the exercise of the personal representative's powers.

History.—s. 1, ch. 74-106; s. 78, ch. 75-220; s. 3, ch. 76-172; s. 31, ch. 77-87; s. 1, ch. 77-174; s. 271, ch. 79-400; s. 1009, ch. 97-102; s. 135, ch. 2001-226.

733.6121 Personal representative; powers as to environmental issues relating to property subject to administration; liability.—

(1)   Except as otherwise provided by the will or by court order, and subject to s. 733.805, the personal representative has, without court authorization, the powers specified in subsection (2).

(2)   A personal representative has the power, acting reasonably and for the benefit of the interested persons:

(a)   To inspect or investigate, or cause to be inspected or investigated, property subject to administration, including interests in sole proprietorships, partnerships, or corporations and any assets owned by such a business entity for the purpose of determining compliance with an environmental law affecting that property or to respond to an actual or threatened violation of an environmental law affecting that property;

(b)   To take, on behalf of the estate, any action necessary to prevent, abate, or otherwise remedy an actual or potential violation of an environmental law affecting property subject to administration, either before or after initiation of an enforcement action by a governmental body;

(c)   To settle or compromise at any time any claim against the estate or the personal representative that may be asserted by a governmental body or private party which involves the alleged violation of an environmental law affecting property subject to administration over which the personal representative has responsibility;

(d)   To disclaim any power granted by any document, statute, or rule of law which, in the sole judgment of the personal representative, could cause the personal representative to incur personal liability, or the estate to incur liability, under any environmental law;

(e)   To decline to serve as a personal representative, or having undertaken to serve, to resign at any time, if the personal representative believes that there is or could be a conflict of interest because of potential claims or liabilities that could be asserted on behalf of the estate by reason of the type or condition of the assets held; or

(f)   To charge against the assets of the estate the cost of any inspection, investigation, review, abatement, response, cleanup, or remedial action considered reasonable by the personal representative; and, in the event of the closing or termination of the estate or the transfer of the estate property to another personal representative, to hold moneys sufficient to cover the cost of cleaning up any known environmental problem.

(3)   A personal representative is not personally liable to any beneficiary or any other party for a decrease in value of assets in an estate by reason of the personal representative's compliance or efforts to comply with an environmental law, specifically including any reporting requirement under that law.

(4)   A personal representative who acquires ownership or control of a vessel or other property without having owned, operated, or materially participated in the management of that vessel or property before assuming ownership or control as personal representative is not considered an owner or operator for purposes of liability under chapter 376, chapter 403, or any other environmental law. A personal representative who willfully, knowingly, or recklessly causes or exacerbates a release or threatened release of a hazardous substance is personally liable for the cost of the response, to the extent that the release or threatened release is attributable to the personal representative's activities. This subsection does not preclude the filing of claims against the assets that constitute the estate held by the personal representative or the filing of actions against the personal representative as representative of the estate. In such an action, an award or judgment against the personal representative must be satisfied only from the assets of the estate.

(5)   Neither the acceptance by the personal representative of the property or a failure by the personal representative to inspect or investigate the property creates any inference of liability under an environmental law with respect to that property.

(6)   For the purposes of this section, the term "environmental law" means a federal, state, or local law, rule, regulation, or ordinance that relates to protection of the environment or human health, and the term "hazardous substance" means a substance, material, or waste defined as hazardous or toxic, or any contaminant, pollutant, or constituent thereof, or otherwise regulated by an environmental law.

(7)   This section applies to any estate admitted to probate on or after July 1, 1995.

History.—s. 18, ch. 95-401; s. 1010, ch. 97-102; s. 136, ch. 2001-226.

733.613   Personal representative's right to sell real property.—

(1)   When a personal representative of an intestate estate, or whose testator has not conferred a power of sale or whose testator has granted a power of sale but the power is so limited by the will or by operation of law that it cannot be conveniently exercised, shall consider that it is for the best interest of the estate and of those interested in it that real property be sold, the personal representative may sell it at public or private sale. No title shall pass until the court authorizes or confirms the sale. No bona fide purchaser shall be required to examine any proceedings before the order of sale.

(2)   When a decedent's will confers specific power to sell or mortgage real property or a general power to sell any asset of the estate, the personal representative may sell, mortgage, or lease, without authorization or confirmation of court, any real property of the estate or any interest therein for cash or credit, or for part cash and part credit, and with or without security for unpaid balances. The sale, mortgage, or lease need not be justified by a showing of necessity, and the sale pursuant to power of sale shall be valid.

(3)   In a sale or mortgage which occurs under a specific power to sell or mortgage real property, or under a court order authorizing or confirming that act, the purchaser or lender takes title free of claims of creditors of the estate and entitlements of estate beneficiaries, except existing mortgages or other liens against real property are not affected.

History.—s. 1, ch. 74-106; s. 78, ch. 75-220; s. 1011, ch. 97-102; s. 137, ch. 2001-226.

Note.—Created from former s. 733.23.

733.614   Powers and duties of successor personal representative.—A successor personal representative has the same power and duty as the original personal representative to complete the administration and distribution of the estate as expeditiously as possible, but shall not exercise any power made personal to the personal representative named in the will without court approval.

History.—s. 1, ch. 74-106; s. 78, ch. 75-220; s. 1012, ch. 97-102; s. 138, ch. 2001-226.

Note.—Created from former s. 734.10.

733.615   Joint personal representatives; when joint action required.—

(1)   If two or more persons are appointed joint personal representatives, and unless the will provides otherwise, the concurrence of all joint personal representatives appointed pursuant to a will or codicil executed prior to October 1, 1987, or appointed to administer an intestate estate of a decedent who died prior to October 1, 1987, or of a majority of joint personal representatives appointed pursuant to a will or codicil executed on or after October 1, 1987, or appointed to administer an intestate estate of a decedent dying on or after October 1, 1987, is required on all acts connected with the administration and distribution of the estate. This restriction does not apply when any joint personal representative receives and receipts for property due the estate, when the concurrence required under this subsection cannot readily be obtained in the time reasonably available for emergency action necessary to preserve the estate, or when a joint personal representative has been delegated to act for the others.

(2)   Where action by a majority of the joint personal representatives appointed is authorized, a joint personal representative who has not joined in exercising a power is not liable to the beneficiaries or to others for the consequences of the exercise, and a dissenting joint personal representative is not liable for the consequences of an action in which the dissenting personal representative joins at the direction of the majority of the joint personal representatives, if the dissent is expressed in writing to the other joint personal representatives at or before the time of the action.

(3)   A person dealing with a joint personal representative without actual knowledge that joint personal representatives have been appointed, or if advised by a joint personal representative that the joint personal representative has authority to act alone for any of the reasons mentioned in subsection (1), is as fully protected in dealing with that joint personal representative as if that joint personal representative possessed and properly exercised the power.

History.—s. 1, ch. 74-106; s. 1, ch. 87-317; s. 4, ch. 88-340; s. 1013, ch. 97-102; s. 139, ch. 2001-226.

Note.—Created from former s. 732.50.

733.616 Powers of surviving personal representatives.—Unless otherwise provided by the terms of the will or a court order, every power exercisable by joint personal representatives may be exercised by the one or more remaining after the appointment of one or more is terminated. If one or more, but not all, nominated as joint personal representatives are not appointed, those appointed may exercise all powers granted to those nominated.

History.—s. 1, ch. 74-106; s. 140, ch. 2001-226.

Note.—Created from former s. 732.52.

733.617 Compensation of personal representative.—

(1)   A personal representative shall be entitled to a commission payable from the estate assets without court order as compensation for ordinary services. The commission shall be based on the compensable value of the estate, which is the inventory value of the probate estate assets and the income earned by the estate during administration.

(2)   A commission computed on the compensable value of the estate is presumed to be reasonable compensation for a personal representative in formal administration as follows:

(a)   At the rate of 3 percent for the first $1 million.

(b)   At the rate of 2.5 percent for all above $1 million and not exceeding $5 million.

(c)   At the rate of 2 percent for all above $5 million and not exceeding $10 million.

(d)   At the rate of 1.5 percent for all above $10 million.

Florida Probate Code

(3)   In addition to the previously described commission, a personal representative shall be allowed further compensation as is reasonable for any extraordinary services including, but not limited to:

       (a)   The sale of real or personal property.

       (b)   The conduct of litigation on behalf of or against the estate.

       (c)   Involvement in proceedings for the adjustment or payment of any taxes.

       (d)   The carrying on of the decedent's business.

       (e)   Dealing with protected homestead.

       (f)   Any other special services which may be necessary for the personal representative to perform.

(4)   If the will provides that a personal representative's compensation shall be based upon specific criteria, other than a general reference to commissions allowed by law or words of similar import, including, but not limited to, rates, amounts, commissions, or reference to the personal representative's regularly published schedule of fees in effect at the decedent's date of death, or words of similar import, then a personal representative shall be entitled to compensation in accordance with that provision. However, except for references in the will to the personal representative's regularly published schedule of fees in effect at the decedent's date of death, or words of similar import, if there is no written contract with the decedent regarding compensation, a personal representative may renounce the provisions contained in the will and be entitled to compensation under this section. A personal representative may also renounce the right to all or any part of the compensation.

(5)   If the probate estate's compensable value is $100,000 or more, and there are two representatives, each personal representative is entitled to the full commission allowed to a sole personal representative. If there are more than two personal representatives and the probate estate's compensable value is $100,000 or more, the compensation to which two would be entitled must be apportioned among the personal representatives. The basis for apportionment shall be one full commission allowed to the personal representative who has possession of and primary responsibility for administration of the assets and one full commission among the remaining personal representatives according to the services rendered by each of them respectively. If the probate estate's compensable value is less than $100,000 and there is more than one personal representative, then one full commission must be apportioned among the personal representatives according to the services rendered by each of them respectively.

(6)   If the personal representative is a member of The Florida Bar and has rendered legal services in connection with the administration of the estate, then in addition to a fee as personal representative, there also shall be allowed a fee for the legal services rendered.

(7)   Upon petition of any interested person, the court may increase or decrease the compensation for ordinary services of the personal representative or award compensation for extraordinary services if the facts and circumstances of the particular administration warrant. In determining reasonable compensation, the court shall consider all

of the following factors, giving weight to each as it determines to be appropriate:

      (a)   The promptness, efficiency, and skill with which the administration was handled by the personal representative;

      (b)   The responsibilities assumed by and the potential liabilities of the personal representative;

      (c)   The nature and value of the assets that are affected by the decedent's death;

      (d)   The benefits or detriments resulting to the estate or interested persons from the personal representative's services;

      (e)   The complexity or simplicity of the administration and the novelty of the issues presented;

      (f)   The personal representative's participation in tax planning for the estate and the estate's beneficiaries and in tax return preparation, review, or approval;

      (g)   The nature of the probate, nonprobate, and exempt assets, the expenses of administration, the liabilities of the decedent, and the compensation paid to other professionals and fiduciaries;

      (h)   Any delay in payment of the compensation after the services were furnished; and

      (i)   Any other relevant factors.

History.—s. 1, ch. 74-106; s. 80, ch. 75-220; s. 1, ch. 76-172; s. 5, ch. 88-340; s. 1, ch. 90-129; s. 10, ch. 93-257; s. 1, ch. 95-401; s. 141, ch. 2001-226; s. 109, ch. 2002-1.

Note.—Created from former s. 734.01.

733.6171 Compensation of attorney for the personal representative.—

      (1)   Attorneys for personal representatives shall be entitled to reasonable compensation payable from the estate assets without court order.

      (2)   The attorney, the personal representative, and persons bearing the impact of the compensation may agree to compensation determined in a different manner than provided in this section. Compensation may also be determined in a different manner than provided in this section if the manner is disclosed to the parties bearing the impact of the compensation and if no objection is made as provided for in the Florida Probate Rules.

      (3)   Compensation for ordinary services of attorneys in formal estate administration is presumed to be reasonable if based on the compensable value of the estate, which is the inventory value of the probate estate assets and the income earned by the estate during the administration as provided in the following schedule:

      (a)   One thousand five hundred dollars for estates having a value of $40,000 or less.

       (b)   An additional $750 for estates having a value of more than $40,000 and not exceeding $70,000.

       (c)   An additional $750 for estates having a value of more than $70,000 and not exceeding $100,000.

       (d)   For estates having a value in excess cf $100,000, at the rate of 3 percent on the next $900,000.

       (e)   At the rate of 2.5 percent for all above $1 million and not exceeding $3 million.

       (f)   At the rate of 2 percent for all above $3 million and not exceeding $5 million.

       (g)   At the rate of 1.5 percent for all above $5 million and not exceeding $10 million.

       (h)   At the rate of 1 percent for all above $10 million.

       (4)   In addition to fees for ordinary services, the attorney for the personal representative shall be allowed further reasonable compensaticn for any extraordinary service. What is an extraordinary service may vary depending on many factors, including the size of the estate. Extraordinary services may include, but are not limited to:

       (a)   Involvement in a will contest, will construction, a proceeding for determination of beneficiaries, a contested claim, elective share proceeding, apportionment of estate taxes, or any adversarial proceeding or litigation by or against the estate.

       (b)   Representation of the personal representative in audit or any proceeding for adjustment, determination, or collection of any taxes.

       (c)   Tax advice on postmortem tax planning, including, but not limited to, disclaimer, renunciation of fiduciary commission, alternate valuation date, allocation of administrative expenses between tax returns, the QTIP or reverse QTIP election, allocation of GST exemption, qualification for Internal Revenue Code ss. 6166 and 303 privileges, deduction of last illness expenses, fiscal year planning, distribution planning, asset basis considerations, handling income or deductions in respect of a decedent, valuation discounts, special use and other valuation, handling employee benefit or retirement proceeds, prompt assessment request, or request for release of personal liability for payment of tax.

       (d)   Review of estate tax return and preparation or review of other tax returns required to be filed by the personal representative.

       (e)   Preparation of the estate's federal estate tax return. If this return is prepared by the attorney, a fee of one-half of 1 percent up to a value of $10 million and one-fourth of 1 percent on the value in excess of $10 million of the gross estate as finally determined for federal estate tax purposes, is presumed to be reasonable compensation for the attorney for this service. These fees shall include services for routine audit of the return, not beyond the examining agent level, if required.

      (f)   Purchase, sale, lease, or encumbrance of real property by the personal representative or involvement in zoning, land use, environmental, or other similar matters.

      (g)   Legal advice regarding carrying on of the decedent's business or conducting other commercial activity by the personal representative.

      (h)   Legal advice regarding claims for damage to the environment or related procedures.

      (i)   Legal advice regarding homestead status of real property or proceedings involving that status and services related to protected homestead.

      (j)   Involvement in fiduciary, employee, or attorney compensation disputes.

      (k)   Proceedings involving ancillary administration of assets not subject to administration in this state.

      (5)   Upon petition of any interested person, the court may increase or decrease the compensation for ordinary services of the attorney or award compensation for extraordinary services if the facts and circumstances of the particular administration warrant. In determining reasonable compensation, the court shall consider all of the following factors, giving weight to each as it determines to be appropriate:

      (a)   The promptness, efficiency, and skill with which the administration was handled by the attorney.

      (b)   The responsibilities assumed by and the potential liabilities of the attorney.

      (c)   The nature and value of the assets that are affected by the decedent's death.

      (d)   The benefits or detriments resulting to the estate or interested persons from the attorney's services.

      (e)   The complexity or simplicity of the administration and the novelty of issues presented.

      (f)   The attorney's participation in tax planning for the estate and the estate's beneficiaries and tax return preparation, review, or approval.

      (g)   The nature of the probate, nonprobate, and exempt assets, the expenses of administration, the liabilities of the decedent, and the compensation paid to other professionals and fiduciaries.

      (h)   Any delay in payment of the compensation after the services were furnished.

(i)   Any other relevant factors.

(6)   If a separate written agreement regarding compensation exists between the attorney and the decedent, the attorney shall furnish a copy to the personal representative prior to commencement of employment, and, if employed, shall promptly file and serve a copy on all interested persons. Neither a separate agreement nor a provision in the will suggesting or directing that the personal representative retain a specific attorney will obligate the personal representative to employ the attorney or obligate the attorney to accept the representation, but if the attorney who is a party to the agreement or who drafted the will is employed, the compensation paid shall not exceed the compensation provided in the agreement or in the will.

History.—s. 4, ch. 93-257; s. 2, ch. 95-401; s. 142, ch. 2001-226.

733.6175 Proceedings for review of employment of agents and compensation of personal representatives and employees of estate.—

(1)   The court may review the propriety of the employment of any person employed by the personal representative and the reasonableness of any compensation paid to that person or to the personal representative.

(2)   Court proceedings to determine reasonable compensation of the personal representative or any person employed by the personal representative, if required, are a part of the estate administration process, and the costs, including attorneys' fees, of the person assuming the burden of proof of propriety of the employment and reasonableness of the compensation shall be determined by the court and paid from the assets of the estate unless the court finds the requested compensation to be substantially unreasonable. The court shall direct from which part of the estate the compensation shall be paid.

(3)   The burden of proof of propriety of the employment and the reasonableness of the compensation shall be upon the personal representative and the person employed. Any person who is determined to have received excessive compensation from an estate for services rendered may be ordered to make appropriate refunds.

(4)   The court may determine reasonable compensation for the personal representative or any person employed by the personal representative without receiving expert testimony. Any party may offer expert testimony after notice to interested persons. If expert testimony is offered, a reasonable expert witness fee shall be awarded by the court and paid from the assets of the estate. The court shall direct from what part of the estate the fee shall be paid.

History.—s. 2, ch. 76-172; s. 1014, ch. 97-102; s. 143, ch. 2001-226.

733.619 Individual liability of personal representative.—

(1)   Unless otherwise provided in the contract, a personal representative is not individually liable on a contract, except a contract for attorney's fee, properly entered into as fiduciary unless the personal representative fails to reveal that representative capacity and identify the estate in the contract.

(2)   A personal representative is individually liable for obligations arising from ownership or control of the estate or for torts committed in the course of

administration of the estate only if personally at fault.

(3)   Claims based on contracts, except a contract for attorney's fee, entered into by a personal representative as a fiduciary, on obligations arising from ownership or control of the estate, or on torts committed in the course of estate administration, may be asserted against the estate by proceeding against the personal representative in that capacity, whether or not the personal representative is individually liable.

(4)   Issues of liability as between the estate and the personal representative individually may be determined in a proceeding for accounting, surcharge, or indemnification, or other appropriate proceeding.

History.—s. 82, ch. 75-220; s. 32, ch. 77-87; s. 228, ch. 77-104; s. 1015, ch. 97-102; s. 144, ch. 2001-226.

733.620 Exculpation of personal representative.—

(1)   A term of a will relieving a personal representative of liability to a beneficiary for breach of fiduciary duty is unenforceable to the extent that the term:

(a)   Relieves the personal representative of liability for breach of fiduciary duty committed in bad faith or with reckless indifference to the purposes of the will or the interests of interested persons; or

(b)   Was inserted into the will as the result of an abuse by the personal representative of a fiduciary or confidential relationship with the testator.

(2)   An exculpatory term drafted or caused to be drafted by the personal representative is invalid as an abuse of a fiduciary or confidential relationship unless:

(a)   The personal representative proves that the exculpatory term is fair under the circumstances.

(b)   The term's existence and contents were adequately communicated directly to the testator or to the independent attorney of the testator. This paragraph applies only to wills created on or after July 1, 2007.

History.—s. 15, ch. 2007-74.

PART VII
CREDITORS' CLAIMS

733.701 Notifying creditors.—Unless creditors' claims are otherwise barred by s. 733.710, every personal representative shall cause notice to creditors to be published and served under s. 733.2121.

History.—s. 1, ch. 74-106; s. 83, ch. 75-220; s. 33, ch. 77-87; s. 4, ch. 89-340; s. 145, ch. 2001-226; s. 31, ch. 2003-154.

Note.—Created from former s. 733.15.

Florida Probate Code

733.702 Limitations on presentation of claims.—

(1)   If not barred by s. 733.710, no claim or demand against the decedent's estate that arose before the death of the decedent, including claims of the state and any of its political subdivisions, even if the claims are unmatured, contingent, or unliquidated; no claim for funeral or burial expenses; no claim for personal property in the possession of the personal representative; and no claim for damages, including, but not limited to, an action founded on fraud or another wrongful act or omission of the decedent, is binding on the estate, on the personal representative, or on any beneficiary unless filed in the probate proceeding on or before the later of the date that is 3 months after the time of the first publication of the notice to creditors or, as to any creditor required to be served with a copy of the notice to creditors, 30 days after the date of service on the creditor, even though the personal representative has recognized the claim or demand by paying a part of it or interest on it or otherwise. The personal representative may settle in full any claim without the necessity of the claim being filed when the settlement has been approved by the interested persons.

(2)   No cause of action, including, but not limited to, an action founded upon fraud or other wrongful act or omission, shall survive the death of the person against whom the claim may be made, whether or not an action is pending at the death of the person, unless a claim is filed within the time periods set forth in this part.

(3)   Any claim not timely filed as provided in this section is barred even though no objection to the claim is filed unless the court extends the time in which the claim may be filed. An extension may be granted only upon grounds of fraud, estoppel, or insufficient notice of the claims period. No independent action or declaratory action may be brought upon a claim which was not timely filed unless an extension has been granted by the court. If the personal representative or any other interested person serves on the creditor a notice to file a petition for an extension, the creditor shall be limited to a period of 30 days from the date of service of the notice in which to file a petition for extension.

(4)   Nothing in this section affects or prevents:

(a)   A proceeding to enforce any mortgage, security interest, or other lien on property of the decedent.

(b)   To the limits of casualty insurance protection only, any proceeding to establish liability that is protected by the casualty insurance.

(c)   The filing of a cross-claim or counterclaim against the estate in an action instituted by the estate; however, no recovery on a cross-claim or counterclaim shall exceed the estate's recovery in that action.

(5)   Nothing in this section shall extend the limitations period set forth in s. 733.710.

History.—s. 1, ch. 74-106; s. 84, ch. 75-220; s. 2, ch. 80-127; s. 4, ch. 81-27; s. 160, ch. 83-216; s. 5, ch. 84-106; s. 4, ch. 85-79; s. 6, ch. 88-340; s. 5, ch. 89-340; s. 4, ch. 90-23; s. 1016, ch. 97-102; s. 146, ch. 2001-226; s. 6, ch. 2002-82; s. 26, ch. 2006-312; s. 21, ch. 2010-4.

Note.—Created from former s. 733.16.

733.703 Form and manner of presenting claim.—

(1)   A creditor shall file a written statement of the claim. No additional charge may be imposed by a claimant who files a claim against the estate.

(2)   Within the time allowed by s. 733.702, the personal representative may file a proof of claim of all claims he or she has paid or intends to pay. A claimant whose claim is listed in a personal representative's proof of claim shall be deemed to have filed a statement of the claim listed. Except as provided otherwise in this part, the claim shall be treated as if the claimant had filed it.

History.—s. 1, ch. 74-106; s. 84, ch. 75-220; s. 5, ch. 81-27; s. 5, ch. 85-79; s. 6, ch. 89-340; s. 147, ch. 2001-226.

Note.—Created from former s. 733.16.

733.704 Amendment of claims.—If a bona fide attempt to file a claim is made but the claim is defective as to form, the court may permit the amendment of the claim at any time.

History.—s. 1, ch. 74-106; s. 1, ch. 77-174; s. 148, ch. 2001-226.

Note.—Created from former s. 733.17.

733.705 Payment of and objection to claims.—

(1)   The personal representative shall pay all claims within 1 year from the date of first publication of notice to creditors, provided that the time shall be extended with respect to claims in litigation, unmatured claims, and contingent claims for the period necessary to dispose of those claims pursuant to subsections (5), (6), (7), and (8). The court may extend the time for payment of any claim upon a showing of good cause. No personal representative shall be compelled to pay the debts of the decedent until after the expiration of 5 months from the first publication of notice to creditors. If any person brings an action against a personal representative within the 5 months on any claim to which the personal representative has not filed an objection, the plaintiff shall not receive any costs or attorneys' fees, nor shall the judgment change the class of the claim for payment under this code.

(2)   On or before the expiration of 4 months from the first publication of notice to creditors or within 30 days from the timely filing or amendment of a claim, whichever occurs later, a personal representative or other interested person may file a written objection to a claim. If an objection is filed, the person filing it shall serve a copy of the objection as provided by the Florida Probate Rules. The failure to serve a copy of the objection constitutes an abandonment of the objection. For good cause, the court may extend the time for filing or serving an objection to any claim. Objection to a claim constitutes an objection to an amendment of that claim unless the objection is withdrawn.

(3)   If the objection is filed by a person other than the personal representative, the personal representative may apply to the court for an order relieving him or her from the obligation to defend the estate in an independent action or for the appointment of the objector as administrator ad litem to defend the action. Fees for the attorney for the administrator ad litem may be awarded as provided in s. 733.106(3). If costs

or attorney's fees are awarded from or against the estate, the probate court may charge or apportion that award as provided in s. 733.106(4).

(4)   An objection by an interested person to a personal representative's proof of claim shall state the particular item or items to which the interested person objects and shall be filed and served as provided in subsection (2). Issues of liability as between the estate and the personal representative individually for items listed in a personal representative's proof of claim shall be determined in the estate administration, in a proceeding for accounting or surcharge, or in another appropriate proceeding, whether or not an objection has been filed. If an objection to an item listed as to be paid in a personal representative's proof of claim is filed and served, and the personal representative has not paid the item, the other subsections of this section shall apply as if a claim for the item had been filed by the claimant; but if the personal representative has paid the claim after listing it as to be paid, issues of liability as between the estate and the personal representative individually shall be determined in the manner provided for an item listed as paid.

(5)   The claimant is limited to a period of 30 days from the date of service of an objection within which to bring an independent action upon the claim, or a declaratory action to establish the validity and amount of an unmatured claim which is not yet due but which is certain to become due in the future, or a declaratory action to establish the validity of a contingent claim upon which no cause of action has accrued on the date of service of an objection and that may or may not become due in the future, unless an extension of this time is agreed to by the personal representative in writing before it expires. For good cause, the court may extend the time for filing an action or proceeding after objection is filed. No action or proceeding on the claim may be brought against the personal representative after the time limited above, and the claim is barred without court order. If an objection is filed to the claim of any creditor and the creditor brings an action to establish the claim, a judgment establishing the claim shall give it no priority over claims of the same class to which it belongs.

(6)   A claimant may bring an independent action or declaratory action upon a claim which was not timely filed pursuant to s. 733.702(1) only if the claimant has been granted an extension of time to file the claim pursuant to s. 733.702(3).

(7)   If an unmatured claim has not become due before the time for distribution of an estate, the personal representative may prepay the full amount of principal plus accrued interest due on the claim, without discount and without penalty, regardless of any prohibition against prepayment or provision for penalty in any instrument on which the claim is founded. If the claim is not prepaid, no order of discharge may be entered until the creditor and personal representative have filed an agreement disposing of the claim, or in the absence of an agreement until the court provides for payment by one of the following methods:

(a)   Requiring the personal representative to reserve such assets as the court determines to be adequate to pay the claim when it becomes due; in fixing the amount to be reserved, the court may determine the value of any security or collateral to which the creditor may resort for payment of the claim and may direct the reservation, if necessary, of sufficient assets to pay the claim or to pay the difference between the value of any security or collateral and the amount necessary to pay the claim. If the estate is insolvent, the court may direct a proportionate amount to be reserved. The court shall direct that the amount reserved be retained by the personal representative until the time that the claim becomes due, and that so much of the reserved amount as is not used for payment be distributed according to law;

  (b) Requiring that the claim be adequately secured by a mortgage, pledge, bond, trust, guaranty, or other security, as may be determined by the court, the security to remain in effect until the time the claim becomes due, and so much of the security or collateral as is not needed for payment be distributed according to law; or

  (c) Making provisions for the disposition or satisfaction of the claim as are equitable, and in a manner so as not to delay unreasonably the closing of the estate.

  (8) If no cause of action has accrued on a contingent claim before the time for distribution of an estate, no order of discharge may be entered until the creditor and the personal representative have filed an agreement disposing of the claim or, in the absence of an agreement, until:

  (a) The court determines that the claim is adequately secured or that it has no value,

  (b) Three months from the date on which a cause of action accrues upon the claim, provided that no action on the claim is then pending,

  (c) Five years from the date of first publication of notice to creditors, or

  (d) The court provides for payment of the claim upon the happening of the contingency by one of the methods described in paragraph (a), paragraph (b), or paragraph (c) of subsection (7),
whichever occurs first. No action or proceeding on the claim may be brought against the personal representative after the time limited above, and the claim is barred without court order. If an objection is filed to the claim of any creditor and the creditor brings an action to establish the claim, a judgment establishing the claim shall give it no priority over claims of the same class to which it belongs.

  (9) Interest shall be paid by the personal representative on written obligations of the decedent providing for the payment of interest. On all other claims, interest shall be allowed and paid beginning 5 months from the first publication of the notice to creditors.

  (10) The court may determine all issues concerning claims or matters not requiring trial by jury.

  (11) An order for extension of time authorized under this section may be entered only in the estate administration proceeding.

History.—s. 1, ch. 74-106; s. 86, ch. 75-220; s. 34, ch. 77-87; s. 1, ch. 77-174; s. 1, ch. 84-25; s. 1, ch. 86-249; s. 7, ch. 88-340; s. 7, ch. 89-340; s. 2, ch. 91-61; s. 1017, ch. 97-102; s. 149, ch. 2001-226.

Note.—Created from former s. 733.18.

733.706 Executions and levies.—Except upon approval by the court, no execution or other process shall issue on or be levied against property of the estate. An order approving execution or other process to be levied against property of the estate may be entered only in the estate administration proceeding. Claims on all judgments against a decedent shall be filed in the same manner as other claims against estates of decedents. This section shall not be construed to prevent the enforcement of mortgages, security interests, or liens encumbering specific property.

History.—s. 1, ch. 74-106; s. 86, ch. 75-220; s. 8, ch. 89-340.

Note.—Created from former s. 733.19.

733.707   Order of payment of expenses and obligations.—

(1)   The personal representative shall pay the expenses of the administration and obligations of the decedent's estate in the following order:

(a)   Class 1.—Costs, expenses of administration, and compensation of personal representatives and their attorneys fees and attorneys fees awarded under s. 733.106(3).

(b)   Class 2.—Reasonable funeral, interment, and grave marker expenses, whether paid by a guardian, the personal representative, or any other person, not to exceed the aggregate of $6,000.

(c)   Class 3.—Debts and taxes with preference under federal law, claims pursuant to ss. 409.9101 and 414.28, and claims in favor of the state for unpaid court costs, fees, or fines.

(d)   Class 4.—Reasonable and necessary medical and hospital expenses of the last 60 days of the last illness of the decedent, including compensation of persons attending the decedent.

(e)   Class 5.—Family allowance.

(f)   Class 6.—Arrearage from court-ordered child support.

(g)   Class 7.—Debts acquired after death by the continuation of the decedent's business, in accordance with s. 733.612(22), but only to the extent of the assets of that business.

(h)   Class 8.—All other claims, including those founded on judgments or decrees rendered against the decedent during the decedent's lifetime, and any excess over the sums allowed in paragraphs (b) and (d).

(2)   After paying any preceding class, if the estate is insufficient to pay all of the next succeeding class, the creditors of the latter class shall be paid ratably in proportion to their respective claims.

(3)   Any portion of a trust with respect to which a decedent who is the grantor has at the decedent's death a right of revocation, as defined in paragraph (e), either alone or in conjunction with any other person, is liable for the expenses of the administration and obligations of the decedent's estate to the extent the decedent's estate is

insufficient to pay them as provided in ss. 733.607(2) and 736.05053.

(a)   For purposes of this subsection, any trusts established as part of, and all payments from, either an employee annuity described in s. 403 of the Internal Revenue Code of 1986, as amended, an Individual Retirement Account, as described in s. 408 of the Internal Revenue Code of 1986, as amended, a Keogh (HR-10) Plan, or a retirement or other plan established by a corporation which is qualified under s. 401 of the Internal Revenue Code of 1986, as amended, shall not be considered a trust over which the decedent has a right of revocation.

(b)   For purposes of this subsection, any trust described in s. 664 of the Internal Revenue Code of 1986, as amended, shall not be considered a trust over which the decedent has a right of revocation.

(c)   This subsection shall not impair any rights an individual has under a qualified domestic relations order as that term is defined in s. 414(p) of the Internal Revenue Code of 1986, as amended.

(d)   For purposes of this subsection, property held or received by a trust to the extent that the property would not have been subject to claims against the decedent's estate if it had been paid directly to a trust created under the decedent's will or other than to the decedent's estate, or assets received from any trust other than a trust described in this subsection, shall not be deemed assets of the trust available to the decedent's estate.

(e)   For purposes of this subsection, a "right of revocation" is a power retained by the decedent, held in any capacity, to:

1.   Amend or revoke the trust and revest the principal of the trust in the decedent; or

2.   Withdraw or appoint the principal of the trust to or for the decedent's benefit.

History.—s. 1, ch. 74-106; s. 86, ch. 75-220; s. 35, ch. 77-87; s. 7, ch. 85-79; s. 69, ch. 87-226; s. 20, ch. 93-208; s. 11, ch. 93-257; s. 10, ch. 95-401; s. 1018, ch. 97-102; s. 3, ch. 97-240; s. 150, ch. 2001-226; s. 2, ch. 2010-122; s. 17, ch. 2012-100.

Note.—Created from former s. 733.20.

733.708   Compromise.—When a proposal is made to compromise any claim, whether in suit or not, by or against the estate of a decedent or to compromise any question concerning the distribution of a decedent's estate, the court may enter an order authorizing the compromise if satisfied that the compromise will be for the best interest of the interested persons. The order shall relieve the personal representative of liability or responsibility for the compromise. Claims against the estate may not be compromised until after the time for filing objections to claims has expired.

History.—s. 1, ch. 74-106; s. 86, ch. 75-220; s. 151, ch. 2001-226.

Note.—Created from former s. 733.21.

733.710 Limitations on claims against estates.—

(1) Notwithstanding any other provision of the code, 2 years after the death of a person, neither the decedent's estate, the personal representative, if any, nor the beneficiaries shall be liable for any claim or cause of action against the decedent, whether or not letters of administration have been issued, except as provided in this section.

(2) This section shall not apply to a creditor who has filed a claim pursuant to s. 733.702 within 2 years after the person's death, and whose claim has not been paid or otherwise disposed of pursuant to s. 733.705.

(3) This section shall not affect the lien of any duly recorded mortgage or security interest or the lien of any person in possession of personal property or the right to foreclose and enforce the mortgage or lien.

History.—s. 1, ch. 74-106; s. 50, ch. 75-220; s. 36, ch. 77-87; s. 9, ch. 89-340; s. 152, ch. 2001-226.

Note.—Created from former s. 734.29(1).

PART VIII
SPECIAL PROVISIONS FOR DISTRIBUTION

733.801 Delivery of devises and distributive shares.—

(1) No personal representative shall be required to pay or deliver any devise or distributive share or to surrender possession of any land to any beneficiary until the expiration of 5 months from the granting of letters.

(2) Except as otherwise provided in the will, the personal representative shall pay as an expense of administration the reasonable expenses of storage, insurance, packing, and delivery of tangible personal property to a beneficiary.

History.—s. 1, ch. 74-106; s. 86, ch. 75-220; s. 153, ch. 2001-226.

Note.—Created from former s. 734.02.

733.802 Proceedings for compulsory payment of devises or distributive interest.—

(1) Before final distribution, no personal representative shall be compelled:

(a) To pay a devise in money before the final settlement of the personal representative's accounts,

(b) To deliver specific personal property devised, unless the personal property is exempt personal property,

(c) To pay all or any part of a distributive share in the personal estate of a decedent, or

(d) To surrender land to any beneficiary,
unless the beneficiary establishes that the property will not be required for the payment of

debts, family allowance, estate and inheritance taxes, claims, elective share of the surviving spouse, charges, or expenses of administration or to provide funds for contribution or to enforce equalization in case of advancements.

(2)   An order directing the surrender of real property or the delivery of personal property by the personal representative to the beneficiary shall be conclusive in favor of bona fide purchasers for value from the beneficiary or distributee as against the personal representative and all other persons claiming by, through, under, or against the decedent or the decedent's estate.

(3)   If the administration of the estate has not been completed before the entry of an order of partial distribution, the court may require the person entitled to distribution to give a bond with sureties as prescribed in s. 45.011, conditioned on the making of due contribution for the payment of devises, family allowance, estate and inheritance taxes, claims, elective share of the spouse, charges, expenses of administration, and equalization in case of advancements, plus any interest on them.

History.—s. 1, ch. 74-106; s. 86, ch. 75-220; s. 37, ch. 77-87; s. 1, ch. 77-174; s. 272, ch. 79-400; s. 1019, ch. 97-102; s. 154, ch. 2001-226.

Note.—Created from former s. 734.03.

733.803 Encumbered property; liability for payment.—The specific devisee of any encumbered property shall be entitled to have the encumbrance on devised property paid at the expense of the residue of the estate only when the will shows that intent. A general direction in the will to pay debts does not show that intent.

History.—s. 1, ch. 74-106; s. 86, ch. 75-220; s. 155, ch. 2001-226.

Note.—Created from former s. 734.051.

733.805 Order in which assets abate.—

(1)   Funds or property designated by the will shall be used to pay debts, family allowance, exempt property, elective share charges, expenses of administration, and devises, to the extent the funds or property is sufficient. If no provision is made or the designated fund or property is insufficient, the funds and property of the estate shall be used for these purposes, and to raise the shares of a pretermitted spouse and children, except as otherwise provided in subsections (3) and (4), in the following order:

(a)   Property passing by intestacy.

(b)   Property devised to the residuary devisee or devisees.

(c)   Property not specifically or demonstratively devised.

(d)   Property specifically or demonstratively devised.

(2)   Demonstrative devises shall be classed as general devises upon the failure or insufficiency of funds or property out of which payment should be made, to the extent of the insufficiency. Devises to the decedent's surviving spouse, given in satisfaction of, or instead of, the surviving spouse's statutory rights in the estate, shall not abate until

other devises of the same class are exhausted. Devises given for a valuable consideration shall abate with other devises of the same class only to the extent of the excess over the amount of value of the consideration until all others of the same class are exhausted. Except as herein provided, devises shall abate equally and ratably and without preference or priority as between real and personal property. When property that has been specifically devised or charged with a devise is sold or used by the personal representative, other devisees shall contribute according to their respective interests to the devisee whose devise has been sold or used. The amounts of the respective contributions shall be determined by the court and shall be paid or withheld before distribution is made.

(3) Section 733.817 shall be applied before this section is applied.

(4) In determining the contribution required under s. 733.607(2), subsections (1)-(3) of this section and s. 736.05053(2) shall be applied as if the beneficiaries of the estate and the beneficiaries of a trust described in s. 733.707(3), other than the estate or trust itself, were taking under a common instrument.

History.—s. 1, ch. 74-106; s. 88, ch. 75-220; s. 1, ch. 77-174; s. 1020, ch. 97-102; s. 156, ch. 2001-226; s. 38, ch. 2006-217.

Note.—Created from former s. 734.05.

733.806 Advancement.—If a person dies intestate, property that the decedent gave during lifetime to an heir is treated as an advancement against the heir's share of the estate only if declared in a contemporaneous writing by the decedent or acknowledged in writing by the heir. The property advanced shall be valued at the time the heir came into possession or enjoyment of the property or at the time of the death of the decedent, whichever first occurs. If the recipient of the property does not survive the decedent, the property shall not be taken into account in computing the intestate share to be received by the recipient's descendants unless the declaration or acknowledgment provides otherwise.

History.—s. 1, ch. 74-106; s. 1021, ch. 97-102; s. 157, ch. 2001-226.

Note.—Created from former s. 734.07.

733.808 Death benefits; disposition of proceeds.—

(1) Death benefits of any kind, including, but not limited to, proceeds of:

(a) An individual life insurance policy;

(b) A group life insurance policy;

(c) A benefit plan as defined by s. 710.102;

(d) An annuity or endowment contract; and

(e) A health or accident policy,

may be made payable to the trustee under a trust agreement or declaration of trust in existence at the time of the death of the insured, employee, or annuitant or the owner of or participant in the benefit plan. The death benefits shall be held and disposed of by the trustee in accordance with the terms of the trust as they appear in writing on the date of the death of the insured, employee, annuitant, owner, or participant. It shall not be necessary to the validity of the trust agreement or declaration of trust, whether revocable or irrevocable, that it have a trust corpus other than the right of the trustee to receive death benefits.

(2)   Death benefits of any kind, including, but not limited to, proceeds of:

(a)   An individual life insurance policy;

(b)   A group life insurance policy;

(c)   A benefit plan as defined in s. 710.102;

(d)   An annuity or endowment contract; and

(e)   A health or accident policy,

may be made payable to the trustee named, or to be named, in a written instrument that is admitted to probate as the last will of the insured, the owner of the policy, the employee, owner, or participant covered by the plan or contract, or any other person, whether or not the will is in existence at the time of designation. Upon the admission of the will to probate, the death benefits shall be paid to the trustee, to be held, administered, and disposed of in accordance with the terms of the trust or trusts created by the will.

(3)   In the event no trustee makes proper claim to the proceeds from the insurance company or other obligor within a period of 6 months after the date of the death of the insured, employee, annuitant, owner, or participant, or if satisfactory evidence is furnished to the insurance company or obligor within that period that there is, or will be, no trustee to receive the proceeds, payment shall be made by the insurance company or obligor to the personal representative of the person making the designation, unless otherwise provided by agreement with the insurer or obligor during the lifetime of the insured, employee, annuitant, owner, or participant.

(4)   Death benefits payable as provided in subsection (1), subsection (2), or subsection (3), unless paid to a personal representative under the provisions of subsection (3), shall not be deemed to be part of the decedent's estate, and shall not be subject to any obligation to pay the expenses of the administration and obligations of the decedent's estate or for contribution required from a trust under s. 733.607(2) to any greater extent than if the proceeds were payable directly to the beneficiaries named in the trust.

(5)   The death benefits held in trust may be commingled with any other assets that may properly come into the trust.

(6)   This section does not affect the validity of any designation of a beneficiary of proceeds previously made that designates as beneficiary the trustee of any trust established under a trust agreement or declaration of trust or by will.

History.—s. 1, ch. 74-106; s. 38, ch. 77-87; s. 158, ch. 2001-226; s. 7, ch. 2005-101.

Note.—Created from former s. 736.172.

733.809 Right of retainer.—The amount of a noncontingent indebtedness due from a beneficiary to the estate or its present value, if not due, may be offset against that beneficiary's interest. However, that beneficiary shall have the benefit of any defense that would be available in a direct proceeding for recovery of the debt.

History.—s. 1, ch. 74-106; s. 39, ch. 77-87; s. 1022, ch. 97-102; s. 159, ch. 2001-226.

733.810 Distribution in kind; valuation.—

(1)   Assets shall be distributed in kind unless:

(a)   A general power of sale is conferred;

(b)   A contrary intention is indicated by the will or trust; or

(c)   Disposition is made otherwise under the provisions of this code.

(2)   Any pecuniary devise, family allowance, or other pecuniary share of the estate or trust may be satisfied in kind if:

(a)   The person entitled to payment has not demanded cash;

(b)   The property is distributed at fair market value as of its distribution date; and

(c)   No residuary devisee has requested that the asset remain a part of the residuary estate.

(3)   When not practicable to distribute undivided interests in a residuary asset, the asset may be sold.

(4)   When the fiduciary under a will or trust is required, or has an option, to satisfy a pecuniary devise or transfer in trust, to or for the benefit of the surviving spouse, with an in-kind distribution, at values as finally determined for federal estate tax purposes, the fiduciary shall, unless the governing instrument otherwise provides, satisfy the devise or transfer in trust by distribution of assets, including cash, fairly representative of the appreciated or depreciated value of all property available for that distribution, taking into consideration any gains and losses realized from a prior sale of any property not devised specifically, generally, or demonstratively.

(5)   A personal representative or a trustee is authorized to distribute any distributable assets, non-pro rata among the beneficiaries subject to the fiduciary's duty of impartiality.

History.—s. 1, ch. 74-106; s. 92, ch. 75-220; s. 40, ch. 77-87; s. 160, ch. 2001-226.

Note.—Created from former s. 734.031.

733.811 Distribution; right or title of distributee.—If a distributee receives from a fiduciary an instrument transferring assets in kind, payment in distribution, or possession of specific property, the distributee has succeeded to the estate's interest in the assets as against all persons interested in the estate. However, the fiduciary may recover the assets or their value if the distribution was improper.

History.—s. 1, ch. 74-106; s. 161, ch. 2001-226.

733.812 Improper distribution or payment; liability of distributee or payee.—A distributee or a claimant who was paid improperly must return the assets or funds received, and the income from those assets or interest on the funds since distribution or payment, unless the distribution or payment cannot be questioned because of adjudication, estoppel, or limitations. If the distributee or claimant does not have the property, its value at the date of disposition, income thereon, and gain received by the distributee or claimant must be returned.

History.—s. 1, ch. 74-106; s. 92, ch. 75-220; s. 1023, ch. 97-102; s. 162, ch. 2001-226.

733.813 Purchasers from distributees protected.—If property distributed in kind, or a security interest in that property, is acquired by a purchaser or lender for value from a distributee, the purchaser or lender takes title free of any claims of the estate and incurs no personal liability to the estate, whether or not the distribution was proper. The purchaser or lender need not inquire whether a personal representative acted properly in making the distribution in kind.

History.—s. 1, ch. 74-106; s. 163, ch. 2001-226.

733.814 Partition for purpose of distribution.—When two or more beneficiaries are entitled to distribution of undivided interests in any property, the personal representative or any beneficiary may petition the court before the estate is closed to partition the property in the same manner as provided by law for civil actions of partition. The court may direct the personal representative to sell any property that cannot be partitioned without prejudice to the owners and that cannot be allotted equitably and conveniently.

History.—s. 1, ch. 74-106; s. 164, ch. 2001-226.

733.815 Private contracts among interested persons.—Subject to the rights of creditors and taxing authorities, interested persons may agree among themselves to alter the interests, shares, or amounts to which they are entitled in a written contract executed by them. The personal representative shall abide by the terms of the contract, subject to the personal representative's obligation to administer the estate for the benefit of interested persons who are not parties to the contract, and to pay costs of administration. Trustees of a testamentary trust are interested persons for the purposes of this section. Nothing in this section relieves trustees of any duties owed to beneficiaries of trusts.

History.—s. 1, ch. 74-106; s. 94, ch. 75-220; s. 1024, ch. 97-102; s. 165, ch. 2001-226.

733.816 Disposition of unclaimed property held by personal representatives.—

(1)   In all cases in which there is unclaimed property in the hands of a personal representative that cannot be distributed or paid because of the inability to find the lawful owner or because no lawful owner is known or because the lawful owner refuses to accept the property after a reasonable attempt to distribute it and after notice to that lawful owner, the court shall order the personal representative to sell the property and deposit the proceeds and cash already in hand, after retaining those amounts provided for in subsection (4), with the clerk and receive a receipt, and the clerk shall deposit the funds in the registry of the court to be disposed of as follows:

(a)   If the value of the funds is $500 or less, the clerk shall post a notice for 30 days at the courthouse door giving the amount involved, the name of the personal representative, and the other pertinent information that will put interested persons on notice.

(b)   If the value of the funds is over $500, the clerk shall publish the notice once a month for 2 consecutive months in a newspaper of general circulation in the county.

After the expiration of 6 months from the posting or first publication, the clerk shall deposit the funds with the Chief Financial Officer after deducting the clerk's fees and the costs of publication.

(2)   Upon receipt of the funds, the Chief Financial Officer shall deposit them to the credit of the State School Fund, to become a part of the school fund. All interest and all income that may accrue from the money while so deposited shall belong to the fund. The funds so deposited shall constitute and be a permanent appropriation for payments by the Chief Financial Officer in obedience to court orders entered as provided by subsection (3).

(3)   Within 10 years from the date of deposit with the Chief Financial Officer, on written petition to the court that directed the deposit of the funds and informal notice to the Department of Legal Affairs, and after proof of entitlement, any person entitled to the funds before or after payment to the Chief Financial Officer and deposit as provided by subsection (1) may obtain a court order directing the payment of the funds to that person. All funds deposited with the Chief Financial Officer and not claimed within 10 years from the date of deposit shall escheat to the state for the benefit of the State School Fund.

(4)   The personal representative depositing assets with the clerk is permitted to retain from the funds a sufficient amount to pay final costs of administration chargeable to the assets accruing between the deposit of the funds with the clerk of the court and the order of discharge. Any funds so retained which are surplus shall be deposited with the clerk prior to discharge of the personal representative.

(5)   (a)   If a person entitled to the funds assigns the right to receive payment or part payment to an attorney or private investigative agency which is duly licensed to do business in this state pursuant to a written agreement with that person, the Department of Financial Services is authorized to make distribution in accordance with the assignment.

(b)   Payments made to an attorney or private investigative agency shall be promptly deposited into a trust or escrow account which is regularly maintained by the attorney or private investigative agency in a financial institution located in this state and authorized to accept these deposits.

(c)   Distribution by the attorney or private investigative agency to the person entitled to the funds shall be made within 10 days following final credit of the deposit into the trust or escrow account at the financial institution, unless a party to the agreement protests the distribution in writing before it is made.

(d)   The department shall not be civilly or criminally liable for any funds distributed pursuant to this subsection, provided the distribution is made in good faith.

History.—s. 1, ch. 74-106; s. 95, ch. 75-220; s. 6, ch. 85-79; s. 5, ch. 89-291; s. 10, ch. 89-299; s. 21, ch. 95-401; s. 1025, ch. 97-102; s. 166, ch. 2001-226; s. 1897, ch. 2003-261.

Note.—Created from former s. 734.221.

733.817   Apportionment of estate taxes.—

(1)   For purposes of this section:

(a)   "Fiduciary" means a person other than the personal representative in possession of property included in the measure of the tax who is liable to the applicable taxing authority for payment of the entire tax to the extent of the value of the property in possession.

(b)   "Governing instrument" means a will, trust agreement, or any other document that controls the transfer of an asset on the occurrence of the event with respect to which the tax is being levied.

(c)   "Gross estate" means the gross estate, as determined by the Internal Revenue Code with respect to the federal estate tax and the Florida estate tax, and as that concept is otherwise determined by the estate, inheritance, or death tax laws of the particular state, country, or political subdivision whose tax is being apportioned.

(d)   "Included in the measure of the tax" means that for each separate tax that an interest may incur, only interests included in the measure of that particular tax are considered. The term "included in the measure of the tax" does not include any interest, whether passing under the will or not, to the extent the interest is initially deductible from the gross estate, without regard to any subsequent reduction of the deduction by reason of the charge of any part of the applicable tax to the interest. The term "included in the measure of the tax" does not include interests or amounts that are not included in the gross estate but are included in the amount upon which the applicable tax is computed, such as adjusted taxable gifts with respect to the federal estate tax. If an election is required for deductibility, an interest is not "initially deductible" unless the election for deductibility is allowed.

(e)   "Internal Revenue Code" means the Internal Revenue Code of 1986, as amended from time to time.

(f)   "Net tax" means the net tax payable to the particular state, country, or political subdivision whose tax is being apportioned, after taking into account all credits against the applicable tax except as provided in this section. With respect to the federal estate tax, "net tax" is determined after taking into account all credits against the tax except for the credit for foreign death taxes.

(g)   "Nonresiduary devise" means any devise that is not a residuary devise.

(h)   "Nonresiduary interest" in connection with a trust means any interest in a trust which is not a residuary interest.

(i) "Recipient" means, with respect to property or an interest in property included in the gross estate, an heir at law in an intestate estate, devisee in a testate estate, beneficiary of a trust, beneficiary of an insurance policy, annuity, or other contractual right, surviving tenant, taker as a result of the exercise or in default of the exercise of a general power of appointment, person who receives or is to receive the property or an interest in the property, or person in possession of the property, other than a creditor.

(j) "Residuary devise" has the meaning set forth in s. 731.201.

(k) "Residuary interest," in connection with a trust, means an interest in the assets of a trust which remain after provision for any distribution that is to be satisfied by reference to a specific property or type of property, fund, sum, or statutory amount.

(l) "Revocable trust" means a trust as described in s. 733.707(3).

(m) "State" means any state, territory, or possession of the United States, the District of Columbia, and the Commonwealth of Puerto Rico.

(n) "Tax" means any estate tax, inheritance tax, generation skipping transfer tax, or other tax levied or assessed under the laws of this or any other state, the United States, any other country, or any political subdivision of the foregoing, as finally determined, which is imposed as a result of the death of the decedent, including, without limitation, the tax assessed pursuant to s. 4980A of the Internal Revenue Code. The term also includes any interest and penalties imposed in addition to the tax. Unless the context indicates otherwise, the term "tax" means each separate tax.

(o) "Temporary interest" means an interest in income or an estate for a specific period of time or for life or for some other period controlled by reference to extrinsic events, whether or not in trust.

(p) "Tentative Florida tax" with respect to any property means the net Florida estate tax that would have been attributable to that property if no tax were payable to any other state in respect of that property.

(q) "Value" means the pecuniary worth of the interest involved as finally determined for purposes of the applicable tax after deducting any debt, expense, or other deduction chargeable to it for which a deduction was allowed in determining the amount of the applicable tax. A lien or other encumbrance is not regarded as chargeable to a particular interest to the extent that it will be paid from other interests. The value of an interest shall not be reduced by reason of the charge against it of any part of the tax.

(2) An interest in protected homestead shall be exempt from the apportionment of taxes.

(3) The net tax attributable to the interests included in the measure of each tax shall be determined by the proportion that the value of each interest included in the measure of the tax bears to the total value of all interests included in the measure of the tax. Notwithstanding the foregoing:

(a)　　　The net tax attributable to interests included in the measure of the tax by reason of s. 2044 of the Internal Revenue Code shall be determined in the manner provided for the federal estate tax in s. 2207A of the Internal Revenue Code, and the amount so determined shall be deducted from the tax to determine the net tax attributable to all remaining interests included in the measure of the tax.

(b)　　　The foreign tax credit allowed with respect to the federal estate tax shall be allocated among the recipients of interests finally charged with the payment of the foreign tax in reduction of any federal estate tax chargeable to the recipients of the foreign interests, whether or not any federal estate tax is attributable to the foreign interests. Any excess of the foreign tax credit shall be applied to reduce proportionately the net amount of federal estate tax chargeable to the remaining recipients of the interests included in the measure of the federal estate tax.

(c)　　　The reduction in the Florida tax on the estate of a Florida resident for tax paid to other states shall be allocated as follows:

1.　　　If the net tax paid to another state is greater than or equal to the tentative Florida tax attributable to the property subject to tax in the other state, none of the Florida tax shall be attributable to that property.

2.　　　If the net tax paid to another state is less than the tentative Florida tax attributable to the property subject to tax in the other state, the net Florida tax attributable to the property subject to tax in the other state shall be the excess of the amount of the tentative Florida tax attributable to the property over the net tax payable to the other state with respect to the property.

3.　　　Any remaining net Florida tax shall be attributable to property included in the measure of the Florida tax exclusive of property subject to tax in other states.

4.　　　The net federal tax attributable to the property subject to tax in the other state shall be determined as if it were located in the state.

(d)　　　The net tax attributable to a temporary interest, if any, shall be regarded as attributable to the principal that supports the temporary interest.

(4)　　　(a)　　　Except as otherwise effectively directed by the governing instrument, if the Internal Revenue Code, including, but not limited to, ss. 2032A(c)(5), 2206, 2207, 2207A, 2207B, and 2603, applies to apportion federal tax against recipients of certain interests, all net taxes, including taxes levied by the state attributable to each type of interest, shall be apportioned against the recipients of all interests of that type in the proportion that the value of each interest of that type included in the measure of the tax bears to the total of all interests of that type included in the measure of the tax.

(b)　　　The provisions of this subsection do not affect allocation of the reduction in the Florida tax as provided in this section with respect to estates of Florida residents which are also subject to tax in other states.

(5)　　　Except as provided above or as otherwise directed by the governing instrument, the net tax attributable to each interest shall be apportioned as follows:

(a)   For property passing under the decedent's will:

1.   The net tax attributable to nonresiduary devises shall be charged to and paid from the residuary estate whether or not all interests in the residuary estate are included in the measure of the tax. If the residuary estate is insufficient to pay the net tax attributable to all nonresiduary devises, the balance of the net tax attributable to nonresiduary devises shall be apportioned among the recipients of the nonresiduary devises in the proportion that the value of each nonresiduary devise included in the measure of the tax bears to the total of all nonresiduary devises included in the measure of the tax.

2.   The net tax attributable to residuary devises shall be apportioned among the recipients of the residuary devises included in the measure of tax in the proportion that the value of each residuary devise included in the measure of the tax bears to the total of all residuary devises included in the measure of the tax.

(b)   For property passing under the terms of any trust other than a trust created in the decedent's will:

1.   The net tax attributable to nonresiduary interests shall be charged to and paid from the residuary portion of the trust, whether or not all interests in the residuary portion are included in the measure of the tax. If the residuary portion of the trust is insufficient to pay the net tax attributable to all nonresiduary interests, the balance of the net tax attributable to nonresiduary interests shall be apportioned among the recipients of the nonresiduary interests in the proportion that the value of each nonresiduary interest included in the measure of the tax bears to the total of all nonresiduary interests included in the measure of the tax.

2.   The net tax attributable to residuary interests shall be apportioned among the recipients of the residuary interests included in the measure of the tax in the proportion that the value of each residuary interest included in the measure of the tax bears to the total of all residuary interests included in the measure of the tax.

(c)   The net tax attributable to an interest in protected homestead shall be apportioned against the recipients of other interests in the estate or passing under any revocable trust in the following order:

1.   Class I: Recipients of interests not disposed of by the decedent's will or revocable trust that are included in the measure of the federal estate tax.

2.   Class II: Recipients of residuary devises and residuary interests that are included in the measure of the federal estate tax.

3.   Class III: Recipients of nonresiduary devises and nonresiduary interests that are included in the measure of the federal estate tax.
The net tax apportioned to a class, if any, pursuant to this paragraph shall be apportioned among the recipients in the class in the proportion that the value of the interest of each bears to the total value of all interests included in that class.

(d)   In the application of this subsection, paragraphs (a), (b), and

(c) shall be applied to apportion the net tax to the recipients of the estate and the recipients of the decedent's revocable trust as if all recipients, other than the estate or trusts themselves, were taking under a common instrument.

(e)   The net tax imposed under s. 4980A of the Internal Revenue Code shall be apportioned among the recipients of the interests included in the measure of that tax in the proportion that the value of the interest of each bears to the total value of all interests included in the measure of that tax.

(f)   The net tax that is not apportioned under paragraphs (a), (b), and (c), including, but not limited to, the net tax attributable to interests passing by intestacy, jointly held interests passing by survivorship, insurance, properties in which the decedent held a reversionary or revocable interest, and annuities, shall be apportioned among the recipients of the remaining interests that are included in the measure of the tax in the proportion that the value of each such interest bears to the total value of all the remaining interests included in the measure of the tax.

(g)   If the court finds that it is inequitable to apportion interest, penalties, or both, in the manner provided in paragraphs (a)-(f), the court may assess liability for the payment thereof in the manner it finds equitable.

(h)   1.   To be effective as a direction for payment of tax in a manner different from that provided in this section, the governing instrument must direct that the tax be paid from assets that pass pursuant to that governing instrument, except as provided in this section.

2.   If the decedent's will provides that the tax shall be apportioned as provided in the decedent's revocable trust by specific reference to the trust, the direction in the revocable trust shall be deemed to be a direction contained in the will and shall control with respect to payment of taxes from assets passing under both the will and the revocable trust.

3.   A direction in the decedent's will to pay tax from the decedent's revocable trust is effective if a contrary direction is not contained in the trust agreement.

4.   For a direction in a governing instrument to be effective to direct payment of taxes attributable to property not passing under the governing instrument from property passing under the governing instrument, the governing instrument must expressly refer to this section, or expressly indicate that the property passing under the governing instrument is to bear the burden of taxation for property not passing under the governing instrument. A direction in the governing instrument to the effect that all taxes are to be paid from property passing under the governing instrument whether attributable to property passing under the governing instrument or otherwise shall be effective to direct the payment from property passing under the governing instrument of taxes attributable to property not passing under the governing instrument.

5.   If there is a conflict as to payment of taxes between the decedent's will and the governing instrument, the decedent's will controls, except as follows:

a.   The governing instrument shall be given

effect with respect to any tax remaining unpaid after the application of the decedent's will.

b. A direction in a governing instrument to pay the tax attributable to assets that pass pursuant to the governing instrument from assets that pass pursuant to that governing instrument shall be effective notwithstanding any conflict with the decedent's will, unless the tax provision in the decedent's will expressly overrides the conflicting provision in the governing instrument.

(6) The personal representative or fiduciary shall not be required to transfer to a recipient any property reasonably anticipated to be necessary for the payment of taxes. Further, the personal representative or fiduciary shall not be required to transfer any property to the recipient until the amount of the tax due from the recipient is paid by the recipient. If property is transferred before final apportionment of the tax, the recipient shall provide a bond or other security for his or her apportioned liability in the amount and form prescribed by the personal representative or fiduciary.

(7) (a) The personal representative may petition at any time for an order of apportionment. If no administration has been commenced at any time after 90 days from the decedent's death, any fiduciary may petition for an order of apportionment in the court in which venue would be proper for administration of the decedent's estate. Formal notice of the petition for order of apportionment shall be given to all interested persons. At any time after 6 months from the decedent's death, any recipient may petition the court for an order of apportionment.

(b) The court shall determine all issues concerning apportionment. If the tax to be apportioned has not been finally determined, the court shall determine the probable tax due or to become due from all interested persons, apportion the probable tax, and retain jurisdiction over the parties and issues to modify the order of apportionment as appropriate until after the tax is finally determined.

(8) (a) If the personal representative or fiduciary does not have possession of sufficient property otherwise distributable to the recipient to pay the tax apportioned to the recipient, whether under this section, the Internal Revenue Code, or the governing instrument, if applicable, the personal representative or fiduciary shall recover the deficiency in tax so apportioned to the recipient:

1. From the fiduciary in possession of the property to which the tax is apportioned, if any; and

2. To the extent of any deficiency in collection from the fiduciary, or to the extent collection from the fiduciary is excused pursuant to subsection (9) and in all other cases, from the recipient of the property to which the tax is apportioned, unless relieved of this duty as provided in subsection (9).

(b) In any action to recover the tax apportioned, the order of apportionment shall be prima facie correct.

(c) In any action for the enforcement of an order of apportionment, the court shall award taxable costs as in chancery actions, including reasonable attorney's fees, and may award penalties and interest on the unpaid tax in accordance with equitable principles.

(d)   This subsection shall not authorize the recovery of any tax from any company issuing insurance included in the gross estate, or from any bank, trust company, savings and loan association, or similar institution with respect to any account in the name of the decedent and any other person which passed by operation of law on the decedent's death.

(9)   (a)   A personal representative or fiduciary who has the duty under this section of collecting the apportioned tax from recipients may be relieved of the duty to collect the tax by an order of the court finding:

1.   That the estimated court costs and attorney's fees in collecting the apportioned tax from a person against whom the tax has been apportioned will approximate or exceed the amount of the recovery;

2.   That the person against whom the tax has been apportioned is a resident of a foreign country other than Canada and refuses to pay the apportioned tax on demand; or

3.   That it is impracticable to enforce contribution of the apportioned tax against a person against whom the tax has been apportioned in view of the improbability of obtaining a judgment or the improbability of collection under any judgment that might be obtained, or otherwise.

(b)   A personal representative or fiduciary shall not be liable for failure to attempt to enforce collection if the personal representative or fiduciary reasonably believes it would have been economically impracticable.

(10)   Any apportioned tax that is not collected shall be reapportioned in accordance with this section as if the portion of the property to which the uncollected tax had been apportioned had been exempt.

(11)   Nothing in this section shall limit the right of any person who has paid more than the amount of the tax apportionable to that person, calculated as if all apportioned amounts would be collected, to obtain contribution from those who have not paid the full amount of the tax apportionable to them, calculated as if all apportioned amounts would be collected, and that right is hereby conferred. In any action to enforce contribution, the court shall award taxable costs as in chancery actions, including reasonable attorney's fees.

(12)   Nothing herein contained shall be construed to require the personal representative or fiduciary to pay any tax levied or assessed by any foreign country, unless specific directions to that effect are contained in the will or other instrument under which the personal representative or fiduciary is acting.

History.—s. 1, ch. 74-106; s. 95, ch. 75-220; s. 41, ch. 77-87; s. 273, ch. 79-400; s. 20, ch. 92-200; s. 1026, ch. 97-102; s. 9, ch. 97-240; s. 13, ch. 2000-159; s. 167, ch. 2001-226; s. 39, ch. 2006-217; s. 122, ch. 2010-5.

Note.—Created from former s. 734.041.

PART IX
CLOSING ESTATES

733.901 Final discharge.—

(1)   After administration has been completed, the personal representative shall be discharged.

(2)   The discharge of the personal representative shall release the personal representative and shall bar any action against the personal representative, as such or individually, and the surety.

History.—s. 1, ch. 74-106; s. 96, ch. 75-220; s. 42, ch. 77-87; s. 1, ch. 77-174; s. 6, ch. 81-27; s. 29, ch. 95-401; s. 1027, ch. 97-102; s. 168, ch. 2001-226.

Note.—Created from former s. 734.22.

733.903 Subsequent administration.—The final settlement of an estate and the discharge of the personal representative shall not prevent further administration. The order of discharge may not be revoked based upon the discovery of a will or later will.

History.—s. 1, ch. 74-106; s. 96, ch. 75-220; s. 1, ch. 88-110; s. 169, ch. 2001-226.

Note.—Created from former s. 734.26.

Florida Probate Code

PART I
GENERAL PROVISIONS

734.101 Foreign personal representative.—

(1)   Personal representatives who produce authenticated copies of probated wills or letters of administration duly obtained in any state or territory of the United States may maintain actions in the courts of this state.

(2)   Personal representatives appointed in any state or country may be sued in this state concerning property in this state and may defend actions or proceedings brought in this state.

(3)   Debtors who have not received a written demand for payment from a personal representative or curator appointed in this state within 90 days after appointment of a personal representative in any other state or country, and whose property in Florida is subject to a mortgage or other lien securing the debt held by the foreign personal representative, may pay the foreign personal representative after the expiration of 90 days from the date of appointment of the foreign personal representative. Thereafter, a satisfaction of the mortgage or lien executed by the foreign personal representative, with an authenticated copy of the letters or other evidence of authority attached, may be recorded in the public records. The satisfaction shall be an effective discharge of the mortgage or lien, irrespective of whether the debtor making payment had received a written demand before paying the debt.

(4)   Except as provided in s. 655.936, all persons indebted to the estate of a decedent, or having possession of personal property belonging to the estate, who have received no written demand from a personal representative or curator appointed in this state for payment of the debt or the delivery of the property are authorized to pay the debt or to deliver the personal property to the foreign personal representative after the expiration of 90 days from the date of appointment of the foreign personal representative.

History.—s. 1, ch. 74-106; s. 98, ch. 75-220; s. 1028, ch. 97-102; s. 170, ch. 2001-226; s. 110, ch. 2002-1; s. 16, ch. 2007-74.

Note.—Created from former s. 734.30.

734.102 Ancillary administration.—

(1)   If a nonresident of this state dies leaving assets in this state, credits due from residents in this state, or liens on property in this state, a personal representative specifically designated in the decedent's will to administer the Florida property shall be entitled to have ancillary letters issued, if qualified to act in Florida. Otherwise, the foreign personal representative of the decedent's estate shall be entitled to have letters issued, if qualified to act in Florida. If the foreign personal representative is not qualified to act in Florida and the will names an alternate or successor who is qualified to act in Florida, the alternate or successor shall be entitled to have letters issued. Otherwise, those entitled to a majority interest of the Florida property may have letters issued to a personal representative

selected by them who is qualified to act in Florida. If the decedent dies intestate and the foreign personal representative is not qualified to act in Florida, the order of preference for appointment of a personal representative as prescribed in this code shall apply. If ancillary letters are applied for by other than the domiciliary personal representative, prior notice shall be given to any domiciliary personal representative.

(2)   Ancillary administration shall be commenced as provided by the Florida Probate Rules.

(3)   If the will and any codicils are executed as required by the code, they shall be admitted to probate.

(4)   The ancillary personal representative shall give bond as do personal representatives generally. All proceedings for appointment and administration of the estate shall be as similar to those in original administrations as possible.

(5)   Unless creditors' claims are otherwise barred by s. 733.710, the ancillary personal representative shall cause a notice to creditors to be served and published according to the requirements of chapter 733. Claims not filed in accordance with chapter 733 shall be barred as provided in s. 733.702.

(6)   After the payment of all expenses of administration and claims against the estate, the court may order the remaining property held by the ancillary personal representative transferred to the foreign personal representative or distributed to the beneficiaries.

(7)   Ancillary personal representatives shall have the same rights, powers, and authority as other personal representatives in Florida to manage and settle estates; to sell, lease, or mortgage local property; and to raise funds for the payment of debts, claims, and devises in the domiciliary jurisdiction. No property shall be sold, leased, or mortgaged to pay a debt or claim that is barred by any statute of limitation or of nonclaim of this state.

History.—s. 1, ch. 74-106; s. 98, ch. 75-220; s. 43, ch. 77-87; s. 1, ch. 77-174; s. 1029, ch. 97-102; s. 171, ch. 2001-226.

Note.—Created from former s. 734.31.

734.1025 Nonresident decedent's testate estate with property not exceeding $50,000 in this state; determination of claims.—

(1)   When a nonresident decedent dies testate and leaves property subject to administration in this state the gross value of which does not exceed $50,000 at the date of death, the foreign personal representative of the estate before the expiration of 2 years after the decedent's death may file in the circuit court of the county where any property is located an authenticated transcript of so much of the foreign proceedings as will show the will and beneficiaries of the estate, as provided in the Florida Probate Rules. The court shall admit the will and any codicils to probate if they comply with s. 732.502(1), (2), or (3).

(2)   The foreign personal representative may cause a notice to creditors to be served and published according to the relevant requirements of chapter 733. Claims not filed in accordance with chapter 733 shall be barred as provided in s. 733.702. If any claim is filed, a personal representative shall be appointed as provided in the Florida Probate

Rules.

History.—s. 1, ch. 80-203; s. 10, ch. 89-340; s. 1030, ch. 97-102; s. 79, ch. 99-3; s. 172, ch. 2001-226; s. 12, ch. 2003-154.

734.104   Foreign wills; admission to record; effect on title.—

(1)   An authenticated copy of the will of a nonresident that devises real property in this state, or any right, title, or interest in the property, may be admitted to record in any county of this state where the property is located at any time after 2 years from the death of the decedent or at any time after the domiciliary personal representative has been discharged if there has been no proceeding to administer the estate of the decedent in this state, provided:

(a)   The will was executed as required by chapter 732; and

(b)   The will has been admitted to probate in the proper court of any other state, territory, or country.

(2)   A petition to admit a foreign will to record may be filed by any person and shall be accompanied by authenticated copies of the foreign will, the petition for probate, and the order admitting the will to probate. If no petition is required as a prerequisite to the probate of a will in the jurisdiction where the will of the nonresident was probated, upon proof by affidavit or certificate that no petition is required, an authenticated copy of the will may be admitted to record without an authenticated copy of a petition for probate, and the order admitting the will to record in this state shall recite that no petition was required in the jurisdiction of original probate.

(3)   If the court finds that the requirements of this section have been met, it shall enter an order admitting the foreign will to record.

(4)   When admitted to record, the foreign will shall be as valid and effectual to pass title to real property and any right, title, or interest therein as if the will had been admitted to probate in this state.

History.—s. 3, ch. 74-106; s. 98, ch. 75-220; s. 45, ch. 77-87; s. 229, ch. 77-104; s. 15, ch. 79-221; s. 274, ch. 79-400; s. 11, ch. 89-340; s. 173, ch. 2001-226.

Note.—Created from former s. 736.06.

PART II
JURISDICTION OVER FOREIGN PERSONAL REPRESENTATIVES

734.201   Jurisdiction by act of foreign personal representative.—A foreign personal representative submits personally to the jurisdiction of the courts of this state in any proceeding concerning the estate by:

(1)   Filing authenticated copies of the domiciliary proceedings under s. 734.104;

(2)   Receiving payment of money or taking delivery of personal property, under s. 734.101; or

(3)   Doing any act as a personal representative in this state that would have given the state jurisdiction over that person as an individual.

History.—s. 1, ch. 74-106; s. 99, ch. 75-220; s. 1031, ch. 97-102; s. 174, ch. 2001-226.

734.202 Jurisdiction by act of decedent.—In addition to jurisdiction conferred by s. 734.201, a foreign personal representative is subject to the jurisdiction of the courts of this state to the same extent that the decedent was subject to jurisdiction immediately before death.

History.—s. 1, ch. 74-106; s. 1032, ch. 97-102; s. 175, ch. 2001-226.

Florida Probate Code

CHAPTER 735
PROBATE CODE: SMALL ESTATES

PART I
SUMMARY ADMINISTRATION

735.201 Summary administration; nature of proceedings.—Summary administration may be had in the administration of either a resident or nonresident decedent's estate, when it appears:

    (1)   In a testate estate, that the decedent's will does not direct administration as required by chapter 733.

    (2)   That the value of the entire estate subject to administration in this state, less the value of property exempt from the claims of creditors, does not exceed $75,000 or that the decedent has been dead for more than 2 years.

History.—s. 1, ch. 74-106; s. 105, ch. 75-220; s. 2, ch. 80-203; s. 13, ch. 89-340; s. 179, ch. 2001-226.

735.202 May be administered in the same manner as other estates.—The estate may be administered in the same manner as the administration of any other estate, or it may be administered as provided in this part.

History.—s. 1, ch. 74-106.

Note.—Created from former s. 735.02.

735.203 Petition for summary administration.—

    (1)   A petition for summary administration may be filed by any beneficiary or person nominated as personal representative in the decedent's will offered for probate. The petition must be signed and verified by the surviving spouse, if any, and any beneficiaries except that the joinder in a petition for summary administration is not required of a beneficiary who will receive a full distributive share under the proposed distribution. However, formal notice of the petition must be served on a beneficiary not joining in the petition.

    (2)   If a person named in subsection (1) has died, is incapacitated, or is a minor, or has conveyed or transferred all interest in the property of the estate, then, as to that person, the petition must be signed and verified by:

    (a)   The personal representative, if any, of a deceased person or, if none, the surviving spouse, if any, and the beneficiaries;

    (b)   The guardian of an incapacitated person or a minor; or

    (c)   The grantee or transferee of any of them shall be authorized to sign and verify the petition instead of the beneficiary or surviving spouse.

    (3)   If each trustee of a trust that is a beneficiary of the estate of the deceased person is also a petitioner, formal notice of the petition for summary

administration shall be served on each qualified beneficiary of the trust as defined in s. 736.0103 unless joinder in, or consent to, the petition is obtained from each qualified beneficiary of the trust.

History.—s. 1, ch. 74-106; s. 107, ch. 75-220; s. 1, ch. 77-174; s. 180, ch. 2001-226; s. 12, ch. 2009-115; s. 16, ch. 2010-132.

Note.—Created from former s. 735.05.

735.2055 Filing of petition.—The petition for summary administration may be filed at any stage of the administration of an estate if it appears that at the time of filing the estate would qualify.

History.—s. 47, ch. 77-87.

735.206 Summary administration distribution.—

(1)   Upon the filing of the petition for summary administration, the will, if any, shall be proved in accordance with chapter 733 and be admitted to probate.

(2)   Prior to entry of the order of summary administration, the petitioner shall make a diligent search and reasonable inquiry for any known or reasonably ascertainable creditors, serve a copy of the petition on those creditors, and make provision for payment for those creditors to the extent that assets are available.

(3)   The court may enter an order of summary administration allowing immediate distribution of the assets to the persons entitled to them.

(4)   The order of summary administration and distribution so entered shall have the following effect:

(a)   Those to whom specified parts of the decedent's estate, including exempt property, are assigned by the order shall be entitled to receive and collect the parts and to have the parts transferred to them. They may maintain actions to enforce the right.

(b)   Debtors of the decedent, those holding property of the decedent, and those with whom securities or other property of the decedent are registered are authorized and empowered to comply with the order by paying, delivering, or transferring to those specified in the order the parts of the decedent's estate assigned to them by the order, and the persons so paying, delivering, or transferring shall not be accountable to anyone else for the property.

(c)   After the entry of the order, bona fide purchasers for value from those to whom property of the decedent may be assigned by the order shall take the property free of all claims of creditors of the decedent and all rights of the surviving spouse and all other beneficiaries.

(d)   Property of the decedent that is not exempt from claims of creditors and that remains in the hands of those to whom it may be assigned by the order shall continue to be liable for claims against the decedent until barred as provided in the code. Any known or reasonably ascertainable creditor who did not receive notice and for whom provision for payment was not made may enforce the claim and, if the creditor prevails, shall be awarded reasonable attorney's fees as an element of costs against those who joined in the petition.

(e)   The recipients of the decedent's property under the order of summary administration shall be personally liable for a pro rata share of all lawful claims against the estate of the decedent, but only to the extent of the value of the estate of the decedent actually received by each recipient, exclusive of the property exempt from claims of creditors under the constitution and statutes of Florida.

(f)   After 2 years from the death of the decedent, neither the decedent's estate nor those to whom it may be assigned shall be liable for any claim against the decedent, unless proceedings have been taken for the enforcement of the claim.

(g)   Any heir or devisee of the decedent who was lawfully entitled to share in the estate but who was not included in the order of summary administration and distribution may enforce all rights in appropriate proceedings against those who procured the order and, if successful, shall be awarded reasonable attorney's fees as an element of costs.

History.—s. 1, ch. 74-106; s. 108, ch. 75-220; s. 48, ch. 77-87; s. 1, ch. 77-174; s. 14, ch. 89-340; s. 1035, ch. 97-102; s. 181, ch. 2001-226.

Note.—Created from former s. 735.07.

735.2063 Notice to creditors.—

(1)   Any person who has obtained an order of summary administration may publish a notice to creditors according to the relevant requirements of s. 733.2121, notifying all persons having claims or demands against the estate of the decedent that an order of summary administration has been entered by the court. The notice shall specify the total value of the estate and the names and addresses of those to whom it has been assigned by the order.

(2)   If proof of publication of the notice is filed with the court, all claims and demands of creditors against the estate of the decedent who are not known or are not reasonably ascertainable shall be forever barred unless the claims and demands are filed with the court within 3 months after the first publication of the notice.

History.—s. 3, ch. 80-203; s. 182, ch. 2001-226; s. 13, ch. 2003-154.

PART II
DISPOSITION OF PERSONAL PROPERTY WITHOUT ADMINISTRATION

735.301   Disposition without administration.—

(1)   No administration shall be required or formal proceedings instituted upon the estate of a decedent leaving only personal property exempt under the provisions of s. 732.402, personal property exempt from the claims of creditors under the Constitution of Florida, and nonexempt personal property the value of which does not exceed the sum of the amount of preferred funeral expenses and reasonable and necessary medical and hospital expenses of the last 60 days of the last illness.

(2)   Upon informal application by affidavit, letter, or otherwise by any interested party, and if the court is satisfied that subsection (1) is applicable, the court, by letter or other writing under the seal of the court, may authorize the payment, transfer, or disposition of the personal property, tangible or intangible, belonging to the decedent to those persons entitled.

(3)   Any person, firm, or corporation paying, delivering, or transferring property under the authorization shall be forever discharged from liability thereon.

History.—s. 1, ch. 74-106; s. 111, ch. 75-220; s. 50, ch. 77-87; s. 1, ch. 77-174; s. 275, ch. 79-400; s. 52, ch. 98-421; s. 184, ch. 2001-226.

735.302   Income tax refunds in certain cases.—

(1)   In any case when the United States Treasury Department determines that an overpayment of federal income tax exists and the person in whose favor the overpayment is determined is dead at the time the overpayment of tax is to be refunded, and irrespective of whether the decedent had filed a joint and several or separate income tax return, the amount of the overpayment, if not in excess of $2,500, may be refunded as follows:

(a)   Directly to the surviving spouse on his or her verified application; or

(b)   If there is no surviving spouse, to one of the decedent's children who is designated in a verified application purporting to be executed by all of the decedent's children over the age of 14 years.
In either event, the application must show that the decedent was not indebted, that provision has been made for the payment of the decedent's debts, or that the entire estate is exempt from the claims of creditors under the constitution and statutes of the state, and that no administration of the estate, including summary administration, has been initiated and that none is planned, to the knowledge of the applicant.

(2)   If a refund is made to the surviving spouse or designated child pursuant to the application, the refund shall operate as a complete discharge to the United States from liability from any action, claim, or demand by any beneficiary of the decedent or other person. This section shall be construed as establishing the ownership or rights of the payee in the refund.

History.—s. 1, ch. 74-106; s. 112, ch. 75-220; s. 51, ch. 77-87; s. 1, ch. 77-174; s. 185, ch. 2001-226.

Note.—Created from former s. 735.15.

www.ingramcontent.com/pod-product-compliance
Lightning Source LLC
Chambersburg PA
CBHW051625170526
45167CB00001B/69